21 95

Hermeneutics
and
Medieval Culture

Hermeneutics
and
Medieval Culture

Edited by
PATRICK J. GALLACHER & HELEN DAMICO

State University of New York Press

Published by
State University of New York Press, Albany

© 1989 State University of New York

For information, address State University of New York
Press, State University Plaza, Albany, N.Y., 12246

Library of Congress Cataloging in Publication Data

Library of Congress Cataloging-in-Publication Data

Hermeneutics and medieval culture / edited by Patrick J. Gallacher and
Helen Damico.
  p. cm.
  Includes index.
  ISBN 0-88706-743-3. ISBN 0-88706-745-X (pbk.)
  1. Civilization, Medieval—Sources. 2. Literature, Medieval—
History and criticism—Theory, etc. 3. Hermeneutics.
I. Gallacher, Patrick J. II. Damico, Helen.
CB353.H47 1988   87-25637
909.07—dc19   CIP

10 9 8 7 6 5 4 3 2 1

For Ifigenia and Patricia

Contents

Part III. Discovery of New Meaning

Part IV. Bridging Historical Distance

Preface

☙❦☙

This book contains a selection of original essays written by some of the most insightful, creative, and renowned scholars in the field of medieval studies. The essays are explorations into an important contemporary field of critical inquiry—hermeneutics, or the art of interpretation—and its operation in works of history, art, and literature from the medieval period. The essays represent both the direct involvement with the theoretical approach to understanding (the desired end of hermeneutics) and the indirect display of the process, or the technique of interpretation at work. In this respect, the essays cumulatively illustrate the modern perception of hermeneutics (first put forth in the mid-seventeenth century but not fully established until the nineteenth with the work of Schleiermacher and Dilthey) as referring both to the theory of interpretation (and its accompanying rules and methodology) and to the practice of making understandable that which is indeterminate and strange. As a whole, the essays collected here address the special hermeneutic strategies that illuminate meaning in medieval texts. The collection is the first and only one of its kind, in that it offers a diversity of hermeneutic approaches and themes in the context of medieval works.

The essays are arranged around four hermeneutic principles, an order that came about naturally from the issues raised by the individual works and the interrelationship between these questions. The essays in Part I examine the definition of hermeneutics and the crucial principle of "gaps of indeterminacy" (to use Wolfgang Iser's phrase). The medieval works explored in this section propose that gaps of meaning are essential to a literary work, for they invite interpretation and provide the means by which reader and author may meet, an encounter in which an experience of "true" comprehension may occur. The fragility and vulnerability of this "true" comprehension, subject as it is to the vicissitudes of historical time and political exigencies, concern the essays in Part II of the collection, which focus on the hermeneutic function of subjectivity and objectivity. Can the "true" nature of an event or work be made manifest when the interpreter is burdened by bias and self-interest? The essays in this section illustrate how easily the hermeneutic experience may be manipulated and undermined, so that "true" meaning is concealed rather than uncovered. The discovery of new meaning—brought about by a renewed interaction with and redefinition of the whole and its parts—is the principle that unites the essays in Part III. This is the largest section in the volume because the nine essays contained therein provide a variety of approaches to the hermeneutic principles of transtextuality and difference. Through an exploration of "difference" and "incongruity," disclosure of true meaning may occur. The essays contained in Part IV of the collection represent what could be considered the most important of hermeneutic tenets—the principle of mediation between one historical period and another. The underlying notion has to do with the immortality of an idea formulated by the human mind. Each age interprets, translates, and transforms the testaments of life manifested in the art and literature of an earlier time. The activity is extraordinarily vital to the continuation of Western culture since it propels the past into the present and brings that which was dormant to life.

To readers of medieval historical, literary, and philosophical works, the interpretative activity cited above and discussed in the following pages, would call to mind abundant evidence from medieval texts that hermeneutics, the search for meaning, was a primary concern of medieval authors. Admittedly, no culture or historical period is without interpretation; yet, the Middle Ages seem to have been continuously and explicitly conscious of such activity. The history of medieval thought from Augustine to Aquinas and Ockham illustrates the dialectic of question and answer that is the foundation of hermeneutics. The knowledge of literary conventions on the part of medieval poets enforced a continuous reinterpretation of their literary tradition. Even before the High Middle Ages, society as a whole was remarkably oriented to certain privileged texts, for which interpretation, sometimes on a fairly elementary level, was an obvious necessity.

Some remarks are perhaps in order concerning the limits of the collections. It is limited in its discussion of only four (albeit the most universal) hermeneutic principles. It is limited also in its concern with only the means and the ends of hermeneutic activity, and does not provide a historical survey of hermeneutics from Aristotle to contemporary criticism, or of medieval literary theory. The former would be an appropriate subject for an encyclopedic series, and the latter is already the concern of such scholars as James J. Murphy and Alastair Minnis.

Because the essays in the collection are interdisciplinary and deal with various methodologies and interpretations of medieval history, literature, art, and music, they would be of interest to and invite analysis from scholars and critics in all areas of medieval studies. It is this broadness of scope in addressing the art of interpretation in these various disciplines that makes the collection a valuable book for use in the classroom as well. The interpretative activity in each discipline proceeds from different assumptions, methods, and basic perceptions, and the essays in the collection exemplify this diversity in technique. Thus, the book would be most useful in courses that attempt to provide a general introduction to medieval culture, an introduction that illustrates scope, rigorous scholarship, and methodology. For the general reader who has an interest in the medieval period, in the history of ideas, and, most important, in the processes that bring forth understanding, we hope the book will be a source of enjoyment and information in its rich and varied contents.

Acknowledgments

It has been our good fortune to work with the authors of these essays over a two-year period, and it is with pleasure that we thank them for the charity, flexibility, and good humor they have shown during the publication process. The essays began as papers delivered at the sixty-first annual meeting of the Medieval Academy of America, hosted by the University of New Mexico in April 1986. In a sense, the collection might not have come into being without the support of the University's College of Arts and Sciences and College of Fine Arts. We owe particular thanks to F. Chris Garcia, Vice President for Academic Affairs and former Dean of the College of Arts & Sciences; to Joel M. Jones, former Vice President for Administration and Planning; to former Provost McAllister H. Hull, Professor of Physics; and to Hamlin Hill, former Chair of the Department of English, for their abundant generosity. Others to whom we owe thanks are David C. McPherson, the present Chair of the Department of English, for his encouragement and support; Krystan V. Douglas for her help in proofing the manuscript; Elizabeth Abbott for typing parts of the manuscript; and the office staff of the Department of English for their continuous forbearance. We also thank the English Seminar of the University of Münster for providing Helen Damico the use of their research facilities while she was with them as Visiting Professor. Last, but not least, we wish to thank our colleagues, Professors Susan Patrick and Raymond R. MacCurdy for reading portions of the manuscript, Professor Joseph B. Zavadil for his *felaweshipe* and *curteisie*, and our editor, Carola Sautter, for her patience and helpful criticism.

University of New Mexico, 1988

Illustrations

Introduction

*Ego certe, quod intrepidus de meo corde pronuntio, si ad culmen auc-
toritatis aliquid scriberem, sic mallem scribere, ut, quod ueri quisque de his
rebus capere posset, mea uerba resonarent, quam ut unam ueram senten-
tiam ad hoc apertius ponerem, ut excluderem ceteras, quarum falsitas me
non posset offendere.*

Augustine, Confessions, Bk. XII, 31.[1]

For my part, indeed, and I say this with the greatest confidence and
sincerity, if I were to write anything that was to become supremely authoritative, I would choose to write in such a way that my words would
resound with whatever truth anyone could grasp in them, rather than to put
down one true meaning so clearly as to exclude other meanings, which, if
they were not false, would not offend me.

Augustine's *Confessions,* a seminal work not only for medieval culture,
but for the tradition of the humanities in general, abounds in principles held
by practitioners of contemporary hermeneutics. Paul Ricoeur's notion of multiple meaning, or polysemy—whereby the understanding of polysemic expressions becomes a moment of self-understanding—coincides with Augustine's view quoted above.[2] To unfold multiple levels of meaning implied
in an apparent one is as central an act of interpretation (a hermeneutic experience) to Ricoeur as it was to Augustine.[3] Elsewhere in the *Confessions* (I,
viii), Augustine meditates on the child's first attempts to use language, and
his meditations complement the basic principle of hermeneutics held by
Ricoeur,[4] and Schleiermacher and Dilthey before him,[5] who see the sentence—the act of predication—as the fundamental unit of interpretation from
which the understanding of the whole and its parts derives. We understand the
meaning of a word by seeing it in reference to the whole of the sentence;
reciprocally, the sentence's meaning depends on the meanings of individual
words. For Augustine, all of time is like a sentence, an expression of truth and
beauty, which cannot be fully comprehended until, like the sentence, time
itself is complete (IV, x-xi).

The *Confessions* contain other hermeneutic principles. The contemporary notion of difference—the departure from the ordinary—as an occasion
that instigates hermeneutic activity[6] is clearly delineated in Augustine's story
of how his sick friend refused to join him in their customary derision of

1

baptism (IV, iv). And the phenomenological tenet that corrected misinterpretation serves as a powerful means toward enlightened understanding[7] is a motif which virtually dominates the story of a man whose moral failures eventually made necessary an extensive reinterpretation of the world of late antiquity, and which is nowhere more potently apparent than it is in Monica's correction of her son's misinterpretation of her dream (III, xi). For Augustine and for contemporary theorists of the art of interpretation, hermeneutics is the experience of life itself.[8]

For both Augustine and contemporary theorists, the practice of each of the above hermeneutic principles—polysemy, the relationship of the parts to the whole, the recognition of difference, and the necessary function of corrected misinterpretation in critical inquiry—leads to understanding, the comprehension of the "true" meaning of an event or object as a totality. To achieve understanding is clearly the desired end of the hermeneutic experience. But the achievement of that end is a complicated undertaking, for understanding itself is (1) protean, formed and transformed by the complex interplay of interpreter, object, and cultural environment, and (2) dialectical, characterized by a binary dynamism in which the question determines the answer, and the answer in turn corrects the question.

Augustine's movement from comprehending the sentence (in its particular relationship of the parts to the whole) to the understanding of the whole of time, for example, illustrates Heidegger's model of two kinds of understanding—preunderstanding, and informed understanding.[9] In this model (an illustration of the hermeneutic circle), the understanding of the whole possessed at the beginning of the interpretative process (what can be termed as the sensing of the totality) is different from that possessed at the end. Preunderstanding—biased, fragmentary, nebulous—becomes experientially informed—judicious, integrated, specific. In the dialogue that takes place between object and interpreter during the hermeneutic process, comprehension of "true" meaning moves through successive stages where it assumes various forms, these being open to either correction or confirmation. Mistaken understanding—errors in interpretation—leads to renewed and intensified involvement in the interpretative process. Confirmed understanding provides completion, although this perceived totality is intermediate and becomes the sensing or the preunderstanding of a new totality. Both the process toward and the state of understanding are thus epistemologically hierarchical and kinetic: Each particle, in constant motion, changes its nature in its encounter with other similarly energized particles. The underlying philosophical assumption of both medieval and the best contemporary hermeneutic activity—which separates it from other interpretative processes—is precisely this notion, that understanding, although subject to error, is protean and cumulative.

Interpretation—the technique of giving meaning to an object by means of clarification and explanation—is an ancient art. Stoic commentaries on the Homeric poems, rabbinical interpretations of the Torah, Aristotle's treatise,

Peri Hermeneias, as well as Medieval and Renaissance biblical exegesis, are testaments to the tenacity of this venerable activity.[10] Modern interpretative theory, or hermeneutics, becomes a discipline in its own right—different from the above interpretative activities—in the nineteenth century with the work of Schleiermacher (who broadened the concerns of interpretation from the exegesis of literary, theological, and legal texts to the study of understanding itself) and Dilthey (who extended Schleiermacher's tenets to position hermeneutics historically as a system of understanding for all humanistic and scientific disciplines). In the twentieth century, hermeneutics takes place in the context of phenomenology and existentialism. Heidegger's theory of hermeneutics emerged as an ontology of understanding, a philosophical program later assimilated and developed by Gadamer into the assertion that hermeneutics is the encounter with being through language.[11] In a number of ways, Paul Ricoeur's writings embody all the above concerns. Ricoeur resituates hermeneutics to focus on the text, but emphasizes an extra-textual dynamism, a referential impetus that goes outside the internal structures of both language and text. In medieval texts, the interplay of the literal and tropological interests corresponds to this interrelationship between culture and work. Ricoeur's explorations of latent meanings in a text, his ability to seek out and to incorporate multiple meanings (as revealed by Freudian, Marxist, and religious interpretations), and his stance as arbitrator between different types of interpretation, recognizing them as being grounded in disparate but related experiences in existence itself, correspond to the best medieval hermeneutic activity. It is precisely these aspects—the many voices of the text, and its complementary expressive and referential relationship with the culture—that relate medieval interpretation with contemporary hermeneutics.

The connection between contemporary hermeneutics and medieval literature has been made already by Judith Ferster in *Chaucer on Interpretation,* where she explores such hermeneutical issues as the power of self-interestedness in interpretation (especially in the *Knight's Tale*), interpretation as mediation between author and audience (in *The Parliament of Fowls*), and the illusions of excessive objectivity (in the *Clerk's Tale*).[12] This exploratory activity which interrelates Chaucer's sensibility with interpretative principles, as well as her informative and readable introduction to hermeneutics in general, offers a firm beginning for more intensive application of hermeneutics to medieval literature. Viewing the relationship of hermeneutics and medieval culture from a broader perspective are Joseph Anthony Mazzeo in his *Varieties of Interpretation* and Brian Stock in *The Implications of Literacy.*[13] Mazzeo casts a wide net. Investigating the state and methods of interpretation in Plato, Bultman, and Western culture, he repeatedly focuses on developments in hermeneutics that have a specifically medieval cast, as, for example, Auerbach's attempt to deal with Dante and the hermeneutic development of allegory in European literature. Brian Stock deploys conscious hermeneutics more impressively, perhaps, than any other medievalist to date. Focusing on the written and oral models by which human beings interpret their experience, he examines medieval law, the debate on the nature of the Eucharist, and the role of sacred texts in both reform and heretical movements. His account of the difference between the wise man, who embodies his subject, and the intellectual, who uses knowledge in a professional or social role, vividly demonstrates the increasing awareness of subjectivity and objectivity in interpretation.

The collected essays in this volume augment and broaden the scope of the thoughtful and illuminating discussions presented by these scholars. Each of the essays in the present collection offers insights into the hermeneutical process from a particular discipline—art history, biography, music, political and social history, linguistics, and literature. Cumulatively they present investigations of symbolic forms, confrontations of interpretative styles, and critiques of systems of interpretation. Further, they all examine texts or situations that have multiple meanings and that invite the interpreter to make explicit that which is implied. In methodology and in content, they propose indirectly that the roots of the practice of modern hermeneutics are found in medieval culture.

The group of essays which opens the collection is concerned with definition, symbolic signs, lacunae in understanding, and with the multiplicity of approaches and methodologies practiced by medieval writers. Florence H. Ridley's essay defines hermeneutics as the theory or the process of understanding which holds two assumptions: the first, that there is a gap of indeterminacy between the author's meaning in a particular text and the reader's understanding of it, and, the second, that the text contains the potential to bridge the separation. With particular reference to the Chaucerian canon, Professor Ridley comments on current criticism and notes its manifestation in the extremes of the spectrum of interpretative theory—from the interpretative monism of E. D. Hirsch to the Derridean free play of signifiers to the Fishian notion of reader response (which itself has a history in the rhetorical tradition). Geoffrey Chaucer's interest in language and the anticipated response of his reader is readily apparent in his work. Professor Ridley demonstrates how certain aspects of current criticism, taken with those of classical rhetoric, can help us understand both how the poet constructed his poetry, and why as a fourteenth-century poet he did so.

From our own point of view, Chaucer himself practiced hermeneutics, but not just in an unreflective sense. The Chaucerian narrator is aware not only of the many interpretations which a particular situation can merit, but is intensely conscious also of the vulnerability of meaning.

Hermeneutics is primarily concerned, then, both with means—the technique by which one expresses an understanding of a text—and with ends—with understanding itself.[14] To understand a text is to discover the meaning that emerges from the reciprocal relationship between the whole and its parts.

But in most situations in which the mind seeks to accomplish understanding, either a part or a particular configuration of the whole is incongruent, which brings about a gap in the understanding of the whole—the hermeneutic gap, which must be closed by mediation of some kind.[15] Understanding is circular (as illustrated in the Augustinian notion of the sentence referred to above) in that one must have some sense of the whole in order to understand the parts. Yet, without understanding the parts, one cannot adequately grasp the whole.

Karl F. Morrison's essay addresses exactly this issue of the incongruent or undecipherable fragment and the tolerance of it by the medieval mind. A mode of perception that can endure a high degree of toleration of the ''unfinished and the partial'' was as intrinsic to the thought of the Romantic Schleiermacher, as it was to that of the medieval writers Anselm of Havelberg, Gerhoch of Reichersberg, and Otto of Freising. Crucial to Morrison's analysis of these writers' progress toward meaning—their understanding of the process of understanding—is their acceptance of the fact that the gaps in coherence can be bridged by interpretation. The lacunae themselves are illusionary, for present in them is the potential meaning of the author. The interpreter's task, then, is to make present that portion of the author's thought which is absent. For the medieval writers and for Schleiermacher, meaning is existential and within the grasp of the interpreter.[16]

Responding to the gaps of indeterminacy is, thus, the central objective of the interpreter, and he may use any number of means to achieve this objective. The three essays that conclude the first grouping in the collection focus on the relationship between interpreter and text as the means to understanding. Robert Worth Frank's ''*Meditationes Vitae Christi:* The Logistics of Access to Divinity,'' presents two opposite interpretative responses to the unknown. For Anselm, there is an unbridgeable gap between the divine and his ability to comprehend it. He accepts the notion of the human mind's limited capabilities and, hence, his state of separation from understanding God. In contrast to Anselm, the author of the *Meditationes* treats the hermeneutic gap as if it did not exist. He exhorts the meditant to become one with divinity through the power of imagination and to reduce the distance between her and Jesus by inventing scenes that could have taken place in his life. It is the play of the meditant's imagination by which she familiarizes and domesticizes the divine that first reduces and then finally obliterates the hermeneutic gap.

Chauncey Wood's ''The Author's Address to the Reader: Chaucer, Juan Ruiz, Dante,'' similarly features the author as primary interpreter and guide to understanding, who (through a variety of authorial interruptions) calls the indeterminacy of the text to the attention of the reader. The medieval authors whom Professor Wood discusses both invite their readers to activate their intelligence and instruct them on methodology so that they might arrive at the author's meaning expeditiously. This is reader response in a distinctly medieval cast.

The second group of essays raises the issue of subjectivity and objectivity in interpretation from the point of view of various ideological frameworks. Derek Pearsall examines fourteenth-century interpretations of the Peasants' Revolt and concludes that (except for the *Anonimalle Chronicle*) historians of the day were no more objective in their assessments of the causes of the Peasants' Revolt than were the poets. Dom Jean Leclercq provides an example of two roughly contemporary and significant interpretations of a central medieval institution, knighthood, and addresses the relative compatibility of Christianity and war, an issue that continues to plague the modern world. In contrast to the glorification of war presented in *El Cid*, Bernard of Clairvaux's writings on knighthood attempted to minimize violence, to dissuade the reader from the desire for plunder, and to decry the absurdity of a cleric engaging professionally in acts of violence. The argument is a good example of the failure of what Ricoeur calls interpretative "distanciation," by which he means a kind of suspension of disbelief.[17] The essays of Lorraine Attreed and Joseph J. Duggan analyze misinterpretations of medieval "texts" by a later historical period. The core of their essays is "misunderstanding"— of a historical period (Attreed) and of a literary work (Duggan)—and of the formidable difficulties that poets and historians must overcome to devise correctives toward the truth.

A classic function of interpretation is to discover new meaning in a particular text or to restore a meaningful context to a work no longer fully understood. All of the nine essays that make up the third group of the anthology present new understandings of texts. The new meanings grow out of a dialectic between particular patterns in the text and their resonances in other texts or disciplines. The result is the text's "transtextuality."[18] Paul Beekman Taylor, for example, argues for the etymological model as a critical tool for shaping and interpreting narrative structures. Exploring relationships between Chaucer's *Treatise on the Astrolabe* and the *Squire's Tale,* Marijane Osborn finds verbal echoes of the scientific treatise in the description and function of the magical brass horse. Calvin M. Bower posits that the theory of grammatical parts found in medieval musicologists' texts may serve as a criterion for determining structural pitches (or perhaps a hierarchy of pitches). The essays of Charles M. Atkinson, Calvin B. Kendall, and Anita Riedinger address what is the anomalous element in their respective texts. The principle of congruence often makes an interpretation convincing, but encountering what is different from what is the expected norm is often the feature that invites interpretation.[19] Professor Atkinson examines the different use of the term "modos" in the *Musica enchiriadis* and its resonances in the texts of other medieval musicologists. Calvin B. Kendall defines a corpus of tympanum inscriptions on Romanesque churches and discovers what makes the verse inscriptions on the church of Ste.-Foy of Conques distinctively different. Kendall argues for single authorship for the inscriptions of the tympanum and other verse inscriptions which are found at Conques. His investigations reveal a close working relationship between the artist of the tympanum and the poet. The tympanum verses exhibit congruence between length of verse, meaning, availability of space, suitability of location, and, most important, style. In the same way that Professor Kendall defines a corpus of tympanum inscriptions, Anita Riedinger talks about the corpus of Anglo-Saxon oral formulaic constructions in her examination of the *Andreas* poet's style. Professor Riedinger discovers new meaning by analyzing the poet's manipulation of traditional oral formulas, a critical action on his part that betrays a literate Christian mind, one that is intent on changing the ethos inherent in the Old English oral formulaic tradition.

The remaining three articles in this section present new interpretations that grow out of a dialectic between old views and the new, in which the latter are seen to provide a more inclusive or coherent account of a text. It subsumes more effectively all the parts in a newly configured whole. An old interpretation is surpassed and reintegrated into a new interpretation. In the course of applying a hermeneutic method combining paleographical with textual criticism, Fred C. Robinson has added a new poem to the canon of Old English poetry ("The Rewards of Piety") and, thus, removed two fragments from the corpus. Dependence on existing printed editions of medieval poems separates the interpreter from such manuscript facts as the spacing (or lack thereof) between works, rubricated *explicits* that mark the end of a work, and colored capital letters that indicate lesser breaks within a particular poem. Such obvious visual indicators define the text in its original context and make what might otherwise be anomalous features intelligible.

Dealing similarly with a part-whole relationship and yet at the same time reflecting on the nature of the hermeneutic process itself, Thomas Cable, in "Old and Middle English Prosody: Transformations of the Model," engages the issue of the corrected misinterpretation which distinguishes between two sets of data which are equally factual, but not equally pertinent, and proposes a new pattern for Medieval English prosody.

The discovery of new meaning in Donald K. Fry's "The Authority of *Elde* in *The Parlement of the Thre Ages*" proceeds from an examination of the text itself and of the existing criticism. Fry's thesis that Elde is not the spokesman of the poet, but rather the victim of the poet's irony rests on his survey of the criticism of the poem. His article proposes that "misinterpretation" is built into the framework of the poem and that a "corrected misinterpretation" can provide a deeper understanding of the text, especially in this instance where the reader is meant to correct the mistakes of Elde. More important is Fry's emphasis on the poet's use of the accumulation of Elde's errors (mistakes which any medieval reader could have corrected) as a means by which the poet leads the reader to an understanding of the text. In the process of correcting Elde's mistakes, the reader arrives circuitously at the proposition that wisdom and moral fiber do not of necessity come with age, but rather that in Elde the selfish behavior and obsessions of youth are compounded. Moreover, Fry suggests that the device of activating the reader and making him discover what the writer is doing quite independently of the speaker seems to be one of the conventions of medieval dream vision poetry.

The concluding essays of the collection view the art of interpretation as an act of mediation between the present and the past. Hermeneutics is historical because the interpretation of a text must take into account at least the circumstances (the place, the time, the author, the environment) in which the text was produced. But the hermeneutic experience also understands that what is said is articulated in light of the present, of the actual situation of the interpreter and his world. As Gadamer has pointed out, in both theological and legal interpretation, the moment of application is explicitly necessary and even central to understanding,[20] an element in the history of interpretative theory familiar to medievalists as the tropological, or moral level of biblical exegesis.[21] Every true interpretation must render explicit a work's meaning in the present. It must bridge the historical distance between the horizon of the interpreter and that of the text.

The essays of Madeline H. Caviness, Giles Constable, Joseph M. P. Donatelli, and Paul E. Szarmach are about interpreters who are concerned with this central issue of bridging historical distance. Joseph M. P. Donatelli argues that Thomas Percy, in his *Reliques,* by revising and interpolating medieval texts, created an image of the Middle Ages that influenced and moulded subsequent perceptions of early English poetry. Percy, the editor, serves as a guide for the reader into the unknown, as do the art historians, Wickhoff, Haseloff, Goldschmidt, and the Swarzenskis, the subjects of Professor Caviness's article. These art historians, connoisseurs, and museum curators were the lens through which the twentieth century came to view medieval art. They saw the aesthetic values of early medieval art as anticipations of modern art. Caviness posits a correlation between the development of modern art, and the more enlightened and appreciative reception of early medieval art.

Interpreting medieval institutions for his twentieth-century contemporaries was the professional concern of William Mendel Newman, one of America's leading historians. In describing the complex makeup of this reluctant scholar, Professor Constable points to the binary tension that informed the visible and invisible lives led by Newman, who could perceive so accurately the objective past, but who misinterpreted his own life so extravagantly. Newman's diary—a kind of *Historia Calamitatum*—reveals a man who believed himself to be without friends, racked with misfortune, and misunderstood and undervalued by his teachers. His historical studies, on the other hand, particularly *Les seigneurs de Nesle en Picardie,* reveal an interpreter who is objective, empirical, and balanced. This binary opposition in Newman's role of interpreter exemplifies a central problem in interpretation—the relationship between the subjective interpreter and the objective text. The diaries manifest the psychic disturbance that formed an obstacle to perception, while the historical works suggest that the study of medieval institutions provided the last sanctuary for the historian's troubled spirit.

Opposite to Newman in temperament, but complementary to him in the desire to interpret the past for his time, was Ælfric of Eynsham, whose hermeneutic habits are examined by Paul E. Szarmach. Szarmach argues for Ælfric's mode of interpretation as one which operates on several levels simultaneously, the explanatory (with its insistence on the literal and the factual) and the allegorical (which is manifested by what Szarmach calls Ælfric's "narrative impulse."). Ælfric sought meaning not only in Scripture, but in past interpretations of Scripture. In this regard, the abbot was but one member of an interpretative community which stretched from the disciples to Paul the Deacon, and he identified strongly with them.[22] In his sermon on the Passion, for instance, he made free use of all the gospel sources to bring the event to life. Professor Szarmach illustrates how, in Ælfric's striking use of the first person plural in his interpretative account of the sacred event, Ælfric became, in effect, an evangelist himself. This particular instance is a cogent example of the premise that the interpretation of a text is an act neither of mastery nor of manipulation, but a participation in which the interpreter and the text mutually affect each other. The interpreter is changed by the text, and it is the text itself that holds (and reveals) those elements of meaning that call the transformation into being.[23]

All of the essays in this collection illustrate the stated hermeneutic principles in one way or another. Each article serves as a corrective to received opinion and looks to understand that which is different. In varying degrees, each illustrates the act of predication and the notion of polysemy. Each is dialectical in that it invites controversy, historical in that it recognizes contextual relevance, and existential in that it posits meaning for the intended present. The essays not only exemplify the end of the hermeneutic process, but are themselves a reflection of the process in operation. Finally, the essays embody a central issue of hermeneutics—the relationship between the parts and the whole, in that each is a whole in its own right, and also one part of this collection on hermeneutics and medieval culture.

PATRICK J. GALLACHER and HELEN DAMICO
UNIVERSITY OF NEW MEXICO

Notes

1. The text used is *Les Confessions*, ed. M. Skutella, tr. E. Trehorel, and G. Bouissou (Bruges: Desclée de Brouwer, 1962). The English translation is adapted by Patrick J. Gallacher from *The Confessions of St. Augustine*, trans. F. J. Sheed (New York: Sheed & Ward, 1942).

2. Paul Ricoeur, *The Conflict of Interpretations: Essays in Hermeneutics*, ed.

Don Ihde (Evanston: Northwestern University Press, 1974), 93–96. Hereafter referred to as *Conflict*.

3. Ricoeur, *Conflict*, 62–78.

4. A discussion of the sentence as the basic unit of interpretation occurs in Ricoeur's *Freud and Philosophy: An Essay on Interpretation,* trans. Denis Savage (New Haven and London: Yale University Press, 1970), 20–24. Ricoeur's source for this emphasis is the *Peri Hermeneias* of Aristotle, where the discussion also focuses mainly on the "enunciation," or the sentence. The notion of predication, of saying something to someone about something, has considerable subtlety and extensiveness in Ricoeur's work. See Theodoor Marius Van Leeuwen, *The Surplus of Meaning: Ontology and Eschatology in the Philosophy of Paul Ricoeur* (Amsterdam: Editions Rodopi B.V., 1981), 74 ff.

5. See Richard E. Palmer, *Hermeneutics: Interpretation Theory in Schleiermacher, Dilthey, Heidegger, and Gadamer* (Evanston: Northwestern University Press, 1969), 87–88; 118–21.

6. For an account of difference in modern thought, see Jonathan Culler, *Structuralist Poetics: Structuralism, Linguistics, and the Study of Literature* (Ithaca: Cornell University Press, 1975), 11 ff. et passim. Also the same author's *On Deconstruction: Theory and Criticism After Structuralism* (Ithaca: Cornell University Press, 1982), 97 ff., takes up the further adventures of the concept. As a basic philosophical experience, in Heidegger's vivid language, "der Unter-schied ist das Heissende," "the difference is what calls to us"—quoted by William J. Richardson, S. J., *Heidegger: Through Phenomenology to Thought,* 3rd ed. (The Hague: Martinus Nijhoff, 1974), 578–81. See also Martin Heidegger, *Identity and Difference,* translated and introduced by Joan Stambaugh (New York: Harper and Row, 1969).

7. For Maurice Merleau-Ponty, in *The Visible and the Invisible* (Evanston: Northwestern University Press, 1968), 42, the mistaken perception that is corrected "reveals the prepossession of a totality which is there before one knows how or why, whose realizations are never what we would have imagined them to be, and which nonetheless fulfills a secret expectation within us. . . ." He cites the similar effects of "crossing out" in Husserl, a function that is paralleled in Heidegger and Derrida: see Jacques Derrida, *Of Grammatology* (Baltimore: The Johns Hopkins University Press, 1976), trans. Gayatri Chakravorty Spivak, xiii ff. Frank Lentricchia, in *After the New Criticism* (Chicago: The University of Chicago Press, 1980), 85–88, examines Heidegger's notion of how the broken tool reveals the whole world of equipment in which it functioned, a world which remained invisible as long as the tool functioned well. For the Middle Ages, there is of course the scholastic method of raising objections to a thesis as a means of clarifying and strengthening the argument.

8. Ricoeur, in *Conflict,* 12, quotes Nietzsche as asserting that life itself is interpretation. Also, in his essay, "Existence and Hermeneutics," in *Conflict,* 3–24, Ricoeur associates Freud and the subconscious with an archaeology of the desire to be; Hegel with a teleology of the effort to exist; and the phenomenology of religion with an eschatology of the final end in connection with an ultimate origin.

9. For a discussion of preunderstanding in Heidegger, as well as for the example

of the question and answer, see Joseph Anthony Mazzeo, *Varieties of Interpretation* (Notre Dame: University of Notre Dame Press, 1978), 22. See also Martin Heidegger, *Being and Time,* translated by John Macquarrie & Edward Robinson (New York: Harper and Row, 1962), 194–95, *et passim.*

10. See Ricoeur, *Conflict,* 4.

11. See Palmer's discussion in *Hermeneutics,* 40–43. See also Terry Eagleton's *Literary Theory: An Introduction* (Minneapolis: University of Minnesota Press, 1983), especially 54–90, which discusses phenomenology, hermeneutics, and reception theory.

12. Judith Ferster, *Chaucer on Interpretation* (Cambridge: Cambridge University Press, 1985), 15–16.

13. Brian Stock, *The Implications of Literacy: Written Language and Models of Interpretation in the Eleventh and Twelfth Centuries* (Princeton: Princeton University Press, 1983). For Mazzeo, see note 9 above. See also *Interpretation: Theory and Practice,* ed. Charles S. Singleton (Baltimore: The Johns Hopkins University Press, 1969).

14. Ricoeur, *Conflict,* 6–11, discusses how in Heidegger, the epistemology of interpretation becomes an ontology of understanding. See also Palmer, 227–32; and Hans-Georg Gadamer, *Truth and Method* (New York: Crossroad Publishing Company, 1982), 167, *et passim;* originally published as *Wahrheit und Methode* (Tübingen: J.C.B. Mohr, 1960). *Insight: A Study of Human Understanding* (New York: Philosophical Library, 1970), by Bernard J.F. Lonergan, S.J., is a substantial contribution to this subject.

15. Gadamer, *Truth and Method,* 139, 150, 192, 258 ff. See also Josef Bleicher, *Contemporary Hermeneutics: Hermeneutics as Method, Philosophy and Critique* (London: Routledge & Kegan Paul, 1980), 122, 126.

16. See Karl F. Morrison's essay, "Interpreting the Fragment," 27–37, below. See also Mazzeo, *Varieties of Interpretation,* 8–9, 21–24.

17. Paul Ricoeur, *Hermeneutics and the Human Sciences: Essays on Language, Action, and Interpretation,* edited, translated, and introduced by John B. Thompson (Cambridge: Cambridge University Press, 1981), 131–44.

18. Gérard Genette, *Palimpsestes* (Paris: Seuil, 1982), 8 ff. See also Julia Kristeva, *Semiotikè* (Paris: Seuil, 1969). A concise summary of the subjective and objective aspects of linguistic signs can be found in *The Philosophy of Paul Ricoeur: An Anthology of His Work,* ed. Charles E. Reagan & David Stewart (Boston: Beacon Press, 1978), 123.

19. See note 6.

20. Gadamer, 294 ff., *et passim.*

21. See Henri de Lubac, S.J., *Exégèse Médiévale: Les Quatre Sens de L'Ecriture,* première partie, II, "La Tropologie Mystique," 549–620. The medieval interpretation of literature was dominated by this concern with application: see Judson

Boyce Allen, *The Ethical Poetic of the Later Middle Ages* (Toronto: University of Toronto Press, 1982).

22. See Ricoeur, *Conflict,* 3–4, for a discussion of interpretative communities.

23. See "Appropriation," in Ricoeur, *Hermeneutics and the Human Sciences,* 182–93; and Ferster, *Chaucer on Interpretation,* 13.

Part I
The Hermeneutic Gap

The essays emphasize what Wolfgang Iser called the "gaps of indeterminacy" in a text. Florence Ridley gives an account of how some critics have addressed such gaps in Chaucer's poetry. Karl F. Morrison discusses three authors of the Romanesque period who, because of their hermeneutic ability to supply the whole implied by a fragment, deliberately inserted such gaps into their texts in order to invite interpretation. Robert Worth Frank, Jr., examines the methodology used by the author of the *Meditationes Vitae Christi* to fill in gaps perceived in the Gospel narratives. And Chauncey Wood shows how Chaucer, Juan Ruiz, and Dante, by directly addressing the reader, indicate how the gaps of indeterminacy should be filled.

1. Chaucer and Hermeneutics

FLORENCE H. RIDLEY

In a 1980 address to the Second International Congress of the New Chaucer Society, Morton Bloomfield pointed out that although "very little modern literary theory has been applied to Chaucer, . . . new literary theorizing . . . is about ripe to reach [him]."[1] A number of the excellent papers presented in March 1986 at the Fifth International Congress of the New Chaucer Society bore out this prophecy by applying to his poetry critical theories which fall under the nebulous canopy of modern hermeneutics.[2]

Hermeneutics is a slippery term which covers a multitude of matters: some would say a multitude of sins. One might attack the topic, "Chaucer and Hermeneutics," by commenting comprehensively upon all the psychological, linguistic, philological, theological, and philosophical approaches which can be made to him; but my present aim is more modest. I would like to present a selective view of certain aspects of hermeneutic study of the poet, noting its background and dual manifestation today as analytical and interpretative criticism; then attempt to demonstrate how some aspects of some current critical modes, taken in company with those of classical rhetoric, can help us better to understand both *how* the poet crafted his poetry and *why* as a medieval writer he did so. What follows in no sense aspires to be a survey of modern hermeneutics, whether of literary or philosophical persuasion. My subject is Chaucer's poetry and the new light some, but by no means all, modern theory can shed upon it.

In "The Outline of the 1819 Lectures," F. D. E. Schleiermacher defined hermeneutics as the art of relating discourse to understanding of speech as it derives from language in general and from the mind of the speaker.[3] As Peter Szondi has pointed out, what Schleiermacher really wanted was an analysis of understanding. Today hermeneutics generally refers to the theory or the methods of understanding literary works; and the concerns of its practitioners, if jargon and meretricious distinctions be stripped away, are much the same as they were in 1819 and earlier: the *sensus litteralis,* grammatical interpretation focused on language; and the *sensus spiritualis,* allegorical interpretation focused on meaning.[4]

The distinction between these two modes is old, and appears today in the slightly modified form of analytical vs. interpretative criticism or theory. Interpretative critics, in the tradition of the *sensus spiritualis,* still seek meaning beyond the literal text, and many of them assign meanings born of their own world to signs no longer familiar. Analytical critics, in the tradition of the *sensus litteralis,* focus on language, specifically on the structure or functioning of the textual medium. And certain analysts and interpreters help reveal how Chaucer's poetry functions on the one hand, and to what end on the other.

Thus Robert Jordan, in his recent paper advocating the ascendancy of analytical over interpretative criticism, suggested that there is an affinity between analytical critics like Todorov, medieval French rhetoricians, and Chaucer—an affinity resting on their common interest in language and the fictional process. Jordan redresses the critical imbalance which favored interpretation—the discounting of the text for a too eager pursuit of meaning beyond it. And he quite rightly points to the importance of rhetoric in the shaping of Chaucer's art, an importance in part evidenced by the way in which the poet invites attention to his act of composition by interrupting the story; calling attention to his role in its creation; and commenting on the practice of his art, on the nature of language, and on the dependence of his composition for survival upon his own language. As Jordan demonstrates, there is much to suggest that the poet was interested, as was Geoffrey Vinsauf, in the concept of language as a veil or woven garment for meaning.[5]

Although Chaucer was clearly fascinated by the textual surface of the fiction and by the play of language, he is as far removed in thought as in time from such advice as that of Derrida: "we should cease looking for meaning and merely enjoy the free play of signifiers."[6] Alastair Minnis's work on medieval commentary is uncovering a mine of information as to how a writer of the period would have understood and practiced his art.[7] Application of such information makes ever clearer Chaucer's acute awareness of language, not just in and for itself, but as a conveyor of meaning: his concern was primarily with the interrelation between signifier and signified. In part because of the findings of historically-oriented theorists like Minnis, the future for interpretative criticism which can relate the medium to the message looks very bright, particularly, I believe, hermeneutic approaches which recognize the participation of audience as well as text in the making of meaning—in modern terminology, varieties of reader response criticism.

As a medieval writer, Chaucer had ample precedent for making his audience participate in the fictional process; we may look to classical rhetoric for his ultimate model in doing so. To Aristotle, Quintillian, and Cicero, rhetoric was a process of interaction between orator, language, and audience; a process designed for a foreseen end—to persuade by arousing anticipated response.[8]

For example, to Cicero the lawyer, in his *De inventione,* the persuasive effect of words rested, he said, on interaction between "our own person . . . the jury, and the case itself." To him the *exordium* of a speech was "a passage which brings the mind of the auditor . . . [to be] well-disposed, attentive, and receptive"; the *peroration,* one which appeals to his emotions. If the case were a scandalous one, in the summation the speaker might focus on elements the audience approved of; if they seemed bored, he might tell a joke, or make a startling shift in tone or topic to recapture their attention, creating an affinity between them and himself.[9] And centuries after Cicero, we find Chaucer putting this advice into practice, creating an affinity between himself and his reader. For example the exaggerated outburst, " 'Namoore of this, for Goddes dignitee!'/ Quod oure Hooste," breaks the sing-song doggerel of "Sir Thopas," ends both Harry Bailly's boredom and our own, and provokes a laugh. Similarly, the remonstrance, " 'Hoo!' quod the Knight, 'good sire, namoore of this!,' " happily stops the Monk's tedious tragedies and may call to mind the striking contrast between his dull frame story, and the richly varied frame of "The Canterbury Tales" which encloses it.[10]

Chaucer could have learned of Cicero's rhetorical practice in Italy, where his work had been circulated since the thirteenth century, quoted and praised by Dante, Boccaccio, and Petrarch, and used in legal training. But whether or not Chaucer derived such notions from treatises of classical rhetoric, or commentaries thereon, he would inevitably have been exposed to them in sermons of his own day. For from Augustine on, the orator-preacher shaped his material in Ciceronian fashion, to elicit a response from his audience which would persuade them to right action.[11]

Models for a similar process were equally available in Chaucer's literary sources. Dante and the poets of *The Romance of the Rose* manipulated their audience by causing them to identify with the dreamer and/or poet in sharing sensations, emotions, and perceptions of truth. Like Dante, Chaucer presents visual images which penetrate the imagination and, by stages, draw the will of the reader along. Like de Lorris, he addresses the reader or listener, indicating how the narrative will proceed and the kind of response it is designed to elicit. And like de Meun, he frequently interrupts his narrative to speak in different voices for different purposes, perhaps to lead the reader to a perception of irony or comedy (as when de Meun has himself lavishly praised as a poet of the future by the God of Love, or when Chaucer has himself brutally interrupted as a failed story-teller by Harry Bailly).[12]

In view of his "auctoritees"—rhetorical, theological, and poetic— Chaucer could be expected to evince consistent awareness of his audience with an intent to shape its response. But whereas in classical rhetoric this process is not circular, but rather like that of an arrow's flight from orator to audience, in Chaucer's poetry it more closely resembles the hermeneutic circle. For the response evoked by his poem is to a degree subjective; and the subjective response is to a degree creative, moving back to the text to reshape it and provide further motivation for further evolving response—even though all such response was intended by the medieval poet to lead to a predetermined end. No one denies that Chaucer manipulates his reader to respond. Yet modern interpretations which rest upon or derive from such a supposition, and encompass the inevitable subjectivity of such response, have encountered surprising resistance.

Beryl Rowland's interpretation of the Wife of Bath is reader response— the creative response of a highly intelligent, exceedingly well-informed, faithful, but twentieth-century reader to Chaucer's text—criticism in the mode of the *sensus spiritualis* which ascribes to his signs meanings born of her own conceptual world. Thus Professor Rowland notes that:

> According to recent studies, precocious sexual experience may create in a woman a trauma which makes her hate all men, seek to get revenge on them and try to dominate them. Money is her symbol of power, and taking it from men is her equivalent of castrating them. Between her and her pimp are the unbreakable, solid ties of the man-hater and the woman-hater. With true insight, Chaucer shows why Jankyn alone was able to arouse Alice: he was "daungerous," abnormally sparing in his love-making; and his calculating adroitness produced a mental stimulus, a "queynte fantasye," which excited her physically.[13]

An attempted refutation of Rowland's interpretation in 1980 consisted not of citing misreadings of or omissions from the text—there were none— but of a repeated, firm assertion that Alice is not as charged; that she cannot be, "because I love her and I don't believe it."[14] This vehement rejection of a refreshingly new reading moved me to suggest in 1981 that newer modes of criticism are not dangerous; but rather that to view Chaucer's text in the light of contemporary awareness and modern critical theory can enhance the power of the text by enhancing our imaginative response to it and our understanding of that response.[15] Yet in 1985, when I attempted to demonstrate how reciprocity between poet, text, and reader could lead to a unified, more meaningful *Canterbury Tales* in the mind of a responding reader, I was told once again that such an approach constitutes a total abandonment of the text, is highly irresponsible, and indeed quite dangerous.[16]

Such recoiling from modernism seems to result primarily from three things: repugnance for the convoluted, inflated jargon in which too many theorists wrap up common sense; uneasiness about extreme positions which discount the text; and a firm belief that Chaucer's poetry can have only one meaning, that which was embedded by the author in the poem and is perceived, of course, by the holder of the firm belief.

With the objection to jargon, suffice it to say that I fully agree.[17] As to the second objection: While a number of theorists do assert that the text is self-consuming, or disappears in the process of reception, no responsible interpreter of Chaucer would discount his text altogether. Most of us, in fact, have a strong sense of responsibility toward it, which includes the necessity of reading it as closely as possible in accordance with the milieu in which it was created. We attempt to become optimum, implied, or informed readers, in the words respectively of Nelson, Iser, and Fish,[18] readers as familiar as possible with the expectations and cultural phenomena which shaped the response of Chaucer's first audience, in order better to understand and experience work composed in light of those expectations and responses.

As to the conviction that Chaucer can have only one meaning, is it not time for all would-be interpreters of his poetry to accept the indeterminacy by which he provokes creative response? This most striking aspect of his art has been recognized for a long time. More than 150 years ago, Charles Lamb took William Godwin to task for his "conjecturing spirit," his fondness for filling out the picture by supposing what Chaucer intended "where the materials are scanty."[19] But anyone who ever commented on this poet, before or since Godwin, has done the same thing, whether he knows it or not, because at some point the materials are always scanty, and the conjecturing spirit of the reader is stirred to fill out the picture.[20]

How indeterminacy results from the exposure of any imaginative reader to Chaucer, neither Godwin, nor Virginia Woolf, who noted the unsolved questions he left us, nor perceptive critics like Muscatine, Robertson, or even Donaldson, explained. But certain theorists of the hermeneutics of literary indeterminacy can help to do so.

After I. A. Richards insisted that meaning for texts which are imaginatively experienced must be largely created by the individual reader, Norman Holland demonstrated the difficulty of different minds constructing the same experience from the same text; and Stanley Fish explained how a reader's understanding of a major work of literary art can only unfold as he moves through it, making partial adjustments or temporary closures, his perceptions shifting with his developing response. Paul de Man based a psychological theory on the fact that the intentions of the writer will always remain indeterminate, first because they cannot be made entirely evident in marks on a page; second, because they always depend for realization upon the intentions of the interpreter. Since author and reader each bring to the work their own spatio-temporal perspective, they remain equal in the process of interpretation, and the final meaning of the text will always remain undecided.[21]

Other theorists explain this phenomenon as authorial intent. An author may deliberately leave his work indeterminate because he is aware of the inescapable gap between consciousness and the empirical world, the inability of an individual mind to encompass and convey adequately any segment of that world to another mind. Or he may depict basic human experience, reactions, and types so realistically that they achieve the inevitable ambiguity of life itself.

Frank Kermode, who holds just such a thematic theory, gives a reading of Hawthorne which is quite relevant to Chaucer. Altieri summarizes Kermode's main thesis: Hawthorne employs the conventional structures which give an illusion of a writer's authority, but carefully forestalls perception of any single thematic coherence within the structure. And by doing so, Hawthorne suggests "that the experience presented can only be given coherence by an individual reader in effect creating his own text."[22]

And so we find Chaucer employing conventional structures: "I read a book," "I heard a story," "I dreamed a dream." But then he leaves the task of supplying coherence or significance to the reader by confronting him with hints, implications, unanswered questions which arouse his suspicions, but do not allay them. For example, in the following passages the faithful copyist of other men's words leaves the reader to create for himself an innocent, misguided Criseyde, or a deceptive, fickle one, by providing the basis for either:

> But how it was, certeyn, kan I nat seye,
> If that his lady understood nat this,
> Or feynede hire she nyste, oon of the tweye;
> But wel I rede that, by no manere weye,
> Ne semed it as that she of hym roughte . . .

and,

> Nought list myn auctour fully to declare
> What that she thoughte whan he seyde so,
> That Troilus was out of towne yfare . . .

and,

> . . . for to helen hym of his sorwes smerte,
> Men seyn—I not—that she yaf hym hire herte.
> *(Troilus and Criseyde* I.492–6; III.575–7; V.1049–50).

Kermode is defining and describing *The House of the Seven Gables* as "the modern classic"; but surely we can apply his description of Hawthorne's novel to Chaucer's poetry. This novel's "confusion of the 'traditionary' and the historical, its allegories cunningly too clear or too obscure—are all evasions of narrative authority, and imply that each man must make his own reading."[23]

The theories of Wimsatt and Beardsley, on the one hand, and Fish on the other, can be said to represent extremes of the hermeneutics of literary indeterminacy. The first maintains that an author consciously designs a passage to produce a specific result; the second, that both design and result exist only as they are perceived by the reader.[24] But the intermediate theory of Wolfgang Iser, I believe, is the one most applicable to Chaucer.[25]

Iser's explanation of the phenomenology of audience response points out that every text contains, in his words, "gaps of indeterminacy" in which meaning is only implied and must be supplied by the reader, who makes connections and produces coherence based on his own judgment and experience. Because no two readers share identical experiences, perceptions, and values, no two interpretations of the work can be exactly the same; but interpretative anarchy is avoided because the text guides production of meaning, although the potential for a variety, even an infinity, of interpretations can lie within its frame.

Iser's way provides a useful path through the theoretical jungle because it encompasses both poet and reader, responsibility to the text in its time, and acceptance of the obvious: Chaucer's intentional ambiguity. That ambiguity has made his poetry endure for successive generations of readers, and makes it susceptible to interpretations elicited by reader response, but determined ultimately by the poet.

The best of these that I know of are by Chauncey Wood and Carolyn Collette.[26] Wood applies affective stylistics to the *General Prologue* first to show how the reader's anticipatory adjustments and partial closures, as he responds progressively to details in the description of the Prioress, produce in his mind a scathing satire upon her; then, to show how a reader chooses to belong to a particular interpretative community, one whose characteristic responses will shape passages of *Troilus and Criseyde* for him.

Although Collette acknowledges the distinction between modern semiotics and medieval sign theory, wherein all signs derived their meaning from *a priori* Being and referred ultimately to God, she accepts Eco's definition of metaphor as a cognitive instrument, and his theory of literature as a mazelike world of potential meanings through which the individual mind moves, choosing, sorting, correlating, fusing. She then offers a semiotic reading of parts of the *Merchant's Tale* to show how we can combine medieval and modern understanding to produce an enriched reading of Chaucer's work. For example, "A man may do no synne with his wyf,/ Ne hurte hymselven with his owene knyf" (*The Canterbury Tales,* IV E 1839–40) contains the simple analogy man:wyf = man:knyf. Collette explains that in Eco's theory, a semiotic reading of such a metaphor depends on the codes each sign brings to it and on what happens to the codes once the signs are placed in the dynamic relationship of a metaphor. As each assumes properties of the other, "man" is understood first as "husband", then as "wielder of tools"; and certain questions arise. In this instance can January control his wife as he might a tool? Is May merely passive until he animates her? And is not "knyf" a particular kind of tool, dangerous, powerful, and sharp? Collette concludes, "in the midst of a comparison designed ostensibly to show Januarie's blind confidence that he can control and dominate his wife utterly, we find, following Eco's lead, that Chaucer links the ideas of wife and knife to create the idea of woman as ironically powerful, dangerous, potent. . . . As readers we almost automatically sense the irony of the phrase, as semioticians we understand the dynamics of how that irony comes to exist."

It will be interesting now to follow the lead of interpretative critics such as these. To read semiotically and ask, perhaps, what happens to the codes which signs like the Wife of Bath's 'fire' and 'lion' bring to the dynamic relationship of metaphors in the mind of a reader today.[27] Or to be more fully aware of the closures and adjustments of opinion one must make as he moves through the long speech introducing Criseyde's betrayal of Troilus; or aware of the different meanings different "interpretative communities" will assign it.

For following the firm resolution of:

> "That Grekis ben of heigh condicioun,
> I woot ek wel; but certeyn, men shal fynde
> As worthi folk withinne Troie Town,
> As konnyng, and as parfit, and as kynde,
> As ben bitwixen Orkades and Inde. . . ."
>   (*Troilus and Criseyde*, V. 967–971)

we are given hints which suggest a gradual, progressive shift from Criseyde's rejection of Diomede to her implicit acceptance of him:

> "If that I sholde of any Grek han routhe,
> It sholde be yourselven, by my trouthe."
>
> I say nat therfore that I wol yow love,
> N'y say nat nay. . . ."
>   (*Troilus and Criseyde*, V. 1000–1003).

And surely Criseyde's words would be understood and interpreted quite differently if read by a modern psychiatrist or a modern feminist—or heard by Diomede or by Troilus.

Today a critic may reasonably insist that Chaucer, like the classical rhetoricians and medieval orator-preachers, intended to arouse his audience for a specific, foreseen end. Such a view results in an interpretation of his poetry which fills the gaps of indeterminacy with answers that accord with the concepts of the poet's world—at least as far as historical research has enabled us to know them. Alternatively, the critic can follow the outline of the poet's narrative and characterization, and the literal sense of his language, and then employ a hermeneutic circle to create imaginative constructs which derive from the poetry but agree with concepts of the critic's own world.[28] Personally, I favor the latter mode because it recognizes that while an author may intend to arouse response, he can have no final control over all the responses he arouses.

Either interpretative approach seems valid, as long as it is consciously pursued, and the critic understands exactly what he is doing. Whichever mode we employ to interpret Chaucer's poetry, and whichever theory we use to analyze his poetics, modern hermeneutics—with its awareness of the role played in poetic creation by the response of the reader—has brought us to another turn in a very long road and ushered in a new era of criticism which promises to last at least as long as that of Robertsonian exegesis.

Notes

1. "Contemporary Literary Theory and Chaucer," presented at the NCS Congress in New Orleans, April, 1980; reprinted in *New Perspectives in Chaucer Criticism,* ed. Donald M. Rose (Norman, Okla.: Pilgrim Books, Inc., 1981), 25.

2. Of particular relevance are those by Carolyn Collette, "Umberto Eco, Semiotics, and Chaucer"; Judith Ferster, "Gadamer and Ricoeur: Hermeneutics and Chaucer"; Chauncey Wood, "Affective Stylistics: the Reader in *Troilus*"; James Andreas, "A Bakhtinian Approach to the *Summoner's Tale*"; John Ganim, "Mikhail Bakhtin's Theory of the 'Carnivalesque' and Chaucer"; Robert Jordan, "Tzvetan Todorov and Geoffrey Chaucer"; T. F. Hoad, "Chaucer's Language: or What Is Possible in Stylistic Analysis"; Joseph Gallagher, "Double Voicing the *Miller's Tale*" (not an analysis or critique, but an extremely persuasive demonstration of reader response and the effect upon interpretation of choice of interpretive community); the panel on "Deconstructing the *Canterbury Tales*, Pro- and Con"; and the report on Research in Progress of John T. Hermann, "Poststructuralism and the *Parliament of Fowls.*"

3. "III: Die Kompendienartige Darstellung von 1819," tr. Jan Wojcik and Roland Hass, as "The Hermeneutics: Outline of the 1819 Lectures," *New Literary History* 10 (1978): 1–16.

4. For discussion of Schleiermacher and the traditional distinction between the two hermeneutic modes, see Szondi, "Introduction to Literary Hermeneutics," *New Literary History* 10 (1978): 17–29, especially 18.

5. This paper is to be published in the Proceedings volume of the Fifth International Congress of the New Chaucer Society.

6. Cited by Charles Altieri in "The Hermeneutics of Literary Indeterminancy: A Dissent from the New Orthodoxy," *New Literary History* 10 (1978): 93.

7. See particularly *Medieval Theory of Authorship* (London: Scolar Press, 1983) which analyzes the medieval concepts of the role of the poet and the practice of poetry, concepts which seem to have dictated certain aspects of Chaucer's techniques; and *Chaucer and Pagan Antiquity* (London: Scolar Press, 1982) wherein Minnis studies the pagan sources of key passages in the *Knight's Tale* and *Troilus and Criseyde* in context in order to identify the ideological structure within which Chaucer's ideas functioned, and therefore better to comprehend the multiple layers of his possible meaning.

8. An excellent summary, to which I am deeply indebted, of the relevant background in classical rhetoric and Chaucer's sources is contained in Catherine T. Corman's unpublished dissertation, "Rhetorical Process in Chaucer's Poetry," UCLA

1985. See especially Chapter I, "Rhetoric as Process: Classical and Medieval Foundations," 1–19.

9. In *De inventione, De optimo genere, Topica,* tr. H. M. Hubbell, Loeb Classical Library (Cambridge, Mass. and London, 1949), I.xvi.22, I.xv.20, I.lii.98.

10. *The Canterbury Tales* in *The Works of Geoffrey Chaucer,* ed. F. N. Robinson, 2nd ed. (Boston: Houghton Mifflin Co., 1957), VII 919–20, 2767. All subsequent quotations from Chaucer will be taken from this edition and identified in the text.

11. For transference of theory from classical rhetoric to Christian preaching, see Augustine, *On Christian Doctrine,* trans. D. W. Robertson, Jr., Library of Liberal Arts, 80 (New York: Liberal Arts Press, 1958), Book IV. For discussion of preaching theory and practice in the Middle Ages and citation of relevant documents, see James J. Murphy, *Rhetoric in the Middle Ages* (Berkeley and Los Angeles: Univ. of Calif. Press, 1974).

12. For an analysis of Dante's techniques for persuading his readers, see, as well as Corman, Robert Montgomery, *The Reader's Eye* (Berkeley and Los Angeles: Univ. of Calif. Press, 1979). The parallels between Chaucer, de Lorris and de Meun are apparent throughout the *Romance of the Rose,* but 11. 691–700 and 2067–76, may serve as illustration.

13. "Chaucer's Dame Alys, Critics in Blunderland?" *Neuphilologische Mitteilungen* 53 (1972): 381–95, especially 391.

14. Response to Rowland at the 1980 Conference of the International Association of University Professors of English, held in Aberdeen.

15. Florence H. Ridley, "Questions without Answers—Yet or Ever? New Critical Modes and Chaucer," *Chaucer Review* 16 (1981): 101–6.

16. Response to Ridley, "*The Canterbury Tales:* Unity and Reader Response," at the Medieval Colloquium, held at the Univ. of the South, Sewanee, Tenn., April 1985.

17. One passage may serve to illustrate the point: "What these critics [Holland, Slatoff, and Fish] root in empirical psychology, Paul de Man locates in his complex phenomenological reconstruction of intentionality as it applies to fictional utterances . . . intentionality signs a verbal object with the presence of a desire that can never be determinately recovered, for intentionality means that the signs emanate from a point of view (or what Sartre called a surpassing of the object) that can only be recovered from other points of view." Altieri, "The Hermeneutics of Literary Indeterminacy": 72–73.

18. Cf. Lowry Nelson, Jr., "The Fictive Reader: Aesthetic and Social Aspects of Literary Performance," *Comparative Literature Studies* 15 (1978): 203–10; Wolfgang Iser, *The Implied Reader* (Baltimore: The Johns Hopkins Univ. Press, 1974), especially xii–xiii; Stanley E. Fish, "Literature in the Reader: Affective Stylistics," *New Literary History* 2 (1970): 123–62, rpt. in Jane P. Tompkins, *Reader-Response Criticism, from Formalism to Post-structuralism* (Baltimore: The Johns Hopkins Univ. Press, 1980), 70–100, especially 87. Fish, however, is one of the extremist

critics who tend to repel traditionalists with assertions, designed perhaps for shock value, such as, "I describe the experience of a reader who in his strategies is answerable to an author's intention by pointing to the strategies employed by that same reader . . . . Since the author's intention (represented by specific features of the text), and the reader's interpretation are interdependent, the text as an objective entity disappears, re-emerging only as it is 'written' by each reader," in "Interpreting the Variorum," reprinted in Tompkins, 183.

19. Quoted by Caroline F. E. Spurgeon, *Five Hundred Years of Chaucer Criticism and Allusion (1357–1900)*, The Chaucer Society, ser. 2, nos. 48–50, 52–56 (London and New York: Oxford Univ. Press, 1914–1925), II, 10.

20. For discussion of Chaucer's ambiguity, see Ridley, "Chaucerian Criticism, the Significance of Varying Perspectives," *Neuphilologische Mitteilungen* 81 (1980): 133–34.

21. For de Man see *Blindness and Insight: Essays in the Rhetoric of Contemporary Criticism*, 2nd ed. revised (Minneapolis: Univ. of Minn. Press, 1983), especially 10. Altieri provides a useful, if somewhat critical, survey of various theories of literary indeterminacy.

22. Paraphrase of Kermode by Altieri, "The Hermeneutics of Literary Indeterminacy": 76.

23. Kermode, "Hawthorne's Modernity," *Partisan Review* 41 (1974): 428–41, especially 436.

24. William Wimsatt, Jr. and Monroe Beardsley, "The Affective Fallacy," in *Studies in the Meaning of Poetry* (Lexington: Univ. Press of Kentucky, 1954). See especially p. 21, where they point out that if one focuses upon the psychological effects of the poem, the result is "impressionism and relativism. The outcome is that the poem itself, as an object of specifically critical judgment, tends to disappear"; and Fish, "intention and understanding are two ends of a conventional act, each of which necessarily stipulates (includes, defines, specifies) the other," "Interpreting the Variorum," in Tompkins, 174.

25. For explanation of Iser's theory of 'gaps of indeterminacy' see *The Act of Reading: A Theory of Aesthetic Response* (Baltimore and London: The Johns Hopkins Univ. Press, 1978).

26. Wood, "Chaucer's Use of Signs in His Portrait of the Prioress," in John P. Hermann and John J. Burke, Jr., eds., *Signs and Symbols in Chaucer's Poetry* (University, Alabama: The Univ. of Alabama Press, 1981), 81–101; "Affective Stylistics and the Study of Chaucer," *Studies in the Age of Chaucer* 6 (1984): 21–40, especially 31–35; and the paper, "Affective Stylistics; the Reader in Troilus," cited above; Collette, "Umberto Eco, Semiotics, and Chaucer," also cited above.

27. One might consider, for example, the metaphors implicit or explicit in lines 89, 373, 793, and in 429, 692, 776, 794 of the *Wife of Bath's Prologue*.

28. Such is the actual basis, I believe, of Rowland's interpretation of the Wife of Bath cited above, and of Donald R. Howard's interpretation of the Pardoner in *The Idea of the Canterbury Tales* (Berkeley and Los Angeles: Univ. of Calif. Press, 1976), see especially 345–76.

2. Interpreting the Fragment

KARL F. MORRISON

My point of departure is a judgment by Meyer Schapiro. His subject was Bernard of Clairvaux's condemnation of Cluniac sculpture for its elaborate contortions, its *mira quaedam deformis formositas ac formosa deformitas*. Schapiro commented, "the fact that medieval art is full of such incongruities, accidental and designed, and can tolerate the unfinished and the partial, points to a conception of the beautiful in art fundamentally different from the ancient."[1] At first, this statement surprised me, because those who comment on verbal and visual artifacts, not only of the Romanesque era, but of the whole course of medieval art, commonly demand wholeness in a work of art. Indeed, the evidence with which I am familiar relentlessly called for an organic wholeness, distinguished by proportion and co-ordination of parts, as in a human body. Even ugliness was comprehended in beauty. Dramatically asking himself whether to break off the account that he had just begun, the author of the *Vita Heinrici IV. Imperatoris* answered: "It is a shameful thing to leave material, once begun, in a mutilated condition, and to have painted a head without the members."[2]

From the outset, my notes on aesthetics seemed to lead to a conclusion quite different from that stated by Professor Schapiro. I could have recognized the appropriateness of his judgment, if only it had been applied to the aesthetics of Rodin, who delighted in representing fragments of the human body, or of Roland Barthes, who portrayed his own existence as an aggregation of fragments. But aesthetics of the Romanesque era seemed to me intolerant of the fragmentary, indeed unwilling for a fragment that could not be worked into a greater context to survive. Augustine spoke of old statues deformed with age as being melted down and recast into new and more beautiful ones.[3] And the ensuing annals of medieval art are replete with instances—including Suger's reconstruction of St. Denis—in which fragments of the old were swept away, if they could not be reincorporated into a new, organic whole. After all, was it not a characteristic of heretics that they fragmented Scripture, rejecting the whole and holding only the parts that pleased them?

As far as positive evidence was concerned, I could think of many exceptions to Schapiro's judgment. However, the reverse was true when I turned to negative values: that is, to factors that are present in a work by their visible absence. For example, the author is a negative value in a work, being everywhere present, but nowhere to be seen. For similar reasons, design too is a negative value. The interpretation of fragments is, above all, an exercise in rendering present what is absent, passing, as it were, from fragment to form.

Schapiro's comment on tolerance of "the unfinished and partial" proved directly germane to that central enterprise of Romanesque culture most concerned with hermeneutic gaps: namely, Scriptural exegesis. This brings us to what is present by its absence (that is, to what is unsaid and unsayable) in the artistic medium of words. I am going to speak mainly about three twelfth-century German historical writers, but a preliminary comment is needed.

In this regard, I was able to assemble evidence—not always from the Romanesque period—favorable to Professor Schapiro's judgment. For example, I could counterbalance the statement in the *Vita Heinrici IV.,* that it was shameful to paint a head without the members, with the Monk of St. Gall's use of the prophet Daniel's apocalyptic vision of a great statue. After the statue of the Romans, with its feet of iron and clay, had been destroyed, the Monk wrote, God "raised up among the Franks, the golden head of a second statue"—but only the head, in Charlemagne.[4]

Pursuing negative values, as I hope to suggest, leads one to challenge the propositions that all understanding is linguistic and, more narrowly, that "history is meaning imposed on time by means of language."[5] For it leads beyond the discursive functions of language—definition, interpretation, and explanation—to the assimilative functions of the heart, beyond cognition to aesthetics.

Even before the canon of the New Testament was closed, in the fourth century, Christian interpreters were perplexed by the incompleteness, and, thus, the hiddenness of Scripture. Eusebius of Caesarea was repeating an old observation when he commented on how few and how brief St. Paul's letters were by contrast with the Apostle's power and great vision; and on the incompleteness of the Gospel.[6] He compiled the canon tables to demonstrate that divergences among the Gospels did not disturb their essential harmony. Inconsistencies, contradictions, and "absurdities," no less than assertions of secrecy and partiality in the sacred texts, convinced interpreters that there was a gap between the revelations imparted to the authors of Scriptural books and the words that they wrote.

Exegetes recognized that the records of Scripture—even those concerning the life and preaching of Christ—were fragmentary; but they also came to believe that the very words in the records that did exist were fragments, husks or vessels that hid the true meaning of Scripture. This was due in part to the sacred nature ascribed to the content of Scripture, and also, in great part, to the disabilities of language as a medium. Acknowledging the discrepancy between words and things and the varying capacities of different languages to speak of the same things (emphasized both in daily life and in theological disputes), exegetes realized that speech itself involved both revelation and dissembling. Not only were the grammatical rules of Donatus inadequate to circumscribe the sacred content of Scripture, but, in all linguistic discourse, one needed to love the truth in the words, rather than the words themselves.[7] The predicamental character of knowledge was therefore not exclusively linguistic, although exegetes labored to redress it by expanding the texts of Scripture through linguistic methods of literal and figurative interpretation.

Tolerance of "the unfinished and the partial" derived, not from those linguistic techniques for rendering present what appeared to be absent, but rather from prior assumptions that defined the preverbal contours of the hermeneutic gaps, and that led writers to assume that between the lines and syllables there lay meanings that could be present by their absence: that is, negative values of a nonlinguistic kind. I shall illustrate those assumptions by reference to a sampling of twelfth-century texts: Anselm of Havelberg's *Dialogues* (1149–1150), Gerhoch of Reichersberg's *Exposition on the Psalms* (1144–1169), and Otto of Freising's *Chronicle* (1147, revised 1157).[8] These works all address the fragmentary nature of Scripture. Diverse as they are, they also indicate a common delight in the hermeneutic gap at the heart of the interpretative enterprise.

It is a striking fact that each of these works is characterized by structural discontinuities and even incoherence, and, moreover, that major disjunctions entered, not during composition, but during revision. There is an evident caesura between the broad, exhilarating strokes of historical philosophy in Book 1 of Anselm's *Dialogues* and the minute dramatic portrayal of debate, word by word, in Books II and III. Gerhoch of Reichersberg's commentary on Psalm 64, which he considered the masterpiece of his vast exposition on the Psalms, is full of digressions, false starts, and inconsistencies. This digressive, seemingly desultory style characterizes the entire *Exposition*. Otto of Freising's *Chronicle* betrays a perplexing unevenness in the working out of its main apocalyptic theme of the two cities, and (as Otto acknowledged) the culmination of the *Chronicle,* Book VIII, seems largely irrelevant to the previous seven books.

It would appear that revision provided the occasion for the imposition of logical and structural difficulties, certainly when Anselm (in 1149–1150) incorporated in a larger work his version of a debate that occurred in 1135, when (in 1158) Gerhoch reedited for a new recipient a text that he had presented to Pope Eugenius III six years earlier, and when Otto (in 1157), restored to a joyous frame of mind by the return of his dynasty to the imperial throne, altered the history that, in bitterness of mind, he had cast *in modum tragoediae.*

Anselm and Gerhoch lived long after they completed their treatises. They never revised them to establish coherence where it was lacking, nor did Otto's secretary, Rahewin, who assisted him in the composition of the *Chron-*

icle and who wrote the last three of the four books of the *Deeds of Frederick,* smooth out the rough places in the *Chronicle*. Indeed, they ascribed considerable importance to these works. Anselm prepared the *Dialogues* at the command of Pope Eugenius III to serve as a "white paper" in his negotiations with eastern Christians. Gerhoch regarded his commentary on Psalm 64 as his masterpiece, and presented it, first to Eugenius, and later to a Cardinal legate on his entry into Augsburg. Otto of Freising saw his *Chronicle* accepted as a document of state by Frederick Barbarossa. It would appear, from a sketchy copy, that a splendid illuminated manuscript was prepared, versions of which might have been the copies transmitted to Frederick and to his chancellor, Rainald of Dassel.

Under these circumstances, one hesitates to ascribe discontinuities and incoherence to negligence or haste alone. The constellation of major works, displaying similar traits, points toward common assumptions about authorship. Rhetoric does provide some clues. Gerhoch defended the elaborate use of digression as a rhetorical trick of diversion and delight. I believe that what appear to be structural discontinuities in Anselm's *Dialogues* actually sprang from his deliberate construction of the *Dialogues* in the form of a logical dilemma. At least some of the inconsistencies were not accidents, but feints calculated to ensnare the imagination of the reader in the text. But there is other evidence, beyond rhetoric, for a common way of thinking about the hermeneutic gap.

Each text presents the hermeneutic gap in a distinctive way. Still, the three texts display certain common traits. Most plainly, they locate the moment at which the hermeneutic gap formed: that is, the moment of redaction. In recent times, students of New Testament texts have developed a method of analysis called "redaction criticism."[9] Given the special requirements of New Testament criticism, this method cannot be liberally applied to other philological enterprises. But it does, at any rate, shift critical attention from the text to the pretextual work of redaction, which may also involve the intellectual and aesthetic process of assimilation by the redactor.

A familiar collect from a Renaissance text, Edward VI's first Prayer Book (1549), may clarify this distinction. The collect (for the second Sunday in Advent) is: "Blessed Lord, which hast caused all holy Scriptures to be written for our learning, grant us that we may in such wise hear them, read, mark, learn, and inwardly digest them; that by patience and comfort of thy holy word, we may embrace and ever hold fast the blessed hope of everlasting life, which thou hast given us in our saviour, Jesus Christ."[10]

Redaction may end with a text, but the work of redaction has no necessary relation to texts. In the thinking of twelfth-century authors as well as in that of the author of this collect, redaction culminated in inwardly digesting Scripture. Inwardly digesting presupposed and subsumed earlier events— hearing, reading, marking, and learning. But it also presupposed assimilation that was not cognitive, but affective, and that engaged not reading, but visualizing. I shall merely comment that, so conceived, it was not the writing or the reading of a text that made history mimetic, but the inward digesting of it. Mimetic reflex derived in part from the aesthetic discipline of contemplating Scripture as a mirror in which the contemplator envisioned himself. Understanding—or interpreting—Scripture was redactive in this sense. And, just as digesting is an individual event, something that each person must do alone, so also was Scriptural redaction.

I am suggesting that, for our authors, the hermeneutic gap was not, essentially, a rhetorical one. To be sure, it encompassed tropes and figures (including enigma and paradox), just as it also encompassed the deficiencies of the medium of language. Likewise, genre entered into it. But locating the gap in interpretation as redaction (particularly in the complex event of inward digestion) made closing the hermeneutic circle far more difficult than it is in a strictly rhetorical venture of writing or reading. For inwardly digesting meant contemplating with the eye of the heart, and, in some instances, discounting as irrelevant the intention of the author.

Against critics, Otto of Freising justified the deliberate introduction of verbal obscurity into his own *Chronicle* when he mingled factual narrative with the difficult and hidden testimonies of Scripture. The deliberate construction of redactive interpretation around a hermeneutic gap for delight and edification had venerable precedents. For, Otto wrote, Augustine and the authors of books, both in the Old and in the New Testament, had compacted accounts of worldly miseries with secret oracles of the Holy Spirit. John the Evangelist, Otto recalled, omitted information that he had at hand, even as he gave mystic anticipation of the future life. And God, the supreme exemplar of authorship, put forth at the creation invisible and formless matter, and then imposed order and gave light. By such models, Otto was convinced that an author cheapened his subject by making access to it obvious and easy. Something always had to be reserved for future inquiry.[11] The contents of a work were not exhibited; they had to be discovered. The author played a game of hide-and-seek with his audience.

Such a hermeneutic gap could not be bridged by communication through words. Anselm of Havelberg confronted the fragmentary nature of Scripture, first, in the conflict between conservatives and innovators in the Western Church, and, second, in the mutual repulsion between Greek and Latin Christians. Otto of Freising ran against its impenetrable screen when he tried to explain the misfortunes of his age, especially the ruinous struggle between Empire and Papacy. More than either of the others, Gerhoch of Reichersberg believed that he had extracted from Scripture a guide in his perplexity: Why, he wondered, had the Church been so debased that Babylon, the once fallen, had been rebuilt within the walls of Jerusalem, and why were the righteous few persecuted by the rulers of the Church? But even Gerhoch lamented that full enlightenment had escaped him.

The contours of the hermeneutic gap were therefore defined by redactively interrogating the text; but from their interrogation, the authors could not pretend to achieve anything more than approximate knowledge. For the words of Scripture were silent even as they spoke. In the *Phaedrus* (274–276), Plato spun out a myth of the invention of writing. He evoked a curse over the cradle of the new skill. It would, he said, produce forgetfulness, and, since they delivered not truth, but a semblance of truth, written words "neither [spoke] for themselves nor [taught] the truth adequately to others." Written speeches, he continued, were like paintings. They preserved a "solemn silence," and they were contorted at will by readers who might or might not understand them. From his own perspective, Anselm of Havelberg, like Plato, placed the event of meaning in the mind of the redactor as, from its initial ignorance, the understanding moved over things that could be seen to the formation of words, and then to the formation of visible letters on the visible parchment. There, he said, they spoke as they kept silent, and kept silent as they spoke, arousing the reverse sequence, from visible to invisible, in the mind of the reader.[12] Recognition that ensued from interrogating a text was proportionate to the capacity of the redactor, not to the nature of the thing known.

The object of redactive interrogation was by no means to recover the intent of the men who wrote the texts of Scripture. A long tradition permitted interpreters to affirm meanings quite different from those of the original authors and, perhaps, entirely unknown to them. The overarching rule was to interpret Scripture as one book made up of many segments, each mutually illuminating and illuminated by the others. It was right, Anselm wrote, for interpreters to use "something alien" to the text of Scripture in order to disclose their inner harmony. Reached in "a catholic sense," such interpretations served the law of charity, though they violated the text.[13] No less than Anselm, Otto and Gerhoch assumed a concordance among the parts of Scripture, a harmony transcending the circumstances, the intent, and the understanding of individual writers; for those authors may, indeed, have been ignorant of the prophetic meaning in the words that God inspired them to write. The letter killed; the Spirit gave life. Redactive interrogation passed from the silent, speaking words set down by individual writers, to the concordance of the parts of Scripture, and beyond the text to the Spirit, the underlying source of unity that encompassed both the writers of Scripture and readers in every age.

For our three authors, the Archimedean point of interpretation was not the text, but the redactor. The object of redaction was not the words, but what had been unsaid in the words, and what would eventually be seen to fulfill the saying. The hermeneutic gap that they confronted, from the interpreter's *Sitz im Leben,* was both analeptic and proleptic. For them, history itself was an unfolding revelation in which Scripture and interpretations of Scripture were moments of transition, and redactive interpreters were mediators.

I have now returned to the paradigm of the mutual reflection of parts and whole, but in a different context. Earlier, I mentioned it as a guiding principle of exegesis. Now, I have moved one step further than exegesis from the text: that is, to the level of understanding understanding, or, in other words, of the ways in which interpreters understood their hermeneutic task of rendering the absent present.

Two words sum up the complex ideas about understanding understanding expressed by Anselm, Gerhoch, and Otto. They are participation and play; both, of course, are subsumed in the digestive event of mimesis. Understanding Scripture, they said, was aesthetic. It lay not in reading the text, a carnal event, but in partaking of the Spirit that brought the words to life. The redactor's soul, inflamed by the Holy Ghost, participated mimetically in the nature of its Creator, the author of Scripture, just as, when metal is liquified in fire, it loses the forms of its own nature and takes on the form of the fire itself.[14] Gerhoch wrote that people praised and loved the artist in the work, rather than the work itself.[15] But, when he described how, in contemplating a crucifix, the viewer's soul penetrated the "painted image," the positive, sensory content of the work, to assimilate its inner, negative values, Gerhoch wrote not of the painter, but of the subject, the Crucified. The viewer assimilated, first, the poor and needy man represented in the painting, and, at a higher level, the Lord and God within the tortured body.[16] The subject became identical with the object. Likewise, redactive interpreters of Scripture passed mimetically through the words to the affects of the writers of Scripture, finally in transitory episodes of enlightenment to assimilate the Spirit that had inflamed their affects. In humility, they emptied themselves so that they might be filled as vessels with the Spirit, each proportionate to his own capacity.

In passing, I may observe that the acceptance of the episodic—and thus of the discontinuous—may have been reinforced by the fact that our authors experienced Scripture through pericopes. This method demanded the play of imagination through memory and visualization to establish hidden links among segments of Scripture, and to enable the hearer to see himself in the mirror of the pericope.

Being filled, they were able to speak sounding words; for human prayers, Gerhoch wrote, were mute and inaudible letters in heaven, unless the Word made flesh, the entirely and more than entirely vocal Word, were mixed with human consonants.[17] To the same effect, Bernard of Clairvaux wrote that prayer must be preceded by inspiration: "Dicendum iam inchoet amor noster, quoniam ubi consummetur dictum est."[18]

I would like to underscore the point that the moment of participation was also the moment of understanding; it was episodic (or pericopic), sacramental, and aesthetic. The verbal labor of exposition that followed was, for the three authors, reflection or recollection: that is, memory, not experience.

The subject participated in—and, in that sense, became proportionately identical with—the object through the dynamic of play. Play mediated the dialectical relationship between them and made assimilation possible. It is striking that all three authors used the language of the theater to define their tasks, and that Anselm and Gerhoch quite deliberately cast their treatises in dramatic forms. These rhetorical devices were symptoms of a profound grasp of the dynamic of play in the formation of thought, inherited directly from the Church Fathers, together with a repertory of metaphors of play drawn from the theater (imitation), amphitheater (conflict), the Circensian games (skill and endurance), and hazard (gambling).[19] Without knowing the term, the Fathers knew that play was a device that made empathetic participation possible. In varying modes, the same perception, as well as the language of play, characterized the works of Anselm, Gerhoch, and Otto. For them all, as rhetoricians, reading became performance, and performance, affective union. As diviners of the occult, spiritual adepts, they also knew, with the visionary of the *Apocalypse,* how to see the voice that spoke and, more, how to become what they saw.

This understanding of understanding posited a union of all parts—all interpreters and their moments of illumination—in an organic whole, described as the body of Christ or as God's eternal temple, made of living stones. But it also insisted on the fragmentary character of every instant of understanding, and of the aggregate of all such instants. Certainly, the text itself was a tissue of deliberate obscurities; hide-and-seek was part of the method of composition. But the inescapable fact was that the view of any given redactive interpreter was clouded by many defects, including his own finitude. Moreover, the great panorama of divine instruction had not yet been entirely unfolded. All understanding was predicamental and approximate, certainly while the body of Christ was still being formed and living stones still being added to the eternal temple. Yet more fragmenting was the incommunicability of what had been inwardly digested. The disputes among Christians which prompted and shaped our three treatises were evidence enough for the authors that understanding of truth, whether in the Scripture or in their own writings, was conveyed in unspoken, unsayable, and transitory experience, from faith to faith, rather than in words inscribed on a page; that understanding was proportionate to the capacity of the interpreter; and, moreover, that it was beyond the power of language to express, except as meaning was conveyed through the spirit.[20]

Each of the three treatises is notoriously fragmentary, inconsistent, and, occasionally, self-contradictory. I believe that the presence of these characteristics is due to the way of understanding understanding as episodic (or pericopic) that I have briefly described, a way that centered on the hermeneutic gap, in two regards. The first lay between the negative contents of Scripture and the mind of the interpreter; it was a gap in which words functioned as sacraments, and it was closed by the cycle of emptying and filling by which the interpreter became one with the Spirit in the text through empathetic participation. The second lay between the interpreter and other human beings. It was a gap in which words functioned as signs or symbols.

One object of the author was to keep this gap open by the hide-and-seek methods of composition: that is, by imitating God in the deliberate intrusion of incompleteness, contradiction, and even absurdities into the text. In any event, this significatory, or symbolic, aspect of the hermeneutic gap could be closed only indirectly, through participation in a common source of understanding, not by direct verbal communication. As Gerhoch pointed out, the branches of the vine were connected with one another only through their common stock; the bad could be pruned away and burned without damage to the good. I would like to suggest that this line of reasoning accepted predicaments, incongruities, and fragments as the basis of pericopic perception, and that it is one reason that the treatises by Anselm, Gerhoch, and Otto illustrate Professor Schapiro's judgment concerning Romanesque aesthetics. I also believe that it elucidates the disparity that I at first noticed between the insistence of Romanesque texts on organic unity and the delight that they also expressed in things that were present by their absence.

To summarize: the hermeneutic gap represented in the three texts just considered was not essentially verbal or rhetorical. Consequently, in so far as these texts exemplify common traits, one need not limit discussion of the predicamental core of historical writing to rhetoric. Hegel wrote about ancient works of art as "corpses of stone from which the animating soul has flown, and hymns of praise [as] words from which all belief has gone."[21] Perhaps medieval texts, too, torn from their own world and placed on exhibit in the necropolises of culture are not the same as they once were. But this is only to say that another kind of hermeneutic gap has arisen in reading, not in redaction. To limit scholarly discourse about the hermeneutic gap in medieval historical writing to rhetoric is to treat only the ashes of a culture's physical existence, and to ignore such coals ignited by the vital flame as still burn beneath them.

I must conclude, however, by pointing out that this aesthetic rationale for tolerating the fragment was a trait of Romantic, as well as of Romanesque, aesthetics. Many important differences separated the father of hermeneutics, Friedrich Schleiermacher, from the three authors I have mentioned. They include his secular concept of inspiration, entirely hostile to the concept of supernatural inspiration embraced by our three authors, and the sense of historical alienation among periods and cultures that produced his critical fragmentation of Scripture. Yet, in his Scriptural exegesis and in his aesthetics many elements of the hermeneutic scheme survived, not least the stress on the spectator, rather than on the spectacle, the work of art. A person, he wrote, might find beautiful outlines and relationships in a fragment of a great work of art. From the fragment, it might be possible to deduce the rules governing them. Would not a viewer, on that account, consider the fragment more a work in itself than part of a work? Would he not suppose (in his partial knowledge), that by comparison with the part, the whole work of art would lack verve, boldness, and everything that bespeaks a great spirit? Yet,

Schleiermacher continued, an individual object displayed relationships that could not be fully understood from the object itself. The world is a work of which a person can see only one part, and, even if that fragment were complete, a viewer could not from it form an adequate conception of the whole.[22]

Schleiermacher did indeed teach that all understanding was linguistic, but this, in fact, applied to the philological enterprise of criticism (*Kritik*). Applied to Scripture, criticism led to extreme fragmentation. But, in his exegetical tasks, Schleiermacher applied not criticism, but the expository method (*Auslegung*) from which quite different results came. Schleiermacher's point in the passage just cited is that the internal unity of a work, which may be extrapolated from a fragment, does not disclose the endless inexhaustible unity that encompasses all human works, and that is detected, not by critical analysis of internal, organic unity of the particular composition, but by a divinatory, religious feeling for the endless unity in which it participated. The interpreter enters into the creative process—the mind of the author—that produced the text; he transforms himself, Schleiermacher said, into the author. From this perspective, every utterance, every text or work of art, was a fragment made up of elements that, to a viewer who had no eye to the greater harmony, might mistakenly seem incongruous or unfinished—in fact, *mira quaedam deformis formositas ac formosa deformositas.*

Notes

1. Meyer Schapiro, "On the Aesthetic Attitude in Romanesque Art," *Romanesque Art* (New York: G. Braziller, 1977) 8: 23–24. Schapiro refers to Bernard of Clairvaux's celebrated statement in his *Apologia*, 12. 28. *S. Bernardi Opera*, J. Leclercq and H.M. Rochais eds., vol. 3 (Rome: Editiones Cistercienses, 1963), 104. For more detailed treatments of some points raised in this essay, see my other articles, "Otto of Freising's Quest for the Hermeneutic Circle," *Speculum* 55 (1980): 207–36; "The Church as Play: Gerhoch of Reichersberg's Call for Reform," in Stanley Chodorow, Richard Fraher, and James Ross Sweeney eds., *Festschrift* for Brian Tierney (Cornell University Press, forthcoming); and "Anselm of Havelberg: Play and the Dilemma of Historical Progress," in John J. Contreni and Thomas F. X. Noble eds., *Religion, Culture and Society in the Early Middle Ages: Studies in Honor of Richard E. Sullivan* (Medieval Institute, Western Michigan University, forthcoming). Some aspects of interpretation discussed in this paper are considered at greater length in my book *"I am You": The Hermeneutics of Empathy in Western Literature, Theology, and Art* (Princeton University Press, forthcoming).

2. *Vita Heinrici IV. Imperatoris*, c. 1. *MGH, SSrrG*, 13. In the following notes, the titles of some standard source collections are cited in abbreviated form, as follows: *CSEL = Corpus Scriptorum Ecclesiasticorum Latinorum; Corp. Christ., ser. lat. = Corpus Christianorum, series latina; PL =* J. P. Migne, *Patrologiae Cursus Completus, series latina; MGH = Monumenta Germaniae Historica; SS = Scriptores; SSrrG = Scriptores rerum Germanicarum in usum scholarum.*

3. *Enchiridion*, 23 (89). *PL* 40:273. *City of God*, 22. 19. *CSEL* 40, pt 2, 629.

4. *De Carlo Magno*, 1.1. *MGH, SS* 2, 731.

5. Nancy F. Partner, "Making Up Lost Time: Writing on the Writing of History," *Speculum* 61 (1986): 97.

6. *Historia Ecclesiastica*, 3.24.

7. Cf. Augustine, *De Doctrina Christiana*, 4.11.26. *Corp. Christ., ser. lat.* 32, 134.

8. Anselm of Havelberg, *Dialogi, PL* 188:1139–1248; Gerhoch of Reichersberg, *Expositio in Psalmos, PL* 193:619–1814; 194:9-998. Otto of Freising, *Chronicon, MGH, SSrrG,* 20.

9. For a general introduction, see Norman Perrin, *What Is Redaction Criticism?* (Philadelphia: Fortress Press, 1969).

10. *The First and Second Prayer Books of Edward VI* (New York: Dutton, 1910), 34.

11. *Chron.*, 8. prol.; 8. 35. *MGH, SSrrG,* 392–93, 457.

12. *Dialogi*, 2. 16. *PL* 188:1187.

13. Ibid., 2. 26. *PL* 188:1208.

14. Gerhoch of Reichersberg, *Tr. in Ps.* 72:19–20. *PL* 194:349–50.

15. *Tr. in Ps. 27:2. Tr. in Ps. 144:4. PL* 193:1224. *PL* 194:964.

16. *Tr. in Ps. 40:14. Tr. in Ps. 72:19–20. PL* 193:1486. *PL* 194:350.

17. *Tr. in Ps. 19:2. PL* 193:914.

18. *De diligendo Deo,* 7. 22. J. Leclercq and H. M. Rochais eds., *S. Bernardi Opera,* 3 (Rome: Editiones Cisterciences, 1963), 137–38.

19. See the chapter, "Augustine's Gaming Board," in my forthcoming study, *"I am You."*

20. Cf. Augustine, *De doctrina Christiana,* 3. 26–28. 37–39. *Corp. Christ., ser. lat.* 32, 98–100.

21. *The Phenomenology of Mind,* trans. J. B. Bailie (New York: Harper, 1967), 753.

22. *Reden über die Religion,* 2. Friedrich Daniel Ernst Schleiermacher, *Theologische Schriften,* ed. Kurt Nowak (Berlin: Union, 1983), 95. See the chapter, "Schleiermacher's Anthropology," in my forthcoming study, *"I am You."*

3. *Meditationes Vitae Christi:* The Logistics of Access to Divinity

ROBERT WORTH FRANK, JR.

The *Meditationes Vitae Christi* is a meditative treatise composed in Latin in the late thirteenth century by an unknown Italian Franciscan, presumably for a woman in the Franciscan order of St. Clare, though it soon won a much wider audience among layfolk and clergy. It survives in over 200 manuscripts.[1] There were translations into most of the Western European vernaculars; Margaret Deanesley identified six or possibly seven translations into English in the fourteenth and fifteenth centuries.[2] In its fullest form it is a vivid recounting of the life of Christ, beginning with the early life of the Virgin and the Annunciation, and ending with the Ascension. The narrative is based on the Gospels and on apocryphal materials, but is freely supplemented by the author's inventive powers. Intermingled with the narrative are simple exegesis and sensible moral instruction, including a disquisition on the Active and Contemplative Lives. A shorter version omits portions of the public life and the treatise on the Two Lives. A third consists of the Passion sequence alone, beginning with the Lord's Supper and ending with the Harrowing of Hell.[3] The full version will be used here.[4]

We should note first that, in accordance with the meditation tradition, the *Meditationes* makes specific and intense demands on its reader. Guigo II (†1188?) defined the process of meditation as "an inner understanding . . . , a studious activity of the mind, seeking knowledge of hidden truth by the guidance of one's reason; . . . it diligently seeks out what may be grasped and, digging away, discovers a treasure."[5] The author of the *Meditationes,* though emphasizing imagination more than reason, expects his reader to "seek" and "dig" for the full import and impact of what she is reading. Dante, Chaucer, and Juan Ruiz all display authorial sensitivity to the fragility of meaning, and all offer directives to guide and involve the reader, which Florence Ridley and Chauncey Wood analyze in their essays. These characteristics probably stem from a different tradition, but they have much in common with what we find in the *Meditationes.* Its author is constantly summoning his reader into the creation of his text, calling for her imaginative participation in and contribution to the scenes from Christ's life, and urging her to reflect on the emotional and doctrinal significance of those scenes. The success of the work must in considerable part be due to this demand for involvement.

For successful it most certainly was. Its enormous influence on art has been amply documented by Emile Mâle, Millard Meiss, and others, and its imprint on the medieval English mystery plays is unmistakable. Its pervasive contribution to late medieval affective spirituality has also been fully acknowledged.[6] What will be analyzed in some detail here is the radical reduction in distance between meditant and divinity which the *Meditationes* established. It constitutes a revolutionary reinterpretation of the relationship between God and man.

We can achieve a preliminary sense of this change by looking briefly at the meditations of St. Anselm, written 200 years earlier. They are the principal documents of the Anselmian revolution, which transformed the devotional life of his time. In them, affective piety reached a new level of intensity.[7] This intensity is located in two polar areas. One is Anselm's dramatic, even shocking, sense of his vileness, his abject failure as God's creature. The meditation on "virginity unhappily lost" begins,

> My soul, wretched soul, soul of a wretched little man, shed your sluggishness, shatter your sin, and shake up your mind. Let your heart break with the enormity of sin and let a huge groan break out of your heart. Unhappy man, turn your thought to the horror of your wickedness, and turn yourself to horrible terror and terrible grief.[8]

The other pole is the meditant's aching love and longing for God:

> Most merciful Lord,
> turn my lukewarmness into a fervent love of you. Most gentle Lord,
> my prayer tends towards this—
> that by remembering and meditating
> on the good things you have done
> I may be enkindled with your love.

And, moments later,

> My Lord and my Creator,
> you bear with me and nourish me—
> be my helper.
> I thirst for you, I hunger for you, I desire you,
> I sigh for you, I covet you:
> I am like an orphan deprived of the presence
> of a very kind father. . . .[9]

A dramatic tension vibrates between these two poles of deepest feeling—the meditant poignantly aware of his sinfulness reaching out for God's love: "What shall I say? What shall I do? Whither shall I go? Where shall I seek him? Where and when shall I find him? Whom shall I ask? Who will tell me of my beloved?"[10] The tension arises from the reaching, a vivid awareness of the chasm to be bridged:

> He [the meditant] longs to see you,
> but your countenance is too far away.
> He wants to have access to you,
> but your dwelling is inaccessible.
> He longs to find you,
> but he does not know where you are.
> He loves to seek you, but he does not know your face.[11]

Anselm had a powerful visual imagination, and he re-created the torments of the Passion and the grief of the Virgin Mother in specific, visual terms, but his lament was that he could not be present at the Crucifixion:

> Alas for me that I was not able to see
> the Lord of angels humbled to converse with men,
> [that he might exalt men to converse with angels!] when God, wronged,
> willingly died that the sinner might live.[12]

The distance separating the sinful mortal from his God, a constant theme, is in fact a synergic force, urging the meditant on. But the distance is there.

We enter a world of markedly different perspectives when we come to the *Meditationes*. William of St. Thierry, St. Bernard, St. Francis, and St. Bonaventura have passed along the pilgrim way, as have Abbot Ekbert and Ailred of Rievaulx. The author of the *Meditationes* learned from all of them, but his vision of the relationship between God and humankind is very much his own and is developed with striking imaginative power and remarkable rhetorical skill. He has created a complete incarnational poetic. Leo Steinberg's dismissal of the *Meditationes* as "a work of naïve sentimental piety" could not be wider off the mark.[13]

The *Meditationes* presents, first, a consistently loving God who does not threaten punishment. Meditations frequently invoke the emotion of fear—Anselm's do—as a spur to repentance and reform. But fear plays no part in the affective program here. God the Father is throughout a God of love. Its opening scene is the debate of the Four Daughters of God. In effect, human history begins with a benevolent concern for the salvation of humankind. In his first appearance, God is an accessible god, open to petition on man's behalf. The meditant is urged to imagine God, though he has no body, "as a great lord, seated on a raised chair, with a benign face, compassionate and paternal, almost as though wishing to be or already reconciled." After the

Annunciation scene, the meditant is told that "God had been indignant with the human race because of the fault of the first parent, but now, seeing the Son become a man, He will no longer be angry."[14]

As for God the Son, the *Meditationes* presents him as unfailingly considerate and loving. In the harrowing of hell (which is completely devoid of dramatics) we are told that Christ might have sent an angel to release the "fathers" imprisoned there and bring them to him, but his infinite love and humility would not allow this (*non sustinuisset*); the Lord of all descended that he might visit them as friends and not as servants, and he stayed with them until the dawn of Sunday.[15]

The *Meditationes* also creates a more completely and convincingly human Christ than had ever been seen before. The doctrine of the Incarnation is, of course, the ultimate confirmation of God's love for humankind. But doctrine in the *Meditationes* is never allowed to mark time as mere doctrine: it must be concretized, realized, made flesh. As a consequence, we get a daring working out of the implications of that doctrine, certainly beyond anything in Anselm. Jean Leclercq, observing Anselm's recurring use of the terms "experiri," "experientia," "experimentum," suggested Anselm was seeking "a certain experience" of God.[16] The meditant in the *Meditationes* beyond question has at one level an experience of God, that is, of the human Christ, for he is there to see, to hear, to touch, and most especially to come to know intimately and fondly.

The experiential involvement with the human Christ had been accelerated by the participatory stratagem originated by Ailred of Rievaulx. In his *De Jesu puero* and *Vita inclusorum,* Ailred had invited the meditant to step into a scene—the Nativity, say—and to be immediately present, even to participate by holding the Christ child and fondling him.[17] The stratagem, very much a product of the age's growing preoccupation with the human Christ, dramatizes the human moment and can result in powerful emotional reactions. The author of the *Meditationes* used it brilliantly. Though he employed it for affective ends, his most revolutionary deployment was in invented scenes where no immediate affective purpose is served. These scenes take us, I believe, to the heart of his intention.

An example from the years in Egypt sequence will illustrate the practice. The meditant had been invited to "visit" the Holy Family in Egypt and urged to feel compassion for them in their poverty before she left: "On every side is material for compassion." But a page later the meditant is instructed to

> go back to visit the boy Jesus. You may find him outside with other boys. When he sees you he'll run to you, for he is gentle, kind, and courteous. Kneeling before him, kiss his feet and then take him in your arms and rest with him a while. Then perhaps he'll say to you, "We've been given permission to go back to our own country, and we have to leave tomorrow. You've come at just the right time, because you'll go back with us." Answer

him at once that you're very pleased at this and you want to follow him wherever he goes. You'll be delighted by this conversation with him. I've already told you that this kind of thing, though it seems childish, is very valuable for meditating on, and it leads afterwards to even greater things.[18]

It is a charming moment, made out of whole cloth. But to what purpose? Not for the sake of its charm certainly. And its affective impact is negligible. Yet the narrator calls special attention to its value, for all its seeming triviality (which he also calls attention to), and says that later it will be of even greater consequence. What he has "already told" her is found in an earlier scene invented for the Egyptian years, which tells of the boy Jesus helping his mother find work to support them. There the narrator had said, "Do not disdain humble things and such as seem childlike in the contemplation of Jesus, for they will yield devotion, increase love, excite fervor, induce compassion, allow purity and simplicity, nurture the virtue of poverty, preserve familiarity, and confirm and raise hope"[19]—a large order, and an important statement. For the later scene I would suggest that increasing love and preserving familiarity are especially its consequences. Stored in the memory, brought out later for recollection and reexamination, its primary significance must be this: an unshakable sense of the human reality of the central figure, the boy Jesus, and of closeness to him ("familiarity"). A "memory" is created such as an older sister, or an aunt—or an uncle—might cherish as a golden moment of intimacy with a loved child. The child's responses are unmistakably human. After such an "experience" the meditant could not doubt that Christ was one of the human family.

The *Meditationes* has many such sensitive human moments. In the treatise on the Two Lives, the author disavows all claims to guiding his reader to a vision of "the celestial court and the majesty of God, [higher manifestations] which are reserved only to the most perfect. For this reason [he adds], perhaps one should call this more directly and properly a meditation on the humanity of Christ, rather than a contemplation."[20] And without question the art of the narrator has made Christ a human figure with whom a meditant can most warmly, lovingly, and intimately identify. It has truly incarnated him.

This can be said in full awareness that the Incarnation is a union of the human *and* divine. The great danger of his method is that the divine will be diminished or dwarfed. The *Meditationes,* however, avoids this danger with great skill. By a variety of techniques, the author never permits the divine to leave our field of vision. He has, for one thing, devised what we might call an "incarnational stylistics," using verbal and syntactical parallelisms to bracket the human and the divine. The five-year old Christ leaving Egypt, too big to carry, too little to walk the entire way, is given an ass to ride on and then apostrophized, "O puer egregie ac delicate, rex coeli et terrae" ("Oh, admirable and gracious child, King of Heaven and Earth" [*Meditationes,* 528b]). In a scene before the Purification, we see Joseph regarding the child "quem

sciebat esse Deum suum et Dominum suum'' (''whom he knew to be his God
and his Lord'') and the Virgin embracing him ''quem sciebat esse filium
suum'' (''whom she knew to be her son'' [*Meditationes*, 523b]).

There are more sophisticated strategies. David Jeffrey has commented on
the author's creation of prefigurational moments.[21] The five-year old Christ
riding out of Egypt on an ass prefigures Christ riding into Jerusalem on Palm
Sunday. Leaving Egypt, the Holy Family crosses the Jordan and probably
found John the Baptist already there doing penance, the author says, for it was
the place where he later baptized, said to be where the children of Israel
crossed on their return from Egypt. The invented human moment becomes a
convergence of Old Testament typology and New Testament fulfillment. The
human event in the *Meditationes* again and again urges forward toward spiritual significance.

The incarnational poetics is, however, probably most skillfully deployed
in the narrational method itself. Of the many vividly rendered scenes in the
Passion sequence, I select one where this bifocal awareness of the human and
divine Christ is clearly in control:

> They laugh and mock at Him who is the true and eternal God, and hasten His
> death. He is led back inside, stripped of the purple, and stands before them
> nude, not given leave to reclothe Himself. Pay diligent attention to this and
> consider His stature in every part. And to make yourself more deeply com-
> passionate and nourish yourself at the same time, turn your eyes away from
> this divinity for a little while and consider Him purely as a man. You will see
> a fine youth, most noble and most innocent and most lovable cruelly beaten
> and covered with blood and wounds, gathering His garments from the
> ground where they were strewn and dressing Himself before them with
> shame, reverence, and blushes however much they jeer, as though He were
> the meanest of all, abandoned by God, and destitute of all help. Look at Him
> diligently, therefore, and be moved to pity and compassion: now He picks up
> one thing, now another, and dresses Himself before them. Next return to His
> divinity and consider the immense, eternal, incomprehensible, and imperial
> Majesty incarnate, humbly bowing down, bending to the ground to gather
> His garments together, dressing Himself with reverence and blushes as if He
> were the vilest of men, indeed the servant under their domination, corrected
> and punished by them for some crime (77:330–31/604b–605a).

The narrator plays over the scene three times: divinity, man, divinity; the
actions and reactions remain the same, the union of God and man beautifully
caught in the repeated reaching down for the garments, the blushes, the
humiliation. The oscillation between Christ's human and divine natures never
allows us to forget the divinity, but by the same token the divinity is never
allowed to loom so overwhelmingly that the meditant pulls away in excessive
awe or the compassionate human relationship slackens or fades.

Above all else, what binds human and divine, meditant and God in the

Meditationes is the image of "family." As a metaphor, "family" vivifies both the doctrine of the Trinity and the doctrine of the Incarnation. But here metaphor becomes literal truth. The concept of family dominates the author's inventions. He elaborates on it for its affective power. It is the prime embodiment of his doctrinal message. And it is at the base of his rhetoric, drawing meditant closer and closer to divinity. By means of it he makes the meditant "familiar" with God. "Familiaris" and "familiariter" are, in fact, favorite words.[22]

The image of family is seen most obviously in the tender relationship of Christ and the Virgin: Christ going about as a boy of five to find work for her to support them in Egypt, helping set the table and make the beds at home before the public life, sending the angels to her for his food after fasting forty days in the wilderness, etc.[23] But the family pattern extends far beyond mother and child. Before the birth of Christ, Mary's visitation at the house of Elizabeth (who was pregnant with John the Baptist) becomes a family tableau: "Oh, the house, the room, the bed in which live and rest together the mothers of two such sons, Jesus and John! And those magnificent old men, Zacharias and Joseph are there also" (5:24/517a).

The family circle widens to become ever more inclusive—Magdalene, the other Marys, Martha, the disciples (frequently called "brothers"). The Italian provenance of the *Meditationes* may be relevant here. David Herlihy has coined the phrase "spiritual families" for the bands of followers attached to female Italian saints in the late Middle Ages. The saint called them "children" and they in turn called her "mother."[24] What evolves in the *Meditationes* may be such a spiritual family—for it is a family beyond doubt.

So powerful is this image, in fact, that the Passion becomes almost as much a family drama as the climax to the drama of salvation. It is framed by familial considerations. These begin with the great distress within the group when first the Magdalene and then the Virgin Mother learn that Jesus will not spend Pasch with them. John hastens to the Virgin and her companions "gathered in the house of Magdalene" to tell them of Jesus' capture and torture. The Virgin begs God to employ some other way to redeem mankind than the death of His—her—son. She, John, and her companions witness the crucifixion. They watch at the cross after the crowd has scattered, they assist Joseph of Arimathea and Nicodemus at the deposition and burial. We follow them home afterwards. Incident and conversation are invented for the group for the whole of Saturday, a sequence given more space than the Harrowing of Hell. On Sunday the resurrected Christ goes first to visit and comfort his mother. Then, concerned for Magdalene, he goes to her with his mother's consent. He visits various disciples, scenes where the intent seems as much to comfort and console as it is to manifest the marvel and the truth of the Resurrection. At the close of Easter Sunday the disciples (except Thomas), Magdalene, the Virgin, and Christ are gathered together. Christ stays "familiarly" with the disciples. The Virgin sits "familiarly" next to her son. The narrator bursts out, "Oh, this little house, how pleasant to live in it."[25] The family has been reunited.

At key moments the familial relationship of Father and Son within the Trinity is also stressed. When Christ prays at Gethsemane, God is referred to nineteen times as "Father," and Christ as "Son" five times. The angel Michael tells Christ that "the Father says that He is always with you and that He will protect your mother and the disciples and return them safe and sound" (75: 323/601a). The distinction between the divine and the human family almost disappears.

The diminished distance between God and man measured here results primarily from a reinterpretation of the relation between God and man. A new emphasis on God's love for man and on the human nature of Christ has moved divinity closer to humankind. The human meditant, in turn, has been moved closer to divinity. The exploitation of a specific human faculty, the imagination, has opened up the possibility of an experiential knowledge of the Gospel Christ. New stress on the virtue of humility has revealed a closer identity that is possible between meditant and Christ.

The role of the imagination in spiritual life had been under examination from the twelfth century on, particularly by mystics. Monastic tradition had been suspicious of "carnal images" and of the delusive power of "fantasy."[26] William of St. Thierry had resorted reluctantly to the imagination, doing so only because he was too weak to *see* God and was therefore obliged to dwell on God's lowliness by means of mental images ("mentis imaginatione").[27] But in *De Unione Corporis et Spiritus*, Hugo of St. Victor (c. 1078–1141) had argued that there is a "basic and complementary relation established between body and spirit" by what he called *sensualitas,* the contact of spirit with matter, and the instrument of *sensualitas* was the imagination. Hugo wrote, "Nothing in the body is higher or nearer to the spiritual nature than what the force of the imagination, coming after sense, and beyond the reach of the senses, conceives."[28]

A kind of laboratory evidence of imagination's contribution to spirituality may also have been a potent factor by the time the *Meditationes* was composed. I refer to the accumulating experience of the growing number of mystics; the rewarding experiences of the many users of the many meditations being written and circulated; and perhaps most notably the example of St. Francis. The spiritual fervor of the man who saw the Cross in crossed sticks in the road and who summoned up as he walked about the countryside the Crucifixion so vividly that he sobbed aloud gave more than impelling testimony of the dynamic role of imagination in spiritual life. And our unknown author was a Franciscan.

From the very first he instructed the meditant on the key role of the imagination: "It suffices that you place his [Christ's] deeds and words before your mind's eye and converse with Him and become familiar with Him. In this appears almost the whole fruit of these meditations."[29] Meditation is identified firmly as an activity involving imagination, a human faculty possessed by all, and so this meditation is open to all. The narrative emphasis on the family is particularly effective in evoking imaginative response, appealing to deep-seated memories and basic feelings that could contribute richly and spontaneously to the imaginative creation of scene and close identification.

The meditant moves closer to divinity also through the key virtue of humility, stressed repeatedly. Humility is the hinge on which the fallible human soul pivots from sinfulness to repentance and restoration to grace. Though the Franciscans did not invent humility, it took on heightened dramatic form in the life of St. Francis and became a central teaching. In the Bernardine-Franciscan view, awareness of one's fallible, sinful nature leads not to despair or separation from God (as it tends to do in Anselm), but to humility. And humility makes humankind most like Christ, whose Incarnation was the supreme act of humility. He is "the Master of Humility."[30] The meditant is advised that the more perfect the servants of God, the closer to God and the more excellent their gifts, "the more humble they become, for they claim nothing for themselves except sins and defects. And the closer one comes, the more he is illuminated and therefore he sees more clearly the magnificence of God and his own wretchedness."[31]

And so the meditant, humbly participating in the Nativity, holding the infant Christ, visiting the young boy in Egypt, standing with the crowd at the Crucifixion, was *there,* close to God. By the power of her imagination she was *with* him. By virtue of his love, his humanity, and his humility and her love and humanity and humility, they were "familiar," of one family. Distance had dissolved.

Notes

1. For basic information, see *Meditations on the Life of Christ,* trans. [from the Italian] Isa Ragusa, completed from the Latin and ed. Isa Ragusa and Rosalie B. Green (Princeton: Princeton University Press, 1961), xxi–xxii, nn. 1–4. Very useful also is *Meditaciones de Passione Christi olim Sancto Bonaventurae Attributae,* ed. Sister M. Jordan Stallings (Washington: Catholic University of America Press, 1965), xiii–xviii and 3–14.

2. "The Gospel Harmony of John de Caulibus or S. Bonaventura," *Collectanea Franciscana,* British Society of Franciscan Studies 10 (1922): 10–19.

3. For the Latin text, see the excellent edition by Sister M. Jordan Stallings (n. 1 above).

4. The Latin text used here is that in *Sancti Bonaventurae Opera Omnia,* ed. A.C. Peltier (Paris: L. Vivès, 1868), 12:509–630.

5. *Lettre sur la vie contemplative (L'échelle des moines); Douze méditations,* ed. Edmund Colledge and James Walsh (Paris: Les Éditions du Cerf, 1970), Sources

Chrétiennes, Vol. 163 (Série des Textes Monastiques d'Occident, no. 29): "meditatio secundum interiorem intellectum" (108); "meditatio est studiosa mentis actio, occultae veritatis notitiam ductu propriae rationis investigans" (108); "meditatio quid appetendum sit diligentius inquirit, et quasi effodiens thesaurum invenit et ostendit" (481).

6. See *Smaointe Beatha Chriost,* ed. Cainneach o Maonaigh [Canice Mooney] (Dublin: Dublin Institute for Advanced Studies, 1944), 323–66, for a valuable survey.

7. For the tradition of meditation and prayer in which St. Anselm wrote, see, most conveniently, Sister Benedicta Ward, "Background to the 'Prayers and Meditations,'" in *The Prayers and Meditations of Saint Anselm,* trans. Sister Benedicta Ward, S.L.G. (Harmondsworth: Penguin Books, 1973), 17–50, and "The Prayers and Meditations," 51–59.

8. *The Prayers and Meditations of Saint Anselm,* 225. I have made use of Sister Benedicta Ward's translation but have sometimes (as here) combined her translation with my own. For the reader's guidance, I give the Latin in each instance, based on the edition by Father Francis S. Schmitt, *S. Anselmi Cantuariensis Archiepiscopi Opera Omnia* (Edinburgh: Thomas Nelson and Sons, 1946): The following is from "Deploratio virginitatis, male amissae":

> Anima mea, anima aerumnosa, anima, inquam, misera miseri homunculi, excute torporem tuum et discute peccatum tuum et concute mentem tuam. Reduc ad cor enorme delictum et perduc de corde immanem rugitum. Intende, infelix, intende sceleris tui horrorem et protende horrificum terrorem et terrificum dolorem (3:80).

9. "Converte, misericordissime, meum teporem in ferventissimum tui amorem. Ad hoc, clementissime, tendit haec oratio mea, haec memoria et meditatio beneficiorum tuorum, ut accendam in me tuum amorem." "Domine meus, creator meus, tolerator et nutritor meus, esto adiutor meus. Te sitio, te esurio, te desidero, ad te suspiro, te concupisco. Et sicut pupillus benignissimi patris orbatus praesentia. . . ." From "Oratio ad Christum cum mens vult eius amore fervere," 3:7; in *Prayers,* 94–95.

10. "Quid dicam? Quid faciam? Quo vadam? Ubi eum quaeram? Ubi vel quando inveniam? Quem rogabo? Quis nuntiabit dilecto. . . ?" Ibid. 3:9; *Prayers,* 97.

11. "Anhelat videre te, et nimis abest illi facies tua. Accedere ad te desiderat, et inaccessibilis est habitatio tua. Invenire te cupit, et nescit locum tuum. Quaerere te affectat, et ignorat vultum tuum." From "Proslogion," 1:98; *Prayers,* 240.

12. "Heu mihi, qui videre non potui dominum angelorum humiliatum ad conversationem hominum, ut homines exaltaret ad conversationem angelorum! Cum deus offensus sponte moriebatur ut peccator viveret." Ibid. 3:7; *Prayers,* 95. I have added a phrase Ward dropped.

13. Leo Steinberg, *The Sexuality of Christ in Renaissance Art and in Modern Oblivion* (New York: Pantheon, October, 1983), 57.

14. For convenient cross reference between Ragusa and Green's translation of the

Italian text (see n. 1), the most accessible translation into English of the *Meditationes,* and the Latin text in the 1868 edition of St. Bonaventura (see n. 4), I shall give chapter number, colon, page number in Ragusa and Green, slash and page number in the Latin. So, here, 4:15–16, 21/ 514b, 516a.

15. 85:350/613a.

16. Jean Leclercq, François Vanderbroucke, and Louis Bouyer, *The Spirituality of the Middle Ages* (London: Burns and Oates, 1968), 163.

17. For texts, see Aelredi Rievallensis, *Opera Omnia,* vol. 1, ed. A. Hoste and C. H. Talbot (Turnholti: Typographi Brepols Editores Pontifici, 1971): *De Iesu puero duodenni,* 249–78; *De Institutione Inclusorum,* 636–82.

18. 13:78/528a; my translation.

19. 12:71–72/526b. This is an important statement, and we should be as certain as we can be about the text. Apparently the Italian, from which Ragusa and Green translated, differed somewhat from the Latin here: ''nec parvipendas talia humilia, et quae puerilia videntur, meditari de ipso. Videntur enim dare devotionem, augere amorem, accendere fervorem, inducere compassionem, puritatem et simplicitatem conferre, et humilitatis et paupertatis vigorem nutrire, et conservare familiaritatem, et conformitatem facere, ac spem elevare.'' The latter part of the statement in the Latin is ''join purity and simplicity, nourish the strength of humility and poverty, maintain familiarity, create conformity, and raise hope.'' Several of these ''effects'' are virtues related particularly to life in an order, that is, the Clares, or to personal virtues in the Franciscan ethic. Increasing love and maintaining familiarity, however, address the relation between the meditant and the object of meditation, that is, Christ.

20. 51:265/578a. I translate from the Latin here: ''de humilitate Christi . . . meditatio.'' The Italian apparently did not translate ''Christi.'' Earlier, after listing the benefits (see n. 19 above) the author commented, ''nam ad sublimia ascendere non valemus. . . .''

21. David L. Jeffrey, *The Early English Lyric and Franciscan Spirituality* (Lincoln: University of Nebraska Press, 1975), 48–49.

22. I cite the following instances, with no claim that the list is complete: Pro: 3/510b; Pro: 4/511a; 13: —/529b; 16: —/536a; 18:133/541a; 19:138/542a; 21: 155/545a; 24:161/545b; 24:162/546a; 27:167/546b; 73:311/596b; 73: —/597; 73: 316/599a; 75:320/600b; 88:363/618b; 91:367/620a; 92:368/620b; 92:369/621a; 100:388/629a.

23. 12:69/526b; 15:95, 101/531a, 533a; 17:125/540a.

24. David Herlihy, *Medieval Households* (Cambridge, Mass.: Harvard University Press, 1985), 122–23. The term ''familia'' is applied in the *Meditationes* to the group around Christ: ''benedictam familiam suam,'' 73:314/598a.

25. See chapters 86, 88, 89, 91, 92; for the quotation, see 91:369/621a.

26. Murray Wright Bundy, *The Theory of the Imagination in Classical and Medieval Thought,* University of Illinois Studies in Language and Literature, 12, nos.

2, 3 (May–August, 1927), 177–256. Also John V. Fleming, *An Introduction to the Franciscan Literature of the Middle Ages* (Chicago: Franciscan Herald Press, 1977), 240–46 (for the *Meditationes,* 242–51); Douglas Kelly, *Medieval Imagination* (Madison: University of Wisconsin Press, 1978), 26–56, 266–73; V. A. Kolve, *Chaucer and the Imagery of Narrative* (Stanford: Stanford University Press, 1984), 20–28, 378–83.

27. *Un Traitie de la vie solitaire: Epistola ad fratres de Monte-Dei,* ed. M.-M. Davy, Collection des études de philosophie médiévale (Paris: J. Vrin, 1940), 214.

28. Bundy, 200, 201 (Migne, *PL* 177: 285, 287). St. Bonaventura's psychology further linked sensation with the rational and the spiritual powers: see Etienne Gilson, *The Philosophy of St. Bonaventure,* trans. Dom Illtyd Trethowan and Frank J. Sheed (Paterson, N.J.: St. Anthony Guild Press, 1950), 327; and Jeffrey, 102, citing the *De reductione artium ad theologiam.*

29. 18:133/541a; see also Pro: 5/511a–b; 9:49–50/522b; 21:154/544b–545a.

30. 16:107/535a; 18:134/541b; 24:162/546a; 73:196/551b–552a.

31. 34:196/551b–552.

4. The Author's Address to the Reader: Chaucer, Juan Ruiz, and Dante

CHAUNCEY WOOD

In Chaucer's *Troilus and Criseyde,* Pandarus, paraphrasing Boethius's Lady Philosophy for his own purposes, declares that "By his contrarie is every thyng declared" (I,637).[1] Leaving aside Pandarus's application of this maxim, let me begin this discussion of medieval authors and their readers with the consideration of something distinctly contrary: a modern painting and its modern viewers. The painting in question is Léon Gérôme's "The Death of Marshall Ney," which was done in 1868. The moment captured by the painting is just after the execution of Marshall Ney, whose body lies face down in the right foreground. To our left a group of soldiers marches away, their backs to us. The dominant structure in the painting is a large, bare, rough stone wall covered with scratches, which extends from the right-hand side of the picture, behind the fallen Marshall, to well past the center of the work. Provocatively, there are few graffiti on this wall—a wall that seems particularly fashioned for them—and one art historian has argued that by this realistic blank space and the neutrality of the beholder's viewpoint, the artist meant to imply that history is merely a series of witnessed events, not a source of explicitly political messages.[2]

Another interpretation of this phenomenon would argue that the painter, by creating this invitingly blank wall, has tacitly prompted the viewer to supply his own graffiti—to write in the mind's eye the political interpretation of the execution so prominently lacking on the wall in the painting.[3] The "modernity" I see in this painting is that when the viewer is invited to respond to the painting, the nature of the response is carefully left free by the artist. We are not prompted to agree with a political statement, but rather to make one. As with the two endings of Fowles's *The French Lieutenant's Woman,* the person responding is given a very real freedom of choice.

These two brief examples from the novel and from the pictorial arts will not convince anyone of my generalizations about what is modern about modern art. However, they should serve nicely as introductory contraries to some medieval authorial addresses to the reader, in which the reader is similarly

51

invited to respond, but is not given anything like the same freedom of choice about how to do it. To be sure, we are not really told by medieval authors what to think, but the interesting feature held in common by the three passages we shall look at is that they tell the reader *how* to think. Or, more precisely, how to read.

As Florence H. Ridley shows, hermeneutic theory assumes a gap of indeterminacy between the author's meaning in a particular text and the reader's understanding of it. Undoubtedly, medieval authors had a strong, if unstated, conception of this hermeneutic truism, for they regularly concerned themselves with teaching their readers how to read the texts that they, the authors, were writing. Sometimes this was managed by a kind of third party intervention, as when Monica must correct St. Augustine's interpretation of the dream of the ruler—an example cited by Professors Gallacher and Damico in their Introduction. However, the pedagogical device commonly occurs as an address or aside directly to the reader, and it is this species I wish to concentrate on here.

Writing in 1965, Thomas Bergin complained about the story of the Old Man of Crete in Dante's *Commedia,* saying "the allegory does nothing to advance the tale; indeed it slows it up."[4] Bergin is quite right. This kind of allegorical word picture does indeed slow the narrative movement of the tale, which is, I think, precisely what Dante wanted it to do. An address to the reader is a device that similarly interrupts the progression of the story, and I will argue that Dante introduces such devices in order to procure that exact effect of breaking the mood. Consider, for example, *Inferno* IX, 61–63, one of the first and probably the most famous of Dante's many asides to the reader:

> O voi ch'avete li 'ntelletti sani,
> mirate la dottrina che s'asconde
> sotto 'l velame de li versi strani.
>   * * * *
> O you who have sound understanding,
> mark the doctrine that is hidden under
> the veil of the strange verses![5]

There has been no dearth of readers—of *studiose*—willing to consider themselves among those with "sound understanding," and the *Dantisti* have accordingly offered explanations of the particular doctrine hidden beneath these verses. However, it is not what this passage *means,* but rather what it *does* that is of foremost interest in the present discourse. The pilgrim Dante you will remember has encountered the three Furies, who threaten him by crying out for Medusa to come and turn him to stone. Virgil cautions Dante to keep his eyes closed, for if he should see the Gorgon he would not return to the upper world. Then Dante the poet steps forward in front of Dante the Pilgrim and asks the reader to look beneath the veil of the story for its doctrinal content. Just when things were getting interesting! We are halted outside the gates to the City of Dis, to which Virgil cannot gain entrance, the Furies are calling for Medusa, and, in the middle of this high drama, the poet asks us to lift up the veil that has been so deftly woven, and to "mark" (*mirate*) the doctrine under what he calls, surprisingly, "strange verses" (*versi strani*). Yet, in the Middle Ages, if we may judge by the numerous commentaries that exist on the poem, no one objected to Dante's breaking the spell, to his failure to advance the action of the story. Benvenuto da Imola, for example, says this: "Here the author, because he has made a subtle and accomplished fiction and being sure that the common and uncultivated would not understand it, invites the wise and intelligent to the consideration of the sentences ["sententiae"] lying beneath it."[6] This distressingly inegalitarian and undemocratic reader response does not take exception to Dante's having interrupted the action of the story, nor does it resist the author's direction to look beneath the surface. Indeed, it seems to accept that instruction as something flattering rather than restricting. Contrast, if you will, this medieval acceptance of Dante's injunction to look beneath the surface of his subtle and accomplished fiction, with a modern reaction by Allan Gilbert against any suggestion that there may be more to Dante's poetry than meets the eye. The *Dantisti* have changed over the years:

> I hold that poetical interpretation is free. Granting such freedom to all, for myself I apply to Dante the principle of minimum interpretation. . . .
>
> . . . .
>
> With an allegorical and true meaning a seeker for delight who reads *poetry as poetry* is not primarily concerned.
>
> . . . .
>
> When a modern reads the *poem as poem* he can feel secure. Not only can he lay aside anxiety about medieval thought, but *he can neglect the allegory as produced by the annotators*. . . . If as free reader he wishes to *pause* and ask for meaning, let him do so, even though he pass out of the realm of poetry into that of the puzzle. . . . The *Commedy* offers enough of the reasonably plain to satisfy legitimate desires. If Dante is a great poet, why attempt to raise his stature with *our own inventions?*[7]

If Léon Gérôme wanted us to be free to write our own graffiti, here is a critic who would have us so free that we do not interpret at all, as though the wall in Gérôme's painting already had words on it, saying *Défense d'afficher* (Post no Bills). If we may hypothesize about theory from what the author, Dante, does, and how his reader, Benvenuto, responds, we might argue as follows: poetry was thought to have two levels, one on the surface and one below it, and the story or action proceeds on the former, while sentence or doctrine is available on the latter. Moreover, while meaning is available on the veiled level, it is nevertheless veiled, so it is not available to everyone—rather it is accessible only to one kind of reader and not to another. "The poem as poem" and "poetry as poetry," then, were different both in their execution by poets and their apprehension by readers in the Middle Ages from what they are today. In a sense, then, to ask the reader to switch levels while reading a medieval poem is only a partial interruption, for apprehension continues changed but unbroken.

Having theorized this much from a few lines in Dante and Benvenuto, let us turn now from Dante to Juan Ruiz, the Arcipreste de Hita, who in a long prose piece, usually placed at the beginning of his *Libro de Buen Amor,* does not so much address as harrangue his readers about the need to consider more than just the words of his poem. The placement, the tone, and the function of this address to the reader are very different from those of Dante's address; yet there are provocative similarities. Much like Dante, Juan Ruiz appeals to the wisest in his audience, and just as Dante addresses himself to those of "intelletti sani," the Arcipreste speaks to those of "buen entendemiento." And, with but a slight change of language, where Dante speaks of a doctrine hidden beneath a veil of strange verses, the Arcipreste speaks of a "sentencia"—the same word used by Benvenuto to describe the doctrinal level—and a "buen solaz," which describes the level of the work that is heard: "Si queredes, señores, oír un buen solaz. . . ."[8] (We shall encounter "sentence" and "solace" again in Chaucer.)

Unlike Dante, however, the Arcipreste is playful in the extreme, and cannot resist an address to those of "poco entendemiento" along with the address to those of "buen entendemiento" (11). The mood, needless to say, is in many ways very different from that in the *Inferno.* There is, however, a marked similarity. Both authors clearly want their readers to look beyond the surface of the text. What is added in the Spanish work is instruction, for by means of his long prose prologue, which consists to a large extent of a commentary on Psalm 31, Juan Ruiz teaches the reader how to read. But, as noted, his sense of humor is always present. Having opened his little lesson by quoting Psalm 31 ("Intellectum tibi dabo et instruam te in via hac qua gradieris . . ./ I will give thee understanding, and I will instruct thee in this way in which thou shalt go . . ." [4–5]), the Arcipreste then gives us some instruction. First, he distinguishes among understanding, memory, and will. Through the understanding of the good we will fear God, which is the beginning of wisdom. With good memory and good will we will choose "buen amor," the love of God, over the "amor loco d'este mundo" and we will do good works (7). However, when the utility of his little book is considered, which he says he wrote "en memoria de bien" (9), thereby exercising his own memory, will, and understanding, the Arcipreste directs it to an amusingly broad audience with a hierarchy of understanding and some very different reader responses. Those of "buen entendemiento" will read it and make good choices. Those of "poco entendemiento" will also gain something. By reading about so much sinfulness in the world they will put aside the mad love of it: "E desecharán e aborrecerán las maneras e maestrías malas del loco amor . . . " (11). Finally, those who, in their fallen state, choose wrongly to use "loco amor," which the author advises against, will nevertheless find within his book "algunas maneras para ello . . ." (some ways for this [10–11]). And then, with a now quite equivocal tone, he quotes again Psalm 31, "intellectum tibi dabo . . . " (11). The Arcipreste's "intellectum" extends farther than the Psalmist's, for he not only gives us instruction in the way we should go but also some little instruction in the way we should not.

In a final cautionary word, one that seems to have made an insufficient impact on critics of the poem, the Arcipreste insists that his words follow his intentions, and not the other way around:

> [El] que quiera bien entender a bien juzgar la mi entención por que lo fiz', e la sentencia de lo que y dize, e non al son feo de las palabras; e segund derecho las palabras sirven a la intención, e non la intención a las palabras. (Let him seek to understand well and to judge well my intention in writing [the book] and not just the ugly sound of the words, for according to law, words serve the intention, and not intention the words [10–11].)

Then, lest we missed the joke about the book's utility for the wicked, he says directly

> E dios sabe que la mi intención non fue de lo fazer por dar manera de pecar nin por mal dezir; mas fue por reduzir a toda persona a memoria buena de bien obrar.
> (And God knows that my intention was not to compose the book in order to provide ways to commit sin or speak evil, but was to guide everyone back to good memory of good deeds [10–11].)

Later in this work, "buen amor" is used to define many more things than just the love of God, which is why it is so important to remember that the words serve the author's intentions and not conversely.

Both authors are more than willing either to break the spell, as with Dante, or to caution us against weaving one, as with Juan Ruiz. Dante asks us to look for doctrine beneath his text; the Arcipreste writes a commentary on a text to show or remind us how to do it, albeit he does so with humor. Both addresses, however, definitely slow down the advancement of the action and are tonally reminiscent of the schoolroom. Accordingly, they are inappropriate in tone for the Italian descent into the inferno or the Spanish series of lyrics. But there they are.

My brief examples from Chaucer are chosen to underscore the same theme. In *The Canterbury Tales* Chaucer's addresses to the reader are effected by means of an address by one of the Canterbury Pilgrims to the others. Or at least so I will argue. Consider, for example, Harry Bailly's reference to the criteria he will use to judge the tales. While we might expect a tavernkeeper to be a confirmed subjectivist, someone who doesn't know much about art but knows what he likes, Harry is knowledgeable about standard criteria. The tales "of best sentence and moost solaas" (*General Prologue* 798) will be the winners, he declares. The terminology is the same as that used by the Arcipreste and implies the two levels to which Dante alluded. However, although we and the pilgrims may be counted among those of "intelletti sani" or "buen entendemiento," Harry sounds very much like one of "poco entendemiento," or one who might even choose the "loco amor" of this world. As Alan Gaylord has observed, Harry likes tales about real toads in real gardens. "He is most pleased if it turns out the toads and the gardens belong to someone he knows, and if what is said about them confirms what he had always thought about gardening."[9] Thus, while Chaucer may intend to instruct us through Harry Bailly in how to respond to his tales on two levels, Harry himself may often confuse the one with the other.

The Nun's Priest also addresses the pilgrim audience about literary methodology, and like Dante he is concerned with "doctrine" (*The Nun's Priest's Tale*, B[2] 4632). More strikingly, however, he is like the Arcipreste de Hita in his concern for intentionality and for the right kind of reader response:

> But ye that holden this tale a folye,
> As of a fox, or of a cok and hen,
> Taketh the moralite, goode men.
> For seint Paul seith that al that writen is,
> To our doctrine it is ywrite, ywis;
> Taketh the fruyt, and lat the chaf be stille.
> (B[2] 4628–33)

The Nun's Priest's concern to appeal to "goode men" is reminiscent both of Dante's remarks to those with "intelletti sani" and the Arcipreste's to those of "buen entendemiento," while "fruyt" and "chaf" are the same as sentence and solace. Certainly the goal of appealing to the audience through a mild flattery exists here as it does in Dante and Juan Ruiz, for it is the form of address used by that arch flatterer, the Pardoner. What is most different from the other passages is the hortatory tone. Readers who think the tale is a "folye" are exhorted to take the "moralite" instead, to take the "fruyt and lat the chaf be stille," for if everything is ultimately written for one doctrine, then as readers we must find that level, and to do so we must get past "chaf," past "folye."

In the Nun's Priest's closing words to his ultimate audience, God, we may hear something about the uses to which God can put literature. Having addressed "goode men" he now implores "goode God":

> Now, goode God, if it be thy wille,
> As seith my lord, *so make us alle goode men,*
> And brynge us to his [that is, to "my lord," Christ's]
>   heighe blisse! Amen.
> (B[2] 4634–36. Emphasis added.)

If we are indeed "goode men" it is "goode God" who makes us so, and through the study of "oure doctrine" in poetry we may, with Grace, act like "goode men."

At this juncture in this long preamble of a tale it may fairly be objected that all I have done is talk about the medievalness of medieval art. To which charge I plead guilty with an explanation: the explanation being that a neglected characteristic of medieval art is its concern to compel the reader's attention away from the story and toward the doctrine, sentence, or "moralite." Moreover, I contend that this implies a different kind of reader response from that we commonly speak of today, and, finally, that these reminders to the reader are regularly given with references to literary terminology, which, if not exactly *récherché*, nevertheless has at least a hint about it of what James Joyce, in a very different context, called the "true scholastic stink." At any rate, the direction of the reader's attention and the kind of language employed are arresting or intrusive or serve to instruct and alert.

For a final example, one that I think is a little more arresting than the others, consider Reason's rather schoolmarmish lecture to Amant in the *Roman de la Rose*. Here in the garden of earthly delights we are most remarkably recalled to the classroom. The discourse arises because of Amant's objection to the word "testicles," which are things he thinks are better used than spoken of. Considering its length I cite the passage only in English:

> In our schools indeed they say many things in parables that are very beautiful to hear; however, one should not take whatever one hears according to the letter. In my speech there is another sense, at least when I was speaking of testicles, which I wanted to speak of briefly here, than that which you want to give to the word. He who understood the letter would see in the writing the sense which clarifies the obscure fable. The truth hidden within would be clear if it were explained. You will understand it well if you review the integuments on the poets. . . . There you will want to take your great delight, and you will thus be able to profit a great deal. You will profit in delight and delight in profit, for in the playful fables of the poets lie very profitable delights beneath which they cover their thoughts when they clothe the truth in fables.[10]

This is not an address to the reader, but it prepares us for the address that comes later in the work. Having been reminded of an aesthetic of delight in profit, of "integumenta," of concealed truth and of different ways of understanding the letter, we are perhaps more willing to accept the author's plea to consider his intentions and not just his words. Much later in the poem Jean de Meun addresses a whole series of readers. To "loyal lovers" (25)—whoever they may be—the author promises "an adequate art of love" from which correct responses will be possible only "when you have heard me gloss the text" (258). Those who object to the author's language are reminded that the words must be cousin to the deed, while those who complain about antifeminism are advised to consider that his writing is "all for our instruction" (258). Those who object to what appears to be anticlericalism are similarly told "it was never my intention to speak against any living man who follows holy religion . . ." (259). Finally, the entire work is offered up to Holy Church for correction. It is all quite out of place in the sensual garden, as it no doubt was meant to be.

Basically, medieval authors mistrusted their readers' potential responses and felt obliged to direct that response accordingly. This mistrust was perhaps more conventional than real, but there was a powerful antecedent for it in the writings of St. Augustine. For not only did some of the literary vocabulary of the Middle Ages come from Augustine, whether nucleus and cortex for the two levels or Egyptian gold for the uses of the classics, but also there came a distrust of the pathetic fallacy. In the *Confessions* St. Augustine portrays himself as having an unseemly fondness for tragedy as it happened fictitiously on stage, and also describes his misplaced concern for Dido and Aeneas. In the classroom, he tells us,

> I was compelled to learn about the wanderings of a certain Aeneas, oblivious of my own, and to weep for Dido dead, because she slew herself for love; while at the same time I brooked with dry eyes my wretched self dying far from Thee. . . .[11]

As he says of his schooling, he learned these things "willingly and with delight, and for this I was called a boy of good promise" (16).

In medieval literature the author's address to the reader is not like the address in nineteenth-century fiction to the "dear" or "gentle" reader. However, neither is it designed to provoke more sympathetic vibrations in boys of good promise like St. Augustine. Rather, it is a device by which the author reminds the reader that the fiction is a fiction, reminds the reader of the cerebral rather than the visceral pleasures of the text, calling the reader away from the plot and the characters to a "delight in profit." The author's address to the reader is intended to forestall our weeping for Dido dead and to remind us of our own death in this world. If we object to allegory as interfering with the enjoyment of "poetry as poetry," whatever that may mean, we have not drawn upon a timeless but rather on a modern aesthetic, for delight was thought to be different by our medieval ancestors. For Boccaccio, writing in the *Genealogies of the Pagan Gods,* the true appreciation of poetry involved the very puzzle-solving so repugnant to the critic I cited earlier:

> But I repeat my advice to those who would appreciate poetry and unwind its difficult involutions. You must read, you must persevere, you must sit up nights, you must inquire, and exert the utmost power of your mind.[12]

In the Middle Ages the author's address to the reader was a device to activate the critical intelligence, while deactivating the affections. It was a device to make us aware of our own wanderings while reading about the wanderings of Aeneas, about the threat of the Medusa, about how to use a book on every kind of love, whether written in French or Spanish. Boys of good promise in St. Augustine's school learned only the surface level of the text. What he would have Christians do is to apply those texts to themselves, so as to become promising in a spiritual rather than scholastic sense. Later in the Middle Ages, if Jean De Meun's Lady Reason is correct, the schools themselves taught a different kind of reading, one based on the advice of St. Augustine and designed to insist on moral applications that would permit its "boys of good promise" to grow into the "goode men" that Chaucer's Nuns's Priest would have us be.

Notes

1. All quotations from Chaucer are from *The Works of Geoffrey Chaucer*, 2nd ed., ed. F. N. Robinson (Boston: Houghton Mifflin, 1957).

2. Wolfgang Kemp, "Death at Work: A Case Study on Constitutive Blanks in Nineteenth-Century Paintings," *Representations* No. 10 (Spring 1985): 118. *Cf.* "The artist is no longer the fabricator of solid data and relations; instead he arranges spaces and surfaces, which are open to projective activity of the beholder. The old notion that art 'should stimulate ideas in the beholder, but not demand them' proves brilliantly its applicability to the fragmented construction of Realism" (114).

3. In fact, there are two sketchy graffiti on the wall. One, which says "Vive L'Empereur," has been crossed out, later to be started again, with only the word "Vive" in place. Kemp objects to words in this painting as "overcoding," and so misses the irony of the exhortation to live on the wall behind the dead Marshall.

4. Thomas G. Bergin, *Perspectives on the Divine Comedy* (Bloomington and London: Indiana University Press, 1967), 256.

5. Dante Alighieri, *The Divine Comedy*, trans. Charles S. Singleton (Princeton: Princeton University Press, 1980), I, 93.

6. Benevenutus de Imola, *Comentum super Dantis Comoediam*, ed. J. P. Lacaita (Florence, 1888), I, 316 (translation mine): "Hic autor quia fecerat subtilem et artificiosam fictionem, certus quod vulgares rudes non intelligerent eam, invitat sapientes et intelligentes ad considerationem sententiae hic latentis."

7. Allan Gilbert, *Dante and his Comedy* (New York: New York University Press, 1966), viii; 30; 42.

8. Juan Ruiz, *Libro de Buen Amor,* ed. and trans., Raymond S. Willis (Princeton: Princeton University Press, 1972), 13. Subsequent quotations in both Spanish and English will be from this edition.

9. Alan T. Gaylord, "*Sentence* and *Solaas* in Fragment VII of the *Canterbury Tales:* Harry Bailly as Horseback Editor," *Publications of the Modern Language Association* 82 (1967): 232.

10. Guillaume de Lorris and Jean de Meun, *The Romance of the Rose,* trans. Charles Dahlberg (Princeton: Princeton University Press, 1971), 136. Subsequent quotations will be from this edition.

11. *The Confessions,* Bk. I, chap. 13, in *Basic Writings of St. Augustine,* trans. Whitney J. Oates (New York: Random House, 1948), I, 13.

12. *Boccaccio on Poetry,* trans. Charles G. Osgood (New York: The Liberal Arts Press, 1956), 62.

Part II
Bias and Interpretation

The essays deal with subjectivity and objectivity in interpretation. Derek Pearsall asserts that the historical and literary accounts of the Peasants' Revolt, because of their authors' conditioned horror of rebellion, exhibit a failure to understand the event. In *El Poema de Mio Cid*, Dom Jean Leclercq documents an alliance between Christianity and the warrior, which Bernard of Clairvaux, in his own writings on knighthood, would have found severely lacking in objectivity. Lorraine Attreed, in her examination of Tudor concepts of the Middle Ages, traces a process of increasing objectivity and historiographical sophistication. Joseph J. Duggan shows how France's conflict with Germany between 1837 and 1945 led French scholars to describe the *Song of Roland* as a national epic in spite of intractible geographical and ethnic facts within the poem itself which contradict such a view.

5. Interpretative Models for the Peasants' Revolt

DEREK PEARSALL

The question I want to address in this brief essay is as follows: What is the nature of the relationship between a historical event (something important that happened in historical actuality) and the interpretations placed upon it by contemporary and later writers. The Peasants' Revolt provides a valuable opportunity to ask this question, partly because it undoubtedly was an event, and partly because it has stimulated a rich variety of interpretation. There is also the advantage of the excellent source book on the Revolt edited by Professor R. B. Dobson, which helps an amateur like me to traverse some of this tricky historical terrain.[1] It also gives me some preliminary sightings of my question, particularly as it is divided into seven sections, the first six dealing with "history" the last dealing with "interpretations." The division is suggestive of the existence of a core of historical actuality, more or less objectively to be arrived at by historians—called "history"—surrounded by a penumbra of interpretations, usually the work of non-historical writers, and more or less subjective. This is called "literature," and consists largely of obvious falsehoods.

Now I know that I have presented a laughably crude parody of the relationship between the two disciplines of study, and I know, too, that no historian would be prepared to accept that his role was confined to eliciting and describing "what happened." He would rather endorse Collingwood's assertion that "the history of thought, and therefore all history, is the re-enactment of past thoughts in the historian's own mind."[2]

History is thus an act of imaginative re-creation, in which the historian studies events "from their inner side," in terms, that is, of the processes of "thought" that they spring from and embody. Collingwood still assumes, however, that those processes of thought are accessible to the historian as ascertainable realities, realities of a higher order than actual "events" but alike in their capacity to be objectively known. We need to go further than this, and recognize that our knowledge, our perception of reality, our thought, and no less our thought about past thought, are made available to us in terms of the interpretative models we have grown accustomed to using—so ac-

customed in fact that we begin to take them for the perception of the object as
in itself it really is. No discipline of enquiry is immune from this precondi-
tioning of expectation: a modern scientist would readily acknowledge that the
processes of scientific experiment and enquiry, and the results obtained thereby, are deeply affected, if not determined, by the questions he asks. These
questions are in turn the product of the models for the understanding of his
matter that he has formed, consciously or unconsciously, in his mind. Karl
Popper speaks of the need for "regularity" as the most important determinant
in the drive of the intellect to impose its own laws upon nature: "There is no
observation which is not related to a set of typical situations—regularities—
between which it tries to find a decision. . . . There is no sense-organ in
which anticipatory theories are not genetically incorporated."[3] All knowledge, he concludes, is "theory-impregnated," and "objective knowledge" is
an illusion.

So it is that when Professor Dobson says at one point, very properly, that
"knowledge of the Peasants' Revolt is irrevocably controlled and restricted
by the interests and thought-sequences of its contemporary historians" (Peasants' Revolt, 3), we must acknowledge that what he says is true. However, if
we understood Professor Dobson to imply that the situation might ever be
otherwise, or that the thought processes of the modern historian are not
similarly (if not equally) restricting, his statement might be misleading. If
indeed we could call up one of the anonymous men of Kent, and ask him what
happened, we know that the account would be equally limited and partial, and
the more it attempted to be objective and generalized, the more limited and
partial it would become, because of the increased scope offered to existing
"thought-sequences" by the impulse toward interpretation. Even if our modern historian had been there, armed with television camera and tape-recorder,
the flux of events would still have been distilled to a particular kind of
intelligibility. At another point, Professor Dobson comments: "The medieval
historian's self-imposed duty was not to understand the Peasants' Revolt in its
own terms but to show how it revealed the eternal truths of human life on
earth" (Peasants' Revolt, 7). Although one can see here the appropriateness
of the implied criticism of medieval chroniclers, it is difficult to know how the
Peasants' Revolt "in its own terms" can be invoked. For there are no terms
for its existence as an event except those supplied by its interpreters, contemporary or modern.

This can readily be demonstrated from contemporary accounts of the
Revolt. Writers reach instinctively for the moral absolutes which are the
models or images through which they may understand the Revolt as a violation of divinely ordained social hierarchy, caused by human wickedness.
Mostly it is the wickedness of the rebels that comes in for castigation, and we
can already see the model of understanding in operation in the Commons
Petitions against Vagrants and against Rebellious Villeins in 1376 and 1377,
where the Commons complain against the willful malice of landless labourers

in seeking higher wages and depriving the landowning classes of their profits, and, what is worse, in continuing "subtly and by great malice aforethought" to seek to escape the penalties decreed for such offences by the Statutes of Labourers.[4] This is not so much a conspiracy of class interest on the part of the landowners; it is rather that the impersonal forces directing the movement from traditional labour service to competitive wage service were unintelligible to them, given the prevalent image or model of the well-being of the commonwealth.

It is Gower who gives the most powerful and sustained account of the Peasants' Revolt in terms of the image of reason and nature overturned, in Book I of his *Vox Clamantis*.[5] Other writers allude casually to the great rift in nature by which men, rebelling against the divinely ordained hierarchy of society, become as beasts—Knighton compares them to wolves; the "monk of Westminster" to rabid dogs; Walsingham, with his inimitable gift for the inapposite, to sheep and peacocks[6]—but Gower sustains a long allegorical vision on the theme. In his vision, he sees the various rascally bands of the common mob wandering abroad; the curse of God suddenly flashes upon them, so that they become wild versions of domesticated animals (carriers become asses; plowmen, oxen; domestic servants, dogs and cats) and then mutate again to wild beasts. Certain events of the Rising—the surrender of London Bridge, the sack of the Savoy, the invasion of the apartments of the Princess Joan at the Tower, the murder of Sudbury—are recognizable, if not readily so, in the lurid light of Gower's apocalypse. But Gower is not, to be frank, much interested in the actuality of the event, rather in the image of primal chaos and reversion to bestiality which follows on the challenge to the established political order.

Walsingham essentially sees things in the same way as Gower, though in a broader religious context, rather than in a primarily political one. For him all disasters—and history consists mostly of disasters—are the punishment visited by God on society, or parts of it, for their sinfulness. The causes of the revolt are thus to be sought in the negligence of the clergy, the sinfulness of lords, and the villainy of the commons: "They pursued fraud and falsehood continually, gave way to lust, wallowed in fornication and were polluted with adultery—everyone neighed after his neighbour's wife" (Dobson, 368).

Pausing on this, conscious that he may not have been sufficiently comprehensive, Walsingham adds that the evil times were attributable to the sins of all the inhabitants of the earth—though especially the Mendicant orders. Walsingham is impatient of all fact, and for him history always rushes headlong to interpretation; and since the interpretation is already known and always the same, there seems little point to him in any irritable straining after fact, except in so far as events provide *exempla*. Often his instant moralizing is ludicrously inappropriate, as when he attributes Wat Tyler's fall to God, who "opposes the proud and favours the humble" (Dobson, 177). It is very hard to know who the humble are in this context: the king? Walworth?

Likewise, when the rebels enter the Tower and offer some insult to the royal
ladies, Walsingham comments sharply on the surprising lack of resistance
offered by the knights and squires present, and continues:

> This happened because God wished to show the English that a man's
> strength does not rest in his own bravery nor ought he to rely on arrow or
> sword, but rather on Him who saves us from our affections and is ac-
> customed to confound our gaolers with his mercy and pity (Dobson, 172).

"But enough of these remarks," he continues airily, perhaps momentarily
conscious that his moralizing constitutes a recommendation of the pusillan-
imous behaviour of the king's men that he began by rebuking.

Sometimes writers less single-minded than Gower and Walsingham
show themselves receptive to more than one image of the Rising, and thus
achieve a reputation for objectivity which is based on the neutralizing effect of
mutually incompatible stereotypes. So, in the *Anonimalle Chronicle,* the
Commons are reproved for their "evil actions" in rising against their lords,
but the taxes that caused them to rise are acknowledged to have been "extor-
tionately levied" and "badly spent" (Dobson, 123). Likewise, the poem *Tax
has tenet us alle,*[7] inspired by the Rising, begins with a detailed account of the
origins of the Rising in the oppressive poll tax:

> The kyng therof had smalle
> fuit in manibus cupidorum—,

but this immediately gives way to an explanation in terms of God's vengeance
on the sins of man:

> Vengeance nede most falle
> propter peccata malorum.

There is no recognition that the *malorum* have been specifically identified as a
particular group of *cupidorum.* Thereafter the Rising is treated as wanton
mischief-making on the part of the rebels, put down in the end by heavenly
grace.

Froissart, of course, is a special case. He gives fuller treatment than any
of the other chroniclers to the themes of freedom and equality, as they are
represented in John Ball's sermon, but he regards this as too absurd for much
further comment, and his understanding of the Revolt is wholly filtered
through the images of chivalric idealism and snobbery. Noble and gracious
conversations abound, and Froissart gives to the nobility, whose actual behaviour seems to have been craven in the extreme, a wholly imaginary role in
the Rising. He tells the story as it ought to have been, not as it was. He loves
inventing motives of a traditional romantic or personal kind: Richard Lyon is
murdered because Wat Tyler had once served him in France as his varlet and
had been beaten by him (Dobson, 189). But his pièce de résistance is the

heroic death of Sir Robert Sale at the hands of the Norfolk rebels, an episode which is seized upon by Froissart for a brave combat and feat of arms, with a speech of noble rebuke:

> "Fly away, ye ungracious people, false and evil traitors that ye be. Would you that I should forsake my natural lord for such a company of knaves as ye be, to my dishonour for ever? I had rather ye were all hanged, as ye shall be, for that shall be your end. . . ." With that, he drew out a good Burdeaux sword and began to skirmish with them and made a great place about him, that it was pleasure to behold him. There was none that durst approach him, but that at every stroke he gave he cut off either leg, head or arm . . . he did there such deeds that it was marvel to regard (Dobson, 263).

But there were more than forty thousand of them, we are told, and although he killed twelve and maimed many more, in the end he was cut down. The whole episode, be it noted, appears to have been completely invented by Froissart.

At this point, in the midst of these fantasies of "theory-impregnated" image-making, it is necessary to recall that all these chroniclers are describing an actual event and that at the heart of all their accounts must be some stubborn, irreducible core of actuality. How to isolate this core, however, is not an easy question. The study of "authentic touches" which have "the ring of truth," whether it is done by intuition or by laborious comparison of the written accounts, is in the end successful, not so much in eliciting historical veracity as in recognizing effective touches on the writer's part. An "authentic touch," in carrying home the illusion of actuality, is thus no different from "authenticating detail" in a literary work.[8] Only the *Anonimalle*, for instance, in referring to the bill prepared by Richard's clerks to satisfy the Commons' grievances, mentions the "old chair":

> And he caused it to be read to them, the man who read it standing up on an old chair above the others so that all could hear (Dobson, 160).

This has the air of something seen, not invented: the arbitrariness of the old chair carries authenticity. Yet is it entirely arbitrary? Does not the old chair carry some impression of impropriety and indignity which enhances the image of the reversal of order? Likewise, a vivid touch is given by two chroniclers, the writer of the *Anonimalle* and the monk of Westminster, to the story of Imworth, steward of the Marshalsea. Dragged from sanctuary in Westminster by the rebels, he was torn away, we are told, as he embraced the pillars of the shrine of St. Edward (Dobson, 163, 202). This is a vivid touch, certainly, but also eminently appropriate behaviour for the poor man and, therefore, capable of having been invented to make a satisfactory story. The fact that two chroniclers mention it does not make it more of a fact, since they may both be drawing on the same written account rather than operating with independent evidence from eye-witnesses. The comparison of the commons enclosed by Walworth's men at Clerkenwell to "sheep enclosed within a pen" occurs in

three chronicles (Dobson, 167, 179, 187), but it seems unlikely that it occurred to all three independently. The analysis I am applying here, it will be
seen, is essentially that used for the analysis of the generation of textual
variation in a literary work, and this seems entirely appropriate.

Sometimes we feel we are on firmer ground in identifying the moulding
of events according to pre-existing models. The murder of Sudbury, for
instance, is recognized by all chroniclers to belong to the genre of *passio
sancti,* and all decorate it with appropriate detail. It is no mere accident of
actuality that the archbishop is found saying his mass and prayers devoutly in
the chapel of the Tower, or that he had reached "Omnes sancti orate pro
nobis" in the Litany when he was dragged off to execution (Dobson, 161).
Very occasionally a detail can be detected which seems recalcitrant to interpretation on these lines: the casualness of the allusion to the commons, on
Clerkenwell fields, falling to the ground "among the corn" like beaten men
when they see the head of their leader stuck on a pole, has the arbitrariness of
actuality. No other chronicler but the writer of the *Anonimalle* (Dobson, 167)
mentions the corn: it is of no significance whatsoever, yet no one there present
on a late June day could have failed to notice it.

The powerful influence of interpretative models is nowhere better exemplified than in the climactic events at Smithfield, especially the confrontation between Wat Tyler and the king. The account in the *Anonimalle* of the
drinking episode, where Wat asks for a jug of water because of the heat, and
"rinsed out his mouth in a very rude and villainous manner before the king"
(Dobson, 165), calling then for a jug of ale from which he drinks a great
draught, has a marvellously authentic quality. Yet the whole episode, with its
reminder of the drinking ceremonies that accompany the making of a truce
between armies, has a literary air, the most striking parallel being with the
meeting between Arthur and Mordred on the field of the last battle.[9] Then
again, the mimesis of chivalric ritual may be not so much the model that has
shaped the record and interpretation of events as the model which shaped the
events in actuality, with Wat quite deliberately acting the part of the leader of
an army equal to the king's, and deliberately parodying the chivalric rituals.

As for documentary records, which are generally treated as if they were
intrinsically more reliable as witnesses to the events of the past, they too must
be understood in terms of the assumptions, prejudices, beliefs, and ingrained
habits of mind that color them.[10] The records of the city of London provide a
salutary example: purporting to record how the rebels were traitorously let
into London by a group of prominent London aldermen, they have been
shown to have been doctored in order to discredit the aldermanic opposition to
John of Northampton, mayor of London in 1381 (Dobson, 212). Like all
forms of writing, records are written by persons with reasons for writing, and
those reasons are what will shape their presentation of the "facts." The only
certainly authentic record is one which no one has a reason for writing—and
such records will of course tend to remain unwritten.

I hope I have created some confusion among traditional categories of thought, and done something to suggest that divisions between the modes of understanding appropriated to historical and literary study are rather artificial. That, at any rate, is my main purpose, though I do want to suggest two possible directions we could go from here. One is to continue up the path of Popperian relativism to the assertion that—the historical actuality of the Peasants' Revolt being essentially irrecoverable, and the event itself being perhaps no more than a blip on the giant screen for receiving signals from the past that has been put up by the *Annales* school of historians—the Revolt is significant chiefly as an imaginative reality, that is, as an image of popular insurrection upon which outrage and utopian idealism could alike focus. The Peasants' Revolt becomes part of English history through the process of interpretation. The importance of history is the way it is read.

Against this view, which is persuasive in some ways, but repugnant in its denial of the lives of many brave men and women, as well as dangerous in the way it opens history to ideological and propagandist reconstruction, one could argue a more old-fashioned, positivistic view of the subject. Popper is evidently right in pointing to the limits of scientific and other claims to objective knowledge. But the capacity to perceive these limits is itself a form of objective knowledge. Scientific enquiry may produce hypotheses that are sooner or later demonstrated to be false, but the possibility of falsifiability implies the existence of truth, however difficult of access. (This, of course, is provided we do not follow T. S. Kuhn into the further elaboration of Popper's theories, and the further argument that theoretical presuppositions so affect the way that scientists perceive the world that facts do not even have the power to force falsification: this I take to be the equivalent, in the history of science, of the practice of deconstruction in literary criticism.) So too in historical and literary study: the relativity of perception, and the shaping power of interpretative models, are not unassailably deterministic. We know more, and we know better, than did our predecessors, and we do not need to repeat their mistakes. The great difference between the past and the present is that the past came first: this is not a relative matter. To recognize therefore that the study of history and the study of literature have much in common is not to consume the objectivity of the former in the subjectivity of the latter, or vice versa, but to insist on the importance for both of recognizing the shaping power of interpretative models.

Notes

1. R. B. Dobson, *The Peasants' Revolt of 1381* (London: Macmillan, 1970).

2. R. G. Collingwood, "Human Nature and Human History," *Proceedings of the British Academy* 22 (1936): 97–127, quotation from 109.

3. Karl Popper, *Objective Knowledge: An Evolutionary Approach* (Oxford: Clarendon Press, 1972), 23, 71–2.

4. Dobson, *Peasants' Revolt,* 73.

5. *The Complete Works of John Gower,* ed. G. C. Macaulay, Vol. 4: *The Latin Works* (Oxford: Clarendon Press, 1902). There is a translation by Eric W. Stockton in *The Major Latin Works of John Gower* (Seattle: University of Washington Press, 1962).

6. Dobson, *Peasants' Revolt,* 182, 199, 173.

7. Printed in Dobson, *Peasants' Revolt,* 358–59, but cited here from the text printed in *Historical Poems of the XIVth and XVth Centuries,* ed. R. H. Robbins (London: Oxford University Press, 1959), 55–7.

8. See Morton W. Bloomfield, "Authenticating Realism and the Realism of Chaucer," *Thought* 39 (1964): 335–58.

9. E.g. in *The Works of Sir Thomas Malory,* ed. Eugene Vinaver (London: Oxford University Press, 1954), 867.

10. See G. Barraclough, "The Historian and his Archives," *History Today* 4 (1954): 412–20.

6. Saint Bernard and El Cid: Knighthood and Two Models of Interpretation

JEAN LECLERCQ, O.S.B.

I. The Reality of Knighthood

We are well-informed about the activities of Christian knights, the battles they fought, and their life-style in the Spanish eleventh century, thanks to studies such as those by Ramón Menéndez Pidal, Colin Smith, Robert I. Burns and others. The religious and political situations were all quite varied and complex, and underwent constant evolution. Fighting went on unceasingly among Christian nobles and soldiers who warred either against the Moors or among themselves. These warriors, Christian though they were, were fierce and out for booty, making the most of their gains. These Spaniards, already mighty in battle, became even more so under the influence of their Moslem adversaries, from whom they learned more than the art of war. A historian from Cordoba, Ben Hayyan, quoted by Menéndez Pidal, has described the spirit of these conquerors lured by the exotic pleasures of the harem. The sensuousness of so many beautiful slave girls was their major concern,[1] and in every sphere the rough bravery of the Spaniards was stamped with what Robert I. Burns has termed "the Islamic connection,"[2] with the difference that the Christians were probably less preoccupied with religious matters than were the Moslems. This has been particularly stressed in connection with the historical Cid (1043–1099): "Of any sign of Christian devotion in the Cid, we know nothing."[3]

A few decades later, somewhere between approximately 1125 and 1153, St. Bernard of Clairvaux wrote a description of the knights in France which is no more flattering.[4] He wrote of "this worldly knighthood, or rather knavery." Monk and reformer that he was, he aimed first at the inward dispositions of the knights' hearts, attacking "perverse intentions," "yielding to vice," and the "empty glory" of all who are overcome by "wrath and pride." But he denounced even more "those who kill neither in the heat of revenge nor in the swelling of pride, but simply in order to save themselves."[5] Such knights were not even brave: empty of good intentions, they were full of vanity:

> What then, O knights, is this monstrous error and what this unbearable urge which bids you fight with such pomp and labor, and all to no purpose except death and sin? You cover your horses with silk, and plume your armor with I know not what sort of rags; you paint your shields and your saddles; you adorn your bits and spurs with gold and silver and precious stones, and then in all this glory you rush to your ruin with fearful wrath and fearless folly. Are these the trappings of a warrior or are they not rather the trinkets of a woman? Do you think the swords of your foes will be turned back by your gold, spare your jewels or be unable to pierce your silks? . . . why do you blind yourselves with effeminate locks and trip yourselves up with long and full tunics, burying your tender, delicate hands in big cumbersome sleeves?[6]

There is one particular abuse which Bernard strongly condemns, and which stems from those just mentioned: knighthood is a temptation for members of the clergy, certain of whom have joined the fighting ranks. "It is not lawful for the clergy to fight with the arms of soldiers," states Bernard in a letter to Bishop Atton of Troyes.[7] And in another letter, addressed to Suger, abbot of Saint-Denis, he enlarges on this theme in connection with a deacon "being at the same time so involved in military affairs as to take precedence over the commanders of the army." Says Bernard:

> I ask you, What sort of monster is this that being a cleric wishes to be thought a soldier as well, and succeeds in being neither? It is an abuse of both conditions. . . . Who would not be astonished, or rather disgusted, that one and the same person should, arrayed in armour, lead soldiers into battle and, clothed in alb and stole, pronounce the Gospel in the church? should at one time give the signal for battle on the bugle and at another inform the people of the commands of the bishop . . . ? A man that puts the army before his clerical state, secular business before the Church, certainly proves that he prefers human things to divine and earthly to heavenly things.[8]

These few texts describe certain facts, but probably with some exaggeration. Satire is always based on factual situations and the evidence which will be quoted later proves that such was the case here.

In twelfth-century France, as in eleventh-century Spain, knightly life entailed a certain amount of love-making and, chiefly in the latter period, of love literature. Bernard does not elaborate on this topic, but the few brief mentions he does make of it show that he was well aware of the facts involved.[9]

II. A Twelfth-Century Interpretation of Knighthood: Bernard of Clairvaux

St. Bernard's family was a knightly one, and he was the only member of it not to engage in armed violence. From the time of his youth, before he became a monk at Cîteaux in 1112, he used all his prestige—which was considerable—to persuade his brothers, his uncle, and other knights to convert to the cloistered life. Once he was a monk, he soon showed himself to be a reformer, at all levels of Church and Society, in all walks of life, including knighthood. Scattered throughout his correspondence and his various works, from the time he started writing, we notice evidence that he strove to limit the violence of knights and set their motivations squarely before them, asking them to examine whether they were really fighting for worthwhile reasons. He confronted them with the prospect of the death they might inflict on others or meet with themselves: death, the moment of their encounter with God, he who will judge us according to our merits.[10] The texts previously quoted in which Bernard denounces "worldly knights" are sufficiently eloquent on this point.

Bernard dealt more specifically with the subject on two particular—and exceptional—occasions. The first time was when, somewhere around 1130, he composed a treatise In Praise of the New Knighthood, written for the Templar Knights with the purpose of justifying for them, in their own eyes, their way of life in a social context, which has been carefully explored by M. C. Barber in a recent issue of the Transactions of the Royal Historical Society.[11] But what he said in favor of these "knight monks" was not intended to apply to the normal, secular knights.

The second occasion for dealing with the subject came toward the end of Bernard's life when, from 1146 onward, he was engaged in preparing and encouraging a crusade against the Saracens in the Holy Land.[12] But this again does not reveal his attitude toward knighthood in general. It only shows that for the Crusaders, as for the Templars, Bernard was attempting to "personalize," as it were, the military expedition and to make it an occasion for their individual, interior, spiritual conversion.[13]

However, what is more revealing of his interpretation of the knightly phenomenon is all that he did to put into harness for spiritual ends two major needs deeply ingrained in the nobility of his day: a tendency toward aggression, and a need for human love, this last being the subject of a vast and refined courtly literature. Bernard strove constantly to "transpose" all knightly characteristics, even every detail of the attitudes and actions of knights in battle, and to lift them to a higher plane, giving them a spiritual interpretation immediately applicable to monks, but incidentally to all other knights. Bernard's whole ascetic teaching became a doctrine of the combat for God, expressed in the terms and illustrated with the imagery that was familiar to the one-time knights among the monks he was addressing, or to the still active knights for whom he was writing.[14] They were not knight-monks, as were the Templars, but rather monk-knights, as it were. Having been worldly knights when they were young adults, they were now maturing into knights of God, given to the service of God in hundreds of monasteries, in Clairvaux with its many daughter houses or foundations, and in the other cloisters where Bernard's texts were copied, preserved, read, and meditated on. This process gave a fresh interpretation, grounded on the experience of knighthood, to many biblical texts and to other texts of the monastic literary tradition, which employed Old Testament words and themes of fighting for God's cause, the New Testament theme of the *Militia Christi,* and similar themes in patristic literature.

The other sphere of human nature—which Bernard considered ought to be taken into consideration rather than ignored, repressed, and suppressed in the imagination of the new type of monks—was that of human love. The monks now coming to the monasteries had not been offered as oblates by their parents when still children, as had been the case in the ancient monastic institutions—those of the so-called black monks of the traditional orders: Cluny and so many others which were much later on to be termed the ''Benedictines.'' The recruits coming to the Cistercians and other various new orders of the twelfth century—Carthusians, Grandmontains and so on—were adults, and some of them had even been married. Their knowledge and experience of love, and the language in which they spoke of it, differed from that of monks who had entered in childhood. Bernard made use of all this new psychological material and gave it a new purpose, object, and value: the love affair that they were now to experience was an affair of the heart between them and God. Bernard did not hesitate to use those allegories of love which abound in the Bible, especially in the *Song of Songs,* and to transpose them, to sublimate their spontaneous imagery and lift it to the level of the monk's search for God in Christ, and his spiritual experience of the combat entailed in fighting to win a new Beloved.[15]

In fact, Bernard is proposing a spiritual hermeneutic of knighthood: he transposes what he knows of the historical reality, as it really was, to the spiritual level, as it should be, at least as he himself sees it. He wrote a satire of worldly knighthood and created a model: both are exaggerations. The model was certainly an idealization. However, it was continuously propounded, and presumably partly implemented by innumerable monks, formerly worldly knights and now become spiritual knights for Christ. The model of love literature created by Bernard, and the model of the virtuous combatant he drew up have influenced not only later courtly and epic writings but also the milieux in which they were known and read. Even in the new society of the thirteenth century, the knightly image of the early twelfth century lived on and was an inspiration to many people. It was even applied to St. Francis in the legend woven around this son of a merchant.

III. El Poema de mio Cid *as an Interpretation of Knighthood*

This great epic poem of almost four thousand verses remains partly mysterious. It raises many problems and not all have yet been solved,[16] but we have enough information to let us situate it in the general evolution of the history of literature and spirituality. The author is still anonymous. The date of his writing has long been supposed to be 1140, an opinion firmly maintained by Ramón Menéndez Pidal. But from 1952 onward scholars have tended to give it a later date, which they fixed somewhere in the early part of the thirteenth century. In 1983, Colin Smith argued convincingly that the date was 1207. As for the content, it has been clearly shown to be an idealization: the historical Cid becomes a "poetic hero." Comparisons and contrasts have been drawn up between the real Cid and the paragon he was later depicted to be, namely a man of chivalric virtues and religious concerns.

Here it will be interesting to attempt to discern whether the Cid of the *Poema* fits in with St. Bernard's spiritual interpretation of knighthood. Whoever the author may be, he represents a milieu, a culture for which his work was conceived and in which, as the colophon says, "The Poem has been read."

A careful reading of this work shows three main concerns, prayer, booty, and armed combat, stated in the order of importance they are given. Prayer activities are those most frequently mentioned; greed for booty is the most deeply obsessive. After prayer and booty, we find battles and all the rest.

In 130 passages we find the religious element present in the form of prayers of various kinds: simple mentions of God, short invocations, long formulas of praise or supplication, canonical hours, masses, absolution, prolonged silent meditation.[17] Not only the Cid himself, but his whole entourage appear deeply religious, and it is to be remarked that everyone is engaged in prayer: Ximena, the promised wife; Minaya, the valiant knight and the Cid's *aide de camp;* Alfonso, the king; Elvira and Sol, the Cid's daughters; the Infantes and, of course, the abbot of Cardeña. The French bishop, Don Jerome, who takes part in the battles, prays and fights even more earnestly than the other people. And finally, the Moors also pray. The work is pervaded from beginning to end with the devotional.

As for the central *dramatis persona,* the Cid himself, the first and most obvious image is that of a knight given to praying, a man who trusts in God and has confidence in the value of prayer. God is ever present to him as a counsellor and a good protector. In a dream he has a vision of St. Gabriel, but it is to God that he commends himself. We notice too that God is everywhere present in the words spoken by King Alfonso.

The titles given to God in the *Poema* are essentially Christian even though there may be some exclamations and interjections very much like oaths—*yo lo juro* (3509)—inspired by and perhaps translated from Muslim invocations of Allah. Frequently they depend on the first words of the Lord's prayer as it is in the Gospels: God is a Father who resides in the heights (*en alto*, 8, 497, et passim) and who comes to everyone's help (*que a todos guías*, 241). God is also the Creator, the glorious Lord (*señor glorioso*, 330). These names and titles are sometimes applied to Christ, as being equal to God the Father. There is a long and perfectly phrased passage recalling Christ's whole life. Mary, the Mother of Christ, is mentioned, and devotion is shown to St. James, St. Isidore, the Holy Powers of God, his saints, and, finally, St. Peter, the patron of Cardeña.

The spiritual attitude we find recurring most frequently is gratitude: *Grado a Dios* (614, 792, 924, et passim). Then come recommendations (*os encomiendo*), supplication (*rrogo*). The object of all these petitions is salvation (*Salve*, 420, 1115, 1636, et passim), protection, guidance, preservation from all evil, success in battle, and other affairs. This indicates a sense of constant dependence on God and trust in prayer. We also find expressions of love for God: *Por amor del Criador* (1321, 2787, 2792, et passim). It could be wondered whether all this is just routine formula and nothing more or, to the contrary, an expression of sincere sentiment. One of the Cid's prayers is quite long: it is a *grand ora* (1932) and, it must be said, Ximena's prayer (330–365) is very beautiful indeed.[18]

On the whole, all this prayer activity is correct in so far as expression is concerned, even though the motivations are far from being pure and disinterested. The Creator, the Lord who is in heaven, was ever present, ready to help the Cid who, when he captured Murviedo, was sure that God was on his side. However, the prayer which immediately follows, a long and correctly worded prayer, stems from motivations which have nothing to do with union with God, for, as we shall point out later, in the Christian regimen, prayer is not everything. But let us now make acquaintance with a person who is the exact opposite—the anti-model, so to speak—of all that St. Bernard had demanded of the clergy: Bishop Don Jerome.[19]

Don Jerome volunteers to fight the Moors, and his friend, the Cid, thanks God for the timely help the bishop will afford him. He further promises to establish him as bishop of Valencia. A question may be asked here: when Jerome came to serve in the battle ranks, was he entirely disinterested, having no ambitions for his own career? He is pious and joins with the clerics who are chanting the canonical hours in the chapel. On the eve of the battle he has a long conversation with the Cid during which both men speak of God and St. Mary. Before going onto the battlefield he celebrates mass and gives the combatants a *grant* absolution for all their sins, promising that "the one who will die here with his face to the enemy (may be sure) that God will receive his soul" (1705). And the bishop goes on to add, "Let me have the honor of striking the first blows" (1709). St. Bernard, in his own day, was aware of this noble desire burning in the hearts of fighting clerics. And Jerome makes the same request before another combat: "Today I have said the mass of the

Holy Trinity for your success." He then adds that he wishes to have—for the honor of his order, as a bishop—the privilege of striking the first blow since he has come to slay as many Moors as possible. "I want to essay my arms, if it may please God to give me joy." And, in fact, from the very first thrusts of his lance, Don Jerome slays two Moors "by good fortune and the love of God, of the God he loved" (*Dios quel amava* [2370–85]). Thus, in his own conduct, still more than in that of others—does he not profess religion?— God is mixed up with every cause. They all profess and practice the Christian religion. But their nature and their culture are in no way eliminated: whatever faith and charity they have are assimilated to the humanity of which they themselves are a part. And greed is one of the elements of this humanity. Hence the importance given to booty in the general mentality. In all this looting, Jerome is not the last to claim his share.

As to warrior violence, it is described with realism and even complacency. It is premeditated: twice, before a battle, the Cid and his knights incite one another to violence, and always in the name of God (1133–1139, 1188). "Strike them hard, knights, with all your might": in Spanish, "d'amor e de grado e de gran voluntad" (1139). In a short space of time, calling upon God, they kill 1,300 enemies (732). It is God himself who gives battle. After an enemy has been killed, thanks are given to God (2398). In the very heat of battle, during man-to-man combat, the Cid cries out: "Help me great God. Protect me from this sword" (3665). And at the end the conclusion is evident: "They won the fight by God's grace" (3696). What more do we need to be convinced of the seductive persuasiveness of the words "Gott mit uns"?

The Cid is praised for being faithful to his word (1080), but especially for his bravery when he goes from one battle to another during those local wars and political strifes with neighboring princes and against which St. Bernard had protested. The Cid is seen as a model of the great conqueror, an image which is the exact opposite of the Bernardine model. He seems to have but one aim in life: to conquer enemies and to gain wealth for himself and for his men. Now, he did all this with God's help (831)—"God was on his side." And what about his intentions, those which Bernard insisted should be purified? In a very explicit sentence the Cid justifies all this violence as being a necessary and legitimate means of self-defence: "We are obliged to defend ourselves with lance and sword. If we did not do so, we could not live in this impoverished land" (833–835). But he can also prove generosity and greatness of soul, being magnanimous in victory, with no abuse of the power that is his. He goes from battle to prayer, and more than once he mingles one with the other, like the strong and courageous knight that he is, penetrated with Christian faith, even though he does not show all the detachment from the goods of this world that would be proper to a demanding spirituality.

The Cid's dress betrays a leaning to vanity and there are allusions to his elegance: "He is magnificently dressed" (2610). He also insists upon his knights being dressed with brilliance and elegance for solemn occasions.

Fifteen or so lines describe every item of his attire when he is preparing to
present himself at the royal court at Toledo, and certain of the details given
evoke those which St. Bernard had held up to ridicule (3084–3100).[20] Of
course, when thus attired, the Cid is not going into battle. But even his martial
attire has a certain splendor.

As to his offensive and his defensive arms, those mentioned in the
Poema are proper to the times;[21] they have already been mentioned in the
Sentences where St. Bernard describes Goliath, or when he talks to his monks
about the inner combat of the spiritual life. Bernard's panoply is richer than
that in the *Poema* because, in addition to all the rest, he includes elements
from the Bible.[22]

We could, too, draw parallels between the two approaches to marriage
and marital love: the same stress is laid on monogamous fidelity in contrast
with other forms of union admitted by the society of the times of both St.
Bernard and the author of the *Poema*.[23] The latter informs us more about the
functioning of rites and institutions, whereas St. Bernard enlarges upon the
symbolic meaning of marriage.[24]

We also find the same attitude in both authors with regard to Jews: an
attitude of peaceful relations. But in Bernard this is based on a doctrine,
whereas in the Cid it is empirical.[25] The former defends the Jews in the name
of Scripture; the latter is content to have with those whom he calls (with
perhaps a certain irony) "my dear friends" (103), useful relationships, even
though he may on occasion be deceitful when dealing with them. Does this
"jovial antisemitism"[26] reveal deep but unconscious feelings?

One last parallel which cannot be left aside is the question of St. Bernard's and the Cid's attitudes towards Islam. St. Bernard scarcely mentions
the Moslems, but considers them to be adversaries of both the Christian faith
and of the presence of Christians in the Holy Land: he contemplates absolutely no compromise with them. The historical Cid had not fought against the
Moors in any particular way and he had even been, occasionally, their political ally. As for the Cid of the *Poema*, he has a few positive values in common
with them. Camón Aznar once characterized him as a "mozarabian person."[27] This fits the picture quite well, but it must be made clear what sort of
"mozarabism" he represents: it is a thirteenth-century conception, and as
such is richer in meaning than it would have been in the eleventh century.
Line twenty of the very first page of the *Poema* contains a frequently recurring
formula: "Dios, qué. . . ." It crops up several times afterwards, in either the
same words or in equivalent expressions. It is a fairly good equivalent to the
modern *Ojalá* of the Castilian tongue.[28] There is a slight difference of meaning between the formula of the *Poema* and the Moslem "Hinshallah": but
even so, it concludes with the name of God as in the Koran.[29] It can be
noticed, then, that throughout the *Poema* we find traces of Islamic influence
on language and even on certain points of morals in medieval Spain.[30]

However, the culture and the spirituality of the Cid—that is to say of the author of the *Poema*—are entirely Christian. Many examples of vocabulary and style proper to the Bible and the tradition of the Church have already been pointed out.[31] The list could be lengthened, especially in what concerns allusions to liturgical formulas.[32] The truly Christian atmosphere, in some ways, paradoxically devoid of aggression and animosity—even the Moors pray—shows that we are dealing with Spanish Africans and not Arabs.[33] One of them, Avengeluón, presented as being a friend of the Cid, a peaceful friend—*amigo de paz*—gives the Infantes a lesson in good behavior.[34] The very name of the knight—*el Cid* or *mio Cid,* comes from the Arabic.[35] It seems to have been given him already in the eleventh century by Moslem allies. In many ways this knight of the early thirteenth century seems to have achieved in himself a synthesis of elements coming from both the Islamic and the Catholic conception. It has been said that he is a "courtly hero,"[36] but he is, rather, a "mozarabian" hero of the beginning of his own era. Between the Cid of the eleventh century and the Cid depicted by the *Poema,* a hundred years later, we see a certain progress in the way the knightly phenomenon is interpreted. St. Bernard and the great century of courtly literature certainly contributed to this progress. Not all the refinements they offer were retained, but even so, progress, though limited, was real.

Much of what we find in the *Poema,* then, is far removed from the program proposed by St. Bernard. The abbot of Clairvaux had aimed too high, but chivalric combativeness, even though it is not moderated by religious concerns, is at least concordant with such ideals. The author of the *Poema* gives an interpretation of the real Cid as he was known to history. Such an interpretation was possible because of the culture of both the author himself and of the surrounding society of Castille at the beginning of the thirteenth century. Throughout the following centuries the image of the Cid was constantly modified and enriched with new and generally more beautiful tones and shades. A long series of Spanish legends contributed to the process, laying stress on one or other aspect of the Cid's personality as it is found in the *Poema.* In France in the seventeenth century Pierre Corneille's play, *Le Cid,* presented a still further interpretation based mainly on the fact that the love between the Cid and Ximena fused harmoniously with the heroism of their respective characters and that of several people in their entourage. In 1961, a Hollywood film greatly stressed the role of Ximena. It is a work of sustained interest and proves to be a modern American interpretation of both the knight and his lady.[37]

And in our own day, progress is still being made in the way the knightly phenomenon is interpreted. In the United States, cinema and video have taken over from literature for the benefit of so many of our contemporaries who no longer know how to read, but who look and listen instead. And it so happens that in many European countries there is a wave of Spanish inspiration; all those sentiments which were pent up during Franco's time are now being released. It is in this context that we have a new hermeneutic of the "Cid phenomenon.'' In April, 1986, Corneille's *Le Cid* was being performed at a Paris theatre. And the producer—who is the real creator of the show—has deliberately borrowed some cultural elements from Shakespeare. The new knight is more akin to Hamlet than to the Spanish model. But the deep underlying psyche behind it all is that of a young person today, a fundamentally non-violent person who is caught up in the business of making war. The hero of the play has a shorn head, he has set aside his elegant attire and his heavy armor. He does not fight for a country, as does the historical Cid; nor for God, as St. Bernard would have him do; nor for honor, as in the times of Louis XIV; nor even for a girl, in the Hollywood manner. He fights for peace.[38]

Notes

1. Ramón Menéndes Pidal, *La España del Cid*, sexta edición, versión abreviada (Madrid: Espasa-Calpe, 1967), 127.

2. Robert I. Burns, S. J., *Muslims, Christians and Jews in the Crusader Kingdom of Valencia: Studies in Symbiosis* (Cambridge: Cambridge University Press, 1984), 285.

3. Colin Smith, *The Making of the* Poema de mio Cid (Cambridge: Cambridge University Press, 1983), 50. On knighthood in general see the recent synthesis of Maurice Keen, *Chivalry* (New Haven: Yale University Press, 1985).

4. Bernard of Clairvaux, *In Praise of the New Knighthood*, here quoted according to the translation of Conrad Greenia, in *The Works of Bernard of Clairvaux*, Vol. 7, Treatise 3 (Kalamazoo: Cistercian Publications, 1977), 133–34. Similar descriptions of knighthood are given by other twelfth-century authors, such as Orderic Vitalis, quoted and commented on by Brian Stock, *The Implications of Literacy: Written Language and Models of Interpretation in the Eleventh and Twelfth Centuries* (Princeton: Princeton University Press, 1983), 482–83.

5. *In Praise of the New Knighthood*, 131.

6. Ibid., 132–33.

7. *Epist.* 203, here quoted as number 262, in *The Letters of St. Bernard of Clairvaux*, trans. Bruno Scott James (Chicago: Henry Regnery Company, 1953; reprint, 1980), 342.

8. Ibid., 116–17: *Epist.* 80, 11; quoted in James as number 136.

9. This has been demonstrated by J. P. M. Deroy, *Thèmes et termes de la* fin'amor *dans les* Sermones super Cantica Canticorum *de Saint Bernard de Clairvaux*, in *Actes du XIIe Congrès International de Linguistique et de Philologie romanes* (Québec: Université Laval, 1976): 865.

10. Jean Leclercq, *Saint Bernard's Attitude toward War*, in *Studies in Medieval Cistercian History*, II, ed. John R. Sommerfeldt (Kalamazoo: Cistercian Publications,

1976), 24–25. A. J. Forey, "The Emergence of the Military Order in the Twelfth Century," in *Journal of Ecclesiastical History*, 36 (1985): 186–87.

11. M. C. Barber, "The Social Context of the Templars," in *Transactions of the Royal Historical Society*, Fifth Series, vol. 34 (London, 1984), 27–46.

12. Bibliography in Benjamin Z. Kedar, *Crusade and Mission: European Approaches toward the Muslims* (Princeton: Princeton University Press, 1985), passim.

13. Giles Constable, "A Report on a Lost Sermon by Saint Bernard on the Failure of the Second Crusade," in *Studies in Medieval Cistercian History Presented to J. F. O'Sullivan*, Cistercian Studies Series, 13 (Shannon, 1971), 49–54.

14. Many of these texts have been assembled and translated into French in *Saint Bernard de Clairvaux: Les Combats de Dieu* (Préface de Dom Jean Leclercq), Textes choisis et traduits par Henri Rochais (Paris: Stock, 1981). See also my *Monks and Love in Twelfth Century France: Psycho-Historical Essays* (Oxford: Clarendon Press, 1979), 88–99.

15. *Monks and Love in Twelfth Century France*, 8–26, 99–105.

16. For the present summary of the acquired results concerning the *Poema de mio Cid*, I made use of the various works of Ramón Menéndez Pidal, who died in 1968, and to whom I am also indebted for all that I learnt in conversation with him. A collection of his essays on the *Poema* has been published under the title *En torno al Poema del Cid* (Barcelona: Edhasa, 1970). See also Edmundo de Chasca, *The Poem of the Cid* (Boston: Twayne Publications, 1974); M. E. Lacarra, *El Poema de mio Cid: Realidad histórica e ideología* (Madrid: J. Porrúa Turanzas, 1980); Amando Represa, *El pendón de Castilla y otras consideraciones sobre el reino* (Valladolid: Ambito Ediciones, 1983); and Smith, *The Making of the* Poema de mio Cid. On the historical Cid a recent contribution has been made by Geoffrey West, "Mediaeval Historiography Misconstrued: The Exile of the Cid, Rodrigo Diaz, and the Supposed 'Invidia' of Alfonso VI," *Medium Ævum* 52 (1983): 286–99.

17. For my analysis of the poem, I have used the Spanish text edited by Colin Smith, *Poema de Mio Cid* (Madrid: Catedra, 1984) and the text edited by Ian Michael, *The Poem of the Cid: A New Critical Edition of the Spanish Text* (Manchester: Manchester University Press and New York: Barnes and Noble, 1975). I quote the English translation by Rita Hamilton and Janet Perry in the same volume, except when I deem it appropriate to make modifications, especially in the case of formulas referring to religion, such as, for example, the names given to God. Here I shall not be dealing with matters concerning literary parallels, sources, and influences, but simply considering the *Poema* in general as a model of the interpretation of knighthood. The bibliography concerning the Cid is being constantly enriched as is seen, for example, by the list of references given in *Cahiers de civilisation médiévale*, X-XIIIe siècles, 28 (1985): Bibliographie, 114*–115*, nos. 2157–2176. To the prayers of the *Poema* as we find them in the text, we may also add those which are in the beginning, missing but reconstructed by Colin Smith, *Poema*, 356–57.

18. The narrative prayer of Don Jerome to the Virgin Mary shows certain parallels with prayers of the same kind which we find in French epic poems. Does it depend on them, or has it rather influenced them? This has been discussed by Menéndez Pidal,

En torno al poema del Cid, 30–33; Smith, *Poema,* 281–82; and others. Represa, *El pendón,* 130, thinks that it was merely one of those "Romanesque prayers" inspired by the sculptured tympanums in churches to the juggler of Medenaceli, San Esteban.

19. On the historical Don Jerome, see Smith, *Poema,* 349–50. He was one of those bishops born outside Spain who have been studied by Bernard F. Reilly, "On Getting to be a Bishop in León-Castile: The 'Emperor' Alfonso VII and the Post-Gregorian Church," in *Studies in Medieval and Renaissance History* I (1978), 37–40. In the *Poema,* 2382, Don Jerome is described as being an *abad.* Smith, *Poema,* 300, points out that he was a bishop, not an abbot. Antonio Linage has given details about the different forms of *abad* and its various meanings in Spanish in "Entorno a la benedictinización: La recepción de la Regla de San Benito en el monacasto de la Península Ibérica a través de Leyre y Aledanos," in *Príncipe de Viana* 46 (1983), 90–91.

20. On the clothes worn by the Cid, see de Chasca, *The Poem of the Cid,* 122–23.

21. On the arms of the Cid, see Menéndez Pidal, *El Poema,* 85–89.

22. On the arms mentioned by Saint Bernard, see *Saint Bernard de Clairvaux: Les combats de Dieu,* as in note 14, 223 and passim.

23. Represa, 140–48.

24. Leclercq, *Monks and Love,* as in note 14.

25. Represa, 127–29.

26. Smith, *Poema,* 293.

27. Camón Aznar, "El Cid Personaje Mozárabe," in *Revista de estudios políticos* 17 (1947): 109–41.

28. Smith, *Poema,* 293.

29. Juan Corominas and José Pascual, *Diccionario crítico etimológico castellano e hispánico,* vol. IV (Madrid: Gredos, 1981), 268–69.

30. Smith, *Poema,* 283, 312, 325, 346.

31. Ibid., 280, 283, 286.

32. For example, line 360, in the Prayer of Doña Ximena, about which Represa, 131, says that it is written "con un vigor casi hiriente," is inspired directly by the liturgical texts for the feast of the Ascension and which, some years ago, I brought together under the title, "L'Ascension, Triomphe du Christ," in my *La liturgie et les paradoxes chrétiens* (Paris: Éditions du Cerf, 1963), 25–36.

33. Represa, 127.

34. Smith, *Poema,* 351.

35. Ibid., 357.

36. B. Matulka, *The Cid as a Courtly Hero* (New York: Columbia University, Institute of French Studies, 1928), 3ff.

37. The film stars Charleton Heston and Sophia Loren and is available as a video recording released by Allied Artists.

38. See for instance Colette Godard, ''Francis Huster: Il est le Cid au Rond-Point,'' in *Le Monde:* 28 November 1985, 13.

7. England's Official Rose: Tudor Concepts of the Middle Ages

LORRAINE ATTREED

During 1985, that small corner of the world that is forever England celebrated the five hundredth anniversary of the death of King Richard III and, consequently, the birth of the Tudor dynasty. Commemorative events included a memorial service in Leicester Cathedral (for Richard III's immortal soul); a historical debate (on the front page of *The Times*) over the precise location of Bosworth field, where body and soul were separated; and a British Tourist Authority campaign to encourage visits to Welsh castles, "where the Tudor legend began." But few people stopped to contemplate the overwhelming uneasiness with which Henry VII must have taken the reins of command in August 1485. A young man of twenty-eight, Henry had spent half his life in Breton exile, dependent on the charity and decisions of others, not a situation that provided the best training for future kings. However he interpreted his checkered past, the present and future could only have seemed uncertain.

It is an oversimplification to suggest that Henry spent his entire reign searching for ways to bolster his claim to power and forcefully wield his authority. However, the king did propose and support an imaginative use of history and historical interpretation that created a scenario of Tudor order and calm, and of his own singlehanded rescue of the realm from turmoil. Henry would have approved of Shakespeare's later depiction of the young conqueror, concluding both the play *Richard III* and the Wars of the Roses with acts of justice, forgiveness, and an invitation to embark on more orderly and prosperous days. By giving Henry victory, God had shown His hand, promising to "enrich the time to come with smooth-faced peace,/With smiling plenty, and fair prosperous days."[1] Henry's interpretation depicted the past in terms which changed the nature of historiography radically. With optimism and a sense of purpose, historians came to believe that the past could be interpreted and even manipulated to emphasize the inevitable glories of their own day. There developed as well an interest in historical research in primary sources and factual accuracy which soon clashed with those interpretations not based so soundly on verifiable events. The conflict discouraged some historians, but challenged many others to find interpretations both reassuring and accurate.

By the sixteenth century, with help from Henry Tudor's interest and financial support, humanist ideas became known in England and began to have profound effects on historical investigation. The Christian conception of history as the working out of God's will was not totally abandoned, but rather was joined by concerns with secular events, organization and synthesis of material, and factual accuracy. God remained the prime mover; He still disposed whatever man proposed, but exactly what man proposed, and the secondary and natural causes that formed those human proposals, were found increasingly worthy of study. The sixteenth century witnessed a slow growth of anachronism, the belief that the past differs from the present, but the past was not yet perceived to be so different that comparisons and parallels could not be drawn.[2] Well past the Renaissance, history retained its moral character, along with a Ciceronian belief that history was the light of truth, the teacher of life, the witness of time, the messenger of antiquity.[3] Secular, political morality, applicable to individual citizens active in society, may have replaced a more introspective medieval view, but the lessons that history taught were still expected and valued by its readers.

The first Tudor appeared at just the right time and place to take advantage of these developments. Most important, Henry and his writers declared that the present had started on that hot summer's day in late August 1485, and that every event that had occurred before it was the past. They gave a sense of an ending to history, and decided that the past could be studied and learned from. They were in no sense victims of the past, but rather its interpreters. This was an entirely optimistic view which spanned the latter part of the fifteenth and the entire sixteenth centuries. It accepted the existence of present prejudices and conditions that shape one's view of the past, but used those Tudor values both to interpret the past and to validate present beliefs. It was in fact, hermeneutic preunderstanding writ large. These historians made a virtue of the inevitable, using sixteenth-century assumptions and prejudices to interpret the past so as to strengthen contemporary values of order, loyalty, obedience, and patriotism.

Divine Providence became a device in this interpretation, by making the past ever accessible to the present. No matter what the specific conditions of the present might be, God's hand in events made the past ever relevant to the present, and entirely knowable. In fact, the belief in Divine Providence validated present concerns and values by showing that God (through time) blessed and brought about those things most dear in the present. For the sixteenth-century, those things were order, peace, and stability.

Two of the most important themes of the Tudor dynasty—the Tudor achievement story and the British origins myth—developed in the last years of the fifteenth century, and influenced historiography as well as the way

Henry VII wished his reign to be assessed. The achievement story was the easier of the two myths to establish. With the help of court poets and historians Bernard André, Pietro Carmeliano, and Giovanni de Gigli, Henry presented to the world (and particularly to the European world) a scenario of salvation in which he had the starring role. The literary works went beyond the mere fact of Henry's victory at Bosworth and the termination of the House of York. Poems, histories, and chronicle entries proclaimed the fact that Henry's victory on the battlefield was matched by one in the bedroom—that his marriage to York heiress Elizabeth was made in heaven, and that it was destined to bring blessings on the land, the major blessing arriving nine months after the wedding in the form of a son and heir Prince Arthur.[4] The symbol of this Golden Age was the Tudor rose, often depicted at this early date as both white and red roses growing from the same plant.[5]

When not stressing the stability he had wrought in the present out of the immediate and violent past, Henry looked to the distant, and almost entirely unrecorded, past of Britain. He claimed its reflected strengths and glories as his rightful heritage, and he presented himself as the most recent fulfillment of a long line of heroes in the British origins myth. The myth came in several parts, including the tale of the Trojan origins of Britain and its first kings; the prophecy of the last British king Cadwallader of the ultimate British triumph over the Saxon invaders (the British red dragon over the Saxon white dragon); and the importance of King Arthur.[6] Henry VII was not the first king to remember and claim British roots: his predecessor Edward IV had been just as assiduous about investigating them, and Edward I has been called an Arthurian enthusiast.[7] But Henry Tudor was the first to carry the historical interpretation of those roots to a conclusion both logical and highly supportive of his rule. In his first ceremonial action after Bosworth, he presented his red dragon standard—one of the symbols of the British origins myth[8]—to St. Paul's in London.[9] At the coronation, his champion's horse wore trappings decorated with Cadwallader's arms, and after the ceremony Henry created a new pursuivant named Rougedragon.[10] Civic pageants, even those not publicly performed, stressed not only Henry's claim to power by divine election, victory and popular assent, but they traced his descent back to British and Arthurian lines as well.[11] Henry even quartered his arms with those of Arthur.[12] When his queen was due to give birth a year after Bosworth, he rushed her to Winchester Castle, ancient seat of British kings and a legendary home of the hero for whom the child was named, Arthur. Historian Edward Hall later commented, "Englishmen no more rejoiced than outward nations and foreign princes trembled and quaked, so much was that name [Arthur] to all nations terrible and formidable."[13] Nor did hopes of the Golden Age that Carmeliano and others predicted would accompany the heir die with the young man in 1502, for Henry had been careful to identify King Arthur with his entire line, not just with one frail prince. Arthurian symbols lasted through Henry VIII's reign, especially in his dealings with Emperor Charles V; and even if the image of King Arthur failed to clinch the Reformation with European ambassadors, Henry's daughter Elizabeth identified with the British monarch, as did the Stuarts and even William of Orange.[14]

Thus did Henry VII claim for himself success blessed both by God and by Britain's greatest hero. His confidence had effects down to the present, for even Tudor specialists today are likely to pass quickly over events such as Stoke and Blackheath; to remember Perkin Warbeck and Lambert Simnel as little more than charismatic failures; and to forget all the other pretenders to the throne. Yet all of these were serious threats in Henry's time, and many of his contemporaries feared a continuation of the violence and disorder known under the Plantagenets.[15] Henry prevailed, and so did a sanguine view of his times, an assessment based primarily on the interpretation that writers of his own day made of the past.

But not everyone was ready to accept all the rules of Henry's personal hermeneutics game. One of those rebels was humanist historian Polydore Vergil, who arrived in England from Urbino in 1502 and soon after acted on Henry's urging to write a history of his new home. At the king's command, it was to be a history on humanist lines that all Europe would respect. Vergil researched the topic for six years, and his findings led him to reject the figure of Arthur (particularly as recorded by twelfth-century historian Geoffrey of Monmouth). Logic alone accounted for the rejection, although Vergil had preceded publication of the history with an edition of the sixth-century writer Gildas, whose total silence on Arthur boded badly for the heroic figure.[16] Vergil's rejection did not just threaten Tudor claims to legitimacy and reflected glory. He implied that the present could not know anything about a past so dim, that even the chronicle sources were either silent or confused about it. Vergil, at least to his enemies, seemed to be saying that the past is unknowable and cannot teach anything, and certainly could not be used to support values of the present day.

Vergil's *Anglica Historia* provided historiography with more than just negative lessons. Vergil, after all, was neither the first man nor the last to doubt Geoffrey of Monmouth's version of Arthur and British history.[17] Truth was important to Vergil: "the first office of an historiographer is to write no lie; the second that he shall conceal no truth, for favor, displeasure or fear."[18] Vergil, who insisted that "history is a full rehearsal and declaration of things done, not a guess or divination," deplored the fictions many writers invented to give their homelands noble histories.[19] He felt that as an Italian, he could write more honestly about England than could a native. Of course, for that reason as well as for his religion, his writings were reviled and he himself charged unfairly with the crime of exporting to Rome and destroying evidence which contradicted his theses.[20] Using a structure strongly influenced by Suetonius, Vergil intended to instruct his readers, both princely and common, with examples of virtue, courage, and God's direct intervention. Henry VII was the hero of his narrative, overcoming opponents with great ease. Despite his rejection of Geoffrey of Monmouth and Arthur, Vergil believed that the

past could be instructive, for the motives of men remained always the same
and a lesson from the past was entirely relevant to conditions in the present
and future.[21]

Like Vergil, many historians of the mid-sixteenth century struggled to
depict the past in terms both honest and edificatory. Simon Grynaeus realized
that history was neither simple nor easy, but like life itself, filled with good
and bad, and mined for lessons by men who took from it according to their
characters.[22] Not everyone was so tolerant. John Leland, "a man with the
seeds of genius and of madness in him,"[23] is as well-known for his impas-
sioned defense of the historicity of Arthur as for his topographical studies. In
1533, Leland convinced Henry VIII that an inventory of monastic libraries
was needed before political dissolution created irrevocable archival disaster
and loss.[24] Some materials went to Henry's Royal Library, but Leland examined even more, and his investigations into medieval sources and chronicles
convinced him that Vergil was wrong. Vergil had demolished Geoffrey of
Monmouth's assertions by logic and negative argument. With lessons learned
from Lorenzo Valla and other humanists, Leland scoured the sources and
concluded that Arthur and the myth of British origins had to be correct. He
never considered for a moment that his medieval sources might have been
incorrect or even forged. Yet Leland's methods proved more influential than
his conclusions, for not only did he give increased value to the study of
original documents, but when his literary record was silent or unreliable, he
turned to archaeology, linguistics, place names, and topography to tell him
about the past. Leland's methods of historical research proved to be an inspiration for many of his successors.

The most famous of those successors was William Camden, who in 1586
wrote the history *Britannia*. As skeptical as Vergil of the British myths,
Camden searched for England's Roman and classical roots, thereby placing
the island firmly and with dignity "within the world of antiquity and that of
international Renaissance scholarship."[25] Camden himself stated, "[This is]
not collecting [history] from fables . . . but from the genuine monuments of
Antiquity."[26] Unfortunately, the medieval era suffered the most for this
emphasis. To Camden, the Middle Ages were "so overcast with dark clouds
or rather thick fogs of ignorance that every little spark of liberal learning
seemed wonderful."[27] The message was one of progress, and to support it
Camden showered readers with geographical and historical detail. He had a
lasting influence: careful to check his interpretations by using several lines of
reasoning, Camden was diligent in his use of references, and he served as
instructor to the following generation of historians.[28]

But some critics feared that writers were ignoring the didactic element of
history by concentrating merely on the validity of individual facts. At the end
of the century, Sir Philip Sidney characterized the historian of his age as

> loaden with old mouse-eaten records, authorizing himself for the most part
> upon other histories whose greatest authorities are built upon the notable

foundation of hearsay . . . better acquainted with one thousand years ago
than with the present age . . . curious for antiquities, inquisitive of novel-
ties, a wonder to young folks and a tyrant in table talk. . . .[29]

Sidney should not have worried, for throughout the sixteenth century
there flourished a strong tradition of moral, providential histories praising the
present by contrasting it to a barbaric and violent past. Edward Hall and John
Stow stressed themes of order and Tudor success in their works, retaining
faith in didactic history and believing it was as impossible for readers to
ignore history's lessons as it was for sunbathers to avoid sunburns.[30] Their
influence and their optimism were vital to one writer in particular, William
Shakespeare.

Mere mention of Sidney and Shakespeare introduces the question of
moral purpose, and whether history or poetry better communicated that
theme. As many realized, poets and playwrights could more easily shape
events to show the moral lesson than could historians, especially those ob-
sessed with antiquarian detail. But one historian, unique in his reflections
about his craft, thought that the two themes could be combined successfully.
Samuel Daniel's writings and career best illustrate the changes historiography
underwent in the sixteenth century. In his poem *The Civil Wars* (1594),
Daniel studied England's history from the reign of Richard II to the glory of
Elizabeth. While establishing himself as an epic poet, he supported the Tudor
salvation myth, assuming that there was nothing new under the sun and that
the past was easily known.[31] His aim was "to show the deformities of Civil
Dissension and the miserable events of Rebellions, Conspiracies and bloody
revengements," but problems developed so quickly that he never finished the
poem.[32] The more he investigated the Wars of the Roses and people like
Henry V and Richard of York, the harder it became to see events and people
in simplistic terms and to condemn the medieval past as a time of relentless
turmoil and ignorance. Growing out of this uneasiness was a nostalgia for the
medieval past, not rooted in chivalric fantasy, but in a respect for the structure
of medieval politics and society.[33]

Disenchanted by poetry, for a time Daniel feared that nothing of the past
could be known.[34] In his work "Musophilus" (1603), the narrator contemplates Stonehenge with a sense of awe and wants to know its origin and reason
for construction. Realizing he will never know the answer, he mourns "the
misery of dark forgetfulness" that history cannot enlighten. Worst of all, it is
an "ignorance with fabulous discourse/ Robbing faire arte and cunning of
their right" and telling a false tale which is worse than knowing nothing at
all.[35] As much as Daniel wanted to write about England's origins, he was
discouraged by the fictions that such a topic spawned. He was all too aware
that early times contained a large share of "poverty, piracy, robbery and
violence, howsoever fabulous writers, to glorify their nations, strive to abuse
the credulity of after ages with heroical or miraculous beginnings."[36] Daniel
turned to prose to work out these problems with greater freedom, and in his

critical study *A Defence of Ryme* (1602–3), he defended at length the value
and intelligence shown by times other than the glorious Elizabethan present:

> The distribution of gifts are [*sic*] universal and all seasons hath them in some
> sort. Modern man should neither be intimidated by classical authorities, nor
> quick to assume the culture between Rome and the present was blank or
> deformed. Only present prejudices and judgments make it seem so, and the
> complacency his contemporaries feel in contrast is built on sand, so that it is
> but the clouds gathered about our own judgment that makes [*sic*] us think all
> other ages wrapped up in mists, and the great distance between us, that
> causes us to imagine men so far off to be so little in respect of our selves.[37]

If the present *is* glorious, as Daniel truly believed, that glory was largely the
result of the strength and dignity of the past. With renewed interest, Daniel
turned to a prose history of England, one which respected the unique character
of every past epoch. He succumbed only to the fear that the mists of which he
wrote might be too thick, and that the present might not be able to understand
the past at all accurately:

> Pardon us, Antiquity, if we mis-censure your actions, which are ever (as
> those of men) according to the vogue and sway of times, and have only their
> upholding by the opinion of the present. We deal with you but as posterity
> will with us, which ever thinks it self the wiser, that will judge likewise of
> our errors according to the cast of their imaginations.[38]

By the end of the sixteenth century, the study of the medieval past could
lead to cultural discouragement, or could be dangerous in itself. Historians
faced an old dilemma with new and more intense fear: how to tell the truth of
medieval events without seeming to praise kings like Henry IV and even
Henry VII, who usurped the thrones of solemnly-annointed monarchs. Seeking the truth and drawing didactic parallels could be a dangerous game, as Sir
John Hayward discovered late in Elizabeth's reign with his suggestive *History
of Henry the Fourth* (1599). The history's untimely dedication to the earl of
Essex, its narrative of Richard II's weaknesses, and its sympathy for usurper
Henry IV led its author to arrest and trial. Queen Elizabeth identified closely
with Richard Plantagenet: she told historian William Lambarde in an inter-
view the following year, "I am Richard the Second, know ye not that?"[39]
Attorney General Edward Coke read the offending text and commented that
"[Hayward] pretende to wright a history past, but entend to point at this very
tyme."[40] Although this was what history was supposed to do, such a purpose
was commendable only as long as it praised the present and its morals at the
expense of a violent and more degenerate past. Writers like Daniel and Hayward made their contemporaries feel uneasy: they suggested that the present
was not the only age of glory, and that any comparison might be specious,
thereby displeasing both readers and rulers.

By the early seventeenth century, newly discovered and interpreted information about the medieval past made it difficult to depict the Middle Ages as a uniformly barbarous time. In one sense, this made it harder for the present to reap the past of clearcut lessons filled with morals which relied on contrast to praise present conditions. It was almost as though there developed a crisis of faith in hermeneutics, or an inability to believe that the past could be known and that present prejudices could be an asset in that process and not a hindrance. But histories in the older, more optimistic form, such as the writings of Sir Walter Raleigh, survived and thrived, proving especially popular with the poor and the newly-literate groups of early modern society.[41] Even more important, past events soon proved all too applicable to the present, as Elizabeth found out in her time of "the wit of the fox,"[42] and as James I and his son would discover, when historical precedent moved into the halls of Parliament and threatened to turn both world and historiography upside down.

Notes

1. William Shakespeare, *Richard III*, Act V, Scene 5, lines 33–34.

2. Antonia Gransden, "Antiquarian Studies in Fifteenth-Century England," *Antiquaries Journal* 60 (1980): 75–80.

3. Antonia Gransden, *Historical Writing in England, Volume II, c.1307 to the Early Sixteenth Century* (London: Routledge and Kegan Paul, 1982), 426–28. For Petrarch's influence, see Myron Gilmore, "The Renaissance Conception of the Lessons of History," *Facets of the Renaissance*, ed. William Werkmeister (Los Angeles: University of Southern California Press, 1959), 76.

4. The papal dispensation for the marriage also stressed the political unity it was likely to bring about: Sydney Anglo, "The Foundation of the Tudor Dynasty: The Coronation and Marriage of Henry VII," *The Guildhall Miscellany* 2 (1960): 10; *The Camden Miscellany Volume I*, Camden Society, old series 39 (London: Royal Historical Society, 1847), 5–7.

5. For details of these poems, see Henry A. Kelly, *Divine Providence in the England of Shakespeare's Histories* (Cambridge, Mass.: Harvard University Press, 1970), chapter 3. Roses are depicted in Carmeliano's work, British Library Additional MS. 33736, ff. 1 and 2, and in de Gigli's work, British Library Harleian MS. 336, f. 70.

6. Sydney Anglo, "The 'British History' in Early Tudor Propaganda," *Bulletin of the John Rylands Library* 44 (1961): 18.

7. Ibid., 35, n. 4; Roger Loomis, "Edward I, Arthurian Enthusiast," *Speculum* 28 (1953): 114, 126.

8. J. S. P. Tatlock, "The Dragons of Wessex and Wales," *Speculum* 8 (1933): 223–35, has the last word on dragons.

9. A. H. Thomas and I. D. Thornley, eds., *The Great Chronicle of London* (London: Library Committee of the Corporation of London, 1938), 238–39. The other two standards depicted St. George and the Dun Cow emblem of the Beaufort line. The red dragon was depicted on white and green sarcenet, the Tudor colors since the twelfth century: Francis Jones, "The Colours of Wales," *The Coat of Arms* 6 (1960): 141–44.

10. Anglo, " 'British History', " 38.

11. John C. Meagher, "The First Progress of Henry VII," *Renaissance Drama*, new series 1 (1968), 45–73; Sydney Anglo, *Spectacle, Pageantry and Early Tudor Policy* (Oxford: The Clarendon Press, 1969), chapter 1; John Leland, *Collectanea*, 6 vols. (London: G. and J. Richardson, 1770), IV, 185–203.

12. British Library Additional MS. 46354, f. 72v (p. 144), Sir Thomas Wriothesley's book of arms.

13. Anglo, " 'British History', " 29.

14. Hugh A. MacDougall, *Racial Myth in English History* (Hanover, New Hampshire: University Press of New England, 1982), 17–26; *Calendar of State Papers, Spanish, 1531–1533* (London: Her Majesty's Stationery Office, 1882), 22–28.

15. For Henry's own concerns and the worries he had about one of the pretenders, see L. C. Attreed, "A New Source for Perkin Warbeck's Invasion of 1497," *Mediaeval Studies* 48 (1986): 514–21.

16. Henry Ellis, ed., *Polydore Vergil's English History, Volume I*, Camden Society, old series 36 (London: J. B. Nichols & Sons, 1846), 121–22.

17. In the twelfth century, Alfred of Beverley, Giraldus Cambrensis, and William of Newburgh expressed doubts, as did Ranulf Higden in the fourteenth century, and Flavio Biondo, Fabyan, and John Rastell in later years: MacDougall, *Racial Myth*, 12; John E. Housman, "Higden, Trevisa, Caxton and the Beginnings of Arthurian Criticism," *Review of English Studies* 23 (1947): 212; Beatrice R. Reynolds, "Latin Historiography: A Survey 1400–1600," *Studies in the Renaissance II*, ed. M. A. Shaaber, (New York: Renaissance Society of America, 1955), 11; T. D. Kendrick, *British Antiquity* (London: Methuen, 1950), 41–42. For Vergil's threats to Tudor claims, see F. J. Levy, *Tudor Historical Thought* (San Marino, California: The Huntingdon Library, 1967), 66.

18. Levy, 63.

19. Ellis, *Vergil's English History*, 26.

20. Henry Ellis, ed., *Three Books of Polydore Vergil's English History*, Camden Society, old series 29 (1844), xxvi. See also Denys Hay, *Polydore Vergil* (Oxford: The Clarendon Press, 1952), 159.

21. Gransden, *Historical Writing*, 433–35; Levy, *Tudor Historical Thought*, 60; Peter Iver Kaufman, "Polydore Vergil's Fifteenth Century," *The Historian* 47 (1985): 518–19.

22. Leonard F. Dean, "Tudor Theories of History Writing," *University of Michigan Contributions in Modern Philology* 1 (1947): 8–9.

23. Joan Evans, *A History of the Society of Antiquaries* (Oxford: Oxford University Press, 1956), 3.

24. May McKisack, *Medieval History in the Tudor Age* (Oxford: The Clarendon Press, 1971), chapter 1; Levy, *Tudor Historical Thought*, 67, 131–32.

25. Stuart Piggott, "Antiquarian Thought in the Sixteenth and Seventeenth Centuries," in *English Historical Scholarship in the Sixteenth and Seventeenth Centuries*, ed. Levi Fox (Oxford: The Dugdale Society, 1956), 102–105.

26. F. J. Levy, "The Making of Camden's *Britannia*," *Bibliothèque d'Humanisme et Renaissance* 26 (1964): 90.

27. Stuart Piggott, "William Camden and the *Britannia*," *Proceedings of the British Academy* 37 (1951): 204.

28. Levy, *Tudor Historical Thought*, 159.

29. *Defence of Poesie*, published 1595, cited in Dean, "Tudor Theories": 1–2.

30. Louis B. Wright, *Middle-Class Culture in Elizabethan England* (Ithaca, NY: Cornell University Press, 1935), 309.

31. Levy, *Tudor Historical Thought*, 224; Joan Rees, *Samuel Daniel* (Liverpool: Liverpool University Press, 1964), 125, 132–33.

32. Samuel Daniel, *The Civil Wars*, ed. Laurence Michel (New Haven, Conn.: Yale University Press, 1958), 67.

33. May McKisack, "Samuel Daniel as Historian," *Review of English Studies* 23 (1947): 238.

34. See "Musophilus," lines 343–52, in Samuel Daniel, *Poems and A Defence of Ryme*, ed. Arthur C. Sprague (Chicago: University of Chicago Press, 1965), 79.

35. Ibid.

36. McKisack, "Samuel Daniel," 236.

37. Daniel, *Poems*, ed. Sprague, 143.

38. Rees, *Samuel Daniel*, 153.

39. Retha M. Warnicke, *William Lambarde, Elizabethan Antiquary 1536–1601* (London: Phillimore, 1973), 136; Robert M. Smith, *Froissart and the English Chronicle Play* (New York: B. Blom, 1915), 99.

40. Elizabeth was already upset by the public performances of William Shakespeare's *Richard II* and ordered the 1597 quarto severely edited: Margaret Dowling, "Sir John Hayward's Troubles over his Life of Henry IV," *The Library*, 4th series, 11 (1930–31): 212–14. Coke's notes can be found in *Calendar of State Papers, Domestic Series, Elizabeth, 1598–1601*, ed. Mary Anne Everett Green (London: Her Majesty's Stationery Office, 1869), 405, 449–51, 539.

41. Levy, *Tudor Historical Thought,* 211; Wright, *Middle Class,* 332; Charles H. Firth, "Sir Walter Raleigh's History of the World," *Proceedings of the British Academy* 8 (1918): 434–35.

42. "In those days [of the Middle Ages], force and arms did prevail; but now the wit of the fox is everywhere on foot, so hardly a faithful and virtuous man may be found": Warnicke, *William Lambarde,* 136.

8. Franco-German Conflict and the History of French Scholarship on the *Song of Roland*

JOSEPH J. DUGGAN

The reception of a literary work by society is a complex topic. Readers come to the text not naively but with a set of expectations: their interpretations are circumscribed by what they have been told of the work's character and by their views both of themselves and of the collectivities to which they wish to belong. Scholarship in turn is affected by the way in which well-known works are received in the culture at large. Indeed scholarship is itself a set of hermeneutic acts at once mediating between ancient artifacts and modern readers, and adapting itself—in a reciprocal relationship—to the history both of its own and of popular readings of a given text.

In this essay, I examine the interplay between an interpretation of the *Song of Roland* as the French national epic and some aspects of the history of scholarship dealing with the poem, in the period 1837 to 1945, that is between the publication of the first edition of the *Roland* and the end of the last period of major hostility between France and Germany.

In his remarkable introduction to the poem's *editio princeps* of 1837,[1] based on the Oxford manuscript, that is to say on the version that has been accepted to the present day as the canonical text, Francisque Michel avoided any semblance of nationalistic fervor. This strictly scholarly stance provoked one of his reviewers, the historian and literary critic Raimond Thomassy, to reproach Michel for not providing an appreciation of the poem with the remark:

> Se dispenser d'apprécier, sous le rapport de l'art, ce que l'on connaît à fond sous le point de vue scientifique, est une disposition si incompatible avec le génie français, qu'on ne saurait jamais trop la combattre. —C'est une importation d'outre-Rhin et d'outre-mer qu'il aurait mieux valu arrêter à la frontière, que l'accepter telle quelle, avec son caractère brut et étranger, et s'en servir avant de lui avoir imprimé le cachet d'une facture nationale.
> (To excuse oneself from appreciating as art what one knows well from the scientific point of view is a stance so incompatible with the French genius

97

that it can never be opposed too strongly. —It is an import from beyond the Rhine and from overseas that would better have been stopped at the border rather than accepted as is, with its raw and foreign nature, and used before one could impress upon it the seal of a national construct.)[2]

Michel's failure to posit the poem's 'national character' was quickly compensated for in the popular press. Xavier Marmier, Romantic poet and author of a history of German literature, reviewed the edition in *Le Monde*,[3] commenting that the *Roland* was "peut-être notre plus ancienne, notre véritable épopée nationale" (perhaps our most ancient, our true national epic), and remarking with envy that if an analogous work had been discovered in German, all of German scholarship would be occupied writing commentaries and bestowing praise. Such expressions of intellectual insecurity in the face of the dynamic achievements of Romance philology in Germany were not uncommon in the period,[4] but what is more important for our purposes is that immediately after the *Roland*'s very first publication a homology was established between the nineteenth-century French nation on the one hand and, on the other, the France of the poetic Charlemagne. The poem was already being characterized as a national epic.

Despite the intellectual problems that it posed, no one challenged this rapprochement, and in fact the Oxford text's second editor, François Génin, in 1850, reinforced the idea by maintaining that the *Roland*'s subject "est national pour les Français autant que l'étaient pour les Grecs les événements de la guerre de Troie" (is national for the French to the same degree as the events of the Trojan War were for the Greeks).[5]

Génin's edition also gave rise to a number of reviews in the popular press, of which I will only cite one here. Frédéric Lacroix, writing in *L'Illustration,* a widely read paper with moderate republican leanings that adopted a popularizing stance on cultural matters, declared of the poem:

> Il règne, d'ailleurs, dans toute cette œuvre épique un si vif sentiment de patriotisme, l'amour de la terre de France y éclate, presque à chaque vers, avec une si naïve énergie, qu'on peut la dire hardiment nationale au premier chef.
>
> (In any case such a vivid feeling of patriotism reigns in this entire epic work, the love of France bursts forth in almost every line with such a naive energy, that one can qualify it as boldly national from the very start.)[6]

Ludovic Vitet, politically conservative author of a trilogy of Romantic dramas and a number of studies on art and archeology, published an intelligent article on the *Roland* in 1852 in the *Revue des Deux Mondes* in which he posed the question: "[Le poëme] peut-il, à titre d'épopée nationale, prendre la place restée vide dans l'histoire littéraire de la France?" (Can the poem assume the position of national epic that has remained empty in the literary history of France?).[7] Vitet chose the *Roland* from among the other *chansons de geste* as particularly patriotic, since it alone invoked "la France, la douce France . . ., l'amour de la patrie, le dévouement à la mère commune, ces nobles sentiments qui répandent sur tout le poëme je ne sais quel coloris tendre et mélancolique" (France, pleasant France . . ., love of the fatherland, devotion to the common mother, those noble feelings that cast over the entire poem an indefinably tender and melancholy coloring).[8] And, Vitet goes on:

> ce qui n'est pas un moindre titre pour notre orgueil national, ce qui ne laisse pas de compenser bien des imperfections, au temps où fut créé notre poëme, aucun peuple en Europe, aussi bien au midi qu'au nord, n'était capable de produire son pareil. . . . Car Roland, c'est la France, c'est son aveugle et impétueux courage: Azincourt et Poitiers, aussi bien que Roncevaux sont là pour confirmer l'exacte ressemblance, la prophétique vérité de ce caractère de Roland.
> (no less a motive for our national pride, and indeed a continual compensation for many an imperfection, is that fact that, in the period in which our poem was created, no people in Europe, northern or southern, was capable of producing its equal. . . . For Roland is France, he is her blind and impetuous courage: Agincourt and Poitiers as well as Roncevaux are there to confirm the exact resemblance, the prophetic truth of this character of Roland.)[9]

Consequently, by the middle of the nineteenth century, the *Song of Roland* was taken not merely as a national work, but also as proof of the superiority of the French over every other European people during the age that the Romantic theorists had appropriated as the repository of ultimate values, the period of origins.

The city of Paris had been under siege by German troops for nearly three months in 1870 when the most accomplished French literary medievalist of the nineteenth century, Gaston Paris, delivered a lecture at the Collège de France entitled "La *Chanson de Roland* et la nationalité française" (The *Song of Roland* and the French nation). Although convinced that scholarship should in principle abstract from patriotism, Paris nevertheless affirmed that the literary history of a people was also the history of its national consciousness.

In the early Middle Ages, according to Paris, Franks and Gallo-Romans merged under the influence of Christianity into a new nation. After the ferment of the Carolingian period, French national life was dominated by two great tendencies: toward unity and toward expansion. France took from Charlemagne's ideal the task of exercising a moral hegemony over the rest of Europe, and poetic traditions on the great emperor, soon effaced in Germany, were transformed in France into the great national epic in which was acted out the Frankish ambition of propagating Christianity, but upon the Muslims rather than the Germanic pagans.[10] In nineteenth-century France, maintains Paris, "ce noble besoin d'expansion qui a fait et fera dans le monde la grandeur de notre pays'' (this noble need for expansion that has constituted and will constitute the greatness of our country in the world) persisted.[11]

These impulses toward unity and expansion inspire the *Song of Roland*, according to Paris. Eight centuries before, when other European nations were still not conscious of their own existence, national sentiment was already alive in France, in the form of love of the land, signified by the expression *la douce France* (pleasant France) in the *Roland;* exalted concern for the honor of the country, as expressed in Roland's refusal to call back the main body of Charlemagne's army; and attachment to national institutions, which in the *Roland* takes the form of loyalty to the emperor Charlemagne. These three features of love, honor, and devotion combine to make the *Roland* an incomparable monument of French national feeling for Gaston Paris.

Like so many of his scholarly predecessors, Paris also envies the Germans, but he envies them because figures such as Jacob Grimm succeeded in regenerating a sense of national consciousness by instilling in their readers a love of medieval poetry. Now, he says, even when the soil of France is trembling under the weight of German armies, two of the three ideals expressed in the *Roland* remain: love of *douce France,* and feelings of national honor.[12] Paris maintains that the third ideal, attachment to national institutions, is missing—no doubt he is reflecting on the recent collapse of the Second Empire—but can still be reinstated as an enduring ideal. He concludes with an appeal to the exemplary function of the *Roland:* ''Faisons-nous reconnaître pour les fils de ceux qui sont morts à Roncevaux et de ceux qui les ont vengés. . .'' (Let us make ourselves known as the sons of those who died at Roncevaux and of those who avenged them).[13]

Behind this appeal to national consciousness lie two qualities of the *Song of Roland* just barely alluded to that make its evocation pertinent at one of the points of lowest morale in the history of nineteenth-century France: the poem is the story of a great defeat; it is the tale of an imperialistic adventure. By 1870 the French army had been in Algeria for 40 years, and the significance of Charlemagne's victory over the dark and vaguely Muslim Saracens of the *chanson de geste* could not have been lost on French readers. This is, I believe, one of the main reasons why the *Song of Roland,* taking place in a foreign land, pitting against the north-African emir of Islam (Baligant of Babylone, i.e. Cairo) the figure who is—in French historical consciousness—the founder of France, and depicting the forced conversion of the Saracens, took on such a disproportionate role in the image that Frenchmen forged of their past in the age of French imperialism.

Aside from Francisque Michel, the most important nineteenth-century editor of the *Song of Roland* was Léon Gautier, who was Professor of Paleography at the École des Chartes for most of his professional life. Gautier was profoundly affected by the siege of Paris, and his experience during the Commune led him to found the Cercles Catholiques d'Ouvriers. Gautier's text of the *Roland* was immensely popular; it went through 26 editions between

1872 when it was first published and 1903, continued to be reprinted well into the 20th century, and was really only supplanted by Joseph Bédier's bilingual edition of 1921.[14]

That the *Roland* was the national epic of France had by now become a commonplace; Gautier made that notion the centerpiece of his interpretation. His introduction, entitled "Histoire d'un poëme national" (History of a national poem), declares from the start that Roland "résume dans sa personnalité puissante les idées, la mission, la générosité, et le héroïsme antiques de la France. Roland, c'est la France faite homme" (sums up in his powerful personality the ancient ideas, mission, generosity, and heroism of France. Roland is France personified).[15] Gautier wrote those words, as he hastens to tell us, "au milieu des malheurs de la Patrie" (amid the misfortunes of the Fatherland), that is to say during the siege of Paris, with the express intention of consoling his compatriots.

Following the line of argument that Vitet had initiated, Gautier uses the platform of his edition to attack the national enemy at the privileged moment of origins. The French were, he claims, the first to develop a sentiment of patriotism: "Jamais, jamais on n'a tant aimé son pays. Et écoutez bien, pesez bien les mots que je vais dire, ô Allemands qui m'entendez: IL EST ICI QUESTION DU XIᵉ SIECLE. A ceux qui étouffent aujourd'hui ma pauvre France, j'ai bien le droit de montrer combien déjà elle était grande il y a environ huit cents ans" (Never, never has a country been so loved. And listen well, weigh the words I am about to utter, oh Germans who are listening to me: WE ARE SPEAKING HERE OF THE ELEVENTH CENTURY. I have indeed the right to show those who today are suffocating my poor France how great she already was approximately eight hundred years ago).[16] In contrast, the ancestors of the nineteenth-century Prussians were at the same period savages:

> Où étaient-ils, quand notre Chanson fut écrite, ou étaient-ils, nos orgueilleux envahisseurs? Ils erraient en bandes sauvages sous l'ombre de forêts sans nom: ils ne savaient . . . que piller et tuer. Quand nous tenions d'une main si ferme notre grande épée lumineuse près de l'Eglise armée et défendue, qu'étaient-ils? Des Mohicans ou des Peaux-Rouges.
> (Where were they when our Song was written, where were they, our proud invaders? They were wandering in wild gangs in the shade of nameless forests: they knew . . . only how to pillage and kill. While we were raising our great luminous sword beside the armed and defended Church, what were they? Mohicans and Redskins.)[17]

Gautier was willing to admit that the *chansons de geste* were Germanic in their spirit, their ideas, in military and political concepts, in the law reflected in them, and in the poetic habits of those who sang them, but what he calls vaguely "la lettre des traditions positives" (the letter of positive traditions)[18] that one finds in them is not Germanic. For him the *Roland* is the "le chant roman des Germains christianisés" (the Romance song of the Germans converted to Christianity).[19]

Even Gautier's stance in favor of the Germanic origins of the *chansons de geste* is fundamentally anti-German, however: in his monumental work of synthesis *Les Épopées françaises (The French Epics)*, for example, he maintains that the women found in the *chansons de geste* must have Germanic models, since they are utterly shameless. He recognizes that the French have Germanic blood in their veins, but "nous appartenons à la race des Germains qui ont fait halte; et nous ne sommes pas de ceux qui perpétuent les invasions" (we belong to the race of the Germans who stopped; and we are not related to those who perpetuate the invasions).[20]

Roland loved France, but, according to Gautier, without knowing too well her geographical limits.[21] This question of the limits of France is, in fact, perplexing for those who have held that the *Roland* is a national poem, since Charlemagne's poetic army includes among its contingents, in addition to peoples settled in areas that would later be within the borders of modern France, Bavarians, Alemanians, Flemish, and Frisians. Gautier admits that it is rather difficult to specify the exact moment at which these different nations belonged to a single empire and to a single Frankish kingdom.[22]

Like his predecessors, Gautier is jealous of the German achievements in scholarship. A propos of Michel's *editio princeps* he writes: "Grâces en soient rendues à Dieu, dont la Providence s'étend aux études littéraires: c'est un Français qui eut cette gloire et non pas un Allemand" (God be thanked, whose Providence reaches out to encompass literary studies: it is a Frenchman who had this distinction and not a German).[23] While admitting that Génin's edition harbored many a defect, Gautier finds that the editor's patriotism makes up for them. Grudgingly he praises the German Theodor Müller's second edition as the only critical text to have appeared up until then.[24]

Gautier campaigned to have the *Roland* included as a standard component in the French school curriculum; he succeeded, beginning with the school year 1880.

The textual tradition of the *Song of Roland* is extremely complex. Aside from the much-studied Oxford version, which is composed in assonance, six substantial manuscripts of longer redactions and three fragments have been preserved. Access to the non-Oxford tradition was acquired only slowly and partially, most scholars making do with the diplomatic transcription of the rhyming manuscripts published in the 1880's by Wendelin Foerster, although Foerster's texts lack notes and a glossary and are marred by numerous paleographic errors.

Between 1940 and 1944, during the German occupation of Paris, Raoul Mortier took steps to remedy this lack of a major research tool.[25] His edition comprises the texts of Oxford, the Venice IV redaction that is fairly close to Oxford for most of the text but then deviates in a long series of episodes that follow Roland's death, the five rhyming manuscripts, the two fragments in rhyme that were known at the time, and four of the ten non-French versions. The edition was to have included six other non-French versions and onomastic tables, but was never completed although Mortier published a work on the *Roland* in 1945 and lived until 1951. The ten volumes that did appear were issued clandestinely in defiance of the German occupation forces under the imprint of "La Geste Francor," a publishing house that apparently only existed for this one enterprise. With the Allied victory, the edition ground to a halt.

Mortier was a scholar who was primarily interested in popular education, serving for a time as director of the Office National des Recherches Scientifiques and supervising the publication of two reference dictionaries for the house of Quillet in Paris. Unfortunately his knowledge of Old French was inadequate to the *Song of Roland,* as the editors of an edition of all the French manuscripts that is now being prepared can attest.[26] For example, Mortier sometimes resolves abbreviations in a way that makes it plain he did not understand the two-case system that is the basis of the morphology of Old French nouns. Mortier repeated nearly all the errors found in Foerster's edition of the *Roland,* revealing that he depended on his predecessor rather than on photographic copies, which were no doubt difficult to obtain in wartime conditions. In addition, of course, Mortier introduced his own errors, so that, although the line correspondences he provides have served as a guide for those who have wished to compare the various *Roland* versions to each other, the texts themselves are not reliable.

To summarize, early French Romantic critics perceived a lack in the corpus of medieval texts, since, with the Homeric model in view, for them any literature that did not possess a great epic was defective. When the Oxford *Song of Roland* was published, it was used to fill the hitherto empty slot of the national epic in French literary history. The apogee of the *Roland*'s use as an offensive intellectual weapon in the conflicts between France and Germany came in 1872, shortly after the Franco-Prussian War. The three most important editions of the poem published by French scholars prior to 1950 were conceived during the three great wars involving France and Germany: Gautier's in the Franco-Prussian War, Bédier's in the First World War, and Mortier's in the Second World War.[27] The last of these was of such a scope that it should have become the standard reference edition. Actually it probably retarded *Roland* scholarship considerably, since it discouraged the preparation of a reliable comprehensive edition.

The period in which the Oxford *Roland* came more and more to be accepted as the great national poem, and in which it was finally enshrined as a standard class text, corresponded to the ascendance of French imperialism in North Africa, between the initial establishment in Algeria in 1830 on the one hand, and on the other the brutal crushing of the Algerian revolt in 1871 and French colonization on an ambitious scale beginning in the same decade. The

Oxford text has unquestionably the most imperialistic cast of any of the French *Rolands,* including as it does the Baligant Episode but not the extended treatment of Roland's fiancée Aude, and was perhaps itself shaped by the expansionist needs of the eleventh-century Norman duchy.[28]

In my opinion, the *Roland* is not really a national poem in the sense that it reflects a unity of France in the Middle Ages that corresponds in some way to modern French unity; but the political climate in which writers and scholars like Thomassy, Marmier, Génin, Gaston Paris, and Gautier were working colored their hermeneutic judgments, leading them to impose on the text a nationalistic interpretation that was embraced by the public. The word "France" has several meanings in the text, the primary of which is "Francia, the land of the Franks," corresponding roughly to the French-speaking area north of the Loire, the area in which, the poet specifies, the earth trembles in anticipation of Roland's death. As I have mentioned, however, Charlemagne's poetic army also includes contigents from the region of his historical empire in which Germanic languages were spoken. The two principal geographical areas that one sees associated with Charlemagne in the poem, then, respectively transcend and fragment the modern surface of France. Only the phrase *douce France* has led people to think otherwise, but that refers to the Frankish land, not to modern France. When the Frankish army crosses the Pyrenees toward Gascony, the poet calls what they see a view not of France but of *Tere Majur* (the Land of Ancestors).

Only in the post-1950 period, during which Charlemagne's empire was geographically reconstituted in the European Economic Community, have Franco-German conflicts ceased to play a role in *Roland* scholarship. Is the fact that German scholars, who historically have made major contributions to the study of the *Song of Roland,* have rarely been represented in the bibliography of studies devoted to the poem since 1950 a sign that German academics not only no longer lay claim to it, but have overreacted to the controversies of the past?

Notes

1. Francisque Michel, *La Chanson de Roland ou de Roncevaux du XIIe siècle publiée pour la première fois d'après le manuscrit de la Bibliothèque Bodléienne à Oxford* (Paris: Librairie Silvestre, 1837).

2. Raimond Thomassy, Review of Francisque Michel in *Revue Française et Etrangère* 1 (1837): 472.

3. Xavier Marmier, Review of Francisque Michel in *Le Monde* (February 17, 1837): 3.

4. Hans Ulrich Gumbrecht, " 'Un Souffle d'Allemagne ayant passé': Friedrich

Diez, Gaston Paris, and the Genesis of National Philologies,'' *Romance Philology* 40 (1986): 1–37.

5. François Génin, *La Chanson de Roland, poëme de Theroulde. Texte critique accompagné d'une traduction, d'une introduction et de notes* (Paris: Imprimerie nationale, 1850), v.

6. Frédéric Lacroix, Review of Génin in *L'Illustration, journal universel* (April 19, 1850): 250.

7. Ludovic Vitet, "La *Chanson de Roland*," *Revue des Deux Mondes* 14 (1852): 823.

8. Ibid., 855.

9. Ibid., 863–64.

10. Gaston Paris, "La *Chanson de Roland* et la nationalité française," *La Poésie du moyen âge: Leçons et lectures,* 2nd. ed. (Paris: Librairie Hachette, 1887), I, 106.

11. Ibid., 107.

12. Ibid., 116.

13. Ibid., 118.

14. Léon Gautier, *La Chanson de Roland, texte critique accompagné d'une traduction nouvelle et précédé d'une introduction historique* (Tours: Alfred Mame et fils, 1872); and Joseph Bédier, *La Chanson de Roland, publiée d'après le manuscrit d'Oxford et traduite* (Paris: Piazza, 1921).

15. Ibid., vi.

16. Ibid., lxxvi.

17. Ibid., cc.

18. Ibid., xxviii.

19. Ibid., xxix.

20. Ibid., xxxii.

21. Ibid., lxxi.

22. Ibid., lxiii.

23. Ibid., clxxiii.

24. Ibid., clxxxviii.

25. Raoul Mortier, *Les Textes de la Chanson de Roland,* 10 vols. (Paris: Editions de la Geste Francor, 1940–44).

26. Ian Short, Robert F. Cook, Annalee C. Rejhon, Wolfgang G. Van Emden, William W. Kibler, and Joseph J. Duggan.

27. John Benton, in " 'Nostre Français n'unt talent de fuïr': The *Song of Roland* and the Enculturation of a Warrior Class," *Olifant* 6 (1979): 237–58, notes that an audience at the École Spéciale Militaire at Saint-Cyr was told in 1900 that "la *Chanson de Roland* est notre *Iliade*" (the *Song of Roland* is our *Iliad* [237]).

28. David C. Douglas, "The *Song of Roland* and the Norman Conquest of England," *French Studies* 14 (1960): 99–116; and Joseph J. Duggan, "The Generation of the Episode of Baligant: Charlemagne's Dream and the Normans at Mantzikert," *Romance Philology* 30 (1976–77): 59–82.

Part III
Discovery of New Meaning

One hermeneutic principle posits that what is outside the text may actually be necessary to its total meaning. Redefinition of the whole, then, to which parts belong, can radically change context. The revised perspectives that result yield new understanding. All the essays in Part III deal with transtextuality and uniqueness through contextual definition. Their focus, however, is various.

The first group illustrates the relationship between a text and an extraneous, but related, body of knowledge. In an account of the etymological style, Paul Beekman Taylor examines the smallest part of a text, the etymon of an individual word, in regard to wholes of varying inclusiveness, such as character, plot, and the whole literary tradition. Marijane Osborn adds new meaning to Chaucer's *Squire's Tale*, *Knight's Tale*, and *General Prologue* by introducing the astrolabe to the interpretative context. Calvin M. Bower similarly demonstrates how medieval musical theorists employed grammatical terms and concepts in order to define their own discipline.

The essays of Charles M. Atkinson, Calvin B. Kendall, and Anita Riedinger show that what is different from the expected norm is often the feature that invites interpretation. By examining a crux in the *Musica enchiriadis*, Atkinson demonstrates how the redefinition of the individual words *modus* and *tonus*, under the influence of Boethius, affected the whole development of music in the Middle Ages. By comparing the same and the different in the verse inscriptions on fourteen tympana, Calvin B. Kendall proposes single authorship for those at Ste.-Foy of Conques and offers a more precise dating for its combination of poetry and architecture. Anita Riedinger examines the changing functions of the Anglo-Saxon poetic formula in the new context of Christianity.

The remaining three essays present new interpretations that grow out of a dialectic between old views and the new, in which the latter are seen to provide a more inclusive or coherent account of a text. By considering two Anglo-Saxon poems in their manuscript context, the original physical whole, Fred C. Robinson discovers that they are actually one poem. By challenging the interpretative assumptions of empiricism, Thomas Cable offers a new pattern to account for Medieval English prosody. Through a dissenting engagement with other interpreters, Donald K. Fry finds, in *The Parlement of the Thre Ages*, a new coherence between the factual errors of a chief character and the whole meaning of the poem.

9. Some Uses of Etymology in the Reading of Medieval Germanic Texts

PAUL BEEKMAN TAYLOR

"By ringing small changes on the words *leg-of-mutton* and *turnip* (changes so gradual as to escape detection), I could demonstrate that a turnip was, is, and of right ought to be, a leg of mutton" boasted Edgar Allan Poe, with some tongue in cheek (*Marginalia*, 1844–1849).[1] He exaggerates, but not much, the extravagancies of historical linguists who isolate words from their contexts, peeling away layers of sound and sense as if a word were an onion whose true culinary worth were its core. From its beginnings, the "science" of etymology has suffered the scorn of the wise. Plato has Socrates insist that the 'truth' of a word is in its *natural* tie to the thing it designates, and those sophists who would have *heroes* born of love—*eros*—are denaturing language (*Cratylus*, 398c-d). "If a person goes on analyzing names into words," continues Socrates, "and inquiring also into the elements out of which the words are formed, and keeps on always repeating this process, he who has to answer him must at last give up the inquiry in despair" (433e).[2] Poet-legislators, however, are exempt from such charges, for their rightness (*orthos*) of style "keeps in view the name which *by nature* belongs to each particular thing and is able to embody its forms in the letters and the syllables" (390d-e, italics mine). In *Theatetus*, 202, Socrates describes *logos* as an account of something in a combination of etyma which are in themselves renderings of knowledge. Names in the Old Testament comprise an allegoresis of God's design.[3] In the *Vita Nuova*, 13, Dante recalls the popular adage: *nomina sunt consequentia rerum*, and Marbod has *nomen commendat res nomine significata*.[4] In the first tale of the *Decameron*, Boccaccio demonstrates how names affect truth in the story of Ceparello "little stump" (an apt name for one whose manliness is deficient). His French associates misread the name for *capello* (chaplet, rosary) and then nickname him Ciapelletto because of his slight stature. As his name improves in sense, his fame increases as the local populace read his acts as emanations of his saintly name, with the result that a villain is beatified.

There is more "game" than "earnest" in such playing with words, and

Florence Ridley in an earlier essay in this volume draws attention to such Derridean free-play of signifiers in relation to medieval texts (at the same time, for instance, in his *Knight's Tale,* Chaucer draws on a sober patristic convention known to him through Bernardus Sylvestris which has *Theseus* glossed as *deus bonus*).[5] In the past few years Fred C. Robinson and Roberta Frank have shown the presence of this sort of etymological play in Old English poetry.[6] Robinson's study of the poetic exploitation of latent meanings in the names *Gūðlāc* and *Hygelāc* raises the question whether etymological play is a native Germanic category of thought as well.[7] It is my purpose here to pursue the question with a shallow, but wide scan of medieval Germanic poetry and prose.

In traditional, or native, Germanic literatures, there is a recognizable style which draws attention to verbal polysemy, a style that is etymological in the sense that it isolates word elements so that they manifest latent meaning. A meaning may be retrieved from an earlier, or original use, or may be discovered, or made, in context. Etymological style, in short, draws attention to significations beneath designations—*les mots sous les mots*—or to a word's signifying source as well as to its signified sense.[8] The signifying pointer of this style is the textual environment of the word, which may gloss a name or word, group together cognate forms, suggest similar meanings for words of similar sounds, pun, and so forth. What I shall concentrate on below is the range of style where attention to etymology both limits and expands meaning, shapes character description and plot contour, and, finally, performs textually and metatextually.[9]

Drawing attention to a word's etymological source by glossing is a common, though banal, technique.[10] Snorri Sturluson explains the name *Niflung* in his account of the attack on Jörmunrek by the brothers Hamðir and Sörli by noting, ''þeir váru allir svartir sem hrafn á hárslit sem Gunnar ok Högni ok aðrir Niflungar'' (they were all black as ravens in the color of their hair, just as Gunnar and Högni and the other Niflungs [*Skáldskaparmál,* 50]).[11] This is etymological camouflage, for a derivation of the name from the root *nifl* (mist, fog, OHG *nebul*) hides the earlier use of the name as an identification with the dark-elves from which, according to *Þiðreks saga* (169), Högni descends. Snorri is simply removing pejorative associations in order to enhance the stature of the brothers.[12]

More interesting is the translation of a name into a more recognizable and local form, what the historical linguist calls a ''calque.'' So Wulfstan draws attention to the implications of his name in his eschatological sermon *Sermo Lupi ad Anglos,* hinting at the apocalyptic wolves of John 10:12, and perhaps as well to the sun- and moon-swallowing wolves of Scandinavian eschatology. More frequent are the telling mistranslations of foreign names. Asser's *Life of Alfred* lists a certain *Frēalāf* among his ancestors. An Icelandic compiler of Haraldr the Fair-haired's genealogy borrows that name in the form *Frjálafr* understanding the Old English *frēa* as identical with Old Icelandic *frjá* (love), and being ignorant of the fact that the cognate Norse name *Frið-leifr* figures already in the king's genealogy.[13] The same ancestor, then, acquires two names. The *Beowulf* poet uses the English *Wæls* for Völsi, the ancestor of Sigemund. Klaeber's glossary assumes that the name must reflect Gothic *walis* (chosen), though the English form means "belonging to slaughter," while the Norse *völsi* is a cult name for a horse's penis.[14] Something similar is at work in the English rune-name *os* (mouth) which derives from a proto-Germanic form *ansuz* (god, OI *áss*). These examples are not indicative of etymological play so much as they are of phonologico-semantic shift. Such folk-etymologizing, however, can be put to poetic purpose. The Old Icelandic poet of the *Prymskviða* uses a familiar Old English word for strength, *prym*, as a name for Pórr's antagonist. The Old Norse cognate is *prúð-*, an element traditionally associated with the god and not with the giant, since Pórr's home is *Prúðheim* (house of strength), and one of his nicknames is *Prúðvaldr* (strength-wielder). The poet's etymological play creates a confrontation of foreign with familiar strength, and Pórr's victory is a form of linguistic patriotism.

Translating foreign names into the local idiom can also indetermine sense, or open name significance to a number of readings. The Old English poem *Deor* has the names *Nīþhād* and *Beaduhild* where the Old Norse *Völundarkviða* has *Níðuðr* and *Böðvildr*. It is assumed by critics that these names are equivalent, but their significations in their respective languages would certainly be distinct, if not ambiguous. *Böðv-* and *Beadu-* are indeed identical, but *-ildr* for *-hild,* though possible, would be obscured by the preceding *v* because *vildr* is a perfectly good word meaning "choice, volition." *-Hād* and *-uðr* are more complicated in their relationship. There is no Old Norse equivalent cognate for Old English *-hād*. Old Norse *heið-* signals "brightness, sunshine," and Old Norse *-uðr* can reflect either *-urð/-varðr* (guardian), *-friðr* (love), or *-fríðr* (handsome); compare ON *Sigurðr* and OHG *Seifríd*, ModG *Sigfried*, for example. As a simplex, *uðr* has still another meaning; it means "wave."

Polysemy is likewise operative in the myths of Óðinn, for his name reflects the adjective *óðr* (mad, frantic) as well as the noun *óðr* (mind, wit, poetry). The etymologists can prove that the adjectival form is the root of his name, but Óðinn's role as thief of the mead of poetry *óðrerir* as well as his acquisition of runic knowledge and his status as prophet insist on the relevance of the noun root as well. The suffix *-aðr* in the name of the Danish hero *Starkaðr* can reflect either *óðr* (frantic), *höðr* (destruction), or *varðr* (guardian), but most likely suggests all three. The name of the Old Norse god of war, Týr, also carries a multiple sense according to context. The form reflects divinity (OE *tīu*, OHG *ziu*) in Óðinn's epithet *Valtýr* (god of the slain), though *-týr* is also a derivative of the verb *þjá* (to serve), making Óðinn a "servant" of the dead. An alternative form with the same sense is *-þér*, as in *Eggþér* (servant of the sword) (cf. Beowulf's father *Ecgþeow*). So *Angantýr*

(OE *Ongenþēow*) suggests both "lord of soft breezes" and "servant of soft breezes" (though ON *angan-* can also be understood as "joy, beloved"). By the same token, Wealhþēow's name echoes Óðinn's agnomen *Valtýr*.[15]

These examples are sufficient to illustrate the etymological style that expands name-force by multiplying name-significance. The same effect can be accomplished by alternating the forms of a name, using one form in one context and another in a different context. In the Old High German *Hildebrandslied* both the hero and his son carry two names, *Hildtibrant/Hiltibraht* and *Hadubrant/Hadubraht*. The suffix *-brant* means "sword" and the suffix *-braht* means "din, noise," and the attribution of both names tends to characterize their speech as well as their arms.

A word's or name's particular context can also release a latent sense of a word. When the *Beowulf* poet uses—or invents—the terms *untýdras* to describe the progeny of Cain (*Beowulf* 111), he is playing not only with meanings of associated forms such as *týdran* (to propagate, bring forth) and *tūdor* (progeny), but also with a deprivative prefix which signals "lack" or "absense." So, *untýdras* not only designates a progeny, but signifies its misbegotten aspect. In the context of the song of creation with which Heorot is celebrated, its enemy, Grendel, is qualified as being miscreated, an unnatural enemy of a hall rendered natural by its own name "Hart." A clearer example of a context releasing an etymological signification can be seen in Beowulf's dying consolation that, although sonless, he has begotten (*gestrȳnan*) a treasure for his people. *Gestrȳnan* refers to the act of winning a treasure, but its signification "to engender" (cf. ModE "strain") binds together the idea of treasure and of genealogy. Beowulf's treasure is, in effect, a legacy for his people, a begotten good, identifiable with a son; for treasure is a sexual fetish.[16]

I find the most effective manner of drawing attention to the etymological significance of a name is *refracting,* breaking the name into its elements to point to its appropriate or inappropriate meaning.[17] When Æthelred was in his own day known popularly as *Unrǣd* (unready), this was a case of refraction to draw attention to an inappropriate name element. A fine example of etymological refraction occurs in *Beowulf* when the poet introduces Wiglaf, as the young hero enters battle alongside his lord for the first time. The poet remarks that *nē his mǣges* [MS. *mǣgenes*] *lāf/gewāc æt wīge* (*Beowulf* 2628b-29a), translated usually something like "nor did his kinsman's heirloom (his father's sword) fail in battle." The separation and reversal of the elements of the name *Wīglāf* in this line, however, release a number of other meanings. First of all, *mǣges lāf* is not only an heirloom, but his father's *living* legacy, begotten product, heir and survivor. Neither Wiglaf nor the sword fail in battle. *Lāf* recalls here its cognate *līfian* (to live) and regularly signifies something which is given life—both son and sword. If the manuscript *mǣgenes* (of strength) is retained in line 2628b, as I believe it should be (and not emended to *mǣges*) then Wiglaf and sword alike are both products and inheritors of strength. The refraction of his name in the line also suggests that *Wīglāf* is a name made and fulfilled in battle. Wiglaf may indeed be recognized as survivor of battle, but he is also a product of battle. The echo of the first element of his Father's name, *wīh-* (homophonous with *wīg-*), may even carry a hint of the sense of *wēoh-* (sacred, ritual) in its other manuscript form, adding a sense of ritual to battle, appropriate to a young warrior's initiation into war. It is unnecessary to insist that any one sense discernible in the name is submerged by another. One might argue for better senses, but all of these are collectively as well as individually good.

In *Beowulf*, Hunferð's name likewise undergoes refraction. Editors and critics, alas, compete with the poetic text by removing the *H* from the first name element and read the second as *frið* (peace) instead of *ferhþ* (spirit, temper), as if the poet had missed an allegorical possibility. The text needs no doctoring in the passage which describes Hunferð at the feast which celebrates the outcome of the fight with Grendel:

> Swylce þær Hunferþ þyle
> æt fotum sæt frean Scyldinga;   gehwylc hiora his
> ferhþe treowde,
> þæt he hæfde mod micel,   þeah þe his magum nære
> arfæst æt ecga gelacum.
>
> (1165b–1168)[18]

> So there sat the counsellor Hunferð at the feet of the lord of the Shield-ings. Each trusted in his spirit (?), that he had great temper, though he had not been honor-fast in swordplay with kinsmen.

The trust in Hunferð's *ferhþ* is a trust in the quality signalled by name, though the trust in person is at once put in doubt by the recollection of a fault in deed.

The larger narrative context of this passage also heightens the contrastive coloring which characterizes *ferhþ* as a name-element. Hroðgar has just presented Beowulf with gifts, some associated with his own heroic "swordplay" in the past, although the kind of swordplay is unspecified. Immediately following the gift-giving, the court poet sings of Finnsburh and the tragic fight between and the treachery of kinsmen before the final rescue of the queen and the winning of treasure. Then, after the presence of Hunferð is noted at Hroðgar's feet, Wealhþeow is described approaching Hroðgar and Hroðulf— another set of kinsmen soon to fall into dispute—after which she asks the newly adopted Beowulf to guard her own sons' interests, before presenting him with gifts. Among these is a neckpiece comparable to the legendary *Brōsinga mene,* which in Nordic tradition is the fecundity ornament (*Brīsinga men*) forged for the fertility goddess Freyja. What this elaboration of details intends to show is the appropriateness of Hunferð's *ferhþ* to a packed collocation of images of generation, kinship, and treasure. Etymologically, of course, *ferhþ* reflects *feorh* (life) as well as being a metathetical echo of *friþ* (love, peace). These senses of *ferhþ*, however, rub wrong with Hunferð's lack of *ār* (honor, kindness), whose etymological history includes "goods" and "harvest," and whose meaning "glory, honor" derives from these concrete elements. Hunferð's lack of *ār* links him, then, with destroyers of life and with breakers of bonds of kinship. While Hroðgar's swordplay gains treasure, Hunferð's vitiates it (*lāc* as a simplex means only "treasure" in the poem). Perhaps a more significant example of refraction is Beowulf's play on Hunferð's father's name when he presents him with his sword: *"ond þu, Hunferþ, læt ealde lafe . . . heard ecg habban"* ("and you, Hunferth, I let have the old heirloom, the hard edge"; 1488–90). The name of Hunferð's father is *Ecglāf*, and the sword which Hunferð gives Beowulf in return is called *Hrunting*, whose Old Norse etymon *hrotti* means, appropriately, "rough, coarse fellow." Beowulf's gift of a *lāf*, with its own discrete etymological associations with life, is in effect a restitution of a signification for *ferhþ*. It is a giving Hunferð back his name value. This complex relationship between Beowulf's action and the name of his one-time antagonist may shed some light on the name-element *Hun-*.[19] First, the element is attested to elsewhere. Hunferð and Hunfrið are both names associated with an eighth-century bishop of Winchester, and Hunwald is a Anglo-Saxon place name. Klaeber points to a hypothetical sense "noble, high" to explain the name *Hunlāfing*, but denies that aristocratic sense for Hunferð. *Hūn* designates a bear-cub. *Hun* as a reference to Huns or Finns is possible, but the sense "bear-cub" is in keeping with both the apparent sense of Beowulf's name— "wolf of bees," that is, "bear"—as well as with the similarity of their respective fathers' names, and with the word play used by the poet to link the two characters together.

The poet is more direct in treating Heremod's name, for it is undone in the same line in which it appears, as a contrast with Sigemund: *Heremōdes hild sweðrode* (The Battle-Minded One's battle-powers ceased [901]). In contrast, in the Old English poem *Deor*, the speaker seems to identify the sense of his own name by its alliterative link: *"dryhtne dȳre mē wæs Deor nama"* ("dear to my lord, my name was Deor" [37]).[20] A similar fracturing takes place in *Njáls saga* (145), when Snorri Priest responds to Flosi's demand to know who is blocking his path with the cryptic, *"mun ek segja þér ófregit, at þeir valda því Þorvaldr kroppinskeggi ok Kolr"* ("I can tell you unasked that they, Thorvald and Kol, are in control" *[valda]*).[21] This is a grim pun, but it illustrates one important aspect of etymological style: he who can play with another's name has some particular and effective power over that person. Beowulf's playing with the name of his opponent is an earlier example. Further, he who can play with his own name has yet greater powers, for it appears that he can fulfill the latent force in the name-elements. I would reluctantly argue that I have found a revealing play on Beowulf's name, but when Beowulf is very near death, he gives Wiglaf orders to build a monument, and he offers a name for it: *"þæt hit sǣ-līðend syððan hātan Biowulfes biorh.* . . ." ("That sea-voyagers afterward will call it Beowulf's barrow" [2806–7]). Having just been the instrument for the "wolfing" of the dragon's barrow, it could appear that Beowulf is giving himself a new and final name—*Beorhwulf.*

The best example of a hero naming himself by isolating name-element values is afforded by *Njáls saga* when the Icelandic hero Skarpheðin Njálsson refracts his own name in a series of heroic boasts. As Njál and his sons go about the Icelandic parliament seeking support for their defense in a legal proceeding, each chieftain they approach is struck by Skarpheðin's appearance and each questions his identity (*Nj* 119–120). When Snorri Priest asks, "Who is that man, fifth in line, the pale sharp-featured man with a grin on his face and an axe on his shoulder?" Skarpheðin answers with a play on "sharp-featured" (*skarpleitr*): "*Heðinn heiti ek . . . en sumir man kalla mik Skarpheðin öllu nafni*" ("I am called Heðin, but some men call me Skarp-Heðin in full" [119]). This isolation of the element "sharp" asserts that the name is earned as well as given (his father Njál had given him the name, but Njál had also given Gunnarr of Hliðarend the name *Kaupaheðin* [Hawker-Heðin]; and giving one name to different persons is often a tragic misuse of name power). The isolation of the first element in the name calls into question the second. The etymology of *heðin* is not certain. As a simplex, *heðin* is an animal pelt or fur jacket, and thus, like the English *hood,* a possible figure for "cover, protection." *Heiðr* signals "value, worth" and *heið* is "bright sky, brightness." The common name-element *höðr* (OE *heaðu*) means "destroyer." Heðin is the name of a divine king in Snorri Sturluson's exposition of Nordic kennings (*Skáldskaparmál* 61), as well as the name of several heroes of the legendary sagas. *Skarpheðin* is the name of this hero's maternal grandfather, but the name seems to be unknown outside of these two instances in the sagas, except for a single appearance in the *Landnámabók.* All of these name values fit this particular hero, and yet the only meaning given the element in the saga is none of these, but one Skarpheðin makes up himself in reply to another chieftain, Þorkell Braggart, who makes scornful reference to his features: "*Ek heiti Skarpheðin, ok er þér skuldlaust at velja mér hæðiyrði, saklausn manni*" ("I am called Skarpheðin, and you have no reason to pick me out, an innocent man, for taunts"). His name plays on ON *hæði* (taunt, insult); and *velja* (to pick out or to choose) is a term appropriate for choosing a name.[22] He then exercises this name-force for "sharp taunts" by accusing Þorkell of having feasted recently on mares' arses. No one would hold that *hæði* (cf. OE *hēan*) is a true etymon for *heðin,* but Skarpheðin is a poet himself and capable of making name values to fit the occasion.

Besides refracting names to reveal latent forces within them, etymological style draws attention to an uncontrollable force within a name, what Heidegger might call the ontological Being of a name, that shapes character and literary structure. In *Njáls saga* (116), Flosi Þorðarson, modest and resourceful by nature, is incited by his niece Hildigunn to blood revenge against the Njálssons for the killing of her husband. Hildigunn charges him with feud obligation, or, as she threatens, he will *"heit hvers manns níðingr ella"* ("be called base by all men" [*NJ* 116]). With this, Flosi's face changes color from red as blood to pale as withered grass, then to black as death. The threat of *níðingr*, with its implications of degeneracy or perversity, would certainly upset Flosi, but the nature of its effects upon him seem to be nothing less than a realization of the apparently trivial potential of his name; for *flosi* (a form of ON *flása* [to rush precipitously]) means "irresponsible, deceitful, fickle." The effects of Hildigunn's calling his name into Being are lasting, for Flosi pursues vengeance in a series of rash acts that culminate in the burning of Njál and his household, an act that qualifies him unequivocally as *níðingr*. Although Flosi eventually regains his former nature, as long as he is under Hildigunn's charge his character is directed by the force of his given and threatened name.[23]

A contrasting example of etymological pointing from the same saga is Kári Sölmundarson, who survives the burning by leaping through the flames. Earlier in the saga he had rescued two of the Njálssons, first from pirates at sea (84), and later from the king of Norway (89). When he pursues the Burners, he catches up to a group of them in the Orkneys, despite a late start, because favorable winds drive him to the spot where Flosi and others had been shipwrecked (154). Satisfied at the end of his quest for vengeance, he sails back to Iceland where he is cast ashore in a snowstorm just beneath Flosi's farm, where he makes his way for the saga-concluding reconciliation. Kári's felicity among the elements of weather reside in his name, for *kári* signifies the sea-wind which curls waves (ON *kárr*, OE *cerr* [turn]). The force in the name would be all the more obvious to the saga audience, because Kári as a name is a metatextual link to a body of Nordic myth. Kári is the name of a mythological ancestor of the kings of Norway whose brothers are Sea and Fire, his son Ice, and his grandson Snow.[24] Neither Kári nor Flosi are names invented to provide an allegorical structure to the saga, for the names are attested in the chronicles of the settlement of Iceland. It is the style of the saga compiler that has seized upon the potential in the names to shape his story.

The hypothesis that etymology is a Germanic habit of thought is neither radically new nor critically surprising, but the prominent features of the style which exploits that habit invite investigation. It appears to me from my own study that more attention must be paid to the metatextual nature of early Germanic literatures on the one hand, and to the manner in which etymological style appeals to a calculable reader-response on the part of the poets and saga compilers. Such studies of style belong to the critic rather than to the formal etymologist, for writers, or singers, can make new words as well as make old words anew. In the world of early Germanic art, words are part of nature, and the style that lets loose their potential is the artist's midwife, collaborating with the vitality of the language, restraining its monsters, and loosing its treasure.

Notes

1. *Marginalia* 1844–1849, ed. John Carl Miller (Charlottesville: University of Virginia Press, 1981), 41.

2. The translation is from *The Collected Dialogues of Plato,* ed. Edith Hamilton and Huntington Cairns (New York: Pantheon Books, 1961). The Latin Middle Ages were full of what Curtius has called "insipid trifling" (Ernst Robert Curtius, *European Literature and the Latin Middle Ages,* trans. Williard R. Trask [New York: Pantheon Books, 1953], 496). Current opposition to "scientific" etymology as a critical tool is heavy. Jost Trier, *Der Deutsche Wortschatz im Sinnbezirk des Verstandes* (Heidelberg: Carl Winter, 1973), 6, notes: "die Geltung eines Wortes wird erst erkannt, wenn mann sie gegen die Geltung der benachbarten und opponierenden Worte abgrenzt. Nur als teil des Ganzen hat es Sinn; denn nur im feld es bedeuten." Hans-Georg Gadamer, *Truth and Method (Wahrheit und Methode)* (New York: Seabury Press, 1977), 92, prefers the word "play" for the style that retrieves original meanings, since etymology is "not performed by language but by linguistic science, which can never be wholly verified by language itself; that is, by their actual usage." By their common ancestor in the Indo-European root *ghrei* "to rub, smear" the monster Grendel (if his name derives from *grindan* "to grind") would be cousin to Christ "the anointed"!

3. See Northrop Frye, *The Great Code: The Bible and Literature* (New York: Harcourt Brace & Jovanovich, 1983). In Scripture, Frye notes, "puns and popular etymologies . . . affect the character of whatever thing or person is given the name" (6).

4. Cited by Curtius, 498.

5. *Commentum Super Sex Libros Eneidos Virgilii,* vii, 8: *Theos enim deus, eu bonus,* ed. J. W. Jones and E. F. Jones (Lincoln and London: University of Nebraska Press, 1977), 56.

6. Fred C. Robinson, "Names in Old English Literature," *Anglia,* 86 (1968): 14–58; Roberta Frank, "Some Uses of Paronomasia in Old English Scriptural Verse," *Speculum,* 47 (1972): 207–26. Most recently, Fred C. Robinson (*Beowulf and the Appositive Style* [Knoxville: University of Tennessee Press, 1985], 67–8) has noted that in Old English "the poet systematically exploits the semantic layering of vocabulary, rejuvenating meanings. For a recent appreciation of the Medieval French etymological style, see R. Howard Bloch, *Etymologies and Genealogies: A Literary Anthropology of the French Middle Ages* (Chicago: University of Chicago Press, 1983).

7. Of course, Heidegger and, following him, Derrida, have concentrated on the interpretative aspects of etymology, but it is difficult to assess the importance of their work to literary criticism. In his *Unterwegs zur Sprache* (1959), translated by Peter D. Hertz as *On the Way to Language* (New York: Harper and Row, 1971), in talking of the playful thinking of etymology that is more "compelling" than the rigor of science, Heidegger is concerned with etymologizing as the act of bringing a word into Being, of realizing a word's ontological force, of putting into language an experience with

118 	Discovery of New Meaning

language. Heidegger's own critical reading of the poetry of Trakl, however, shows little use of etymology as a tool for critical reading, but rather as a tool for philosophic inquiry. Derrida is more concerned with word play as expressing philosophical and psychological associations.

8. The use of the term "signification" for a root sense and "designation" for a secondary sense follows current French practice. Michel Foucault, for one, in *Les mots et les choses*, translated as *The Order of Things* (New York: Pantheon Books, 1970), 104ff. discusses the semantic tension between the two, and adds that "to bring the origin of language back into the light of day means to rediscover the primitive moment in which it was pure designation." Plato contrasts primary (*proto*) meanings with those 'less true' (*kallio*). Augustine contrasts 'proper' with 'figurative' senses throughout his writings.

9. The term "metatextual" is from Gérard Genette, *Palimpsestes* (Paris: Seuil, 1982; see note 18 of the Introduction to this volume). Metatextuality is a form of "transtextuality" in which one text is related to another by allusion and not by direct citation.

10. For a recent study of poetic glosses, see Alfred Bammesberger, *Linguistic Notes on Old English Poetic Texts* (Heidelberg: Carl Winter, 1986), who notes that poetic glossing often disrupts, or disorganizes, the poetic form and, in some cases, should be emended.

11. *Edda Snorra Sturlusonar*, ed. Finnur Jónsson (Reykjavík: Sigurður Kristjánsson, 1907).

12. Roberta Frank ("Snorri and the Mead of Poetry," *Speculum Norrænum: Norse Studies in Memory of Gabriel Turville-Petre*, ed. Ursula Dronke et al. [Odense: Odense University Press, 1981]: 155–170) demonstrates that Snorri is inclined to invent a myth to explain a metaphor or a name.

13. See *Annals of the Reign of Alfred*, ed. J. A. Giles (London: George Bell, 1896), 43. The Icelandic genealogies are found in "Hversu Noregr bygððist," *Fornaldar sögur Norðurlanda*, ed. Guðni Jónsson, vol. II (Reykjavík: Íslendingasagaútgáfn, 1950).

14. Fr. Klaeber, ed., *Beowulf*, 3rd ed. (Boston: D. C. Heath, 1950), 420. The *Völsaþáttr*, which forms part of the *Bárðar saga*, tells us the story of the worship of Völsi. *An Icelandic-English Dictionary*, ed. Richard Cleasby, enlarged and completed by Gudbrand Vigfusson (Oxford: Clarendon Press, 1957) notes that the form *völsi* corresponds etymologically to *phallus*.

15. Such poetic ambiguities hinder scientific precision. Jan de Vries, *Altnordisches Etymologisches Wörterbuch* (Leiden: Brill, 1963), uneasily covers both positions in his entry for *Angantýr*: "*Aus *Anganþér (unter einfluss des götternames Týr?)*." For a thorough discussion of the etymological possibilities for *Wealhþēow* see Helen Damico, *Beowulf's Wealhtheow and the Valkyrie Tradition* (Madison: University of Wisconsin Press, 1984), 58ff. John of Salisbury (*Policraticus* II, 16) asserts that words have as many meanings as similitudes to other words, an idea he may well have borrowed from Augustine (*Confessions* XIII, 36) who said that one corporeal

expression may be understood in many ways. See also Augustine's *De Doctrina* II, 10–11 where, in reading and translating Scripture, he notes that different understandings and expressions complement one another.

16. For a fuller discussion of the language of treasure as reflecting the language of sexual generation, see Paul Beekman Taylor, "The Traditional Language of Treasure in *Beowulf*," *Journal of English and Germanic Philology*, 85 (1986): 191–205.

17. The model for refractive etymologizing is Chaucer's Prologue to *The Second Nun's Tale* (*The Canterbury Tales*, VIII, 95–98), where the Second Nun breaks up the name *Cecilia* into semantic components to discuss etymological possibilities. Chaucer's term for the process is "conjoynynge." Current French criticism uses the term *conjointure* for the medieval style which expands a conventional literary figure or generic form by doing something new with it.

18. Quotations from *Beowulf* and other Old English poems are from the *Anglo-Saxon Poetic Records*, 6 vols, ed. George Philip Krapp and Elliott Van Kirk Dobbie (New York: Columbia University Press, 1931–53).

19. Stanley B. Greenfield (*The Interpretation of Old English Poems* [London and Boston: Routledge & Kegan Paul, 1972], 103–107) reviews the etymological possibilities in the name and considers *giant* as appropriate for *Hun-* in this context.

20. A play on the scop's name was noted by Norman Eliason in "Two Old English Scop Poems," *Publications of the Modern Language Association*, 81 (1966): 191 n. There is considerable tantalizing evidence to point to etymological play on Heremod's name throughout the Old Norse corpus, and though I feel it pertinent to scan the evidence briefly, I would be amiss to argue a conclusion from it. The name *Heremod* is unusual. A certain *Hermóðr* is mentioned in the Norse poem *Hyndluljóð*, along with a certain Sigmund (as in *Beowulf*), as a recipient of Óðinn's war gifts, but nothing further is said of them. Snorri mentions the Heremóð who is a son of Óðinn sent to the Underworld to retrieve Baldr (*Gylfaginning*, 49). On his way he confronts a maiden whose name, *Móðguðr*, mirrors his own name's meaning. He enters Hel through a gate *Helgrind*, whose name would be otherwise unremarkable if its name-elements were not, in reverse order, an echo of *Grendel* (himself one whose knows the secrets of Hell, being a *helrune*, *Beowulf* 163). This Heremóðr is probably the same person mentioned in the fragments of *Skjöldunga saga* published in *Íslenzk Fornrit*, 35 (Reykjavík: Fornritafélag, 1982), 55, in a reading of a dream that sees gods as reflections of heroes: "*Hverr var Helgi inn hvass með Ásum. . . ? Hann var Hermóðr, er bazt var hugaðr, ok þér óðarfr* (Who was Helgi the keen among the gods? He was Heremod, who was best of courage, but unuseful to you)." There is some similarity between the story of Lotherus in Saxo Grammaticus' *Gesta Danorum*, I, and *Beowulf*'s Heremod, in that Lotherus is forced into exile by his people, and he is the father of Skiold. Neither Anglo-Saxon nor Norse genealogies allude to the story of Lotherus, but most of them include Heremod as father of Scyld. The *Anglo-Saxon Chronicle* lists *Itermon* as Heremod's father, Sceldwea his son. Snorri has the sequence Ítrmann, Hermóðr, Skjaldun (ON *ítr* [noble]). This is only slight circumstantial evidence to link Saxo's Lotherus with the Heremod of *Beowulf*, but there is some etymological weight as well. *Lotherus* is a latinization of Old Norse *Hlöðr* (OHG *Hluduco*), the name of a hero of *Hreiðreks saga ok Hervarar*, half-brother of Angan-

tyr. He too is outcast from his people, but attacks his half-brother to regain his former role. *Hlöðr* signifies "destroyer, slayer" (ON *hloð* [booty, troop of warriors]; ON *hlaða* [to kill]; and OE *hladan* [to load]). Old Norse *hlóð* is a mass, or load. *Hlóðyn* (*Hludana*) is an earth-goddess. The similarity of meaning between *her-* and *hlöð* suggests the possibility that the one name is a substitution for the other, or that *hlöð* is a prefix with pejorative connotations, reflecting the falling off of the martial dignity of him who carried the element *her-* previously. This is, alas, desperate conjecture.

21. The text is from the *Fornrit* edition of Einar Ól Sveinsson (Reykjavík: Íslenzka Fornritafélag, 1954). The translations from *Njáls saga* follow Magnus Magnusson and Hermann Pálsson (Harmondsworth: Penguin, 1960).

22. William Ian Miller ("Justifying Skarpheðinn: Of Pretext and Politics in the Icelandic Bloodfeud," *Scandinavian Studies* 55 [1983]: 319), discusses this boast as a rhetorical pose for political advantage in answering charges of murder.

23. *Flosi* appears elsewhere as a name in *Landnámabók*, 7.

24. Kári Sölmundarson is mentioned in both *Landnámabók*, 43, and *Grettis saga*, 10, as *Sviðu-Kári* (Scorched-Kári). In *Hellismanna saga*, 9, Kári Kýlansson has his household burned in similar fashion just after his own death.

10. The Squire's "Steed of Brass" as Astrolabe: Some Implications for The Canterbury Tales

MARIJANE OSBORN

In this essay I suggest that Chaucer conceived of time in *The Canterbury Tales* as a graphic image derived from the astrolabe, an instrument used for celestial observation in navigation and timekeeping (and having only incidentally anything to do with astrology). After showing how Chaucer introduces the astrolabe obliquely into one of his stories, I shall offer two examples of how its diagrams and operations can clarify our understanding of both time and place in the tales.

One of the less familiar *Canterbury Tales* is the baroque and curtailed romance told by the young squire. He begins his tale with a knight coming to the king of Tartary bearing four magical gifts: a ring, a sword, a mirror, and—as a special gift to King Cambyuskan from the knight's liege lord, "the king of Arabe and Inde"[1]—a steed of brass. The nature of this steed is an anomalous element in the received story, for in Chaucer's source (which we do not know for certain) the horse was probably made of wood, perhaps of ebony as it is in the *Arabian Nights* version of the tale. Since Chaucer seldom alters his sources arbitrarily, and sometimes even seems to intend, when producing such anomalies, to call attention to the meaning growing from the dialectic between the old version and the new, one wonders when reading this story why the steed is "of brass."

At first it seems like nothing more than a life-sized mechanical toy, the sort of robot-horse that might actually have been introduced at a king's feast in the fourteenth century.[2] But its powers, as the knight explains them to the king, are more than those of a toy. This horse

Kan in the space of o day natureel—
This is to seyn, in foure and twenty houres—
Wher-so yow lyst, in droghte or elles shoures,
Beren youre body into every place
To which youre herte wilneth for to pace,
Withouten wem of yow, thurgh foul or fair.
(F 116–21)

Later that day, after the banquet, the knight explains to the king how to control the horse:

> . . . whan yow list to ryden anywhere,
> Ye mooten trille a pyn, stant in his ere.
> (F 315–16)

The details of the "space of o day natureel" and the pin that must be turned point very clearly to the nature of this steed of brass from Arabia.

The steed of brass in *The Squire's Tale* is no common automaton, but that scientific instrument imported to England and the Continent from Arabia, the brass astrolabe. J. B. Priestly describes the astrolabe as "the most remarkable instrument that the Middle Ages can boast":

> Its origins go back to ancient Greece; a few astrolabes are still made, for educational purposes; so it may reasonably be regarded as the oldest scientific instrument we know. But it owes most to the astronomical researches and the fine craftsmanship of the Middle East about A.D. 1000. Later it came into regular use in Western Europe. . . . As it gave both latitude and time of day, it was used by navigators until about the middle of the 18th century and the arrival of the quadrant.[3]

Chaucer put considerable time and effort into explaining the construction and use of this instrument "in naked English" to "Little Lewis, my son."[4] He wrote the *Treatise on the Astrolabe* sometime around the years 1391–92 while *The Canterbury Tales* were in progress, and around the time when he was composing *The Squire's Tale,* if J. D. North's astronomical dating of that tale is correct.[5] *The Treatise* has been described as "the oldest work written in English upon an elaborate scientific instrument."[6] In it Chaucer first describes the instrument in detail and then instructs Lewis in such simple operations as determining latitude, taking the angle of the sun and stars, and calculating the time of day.[7] In Part One Chaucer explains to little Lewis how the separate plates of his brass instrument are held together (my italics):

> 14. Than is there a large pyn in manere of an extre [axle], that goth thorugh the hole that halt the tables of the clymates and the riet in the wombe of the moder [onto the main plate]; thorugh which pyn ther goth a litel wegge, *which that is clepid the hors,* that streynith all these parties to-hepe. Thys forseide grete pyn in manere of an extre is ymagyned to be the Pool Artik in thyn Astralabie.

> 15. The wombe syde of thyn Astralabie is also divided with a longe cros in 4 quarters from est to west, fro southe to northe, fro right syde to left syde, as is the bakside.

> 16. The bordure of which wombe side . . . shewith the 24 houres equals of the clokke.

By twirling not this astrolabic "horse" itself but the index and the rete, or cut-out star map, that lies under it, one may indeed journey in imagination wherever in the cosmos one wishes, and all within the "space" of the twenty-four hours marking the outer periphery of the largest plate. The "little wedge" or knob in Chaucer's treatise is called a *hors* after its Arabic designation, *alpheraz,* which means "horse," and the name is no doubt why it was occasionally given this shape, especially on Arabic astrolabes,[8] just as Sirius the dog star, *alhabor* in Arabic, may be marked with the silhouette of a dog's head, as it is on contemporary illustrations of Chaucer's treatise.[9] By metonymic extension the *hors* at the center becomes the astrolabe itself.

In the narrative context of *The Squire's Tale,* the steed of brass is simply an exotic magical gift, appropriately from Arabia, where use of both the finest horses and the astrolabe were the prerogatives of rank.[10] But, by placing Chaucer's horse of the imagination within the context of his *Treatise on the Astrolabe,* its capabilities are increased so that it may range anywhere in the cosmos that the mind itself can roam, thereby making it akin to such symbolic beasts as the Dantean eagle of Chaucer's *House of Fame* and, as some people in the story recognize, Pegasus (lines 207–208). Such associations make us wonder whether this astrolabic story-horse, which can bear its rider "withouten wem . . . thurgh foul or fair" (121), perhaps may even carry a rider through *The Canterbury Tales* both foul and fair, without danger of spiritual harm. The fact that there are twenty-four stories[11] is suggestive in light of the day circle of twenty-four hours that circumscribes the astrolabe.

It seems likely that Chaucer did not mean to conceal the astrolabe so effectively as he did, that under the figure of the steed of brass he meant only to call attention to the presence of astrolabic and related allusions in *The Canterbury Tales.* While it is not within the scope of this paper to discuss in detail the most important of these, an horological maneuver that changes our perspective on the journey to Canterbury and perhaps defines the order of the *Tales,* I can offer here two examples of contrasting ways Chaucer uses his astrolabe for vivid graphic reference. The first passage, which concerns time measured in months, comes at the very beginning of the poem, and the second, which refers to time measured in hours, comes in the first story, *The Knight's Tale.* Both kinds of time are schematized on the astrolabe.

In lines 7–8 of the *General Prologue,* Chaucer offers in somewhat oblique terms the approximate date of the frame tale, the time of the pilgrimage that provides a background and reason for the other tales. Here are the opening lines of *The Canterbury Tales,* which all Chaucerians know by heart:

Whan that Aprill with his shoures soote
The droghte of March hath perced to the roote,
And bathed every veyne in swich licour
Of which vertu engendred is the flour;

Whan Zephirus eek with his sweete breeth
Inspired hath in every holt and heeth
The tendre croppes, and the yonge sonne
Hath in the Ram his half cours yronne . . .

When Lydgate continues *The Canterbury Tales* in his poem *The Siege of Thebes,* he phrases this same reference to zodiacal time in a far more accessible manner, saying simply that Phoebus the sun has passed from the Ram into the Bull:

Whan brighte Phebus passed was the ram
Mid of Aprille and into bole cam . . .
(Prologue, lines 1–2)[12]

Clearly the pilgrims have set out, as we know from the more precise date given in the Introduction to *The Man of Law's Tale* (lines 5–6), shortly after mid-April.

It is the "half cours" in Chaucer's *General Prologue* that gives trouble to modern readers. Even so recently as 1982, in a review of Sigmund Eisner's edition of *The Kalendarium of Nicholas of Lynn,* the reference to Aries the Ram in this passage was grossly but typically misunderstood:

We can readily check in the calendarium under review that the sun gets half way through Aries on March 27, hardly consonant with "April and his shoures soote" of the opening line.[13]

As A. E. Brea pointed out in 1851, the sun has not run "half his course" in the Ram as the reviewer above and most of us assume, but "his half-course," just as it says, in the Ram in April. To put it differently, Chaucer has already told us that it is April, so the sun has just run through the *second* half of his course in the Ram.[14]

Words only make this matter more confusing. The description of the date in terms of the April Ram becomes much easier to understand if we look at the scheme of springtime months and the corresponding signs[15] as they are displayed on the back of the "mother" (the large main plate) of the astrolabe. The relevant section of zodiac and months is laid out as follows:

	March /	April /	May
☼ Sun →	/	Aries /	Taurus /
		(Ram)	(Bull)

This zodiacal splitting of the month suggests that Chaucer was visualizing the date, that he either glanced at his astrolabe or had it well in mind, whereas Lydgate refers to the same date in the more classical and literary terms that

Chaucer himself uses elsewhere. It seems unlikely that Chaucer intended to be obscure about the Ram in April; once the sun's course there is seen graphically displayed, the difficulty evaporates.[16]

But he may have intended mystery in our second passage, lines 1885–1913 of *The Knight's Tale,* where he describes the layout of the amphitheater which Theseus orders to be built for the great tournament. Before Palamon and Arcite fight there for Emelye's hand, all three will pray there to their respective gods, Venus, Mars, and Diana, at shrines that Theseus has had incorporated into the amphitheater walls. As in the opening of the *General Prologue,* Chaucer refers to the zodiac, but here his reference is indirect, and his description of the amphitheater involves not the design on the astrolabe itself, but a function derived from that design, making use of the sky not as a calendar but as a clock.

The Oxford astronomer J. D. North, followed by Brooks and Fowler,[17] has offered us a zodiacal design for Theseus's amphitheater based on the signs (rotating clockwise) of Cancer, Taurus, Capricorn, and Scorpio. These signs are traditional domiciles of the planetary gods featured in the story, Venus, Diana (the moon), Mars, and Saturn (who comes in later), and they are important to the astronomical configurations of the calendar date of 1388 which North derives from them. But North's scheme gives us an apparently asymmetrical design for the placement of the oratories to the three planetary gods in the amphitheater:

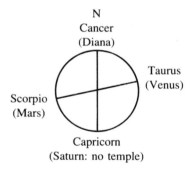

N
Cancer
(Diana)

Taurus
(Venus)

Scorpio
(Mars)

Capricorn
(Saturn: no temple)

—whereas Chaucer has taken pains to describe the plan as symmetrical, particularly in the placement of the gates at east and west in opposition:

> . . . swich a noble theatre as it was
> I dar wel seyen in this world ther nas.
> The circuit a myle was aboute,
> Walled of stoon, and dyched al withoute.
> Round was the *shap,* in manere of *compas,*
> Ful of *degrees,* the heighte of sixty pas . . .
>   Estward ther stood a gate of marbul whit,

Westward right swich another in the opposit.
And shortly to concluden, swich a place
Was noon in erthe, as in so litel space.

(A 1885–90 and 1893–96; my italics)

Indeed, Theseus's "little space" is not simply a few acres which he has circumscribed for human battle, but a representation of the ecliptic itself, like that found "in so litel space" on the back of the astrolabe. Chaucer's description of that instrument for little Lewis in *Treatise* I:21 seems to reflect lines 1889–90 of *The Knight's Tale* (or vice versa), both in language ("degrees," "shapen," "compass") and in concept:

But sothly the ecliptik lyne of thy zodiak is the utterist bordure of thy zodiak there the *degrees* be marked. Thy zodiak of thin Astrelabie is *shapen* as a *compas* . . .

(Part I, Section 21; my italics)

On this main plate of the astrolabe, or on any representation of the zodiac as a sky map, one may see the following design of the zodiacal signs (to which I add here their astrologically associated planets). The first point of each sign occurs at a cardinal point of the compass, in effect dividing the sky "with a longe cros in 4 quarters" (*Treatise* I:15):

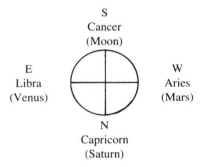

This perfectly symmetrical design gives us the alternative traditional domiciles of Venus in Libra and of Mars in Aries. The problem with this design is that the temple of Diana, the Moon with her domicile in Cancer, is in the south, which is "up" on the astrolabe, whereas Chaucer has carefully located these three temples specifically with that of Venus to the east, that of Mars to the west, and that of Diana to the north:[18]

He estward hath, upon the gate above,
In worshipe of Venus, goddesse of love,
Doon make an auter and an oratorie;
And on the gate westward, in memorie

Of Mars, he maked hath right swich another,
That coste largely of gold a fother.
And northward, in a touret on the wal,
Of alabastre whit and reed coral,
An oratorie, riche for to see,
In worshipe of Dyane of chastitee,
Hath Theseus doon wroght in noble wyse.
(A 1903–13)

Chaucer even alters details in his source, Boccaccio's *Teseide,* to achieve this symmetry, which emphasizes the care he is taking to have the temples correspond to the cardinal directions and the appropriate signs.[19] Therefore, to match his precision as well as his symmetry, the north-south directions on the sky map shown previously must be reversed, or, if the map is turned so that Cancer lies to the north where the oratory of Diana is located, then the east-west directions must be reversed—it amounts to the same thing.

The solution to this problem is simple once one realizes that Chaucer has laid out the amphitheater according to an "observer's horizon" plan, as one may see on a globe—or on an astrolabe furnished with a latitude plate for approximately 52° north, the latitude of Oxford. Then we see that with Cancer in the north and Capricorn in the south, one may after all have Taurus (domicile of Venus) east and Scorpio (domicile of Mars) west. The reason the signs display symmetry in this unlikely way is that the circle of the ecliptic is at an angle to the equator, so that some signs ascend much faster than others. Taurus, for example, ascends obliquely, taking one hour, four minutes to rise, whereas Scorpio ascends directly, taking two hours, forty-eight minutes, at latitude 52° north.[20] At another latitude, for example at the latitude of Boccaccio's Naples or Theseus's Athens, these signs would not fall so due east and west with Taurus rising. It is significant that when Chaucer reversed the entrances of Palamon and Arcite into the amphitheater for the tournament, to have Palamon enter at the east gate and Arcite at the west gate whereas Boccaccio has the opposite, he also changed the date from Boccaccio's autumn to early May. In other words, Chaucer's new arrangement of the amphitheater confirms his revised date for the tournament. But the amphitheater's astronomical symmetry may be perceived only from Chaucer's own latitude.

Chaucer deviates from his original again by introducing Saturn into the story and making him indisputably a planet at line 2454; presumably the "large place" (line 2678) where Saturn enters the action to create his own kind of order is situated at the south of the amphitheater, completing the cardinal directions and the astrolabic design.

The celestial plan, besides associating the amphitheater with the time-circle of the sky, also establishes an image useful for the tales as a whole, an image supporting the hints we are offered at various points for a single celestial day spanning the journey (probably an alternative time scheme, supplementing that of the several days of real time it would take the ambling and tale-telling pilgrims to reach their destination). This elegant "ark," as the host Harry Bailly calls it (B1, line 2), begins with the sun moving out of Aries in the *General Prologue* and concludes as the moon rises with Libra in the *Parson's Prologue,* thus beginning and ending with the two highly symbolic equinoctial signs, situated east and west on the back of astrolabe. This arc also, perhaps incidentally, reminds us of Beatrice's glimpse of the final glory in Dante's *Paradiso* (29:3), when for the barest instant the sun in the Ram and the moon in Libra "fanno dell' orizzonte insieme zona."

The suggestion that Chaucer might have used a single day as a controlling allegorical design in *The Canterbury Tales* has been put forward by several scholars lately.[21] I suggest that this design is related to the navigational use of the astrolabe in which he was so interested, that wondrous "steed of brass" that can bear us into every place "to which [oure] herte wilneth for to pace."[22]

Notes

1. All references to Chaucer's texts are to *The Riverside Chaucer,* ed. Larry D. Benson (Boston: Houghton Mifflin Co., 1987).

2. In *Chaucer in His Time* (London: Longman, 1973), Derek Brewer describes highly ornate mechanical displays that Chaucer would have known about and possibly have seen (182–84); in comparison to such displays, the knight entering Cambyuskan's banquet hall on his steed of brass seems tame.

3. J. B. Priestly, *Man and Time* (Garden City, N.Y.: Doubleday and Company, Inc., 1964), 30.

4. John Reidy writes in his notes on the *Treatise,* "Earlier doubts that Chaucer had a son named Lewis have been dispelled by a document (West Wales Hist. Rec. 4, 1914, 4–8) showing two Chaucers, Thomas and Lewis, both of whom could be the poet's sons" (*Riverside Chaucer,* 1092).

5. J. D. North analyzes the astronomical allusions in *The Squire's Tale* in Part II of "Kalenderes Enlumyned Ben They," *Review of English Studies* 20 (1969): 257–62. He observes that Cambyuskan's wife is named after a star, Elpheta (in modern terms Alpha Coronae Borealis, Alphecca in the almanacs), noting incidentally that this is one of the major star names engraved on the astrolabe; spelled variously, it may be seen on the arm of the rete between Scorpio and Sagittarius. From that observation North proceeds to put forward the interesting idea that other members of Cambyuskan's family also bear star names, some to be found on astrolabes, and that the king himself "is to be equated in an allegorical sense with the planet Mars" (258). It is the planetary associations of the characters from which he derives the date of composition of the story. He concludes with the remark that "Chaucer the astronomer and astrolabist can be seen at work more clearly in *The Squire's Tale* than anywhere outside the *Astrolabe* itself" (262).

6. R. T. Gunther, *Chaucer and Messahalla on the Astrolabe, Early Science in Oxford*, Vol. 5 (Oxford: Oxford University Press, 1929), v.

7. The *Treatise* is edited with notes to aid our understanding by John Reidy in *The Riverside Chaucer* (661–683); one looks forward also to Sigmund Eisner's edition for the Variorum Chaucer currently being produced by the University of Oklahoma Press. J. D. North offers a useful discussion of the instrument in the *Scientific American* for January, 1974 (96–106).

8. See the facsimile and translation of Messahalla's treatise on the astrolabe in Gunther's volume cited in note 6, especially Part I, Section 6, and the manuscript illustration of the "horse" facing page 145, or any number of Arabic astrolabes; for example, that in North's article mentioned in note 7 above (97).

9. See the reproduction of MS Rawlinson D.913, folio 29r, in *The Riverside Chaucer*, 667, an illustration from Chaucer's *Treatise* showing the rete with a dog-shaped Sirius pointer.

10. Samuel Guye and Henri Michel, *Time and Space: Measuring Instruments from the 15th to the 19th Centuries* (New York: Praeger Publishers, 1971), 222.

11. For criticism of that canon see Norman Blake, "The Relationship between the Hengwrt and the Ellesmere Manuscripts of the 'Canterbury Tales,'" *Essays and Studies*, 32 (1979): 1–18, and his rejection of *The Canon's Yeoman's Tale* as spurious in his recent edition of the Hengwrt Manuscript of *The Canterbury Tales* (London: Edward Arnold, 1980).

12. *The Siege of Thebes*, edited by A. Erdmann in *Early English Text Society*, Vols. 108 and 125, extra series (London: Paul, Trench, Trübner, 1911, reprinted 1960), 1. According to the calendar of Chaucer's day, which was ten days "ahead" of ours, the sun was in Aries from March 12th until April 11th.

13. Owen Gingerich, review in *Studies in the Age of Chaucer* 4 (1982): 149. The ease with which this mistake can be made is nicely illustrated by the opening of David Lodge's "Prologue" to his novel *Small World* (New York: Warner Books, 1984):

> When April with its sweet showers has pierced the drought of March to the root, and bathed every vein of earth with that liquid by whose power the flowers are engendered; when the zephyr, too, with its dulcet breath, has breathed life into the tender new shoots in every copse and on every heath, and the young sun has run half his course in the sign of the Ram . . .

14. A. E. Brea, *The Treatise on the Astrolabe of Geoffrey Chaucer* (London: John Russell Smith, 1870), 81. Brea complains at some length, in "Note A," 81–84, that Skeat received the credit and considerable praise for this "greatest gain of late times as to the Prologue," which he published in 1868, seventeen years after Brea had done so.

15. As Brea points out, "In alluding to the zodiac [Chaucer] always refers to the signs, never to the constellations" (76). Because the signs of the zodiac were established so long ago as a means of dividing up the ecliptic into 30° sections, the

precession of the poles has moved these *divisions* off the constellations that have given them their names.

16. In her doctoral dissertation, *Seasons and Months: Studies in a Tradition of Middle English Poetry* (Paris: Librairie Universitaire S.A., 1933), Rosamund Tuve twice suggests (185 and cp. 58) that

> When Chaucer and other poets, in the line immediately before or after the description of a month, note the position of the sun in the zodiac, they are not merely obedient to a literary convention. They also follow an artistic tradition.

As her attention is focused on illustrated books, she does not think to consider Chaucer's familiarity with the design on the astrolabe.

17. North, *op. cit.*, 149–54; Douglas Brooks and Alastair Fowler, "The Meaning of Chaucer's Knight's Tale," *Medium Ævum* 39 (1970): 124–30. Brooks and Fowler comment on the asymmetry of North's scheme for the amphitheater in note 14, 143.

18. Diana's oratory is in the only mentioned "touret" of the amphitheater, which corresponds to the only "toret" that Chaucer mentions in his *Treatise* (I:2), the projection at the top of the astrolabe called a *kursi* or "throne" in Arabic, which holds the ring; it lies above the first point of Cancer as depicted on the back of the instrument. This is the single detail associating the amphitheater of *The Knight's Tale* specifically with the astrolabe, and this "tower over the Moon's domicile" could have been the detail that inspired Chaucer's design of that building.

19. Boccaccio has Arcita pray to Mars, Palemone to Venus, and Emilia to Diana at various locations in Athens, from which their personified prayers travel far away to the gods' houses elsewhere. Chaucer incorporates the temples into the structure of the amphitheater and has the prayers occur in the order of the planetary hours: Venus, Diana, Mars. Boccaccio has Palemone enter the tournament from the west and Arcita from the east; Chaucer reverses these directions to have each combatant enter through the gate associated with his planetary deity. See *Teseida delle Nozze di Emilia* in Giovanni Boccaccio, *Tutti le Opere,* ed. Vittore Branca, 6 vols. (Verona: I Classici Mondadori, 1964), vol. 2.

20. Walter W. Skeat gives the rising times for each of the signs in his edition of Chaucer's *Treatise on the Astrolabe* for the Early English Text Society (London: Oxford University Press, 1872), 36.

21. Most notably Donald R. Howard in *The Idea of the Canterbury Tales* (Berkeley: University of California Press, 1978): "Perhaps the major references to time reveal not facts about the journey but a poetical image, that of a day's passing" (166). V. A. Kolve makes a similar suggestion in *Chaucer and the Imagery of Narrative* (Stanford: Stanford University Press, 1984), 364 and following, and others have spoken of this "day" with varying degrees of commitment to its realism. In "Cosmic Allegory and Cosmic Error in the Frame of *The Canterbury Tales,*" *Pacific Coast Philology* 18 (1983): 77–83, Charlotte Thompson proposes in a powerful and learned

argument that, by associating the rising of the sun with Aries and its setting with Libra, Chaucer made "an allegorical use of time and the stars" echoing eschatological ideas about the beginning and end of the world. I am convinced that she is right.

22. As an outsider to Chaucer studies, I am particularly grateful to two Chaucerians who have taken the time to help me with this material: to Daniel Silvia, who directed me to articles important for the initial stages of this study and who continues to be warmly supportive, and to Sigmund Eisner, who taught me how to use the astrolabe and also directed me to essential articles (such as that by Thompson noted above). I am also grateful to the Committee on Research of the University of California at Davis for a grant enabling me to travel to Oxford to examine the magnificent collection of astrolabes at the Museum of the History of Science, and to see various examples of "the litel wegge, which that is clepid the hors" in its horse-shape on Arabic instruments. I could not have dealt with this material at all without the generous encouragement of my brother, the astronomer Remington Stone, who is helping me to carry the implications of my idea farther.

11. The Grammatical Model of Musical Understanding in the Middle Ages

CALVIN M. BOWER

The meaning of a musical entity, whether it be a single pitch or a complex of pitches forming a larger part, must be interpreted largely through its function in relation to other pitches and parts. Certain musical entities, like some architectural members, are structural: if one removes them, the structure of the whole is destroyed or compromised. Other musical entities, again like some architectural elements, are decorative: they help define the character and style of the whole, but they do not support the fundamental structure. Since music unfolds in time, further dimension is added: an entity which at one moment is elaborative can at another moment become structural, or the reverse process may occur. Musical scholars have barely begun to apply principles of interpretation to the large repertoire of liturgical chant. The lack of clear criteria for determining crucial structural pitches and complexes of pitches in this repertoire has formed a major obstacle to systematic interpretation. The repertoire is remote in time, and the principles of interpretation used in more recent polyphonic and tonal repertoires are obviously inappropriate for analysis of chant. In this study I submit a vocabulary and basis for interpretation of chant drawn from musical theorists not so far removed from the origins of chant. The vocabulary for analysis is based on the ancient grammatical model, but the model goes beyond the mere labeling of parts; it identifies and defines meanings of parts in relation to the structural whole.

One of the principal problems faced by chant scholars is development of a morphology for the analysis of chant. Recent scholarship, particularly that of Treitler and Hucke,[1] has shown the inadequate nature of the old molds into which these melodies had been poured. A second mode gradual is more than a string of patch-work phrases; by labeling an Introit or Communion a "neumatic antiphonal mass chant" we have comprehended little about the dynamics of the melody. Through the work of Treitler and Jonsson[2] we have learned that at least on one level, the structures of melodies are largely determined by the structure of their texts, and as the texts can be analyzed using grammatical principles, so can the melodies. That this principle was integral to medieval theory has been demonstrated in works by Bielitz, Reckow, and Treitler.[3] But these studies have not posed such questions as: What is the hierarchy of parts within medieval musical structures? How does one perceive the relative importance—the functions—of pitches as these melodies unfold? And, perhaps most important, what is the relation between pitches and parts? While all of these questions are familiar to those musicians who analyze tonal music and even those who analyze polyphony, chant scholars have not yet been able to develop a theoretical basis for formulating systematic analysis. The position of this study is that the grammatical model presented in musical treatises from the Middle Ages should play a significant role in forming a system for analysis.

Table I (see p. 135) presents a list of theoretical sources dating from between about 850 and 1100. These treatises represent the mainstream of musical theory which has survived that period.[4] More manuscripts of Boethius's *de musica* survive than any other source,[5] but second to Boethius are manuscripts of Guido's *Micrologus*.[6] Manuscripts containing *Musica* and *Scholica enchiriadis*,[7] and the *Dialogus de musica*[8] follow *Micrologus* in number, each being found in approximately the same quantity of codices. Each treatise in this list contains vocabulary borrowed from the discipline of grammar, a discipline which lay at the core of medieval education. Table II (see p. 136) presents the grammatical terms along with indications of the treatises in which they appear. A few words of definition and explanation are in order:

> Level 1: Terms of this level mark major divisions of a sentence—a clause, for example—or a major phrase in a melody. The most common of these terms is *distinctio*—a word used by the grammarians to indicate major grammatical division. The words *membrum, pars, particula,* and *punctum* are more or less synonyms with *distinctio,* or they may sometimes be treated as subdivisions of *distinctio.* Guido defines *neuma* as a musical *pars*.[9]

> Level 2: the first terms found here—*comma* and *colon*—represent subdivisions of *distinctiones.* Generally speaking, *distinctiones* are said to be broken down into *cola,* which, in turn, are broken down into *commata,* although the terms *comma* and *colon* are sometimes reversed in the hierarchy of parts.[10] The total grammatical (or musical) structure consisting of *distinctiones, commata,* and *cola* is named *periodus* in the *Scolica enchiriadis* and in the treatise of John.[11]

> Level 3: Terms of this level represent subdivisions of terms found in level 2. For lack of a better term, I translate *syllaba* as "melodic gesture," and I translate *vox* as pitch. *Vox* in music would correspond to the letter in grammar.

A hierarchy of completeness is formed in these first three levels. In grammar these levels represent degrees of completeness of meaning; in music they imply degrees of wholeness of a musical structure.

TABLE I

ME	Musica enchiriadis	Musica et Scolica enchriadis una cum aliquibus tractatulis adjunctis, ed. Hans Schmid (Munich: Verlag der Bayerischen Akademie der Wissenschaften, 1981)
SE	Scolica enchiriadis	Ibid.
CB	Commemoratio brevis de tonis et psalmis modulandis	Ibid.
AR	Aurialian of Reome, Musica Disciplina	Aureliani Reomensis Musica Disciplina ed. Lawrence Gushee (Rome: American Institute of Musicology, 1975), Corpus Scriptorum de Musica 21
HM	Hucbald of St. Amand, De musica institutione	in Martin Gerbert, Scriptores Ecclesiastici de musica sacra potissimum (Hildesheim: Georg Olms, 1963), I, 104-122
OD	Oddo, Dialogus de musica	in Gerbert Scriptores I, 252-264
GM	Guido, Micrologus	Guiodonis Aretini Micrologus, ed. Jos. Smits van Waesberghe (Rome: American Institute of Musicology, 1955), Corpus Scriptorum de Musica 4
GE	Guido, Epistola Michaeli monacho de ignoto cantu	in Gerbert Scriptores II, 43-50
GR	Guido, Regulae rhythmicae	Guidonis Aretini "Regulae Rhythmicae," ed. Jos. Smits van Waesberghe (Buren: F. Knuf, 1975), Divitiae Musicae Artis A.IV.
AM	Aribo, De Musica	Aribonis de Musica, ed. J. Smits van Waesberghe (Rome: American Institute of Musicology, 1951), Corpus Scriptorum de Musica 2
CA	Commentarius in Micrologum	Expositiones in Micrologum Guidonis Aretini, ed. J. Smits van Waesberghe (Amsterdam: North Holland Publishing Co., 1957), 93-172
JA	John, De Musica cum Tonario	Johannis Affligemensis De Musica cum Tonario, ed. J. Smits van Waesberghe (Rome: American Institute of Musicology, 1950), Corpus Scriptorum de Musica 1

Level 4: these are special terms which are more or less synonymous with terms in group 2.

Level 5: these represent words borrowed from grammar to describe melodic movement.

Level 6: *Distinctiones* are defined both grammatically and musically by pauses, or by lengthenings of notes. The vocabulary of this level presents terms used to describe these articulations.

Level 7: I include this level because of an interest in "marking time" and to demonstrate the important kinship between *Micrologus* and *Musica enchiriadis*.

TABLE II

Vocabulary:	ME	SE	CB	AR	HM	OD	GM	GE	GR	AM	CA	JA
1.												
DISTINCTIO		x	x	x		x	x	x		x	x	x
MEMBRUM	(x)	x										
PARS					x		x	x	x		x	
PARTICULA	x	x										
PUNCTUM					x							x
(NEUMA)		x			x		x	x	x	x	x	
2.												
COMMA	x	x					x		x		x	x
COLON	x	x					x		x		x	x
PERIODUS		x										x
3.												
SYLLABA					x		x	x	x	x	x	
VOX	x	x	(x)	(x)	x	(x)	x	x	x	x	x	x
4.												
diastema	x	x										x
systema	x	x										x
teleusis												x
clausula							x					
clausura												x
circuitus												x
5.												
arsis	x	x	x				x					
thesis	x	x	x				x					
levatio	x	x										
elevatio	(x)	(x)	x			x	x	x				
positio	x	x	x				x	x				
depositio						x	x					
accentus/ tonus			x									x
gravis												x
circumflexus												x
acutus			x									x
6.												
tenor							x			x	x	
mora	x	x					x			x	x	
morula		x					x				x	
tremula					x		x			x	x	
repauso						x						
pausatio												x
7.												
plaudo		x					x					
metricus		x					x					

(x in parenthesis indicates use not strictly in grammatical context)

An ancient *topos* appears repeatedly in these treatises;[12] it goes something like this: As individual letters are joined together to form syllables, which, in turn form words, and as words are linked together to form phrases and clauses (commas and colons), which in turn become complete sentences (*periodi*), so individual pitches (*voces*) are joined to form melodic gestures (*syllabae*) which, in turn form subphrases (commas and colons), and these combine to make complete phrases (*distinctiones*); several such phrases join together to form a complete melody (a *periodus*). While this analogy seems abstract as a literary *topos*, the application of the analogy to a specific musical composition in the treatise of John serves well to make this basis for analysis concrete. Example 1 serves as musical example for John's text:

EXAMPLE 1

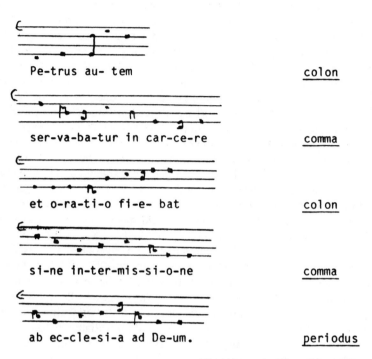

Pe-trus au- tem	<u>colon</u>
ser-va-ba-tur in car-ce-re	comma
et o-ra-ti-o fi-e- bat	<u>colon</u>
si-ne in-ter-mis-si-o-ne	comma
ab ec-cle-si-a ad De-um.	<u>periodus</u>

(Worchester *Antiphonale*, p. 340)

So when a song pauses through an interruption on the fourth or fifth pitch from the final, that is a colon; when it goes back to the final in the middle, that is a comma; when it settles on the final at the end that is a period. Take this antiphon, for example:

Petrus autem represents the colon,
servabatur in carcere the comma,
et oratio fiebat the colon,
[pro eo] sine intermissione the comma, and
ab ecclesia ad Deum the period.[13]

Following John's principles, one can perceive very clearly the structure of the text as reflected in the melody. But information beyond the sphere of grammar is given by John: we are told that the fourth and fifth pitches above the final have significance in marking a division. Likewise we are told that the final note itself indicates a division. Finally, John instructs us that the pause created by the interruption [*per suspensionem*] functions as signal demarking a musical entity.

The full import of grammatical vocabulary in medieval theory is missed if it is viewed merely as a set of terms for analyzing a surface phrase structure independent of deeper, more basic musical meaning. Herein lies one of the fundamental weaknesses in the way this theory has been read and applied. (The other weakness is the use of these passages to argue for a rhythmic performance of chant.) The significance of the grammatical model as a means for interpreting chant melodies lies not so much in the rather simple task of labeling phrases as in the process of perceiving deeper tonal structures. This, of course, should come as no surprise to anyone practiced in analysis of music from more recent periods, for it is impossible to separate the tonal structure of a composition from the articulation of its parts. Moreover, the theorists under consideration have led us to perceive the intimate connection between mode and grammatical structure, for they consistently expound grammatical vocabulary in the context of discussing modes. The theory of grammatical parts is introduced in *Musica enchiriadis* immediately following a chapter discussing the tonal structure of the four *maneria,* and in the chapter introducing and defining the words *tropus* and *modus* (i.e., chap. ix, 20–22). *Scolica enchiriadis* expands the theory of grammatical parts in context of a discussion of species of consonances and the qualities of modes (83–89). In both of these treatises the theory of grammatical parts marks the last element treated in monophonic music, the element treated just before the introduction of organum. The author of *Dialogus* develops his theory of distinctions immediately after defining *tonus vel modus* (157), and immediately before discussing the range of chants and their finals. In *Micrologus*—a treatise striking in its structural similarity to *Musica enchiriadis*—Guido introduces the theory of grammatical parts as the final element in his discussion of the structure of monophonic music; the exposition of *Micrologus*—with exception of a minor excursion—occurs immediately before the introduction of organum. Finally, John presents his discussion of grammatical parts in a chapter entitled *de modis, quos abusive tonos appellamus* (chap. x). Thus, the relation between grammatical entity and musical function should not seem remote.

How, one must ask, can a theory of grammatical parts reveal to us a musical structure beyond the mere level of phrasing? The answer to this question lies in level 6 of the vocabulary in Table II, the terms which are used to discuss pauses or lengthenings at the end of grammatical or musical parts. The lengthening of a pitch in any music imbues that pitch with special significance. But how does one determine which pitch is to be given special structural significance in these melodies? The answer is by determining the points at which a melody articulates the grammatical structure of the text. In the repertoire of chant—a repertoire which is clearly logocentric and which is defined by each of these authors as "modal"—the final pitch takes on the meaning of *tonic,* and, by extension of the same principle, the pitches which occur at the ends of structural parts take on special significance in relation to the final tonic. Guido expresses this principle quite clearly within the metaphor of grammatical function.

> It is not unusual that music determines its functions from the final pitch. For in grammatical parts we often discern the fullness of meaning only in the last letters or syllables through case, number, person, and tense.[14]

Thus one of the first principles in interpreting these melodies must be analysis of the grammatical structure of the underlying text *in order to determine* which pitches will be stressed through lengthening.

The theory of lengthening final pitches of grammatical members finds its first systematic exposition in the *Scolica enchiriadis.* In context of discussing the manner in which pitches unfold within grammatical parts, the author introduces the notion of "measured singing" (*numerose canere*), and illustrates using the antiphon found in Example 2. In "measured singing," the Magister states,

> one observes where more extended lengthenings, where more abbreviated lengthenings should be used, similar to the way in which one observes which syllables are short and which are long. Thus one takes care to notice which sounds ought to be extended and which abbreviated, so that the longs fit together with the shorts in regular ratio. And one marks time as though the song had metrical feet. By way of example let us sing; I will mark time in leading, you imitate in following.

EXAMPLE 2

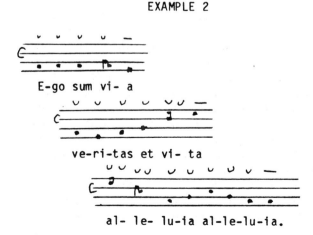

E-go sum vi- a

ve-ri-tas et vi- ta

al- le- lu-ia al-le-lu-ia.

In these three members only the last notes are long, the rest are short.[15]

This musical example is written in dasia notation in the manuscripts, and marks for short and long syllables are written over the notation. Through the systematic lengthening of the final notes in this example, the rather simple grammatical structure of the text is made clear. But grammatical structure could have been articulated on one note; here there is a musical structure unfolding along with the structure of the text: The first member begins with reiteration of the pitch G, and ends with the note F. The second member, again beginning with G, rises a fifth to the note D. The final member descends from the D and settles into the final G. As the text unfolds, a broad musical structure is revealed through reiteration and lengthening of pitches:

Phrase 1: G --- F

Phrase 2: G --- D

Phrase 3: D ------- G

These pitches have obvious structural significance; they form the tonal pillars which support the other notes. The other pitches either elaborate one of these structural pitches or fill the space between them.

Guido, in the famous chapter 15 of *Micrologus,* took the theory of lengthening he found in *Scolica enchiriadis* and refined it. He seems uncomfortable with the limited analysis of the earlier author, and postulates a hierarchy of lengthenings which, in turn, reflects the various strata of grammatical structure. Guido prescribes that the last note of a *syllable* be slightly lengthened, and that the last note of a *pars* (comma or colon) be lengthened more; the most extended lengthening takes place at the end of a distinction. Guido, again following his model, suggests that time be marked with the hand in the manner of counting metrical feet (see level 7 of Table II), but he suggests that the lengthening of syllables, parts, and distinctions be proportional.[16]

Were we left with only the text of Guido's chapter 15 we would be frustrated, for Guido gives no musical examples of these principles. But commentaries on Guido give flesh to Guido's skeleton with clear and numerous examples. Aribo's *De musica* and the anonymous *Commentarius* edited by Smits van Waesberghe use the antiphon *Dixit Dominus mulieri Cananaeae* to present Guido's theory of grammatical parts with particular emphasis on proportional lengthenings at ends of parts. The commentaries analyze only the first phrase of the antiphon, stating that the last *xit* of *dixit* marks a *syllable* and that this note should be slightly lengthened; the final *nus* of *Dominus* marks a "part," and it should be lengthened somewhat more; finally the last *ae* of *Cananaeae* sets off the distinction and it should receive the longest lengthening.[17] Example 3 presents the entire antiphon cited by the commentators.

EXAMPLE 3

1 Di-xit Do-mi-nus mu-li-e-ri Ca-na-nae-ae,

2 Non est bo-num su-me-re pa-nem fi-li-o - rum

3 et mit-te-re ca-ni-bus ad man-du-can-dum.

4 U-ti-que Do-mi-ne nam et ca-tel-li e-dunt de mi-cis

5 quae ca-dunt de men-sa do-mi-no-rum su-o-rum.

6 A-it il-li ie-sus,

7 Mu-li-er mag-na est fi-des tu-a

fi-at ti-bi si-cut pe-ti-sti.

(Worchester *Antiphonale*, p. 94)

I have extended the principles of Guido as exemplified in his commentators to the whole of this antiphon. I have marked with the letter *s* what I judge to be *syllables,* I have marked parts with the comma, and I have indicated distinctions with the colon. One might quibble with my placement of *syllables* in this example, but the markings of parts and distinctions seem clear in each case. Using the structure revealed by the grammatical model, one may interpret these seven phrases as follows:

> Phrase 1 rises from the first pitch D to end the *syllable* (here defined by the medieval theorists) on G, then elaborates the G through repetition and its neighboring pitches F and A.

> Phrase 2, by placing D at the end of a *syllable,* gives it added structural significance, then returns to G to end the part. After dwelling on F through reiteration, it descends to end the distinction on C, the pitch a fifth below G.

> Phrase 3 again stresses F through reiteration, rises to G to end the part, and elaborates the G with neighboring pitches before cadencing on G to end the distinction.

> Phrase 4 continues the elaboration of G, now with slightly bolder gestures, makes a slight pause on F to end a *syllable,* then returns to G.

> Phrase 5 unfolds the five pitches above G, closes the first *syllable* on the higher D, and, after returning to G at the close of the first part, elaborates G for the remainder of the phrase.

> Phrase 6 again unfolds the pitches found in phrase 5, but now as a bold elaboration of G, since G ends both *syllable* and the short distinction.

> Phrase 7, the longest and final phrase, first ornaments G with a gesture recalling the opening of phrase 1, then moves to F for close of the first part, then rises to the pitch a fourth above G, to C, before final elaboration of and cadence on G.

Given this analysis, an interpretation based on the grammatical model articulated by Guido and his commentators, the following generalizations may be offered:

> 1. G is clearly the most important pitch in the tonal hierarchy. It forms the end of more grammatical units than any other pitch, and is the final or "tonic" of the antiphon.

> 2. Pitches a fifth below and above the G, namely C and D, may be said to form the next level in the tonal hierarchy. They—particularly the C—end important structural units and they form the lowest and highest pitches of the antiphon.

> 3. Pitches a fourth below and above the final, D and C, along with F, the pitch a tone below the G, form a final level in the tonal hierarchy.

> 4. Other pitches function to elaborate these structural tones.

At about this point in the analysis I become aware of a certain ambiguity. It is clear, on the one hand, that the text precedes the melody in conception, and that the melody serves to make the textual structure intelligible. But on the other hand, I can view the text as a vehicle used by the musician to establish purely musical functions; the music is not wholly subservient to the text. The "composer" of this antiphon used the text as a foundation on which to build a musical edifice. His musical goal was the elaboration of pitch G by bringing it into relief through articulation of the lower C, the higher D, and other structural pitches. Grammatical units of the basic text aided him in expressing these musical ideas. Perhaps this ambiguity, this balance between textual and musical structure, is one of the reasons that the repertoire of liturgical chant is so satisfying.

In analyzing polyphony of the fifteenth and sixteenth centuries and tonal music, one can establish a hierarchy of pitches using historical rules governing consonance and dissonance, or rules governing chord-tones and non-chord-tones. But criteria for determining consonance and dissonance, chord-tones and non-chord-tones, are obviously no help in establishing a hierarchy of pitches in the repertoire of chant. I am suggesting in this essay that the theory of grammatical parts found in these treatises may serve, indeed should serve, as a criterion for determining structural pitches, even for determining a hierarchy of structural pitches. I submit that the theorists explicated grammatical parts precisely when treating the modes—the tonal bases for the repertoire. I believe contextual treatment of this theory leads us in the direction I suggest. Further, by analyzing and performing melodies according to the principles set down by the theorists—particularly by the author of the *enchiriadis* complex and by Guido and his commentators—the structural moments of melodies can be determined by both eye and ear, and the other parts of the melody can be perceived in relation to them. This criterion obviously functions best in syllabic pieces, and its use is limited in highly melismatic genres. But by achieving some understanding of these principles in syllabic pieces, certain functions can be transferred by analogy to melismatic pieces. Other criteria must be used along with the grammatical model: the importance of intervals a fourth and a fifth above and below the final has been noted in these examples and is stressed in the theoretical texts; similarly, the simple reiteration of a pitch can give it structural significance. Certain techniques, for example the use of neighboring pitches, function to elaborate a structural pitch; elaborative techniques in the repertoire need to be further defined. Finally, the application of analysis according to the grammatical model has obvious implications for the person interpreting this repertoire in performance.

Notes

1. See, for example, H. Hucke, "Toward a New Historical View of Gregorian Chant," *Journal of the American Musicological Society* 33 (1980): 437–67, and L.

Treitler, "Oral, Written, and Literate Process in the Transmission of Medieval Music," *Speculum* 56 (1981): 471–91.

2. R. Jonsson and L. Treitler, "Medieval Music and Language: a Reconsideration of the Relationship," *Studies in the History of Music 1: Music and Language* (New York: Broude Brothers Ltd., 1983), 1–23.

3. M. Bielitz, *Musik und Grammatik: Studien zur mittelalterlichen Musiktheorie* (Munich and Salzburg: Musikverlag Katzbichler, 1977); F. Reckow, "Vitium oder Color Rhetoriens? Thesen zur Bedeutung der Modelldisziplinen Grammatica, Rhetorica, und Poetica für das Musikverständnis," *Forum Musicologicum* 3 (1982): 307–21; and L. Treitler, "Reading and Singing: On the Genesis of Occidental Musikwriting," *Early Music History* 4, ed. Iain Fenlon (Cambridge: Cambridge University Press, 1984), 135–208.

4. All references to page numbers within treatises cited in this study refer to pages of the editions cited in Table I.

5. C. M. Bower, "Boethius's *De institutione musica:* A Handlist of Manuscripts" forthcoming in *Scriptorium*. There are 151 extant manuscripts or fragments containing Boethius's treatise or extracts.

6. See Joseph Smits van Waesberghe, *De musico-paedagogico et theoretico Guidone Aretino eiusque vita et moribus* (Florence: Leo S. Olschki, 1953); also Smits van Waesberghe's edition of *Micrologus*, 4–71. Seventy-eight manuscripts exist containing the *Micrologus*.

7. See Nancy Catherine Phillips, "*Musica* and *Scolica Enchiriadis*. The Literary, Theoretical, and Musical Sources" (Diss. New York University, 1984), Chapter II: "The Manuscript Tradition," 44–119; also Schmid's edition *Musica et Scholica enchiriadis*, vii–viii. There are forty-six extant codices which relate directly to the *enchiriadis* tradition.

8. Concerning *OD,* its author and manuscript tradition, see Michel Huglo, "L'auteur du 'Dialogue sur la musique' attribué à Odon," in *Revue de Musicologie* 55 (1969): 119–171; and Michel Huglo, "Der Prolog des Odo zugeschriebenen 'Dialogus de Musica'," in *Archiv für Musikwissenschaft* 28 (1971): 134–46. Huglo (1969) discusses forty-eight codices related to the textual tradition of *Dialogus*.

9. *GM,* 163, 4: "neumam, id est partem."

10. *ME,* 22: "Sed cola fiunt coeuntibus apte commatibus duobus pluribusve, quamvis interdum est, ubi indiscrete comma sive colon dici potest."

11. For an example of how these terms function in analysis, see John's analysis of *Petrus autem* in note 13. Note that John also reverses the order of colon and comma.

12. *ME,* chapter i (3) and chapter x (23), and *GM,* chapter xv (162–63). The ancient models for these analogies are Chalcidius and Censorinus; see Phillips, op. cit. 273–85.

13. *JA,* chapter x (79–80): Similiter cum cantus in quarta vel quinta a finali voce per suspensionem pausat, colon est; cum in medio ad finalem reducitur, comma est;

cum in fine ad finalem pervenit periodus est. Ut in hac antiphona: *Petrus autem* colon, *servabatur in carcere* comma, *et oratio fiebat* colon, *pro eo sine intermissione* comma, *ab ecclesia ad Deum* periodus.

14. *GM,* chapter xi (145): Nec mirum regulas musicam a finali voce sumere, cum et in grammaticae partibus pene ubique vim sensus in ultimis litteris vel syllabis per casus, numeros, personas, tempora discernimus.

15. *SE* pars 1 (86–87): D. Quid est numerose canere? M. Ut attendatur, ubi productioribus ubi brevioribus morulis utendum sit, quatinus uti, quae sillabae breves quaeque sint longae, attenditur. Ita qui soni producti quique correpti esse debeant, attendatur, ut ea, quae diu, ad ea, quae non diu, legitime concurrant, et veluti metricis pedibus cantilena plaudatur. Age canamus exerctii usu, plaudam pedes ego in praecinendo, tu sequendo imitabere:
Ego sum via veritas et vita alleluia alleluia.
Solae in tribus membris ultimae longae, reliquae breves sunt.

16. *GM,* chapter xv (163–64): Tenor vero, id est mora ultimae vocis, qui in syllaba quantuluscumque est, amplior in parte, diutissimus vero in distinctione, signum in his divisionis existit. Sicque opus est ut quasi metricis pedibus cantilena plaudatur, et aliae voces ab aliis morulam duplo longiorem vel duplo breviorem . . .

It should be noted that both *SE* and *GM* couch the language relating durations of lengthenings with metrical endings in terms such as "veluti" and "quasi." Both texts are clearly suggesting "proportional" durations at endings through analogy, not through strict correspondence, and caution should be exercized in making the lengthenings excessively quantitative or rigid.

17. *CA* (153–54): Tertia pars est proportionis quae describitur his verbis: *aut in ratione tenorum neumae alterutrum conferantur et respondeant.* Tenor est ultimae vocis protensio, quae ad invicem ita confertur, ut numerus vocum et intervalla earum *nunc aequae aequis, nunc duplae vel triplae simplicibus, atque alias collatione sesquialtera vel sesquitertia.* De quo tenore vel protensione dominus Guido dicit: *Tenor vero id est mora ultimae vocis,* et caetera. Dixit Dominus mulieri Cananaeae. Illam unam dictionem "Dixit" habeatis syllabam, "Dixit Dominus" partem, "Dixit Dominus mulieri Cananaeae" distinctionem. In "dixit" finalis "xit" intendatur aliquantulum; in "Dixit Dominus" finalis "nus" producatur amplius, in "Dixit Dominus mulieri Cananaeae" finalis "ae" extendatur diutissime. (Cf. *AM,* chapter 28, 68).

Note that the terms used to describe the lengthenings are not strictly quantitative.

12. On the Interpretation of Modi, quos abusive tonos dicimus

CHARLES M. ATKINSON

As Professors Gallacher and Damico point out in their introduction to this volume, the aspect of difference can be a decisive impulse to interpretation for both medieval and modern writers. For medieval writers on music, an area that provided many such sparks to hermeneutic activity was the confrontation between the theory and practice of plainchant and the study of ancient Greek theoretical writings, translated into Latin, that formed a part of the monastic educational program. Those writings—which in the main transmit Greek harmonic theory that has little to do with sounding music—would eventually have a decisive impact on medieval music theory, particularly in the classification of plainchant into one of the so-called church tones or modes. By the eleventh century, there would be a fully developed system of eight modes (*modi*) that classified chant melodies according to their final pitch in relation to their range (the distance between the highest and lowest notes of the melody), based on the notion of discrete species (arrangements of whole- and half-steps) of segments of the diatonic scale.[1] In the early stages of the confrontation, however, there was a rather large chasm between what the ancient writings said about *tonus* or *modus* and the meanings that were associated with the two terms, particularly with *tonus,* in the ninth century. A telling witness to this difference in theoretical traditions, and one quite sensitive to the difference it could make in facilitating discourse about music, is the *Musica enchiriadis.*

An anonymous treatise written in the second half of the ninth century, the *Musica enchiriadis*[2] occupies a singularly important position in the history of Western music. It is not only one of our most important documents for the theory of plainchant in the early Middle Ages; it is also our earliest source for the theory and practice of polyphonic music, which it refers to as *organum.* The author begins the eighth chapter of his work by saying "Demonstrandum nunc, quomodo haec quattuor ptongorum vis modos, quos abusive *tonos* dicimus, moderetur" (Now we must demonstrate how the power of these four phthongi governs the modes, which we improperly call *tones* [my italics]).[3] He then spends the rest of the chapter describing how the power or force of the *phthongi*[4] creates the character of the four principal tones (*toni*) of plainchant, without mentioning modes again! Indeed, the very title of the chapter itself is "How, from the power of the four sounds, all the *tones* are produced" (Quomodo ex IIII°ʳ sonorum vi omnes toni producantur).[5] The use of the term *tonus* here and elsewhere in chapter eight is in keeping with the usage of the first seven chapters, where the term consistently employed to designate the melodic categories of plainchant is *tonus*, with *modus* appearing only once in its stead.[6]

The passage under consideration here has been an enigma to scholars for years. Why would the author take the trouble to condemn the use of *tonus* when it was not only his own term of choice to describe the fundamental way in which melodies differ from each other, but was also the standard term for this phenomenon in other ninth-century treatises on music?[7] Moreover, why should he introduce the term *modus* to designate melodic category, champion its use over the competing term, *tonus,* and then fly in the face of his own admonition?

Far from being just another example of a medieval author's niggling over minutiae, the question of *tonus* versus *modus* in the *Musica enchiriadis* proves to be a far-reaching one. Implicit in the two terms are two quite different ways of classifying music and, indeed, two different conceptions of its function and character. The term *tonus* is associated with the theory of plainchant, and is closely bound up with the practice of psalmody; the term *modus,* on the other hand, has its roots in ancient Greek harmonic theory, and only gradually comes to have direct relevance for medieval discourse about music. Indeed, the leading edge of its introduction into medieval music theory is represented by its appearance in the *Musica enchiriadis.*

In this essay I offer an interpretation of the use of the terms *tonus* and *modus* in the *Musica enchiriadis* and suggest some of its implications for our understanding of the history of music theory in the early Middle Ages. In order to do this we must first ask ourselves several questions. First, is it possible that the *Musica enchiriadis*—or at least the passage with which we are concerned here—might not have been merely a copy of an earlier work? Second, was *tonus* indeed the term preferred in the ninth century as the designation for the melodic categories of plainchant? Third, if *modus* was not current in ninth-century music theory as a designation for melodic categories, then what was its source?

The answer to the first of these questions must be no. In contrast to several of its contemporary works, the bulk of the *Musica enchiriadis* cannot be explained as the mere copying of an earlier work. It borrows lines from Chalcidius's commentary on the *Timaeus,* Censorinus's *De die natali,* Vergil's *Aeneid,* Fulgentius's *Mitologiarum,* and Boethius's *De institutione musica,* but the work as a whole cannot be traced to a single earlier source.[8] Moreover, as nearly as we can determine, the passage in question here makes its appearance for the first time anywhere in the *Musica enchiriadis.* It then finds its way into any number of later works on music.

In answer to the second question, examination of writings contemporaneous with the *Musica enchiriadis* reveals that *tonus*, not *modus*, is indeed the preferred designation for the categories into which the melody of plainchant can be classified. By way of demonstration, let us consider briefly the terminological usage of other ninth-century writings, in particular that of the early tonaries[9]—St. Riquier, Metz, Regino[10]—that of chapters 8 through 19 of Aurelian's *Musica disciplina,*[11] and that of the *Commemoratio brevis de tonis et psalmis modulandis.*[12] All of these are practical manuals for the singing of plainchant. All are surprisingly consistent in their use of terminology, employing terms that are drawn from the Byzantine theory of the *octoechos.*[13] As an illustration of the terminological usage in these works, several excerpts from the tonary of Regino of Prüm appear as Example 1.

In all the works mentioned one finds eight different melodic categories, called *toni*, each of which is identified by an intonation formula (NONANNEEANE, NOENIS, etc.).[14] Within these eight there are four primary categories, labeled *protus, deuterus, tritus,* and *tetrardus,* with two subcategories of each, called *authenticus* and *plagis* (or *plaga,* as in the middle of the lower right panel [fol. 49r] in Ex. 1). In addition, the tonaries supply one or more *differentiae* for each, indicated over the words *Seculorum amen.*[15] This last relates to the essentially practical function of tonaries—namely, the classification of antiphonal verse-chants in such a way that there might be a euphonious connection between the antiphon and its verses.[16] In none of these documents, including the primary corpus of Aurelian's *Musica disciplina,* does the word *modus* appear as a term designating melodic category; the term of choice is consistently *tonus.*

Viewed against the background we have just been describing, the use of *tonus* in the *Musica enchiriadis* can be seen as being completely consonant with the usage of its contemporaries. Returning to chapter 8 of the *enchiriadis,* the same chapter in which the author inveighs against the use of *tonus,* we are told that:

> When you have sung the first disposition, you will be able to recognize that the power of the first sound ⋎ creates the character of the first tone, which is called *protus autentus.* When you have sung the second, you will perceive the *deuterus* tone to be governed by the *deuterus* sound ⨍. Likewise considering the third you will see that the character of the *tritus* tone depends on the *tritus* sound *I* (etc.).[17]

Later on in this same chapter, the author gives examples of model melodies, one for each *tonus,* as examples of the four principal tones. He explains this as follows:

> In this manner they make use of the customary formulas . . . for investigating a tone and its character . . . As for example NOANNOEANE, NOEAGIS, and others, which we take not to be meaningful words, but rather syllables assigned to modulation.[18]

Fol. 45v.

Fol. 46r.

Fol. 49r.

Example 1. Excerpts from the Tonary of Regino of Prüm (From the facsimile edition of the manuscript Bruxelles, Bibliothèque Royale, 2750/65, reprinted in facsimile by E. de Coussemaker, ed., *Scriptorum de Musica medii aevi*, vol. 2 [Paris, 1867]).

We might recall here that Aurelian, perplexed by the Noannoeane formulas, asked a Greek to explain their meaning. The Greek, certainly a Byzantine, had replied that they were intrinsically meaningless, but that they contained the *modulatio tonorum.*[19]

Further examples could be adduced to show the close affinity of the *Musica enchiriadis*'s use of the term *tonus* with that of other ninth-century treatises. For now it should suffice to say, however, that its usage is not only entirely in keeping with that of contemporaneous treatises, but that it gives us in many ways the most detailed explication of the theory of *toni* as primary categories for the classification of plainchant. Why, then, does the author of the *Musica enchiriadis* state that his own usage is improper? And what could have been his source for *modus* as the preferred usage?

In our search to answer the latter question we are limited essentially to eight authors: Chalcidius,[20] Censorinus,[21] Vergil,[22] Fulgentius,[23] and Boethius[24]—all of whom are either quoted or paraphrased in the *Musica enchiriadis*—along with Martianus Capella,[25] Cassiodorus,[26] and Isidore of Seville,[27] whose works—along with those of Boethius—form the central corpus of ancient theory handed down to Carolingian writers on music.[28] Of these eight authors the only ones who use *modus* as a technical term in music are Chalcidius, Boethius, and Censorinus.[29] And of these, the only author to use *modus* in conjunction with *tonus* is Boethius.

In the fifteenth chapter of the fourth book of his *De musica,* Boethius makes this statement, ''Therefore, out of the species of the diapason consonance arise those things which are called modes, which they also name tropes or tones.''[30] He then describes these modes and gives them the names of Greek peoples, Dorian, Phrygian, Lydian, and so on.[31]

It would appear from the passage just quoted that Boethius conceived modes, tropes, and tones as one substance with three names. As one surveys the entire treatise, however, it becomes apparent that the three designations are not all equal. Throughout the work, Boethius uses the term *modus* to refer to what the ancient Greek theorists call τόνος or τρόπος, specifically in the sense of τρόπος συστηματικός[32] or transposition scale.

Except for its use as equivalent to *modus* or *tropus* in the first part of Bk. IV, ch. 15, the term *tonus* is used as the Latin equivalent of yet another meaning of the Greek τόνος, namely as ''interval'' or ''magnitude of sound.'' This is true even for Boethius's initial discussion of *tonus* in chapter 16 of the first book:

> If a pitch should be higher or lower than another pitch by a duple [proportion] the diapason consonance arises; if a pitch be higher or lower than another pitch by a sesquialtera proportion, or a sesquitertia, or a sesquioctave it produces the consonance diapente, diatessaron, or tone.[33]

After this, *tonus* is consistently used in the treatise to mean an interval whose magnitude is defined by the sesquioctave proportion, 9:8.

Boethius's distinction between *modus* as transposition scale and *tonus* as an interval mathematically defined within acoustic space was probably brought about by his desire to bring clarity to a term, τόνος, that had several different meanings in Greek. This was in turn necessitated by a need to define the divisions of acoustic space precisely in order to discuss the *symphoniae* or consonances which lie at the heart of Boethius's work. Chief among these are the Pythagorean consonances of fourth, fifth, and octave. These "vertical" relationships assumed their cardinal importance because of the nature of Boethius's treatise, which considers music as a part of the technical discipline of harmonics—the system of nomenclature, principles, and procedures which made possible the discussion of the abstract concept of *harmonia,* the joining of inherently dissimilar elements as one—or as Boethius puts it, "plurimorum adunatio et dissidentium consensio."[34] In order to keep *tonus* as a harmonic division of acoustic space, Boethius chose the Latin *modus* to project the Greek notion of τόνος as transposition scale.

We noted above that Boethius is the only ancient author to render the Greek τόνος or τρόπος as *modus*. Other authors, such as Martianus, use the cognates *tonus* or *tropus*. The use of the term *modus* thus assumes special importance as a kind of marker to Boethius and the harmonic theory his treatise contains. The appearance of *modus* in chapter 8 of the *Musica enchiriadis* points unequivocally toward Boethius. This link is reinforced by other aspects of the *Musica enchiriadis* itself.

As mentioned earlier, the term *tonus* appears in the first eight chapters of the *Musica enchiriadis* as the designation for melodic category, the usage common to ninth-century writings on music. These same chapters, however, also use *tonus* in a way not used in the main body of Aurelian's work or in the early tonaries: namely, as a vertical division of acoustic space. Example 2 displays the first occurrences of the term *tonus* in Chapter I of the *Musica enchiriadis,* as it is copied in one of the best manuscripts, Wolfenbüttel, Herzog-August Bibliothek, Gud. lat. 72, fol. 52. Here the author names the four principal sounds and their fixed intervals in relation to each other (see the topmost part of Example 2):

> The first and lowest is called *protos* or *archoos* in Greek; the second, *deuteros,* standing a tone from the first; the third, *tritos,* standing a semitone from the second; the fourth, *tetrardos,* standing a tone from the third. By continuous multiplication an infinity of these sounds is woven, and they continue succeeding each other four by four of the same structure, ascending and descending, until they stop.[35]

As one can see in Example 2 (and also in Schmid's edition), the division of acoustical space that results from the "continuous multiplication" of these sounds is vividly depicted by being set out vertically.

A bit further on in the same section, still in conjunction with the naming

Example 2. *Musica enchiriadis,* Chapter 1, excerpt (Wolfenbüttel, Herzog-August Bibliothek, MS. Gud. lat. 72, fol. 52).

of the four sounds and their grouping into tetrachords, we find the only other use of the term *modus* in the first eight chapters (see the last six lines in the left-hand column of Example 2): "The power of these four sounds determines the character of the eight modes, as will be discussed later in its place." This is, of course, a reference to chapter 8. The author then provides us an important clue as to whence *modus* came and why it is being used here: "Horum sociali diversitate tota adunatur armonia" (All *harmonia* is made one by their conjoined diversity).[36]

Our next encounter with *modus* is in chapter 8, in the passage quoted in the title of this paper. As mentioned earlier, however, the term *modus* does not appear again in that chapter. Instead, the term *tonus* is used—not just in its common meaning as melodic category, but also in its meaning as a discrete division of vertical, harmonic space (see Example 3). After specifying that the same melody should be copied four times, each version higher than the preceding one by a tone or semitone (as shown in Example 3), the anonymous author characterizes them and their effect by saying "In that the four representations are each separated by a tone or a semitone, that is by a *harmonic*

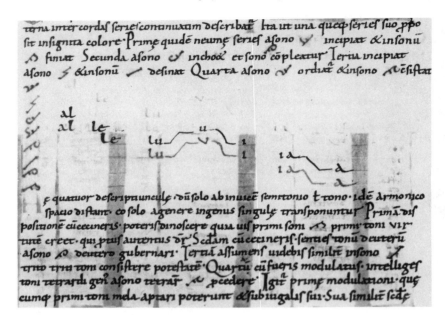

Example 3. *Musica enchiriadis,* Chapter 8, excerpt (Wolfenbüttel, Herzog-August Bibliothek, MS. Gud. lat. 72, fol. 53v).

interval, they are singularly transposed from genus to genus" (my italics).[37] Clearly, the vertical division of acoustic space into the intervals of tone and semitone is conceived here as a harmonic division.

After the hints he has dropped in chapters 1 and 8 about the rationale for *modus* rather than *tonus,* the author finally gives us the solution to the puzzle in chapter 9, which lays the terminological and conceptual foundations first for the study of the symphonies or consonances, then for the theory of organum:

> But from these preliminary exercises that one might call common, granted that they are first principles before understanding, we pursue *harmonic* theories by an easier path. *Harmonia is the suitable joining together of dissimilar pitches* (my italics).[38]

He then sets the vertical divisions of acoustic space necessary for the study of *harmonia:*

> *Tonus* is a fixed magnitude of space from sound to sound. And this interval of musical sounds, because it is in the sesquioctave proportion, is called by the Greek name *epogdous* (my italics).[39]

And since he has just defined *tonus* as a fixed magnitude of acoustic space, he now makes the definitive shift to *modus* as the designation for the melodic categories he had earlier referred to as *toni:*

> The *modes* or *tropes* are species of modulations, concerning which we have spoken above, such as *protos autentus* or *plagis, deuteros autentus* or *plagis,* or the Dorian, Phrygian, Lydian mode, and others, which are designations drawn from the names of peoples (my italics).[40]

From here, the *Musica enchiriadis* goes into the theory of symphonies or consonances, then proceeds to treat organum at the fourth, fifth, and octave, the Pythagorean consonances transmitted by Boethius. Throughout these later chapters, *tonus* is used consistently to mean "a fixed magnitude of space from sound to sound" (that is, a harmonic interval), while *modus* is used consistently to signify melodic category.

As the reader will have detected already, the fine hand of Boethius is highly evident here. We should recall that Boethius had discussed music as a harmonic science, based on precise divisions of acoustic space, through which the larger principles of *harmonia* could be approached. It was Boethius, moreover, who rigorously derived the mathematical proportions governing music, who restricted his application of *tonus* to the harmonic interval expressed by the proportion 9:8, and most importantly, who employed the term *modus* as the designation for the Greek transposition scales, which he named Dorian, Phrygian, Lydian, and so on.

There are yet other signs of the influence of Boethius in the *Musica enchiriadis*. As shown by Example 4 (see p. 156), when the anonymous author of the *enchiriadis* presents organum at the octave, he uses letter notation, associated with the Greater Perfect System in Boethius, rather than the Dasia notation with which the *Musica enchiriadis*'s own tone system is presented. Inasmuch as the *Musica enchiriadis* system contains augmented octaves (between B$^\flat$ and b$^\natural$, F and f$^\sharp$ using modern nomenclature) a shift to the Greater Perfect System was imperative for organum at the octave. Thus, as Calvin Bower pointed out in 1971, there are two different tone systems operative in this treatise.[41] One, the *Musica enchiriadis* system itself, was well suited for plainchant; the other, the Greater Perfect System, was better suited for organum at the octave and the fourth. More important for our purposes, though, the Greater Perfect System was the system which made possible the expounding of the principles of *harmonia,* with its related notions of consonance and dissonance. Those principles in turn were necessary for developing a theory of the vertical relationships between pitches that was essential for the discussion of organum. Since *tonus* had to be reserved as the designation for a fixed magnitude of vertical, acoustic space, the author of the *Musica enchiriadis* reintroduced Boethius's term *modus* as the preferred designation for melodic categories that were being called *toni*—albeit "abusive"—by him-

Musica enchiriadis (Schmid ed., p. 32)

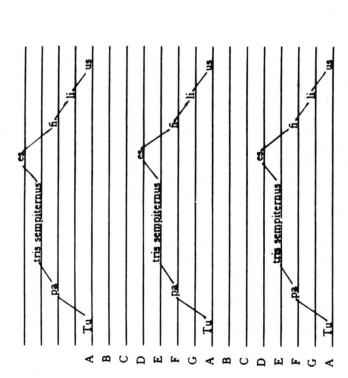

Boethius (Friedlein ed., p. 341)

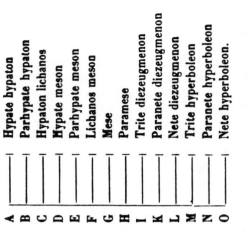

A	Hypate hypaton
B	Parhypate hypaton
C	Hypaton lichanos
D	Hypate meson
E	Parhypate meson
F	Lichanos meson
G	Mese
H	Paramese
I	Trite diezeugmenon
K	Paranete diezeugmenon
L	Nete diezeugmenon
M	Trite hyperboleon
N	Paranete hyperboleon
O	Nete hyperboleon.

Example 4: Organum at the Octave in the *Musica enchiriadis* (chapter 11) and the Letter Designations for the Greater Perfect System in Boethius, *De Institutione musica* (chapter 14, Book IV)

self and his contemporaries. Thus, the terminology of monophonic music has in the *Musica enchiriadis* been adjusted to accommodate the needs of polyphonic music founded on the principles of *harmonia,* and the "modi, quos abusive tonos dicimus" become the signal of a new conceptual mode for music itself.

Notes

1. The diatonic scale corresponds to the white keys on a modern piano. If one plays eight notes in succession, either ascending or descending—for example, from A to a—one will have defined one octave species. Repeating the process, but starting a note higher (B to b) will yield a second species of octave; starting a note higher still (C to c) will yield a third, and so on.

2. Hans Schmid, ed., *Musica et Scolica enchiriadis, una cum aliquibus tractatulis adiunctis,* Bayerische Akademie der Wissenschaften, Veröffentlichungen der Musikhistorischen Kommission, 3 (Munich: Verlag der Bayerischen Akademie der Wissenschaften, 1981). The treatise is also available in Martin Gerbert, *Scriptores ecclesiastici de musica sacra potissimum* ⟨hereafter cited as *GS*⟩, I (St. Blasien: Typis San-Blasianis, 1794), 152–73.

3. Schmid, 13.

4. The term *phthongus* is simply a transliteration of the Greek φθόγγος, which means "a musical sound," or what would usually be called "a tone" in English. One of the reasons the author of the *Musica enchiriadis* chose to use it here must have been to avoid confusion with the term *tonus* (tone) in the same sentence, which here signifies a classificational category for melody.

5. Schmid, 13.

6. The only other appearance of *modus* for *tonus* is in chapter I (Schmid, 5). See discussion on pp. 152–53 in the text.

7. See discussion on pp. 149–51 in the text.

8. For a discussion of the sources and concordant uses of concepts in the *Musica enchiriadis* see Nancy Catherine Phillips, "*Musica* and *Scolica enchiriadis:* The Literary, Theoretical, and Musical Sources" (Diss. New York University, 1984).

9. In its most common form, a tonary classifies antiphonal chants by means of the psalm tones and *differentiae* with which those chants are sung. For more detailed discussion, see notes 15 and 16.

10. St. Riquier, ed. M. Huglo in *Revue grégorienne,* XXXI (1952), 225–37; and in his *Les Tonaires: Inventaire, Analyse, Comparaison* (Paris: Société française de musicologie, 1971), 26–28; Metz, ed. W. Lipphardt, *Der karolingische Tonar von Metz,* Liturgiewissenschaftliche Quellen und Forschungen, 43 (Münster: Aschendorff, 1965); and Regino of Prüm, in facsimile edition in Coussemaker, *Scriptorum de*

musica medii aevi nova series (Paris: Durand, 1864–76; repr. 1931), vol. II, 3–73; hereafter cited as *CS*.

11. Ed. L. Gushee, *Aureliani Reomensis Musica Disciplina, Corpus Scriptorum de Musica* [hereafter cited as *CSM*] 21 (Rome: American Institute of Musicology, 1975); also in Gerbert, *GS* I, 28–63.

12. Ed. T. Bailey (Ottawa: University of Ottawa Press, 1979); also in *GS* I, 213–29, and Schmid, 157–78.

13. The system of eight *echoi* serves a function of melodic classification in Byzantine chant similar to that served by the eight tones or modes in the West. Presented in the singers' manuals, called *papadikai,* that often accompany the collection of psalms, hymns, and other chants known as the *Akolouthia,* the *echoi* are designated one through four (*protus, deuterus, tritus, tetartos*) authentic or one through four plagal. They are exemplified by means of intonation formulas (*enechemata*), short melodic phrases that both introduce the *echos* itself and embody some of its chief features. These formulas are set to meaningless syllables (*ananeanes, neanes, nana,* etc.) that are nonetheless specific to each *echos.* See Oliver Strunk, "Intonations and Signatures of the Byzantine Modes," *The Musical Quarterly,* 31 (1945): 339–55, reprinted in his *Essays on Music in the Byzantine World* (New York: W. W. Norton & Co., 1977), 19–36, and Jørgen Raasted, *Intonation Formulas and Modal Signatures in Byzantine Musical Manuscripts,* Monumenta Musicae Byzantinae, subsidia 7 (Copenhagen: Ejnar Munksgaard, 1966). A particularly clear presentation of the eight *echoi* is that given by the *papadike* in the manuscript Rome, Biblioteca Vaticana, Barberini, Gr. 300, ed. Lorenzo Tardo, *L'antica melurgia bizantina* (Grottaferrata: Scuola Tip. Italo Orientale "S. Nilo," 1938), 151–63. The relevant passages are translated in my article "On the Formation of a Medieval Theory of Mode," *Symposionsbericht* for the symposium "Die Formung einer europäischen musikalischen Kultur im Mittelalter," held in Kiel, W. Germany, June 25–29, 1985 (in press).

14. The intonation formulas in the West seem to have been in most respects analogous to their Eastern counterparts, the *enechemata* of Byzantine chant, although there were differences as well; see Terence Bailey, *The Intonation Formulae of Western Chant* (Toronto: Pontifical Institute of Medieval Studies, 1974). Their primary function in the West seems to have been didactic, based on their embodiment of salient melodic features of their respective tonal or modal categories. They also served a very direct practical function in locating the characteristic final pitch of the tone or mode in relation to the pitches surrounding it. A similar function for modern, tonal music is served in the way the song "Do, Re, Mi" from *The Sound of Music* locates the pitch *Do* as the tonal center in relation to the surrounding pitches *re, mi, fa, sol, la,* and *ti.* Here, too, the syllables are intrinsically meaningless; the song itself imparts meaning to them via a modern version of glossing ("Do(e), a deer, a female deer. . ."). Neither the Byzantine *Neanes* nor the Western *Noeane* syllables were fortunate enough to have an Oscar Hammerstein to gloss them. They remained meaningless throughout the tenure of their use.

15. See particularly the lower section, Fol. 49r, of Example 1, *Divisio tertia (prim)i toni* (on the left) and *Plaga Proti* (on the right). A description of the musical

function of the *differentia* within a psalm tone appears in n. 16. Since the Lesser Doxology (*"Gloria Patri, et Filio, et Spiritui Sancto, sicut erat in principio, et nunc, et semper, et in saecula seculorum. Amen"*) forms the conclusion to each performance of a psalm, the *differentia* of the psalm tone is always sung over the words *"Seculorum. Amen."* These words could therefore serve as a simple means of conveying the *differentia* to the singer. In order to save manuscript space, these words are usually indicated by their vowel sounds alone: E U O U A E.

16. In the performance of psalms during the canonical hours of the Office, consecutive verses of the psalm as well as the concluding Lesser Doxology (*Gloria Patri*) are sung to one of eight simple melodies known as psalm tones, each consisting of an opening melodic phrase or *incipit,* a reciting pitch or *tenor,* upon which most of the text is sung, and the terminating melodic phrase known as the *differentia* (cf. n. 15). The psalm tone itself is framed by a short musical piece known as an antiphon. The practice can be diagrammed as follows:

Antiphon-(a)-Psalm tone ⟨incipit, recitation, differentia⟩-(b)-Antiphon

Since many different antiphon melodies can be sung in conjunction with a single psalm tone, it was necessary to have an efficient system for (a) moving from the end of the antiphon into the beginning of the psalm tone, and (b) moving from the end of the psalm tone into the beginning of the antiphon. The choice of psalm tone was dictated by the final pitch and range of the antiphon; inasmuch as there were only four possible finals (D, E, F, G) the incipit of each psalm tone could be, and was, fixed. Since antiphon melodies had many different ways of opening, however, the ending of the psalm tone had to be flexible in order to accommodate a wide array of opening formulas. The solution to this need for flexibility was the use of alternate endings, or *differentiae* (cf. n. 15), for several of the psalm tones that were sung with large numbers of antiphons. The eight psalm tones with their *differentiae* could thus form a ready means of classification and even subclassification for the repertoire of over 600 antiphons that were sung with them in the Middle Ages (cf. n. 9).

Since there were two points (''a'' and ''b'' in the diagram above) at which the antiphon had to connect with its psalm-tone, and since in the ninth century the antiphon was sung after each verse of the psalm, the smoothness of the connection was obviously of great practical, as well as aesthetic, importance: hence the emphasis by several medieval writers on the importance of euphony in joining an antiphon to its verse. A particularly good example of such discussions occurs in the treatise *De tonis* found in the manuscript Rome, Biblioteca Vaticana, Pal. lat. 235, fol. 39v, ed. Peter Wagner, ''Un piccolo trattato sul canto ecclesiastico in un manoscritto del secolo x-xi,'' *Rassegna gregoriana,* III (1904): 481–84. The relevant passages are translated in my article ''The *Parapteres: Nothi* or Not?'' *The Musical Quarterly,* LXVIII (1982): 49–50.

17. ''Primam dispositionem cum ceceneris, poteris dinoscere, quia vis primi soni Υ *primi toni* virtutem creet, qui *protus autentus* dicitur. Secundam cum ceceneris, senties *tonum deuterum* a sono Ϝ deutero gubernari. Tertiam assumens videbis similiter in sono *I* trito *triti toni* consistere potestatem'' (my italics); Schmid, 15.

18. ''Ad hunc modum consuetis utuntur modulis ad investigandam toni cuiusque vim eadem ratione compositis . . . utpote NOANNOEANE, NOEAGIS, et cetera,

quae putamus non tam significativa esse verba quam syllabas modulationi attributas'';
Schmid, 19–20.

19. See L. Gushee, ed., *CSM*, 21, ch. 9, 84.

20. *Calcidii Commentarius in Timaeum Platonis*, ed. J. H. Waszink, in *Timaeus a Calcidio translatus commentarioque instructus*, vol. IV of *Plato Latinus* in the *Corpus Platonicum Medii Aevi*, ed. Raymundus Klibansky (London: Warburg Institute, 1975). See also J. H. Waszink, "Studien zum Timaioskommentar des Calcidius," *Philosophia Antiqua*, 12 (Leiden: E. J. Brill, 1964).

21. *Censorini de die natali liber ad Q. Caerellium: accedi anonymi cuiusdam epitoma disciplinarum (fragmentum Censorini)*, ed. Nicolaus Sallmann, Bibliotheca scriptorum graecorum et romanorum Teubneriana (Leipzig: Teubner Verlag, 1983).

22. *P. Vergili Maronis Aeneidos Libri XII*, ed. R. A. B. Mynors, *P. Vergili Maronis Opera* (Oxford: The Clarendon Press, 1969).

23. *Mitologiarum libri III*, ed. R. Helm, with addenda by Jean Preaux, in *Fabii Planciadis Fulgentii V.C. Opera*, Bibliotheca scriptorum graecorum et romanorum Teubneriana (Leipzig: Teubner Verlag, 1970).

24. *De Institutione musica*, ed. Gottfried Friedlein, *Boetii De institutione arithmetica libri duo et De institutione musica libri quinque* (Leipzig, 1867; reprint Frankfurt: Minerva, 1966).

25. *De Nuptiis Philologiae et Mercurii*, ed. James Willis, *Martianus Capella*, Bibliotheca scriptorum graecorum et romanorum Teubneriana (Leipzig: Teubner Verlag, 1983).

26. *Cassiodori Senatoris Institutiones*, ed. R. A. B. Mynors, (Oxford: The Clarendon Press, 1937).

27. *Isidori Hispalensis episcopi Etymologiarum sive originum Libri XX*, ed. W. M. Lindsay (Oxford: The Clarendon Press, 1911).

28. On this point, see Michel Huglo, "Le développement du vocabulaire de l'*Ars Musica* à l'époque carolingienne," *Latomus*, 34 (1975): 131–51.

29. Censorinus may not belong in this list. The only use of *modus* as a musical *terminus technicus* among the works ascribed to him occurs in the *Fragmenta*, whose authenticity is not certain. Sallman refers to the author of the *Fragmenta* as a *quidam anonymus*. Cf. Sallman, n. 21.

30. "Ex diapason igitur consonantiae speciebus existunt, qui appellantur *modi*, quos eosdem tropos vel *tonos* nominant" (my italics); Friedlein, 341.

31. Ibid., 342.

32. This is the term used by Aristides Quintilianus in his discussion of the τόνοι in chapter 10 of his *De Musica*. See *Aristidis Quintiliani de musica libri tres*, ed. R. P. Winnington-Ingram, Bibliotheca scriptorum graecorum et romanorum Teubneriana (Leipzig: Teubner Verlag, 1963), 20.

33. "Nam si vox voce duplo sit acuta vel gravis, diapason consonantia fiet, si vox voce sesqualtera proportione sit vel sesquitertia vel sesquioctava acutior graviorque, diapente vel diatessaron vel *tonum* consonantiam reddet" (my italics); Friedlein, 201–02.

34. Boethius, *De Institutione arithmetica,* II, 32. Friedlein, op. cit., 126. For an excellent, concise discussion of *armonia* in the ancient Greek music-theoretical tradition, see Thomas Mathiesen, "Problems of Terminology in Ancient Greek Theory: "APMONÍA," in *Festival Essays for Pauline Alderman* (Provo, Utah: Brigham Young University Press, 1976), 3–18.

35. Cf. Schmid, 4, where the text is laid out just as it appears in the manuscripts.

36. Cf. Ibid., 5.

37. Hae quattuor descriptiunculae, dum solo ab invicem semitonio vel tono id est *armonico spacio* distant, eo solo a genere in genus singulae transponuntur" (my italics); Ibid., 15.

38. "Sed his veluti praeexercitaminibus quibusdam ac vilioribus licet iniciis ante cognitis dehinc faciliori via *armonicas* prosequimur *rationes. Armonia est diversarum vocum apta coadunatio*" (my italics); Ibid., 20.

39. "*Tonus* est spacii legitima magnitudo a sono in sonum. Hocque spacium musicorum sonorum, quia in sesquioctava proportione est, Greco nomine dicitur epogdous" (my italics); Ibid., 21.

40. "*Modi* vel *tropi* sunt species modulationum, de quibus supra dictum est, ut *protos autentus* vel *plagis, deuteros autentus* vel *plagis,* sive modus Dorius, Frigius, Lidius, et ceteri, qui ex gentium vocabulis sortiti sunt nomina" (my italics); Ibid., 21.

41. Paper presented to the Annual Meeting of the American Musicological Society, Chapel Hill and Durham, North Carolina, in 1971.

13. The Voice in the Stone: the Verse Inscriptions of Ste.-Foy of Conques and the Date of the Tympanum

CALVIN B. KENDALL

The remarkable Last Judgment tympanum of the basilica of Ste.-Foy of Conques[1] is situated uncertainly in the history of Romanesque art. Estimates as to when it was carved range widely. Most art historians date it sometime in the second quarter of the twelfth century.[2] The most recent study puts it "close to 1150."[3] If it is as late as this, it falls outside the dynamic period of development in Romanesque art. However, a few scholars believe that the tympanum belongs to the first quarter of the century.[4] The question is crucial, because the earlier date involves an implicit claim that the tympanum of Conques is one of the innovating prototypes of Romanesque monumental sculpture, on a par with the now-destroyed Christ in Majesty tympanum of Cluny III (ca. 1106–1112) and the Ascension tympanum of St.-Sernin of Toulouse (ca. 1112–1115).

I propose to examine a neglected body of material—verse inscriptions which appear in a variety of contexts at Conques, on reliquaries, on tomb sculpture, on the lintels of doorways, as well as on the tympanum itself—for evidence relating to the date of the tympanum. These verses belong to a common Romanesque tradition, yet when they are read against the background of that tradition, contrastive *differences* stand out which allow us to interpret them as the work of a single poet who lived early in the twelfth century and who at one point collaborated with the master sculptor who carved the tympanum.[5]

Conques is one of the great pilgrimage churches built along the routes to Compostella. Work on it began as early as 1042, and it may have been essentially completed by about 1110.[6] Construction proceeded in the usual way from the apse in the east toward the nave in the west. The limestone and schist west facade was built in the last phases of construction.

This sequence is important because of its bearing on the date of the tympanum. The tympanum, which is carved in the same yellow limestone

Figure 1. Tympanum. (Photograph by Calvin B. Kendall)

used for most of the western part of the church, extends the full width of the nave, from tower to tower, and supports the wall above (see fig. 1). The blocks of the tympanum are an integral part of the facade.[7] It would indeed have been strange, as one scholar observes, if the builders had put up the whole structure of the tympanum ''without having any idea of the subject, or of the artist who would treat it.''[8] Further, the fortunes of Conques reached their zenith in the second half of the eleventh century and declined in the later years of Abbot Boniface (ca. 1107–1125).[9] After about 1120 the abbey might have been hard pressed to support a large workshop such as the tympanum master would have required. There are, therefore, practical grounds for assigning the carving of the tympanum as nearly as possible to the time of the completion of the facade.

Church portals and sculptures were often adorned with verses in the Romanesque period. The distribution of the surviving examples indicates that the tradition operated within a broad band stretching from the Lombard plain in northern Italy across the southern two-thirds of France and the northern regions of Spain almost out to Compostella. Sculptors carved verses on historiated capitals, on the socles of statues, on keystones, on banderoles and books held by relief figures, and on arches above or on the background beside relief figures.[10] Above all, sculptors found that the Romanesque tympanum, which was an innovation of the last two decades of the eleventh century,[11] provided an ideal space for their verses.[12]

These verses are invariably in Latin. Poets used only two meters—the dactylic hexameter and the pentameter. With rare exceptions,[13] they rhymed their verses. Leonine rhyme—that is, internal rhyme between the last or last two syllables before the obligatory caesura (the word break in the middle of the third foot) and the last or last two syllables of the line—was fashionable during the Romanesque period, and it is the most common type of rhyme in the verse inscriptions, although disyllabic end-rhyme is also found.[14]

The themes of the inscriptions vary. Sometimes the verses do little more than identify or describe the sculptures. Artists or their patrons may have felt the need to assist churchgoers to recognize what they saw. According to William of Tyre, the Duke of Lorraine passed the time on his way to the First Crusade in 1099 by having priests explain the images which he saw in the churches.[15] Often, however, the verses complement the sculpture in a more significant way. One frequent theme is an invitation to penitence. The voice in the stone urges the pilgrim to change his ways before entering the church.

There are twelve verses inscribed on the tympanum of Conques—more than on any other tympanum that now exists. All of the verses display disyllabic leonine rhyme. They can easily be read from a normal viewing position in front of the church. The letters are for the most part large capitals, carefully formed, equal in size and very legible. There are no superfluous ornamentations, relatively few abbreviations, and only a handful of joined letters. These are characteristics of the epigraphy of the second half of the eleventh and the beginning of the twelfth century.[16]

Christ, seated in majesty in front of the cross, dominates the center of the tympanum. A procession of men and women, led by the Virgin Mary and St. Peter, approaches him on one side. On the other, four angels keep a crowd of damned souls at a distance. An unusual gable-shaped double lintel supports the tympanum. On the left side of the lintel is the orderly Heavenly City. Abraham sits beneath the central arcade holding two souls in his bosom. On the right is the chaotic realm of Hell dominated by the grotesque figure of Satan.

Horizontal inscription bands articulate the various parts of the tympanum. On the upper left, the inscription above the procession of men and women approaching Christ (see fig. 2) reads:

(1) SANCTORVM CETVS STAT XPISTO IVDICE LETVS[17]
The assembly of saints stands joyfully before Christ the Judge.

Although the verse is appropriate to the sculpture, two discrepancies between text and image suggest that the master of the tympanum and the poet indulged in some sly humor.

First, the verse describes the people as an "assembly of saints." However, only Mary and Peter at the head of the line and the four small figures at the rear have halos. The absence of halos on the figures in between indicates that these were persons, apparently connected with the history of the abbey of

Figure 2. Tympanum, upper left. (Photograph by Eleanor K. Kendall)

Conques, whose sainthood was not yet officially recognized. Of course we may assume from their position on the tympanum that the abbey never doubted their ultimate status.

Second, the verse characterizes this assembly (*cetus*) in an emphatic leonine rhyme as "joyful" (*letus*). Most of the saints and prospective saints in the assembly appear to be joyful or at least confident. But not the crowned figure in the middle. This must be one of the imperial benefactors of the abbey—possibly Charlemagne.[18] His hangdog look and shuffling stance, betraying a sadly burdened conscience, are amusingly at odds with the caption. An abbot of Conques leads him firmly by the hand and his attendants carry tokens of his great benefactions to the abbey. If he cannot muster the joy of his companions at this awesome moment, the message of the tympanum is nevertheless clear: his patronage of Conques will see him through in the end.[19]

The corresponding inscription band on the upper right reads:

(2) HOMNES PERVERSI SIC SVNT IN TARTARA MERS[I]
Thus wicked men are plunged into Hell.

The edge of the block on which the band was carved apparently broke off; the gap was filled with a piece of grayer stone. The final *i* of *mersi* was not carved in this new piece, but the leonine rhyme leaves no doubt about the missing letter. *Perversi* (wicked) neatly expresses the physical turning away, the perversion, of the damned from the path of salvation. Pilgrims to Conques whose daily task it was to keep to the path, to avoid "wandering by the way," like the Wife of Bath, could ponder demons tormenting their perverted victims in the most terrible ways in the sculpture. *Homnes* (men) is sometimes misleadingly corrected to *homines* in printed texts of the inscriptions. It is a measure of the poet's metrical virtuosity and linguistic sophistication that he syncopated the middle vowel of the anapestic *homines* to secure the initial long syllable which dactylic hexameter verse demands. Presumably the vernacular form of the word made this syncopation acceptable to his ear.[20] The word *Tartara* is also revealing. Roman poets borrowed the masculine form *Tartarus* from Greek as a synonym for Hades. Occasionally they substituted the Greek neuter plural form *Tartara* for the sake of the meter.[21] Whether the Conques poet got it from classical Latin or from medieval sources, his assured use of this Grecism is indicative of the cultural level of the abbey of Conques.

These inscriptions (1 and 2) are high from the ground and remote from the viewer. Yet they are as visible as the ones below them. To avoid crowding, the poet put these two verses into the shortest possible standard hexameter form of thirteen syllables—spondees in every foot but the fifth.[22] Evidently, he composed his verses with full knowledge of the spatial requirements of the tympanum and of the visual effect on the viewer.

The middle inscription band extends the full width of the tympanum. It is slightly lengthened by a curious jog on the left side. Two leonine elegiac couplets are symmetrically balanced on either side of the center axis. The couplet on the left side above the Heavenly Jerusalem reads:

(3) SIC DATVR ELECTIS AD CELI GAVDIA V[E]CTIS
     GLORIA PAX REQVIES PERPETVVSQue DIES
     Thus is given to the chosen ones, who have been borne to the joys of
     Heaven, glory, peace, rest, and eternal light.

This couplet has never been correctly transcribed. The letter between the *v* and *c* of *vectis* is lost. Mérimée thought the word was *cunctis*.[23] Modern scholars uniformly read *vinctis*. At a casual glance there appear to be traces of a vertical, followed by a right-sloping bar, which may be the cause of the misreading. These are, in fact, two cracks in the stone, made by a chip which has been filled in (see fig. 2). In any case, *vinctis* cannot be right. It makes poor sense ("the chosen ones, united for the joys of Heaven"), and it would be the only exception among all the inscribed verses at Conques, both on the tympanum and elsewhere, to the poet's consistent use of disyllabic leonine rhymes. *Vectis* restores both sense and rhyme. I believe I can see traces of an *e* in red paint in the chip. If so, perhaps an early restorer understood the governing convention. Text and image correspond with charming naiveté in

Figure 3. Tympanum, lower right. (Photograph by Calvin B. Kendall)

the lamps of a style peculiar to Rouergue[24] that hang beneath the arcades of the Heavenly City and provide the eternal light.

Another Grecism is found in the couplet on the right side above Hell (see fig. 3), which reads:

> (4) PENIS INIVSTI CRVCIANTVR[25] IN IGNIBVS VSTI
>   DEMONAS ATQue TREMVNT PERPETVOQue GEMVNT
>   The unjust, burned in fires, are tormented by punishments, and they
>   shudder at the demons and groan endlessly.

The regular accusative plural form of the word for demons (*demones*) is cretic (long, short, long) and therefore cannot be used in a hexameter or pentameter verse. In order to get around this problem and to secure an initial dactyl, the poet adopted the Greek accusative plural in (short) -*as*.

Two leonine hexameter couplets are inscribed on the angled slopes above the Heavenly City on the left and Hell on the right. The former reads:

> (5) CASTI[26] PACIFICI MITES PIETATIS AMICI
>   SIC STANT GAVDENTES SECVRI NIL METVENTES
>   The chaste, the peace-loving, the gentle ones, the lovers of piety—
>   thus they remain rejoicing, secure, fearing nothing.

And the latter:

(6) FVRES MENDACES FALS[I][27] CVPIDIQVE RAPACES
SIC SVNT DAMPNATI CVNCTI SIMVL ET SCELERATI
Thieves, liars, hypocrites, and the rapaciously avaricious—thus they
are condemned and defiled at the same moment.

The final set of verses—another leonine hexameter couplet—is inscribed on the lower edge of the double lintel. The lintel is supported by a broad central pier and spans two doors. Unlike the other verses which refer to the scenes of the tympanum, this couplet is the voice of the church addressing the pilgrims who are about to pass through its portals:

(7) O PECCATORES TRANSMVTETIS NISI MORES
IVDICIVM DVRVM VOBIS SCITOTE FVTVRVM
Sinners, if you do not change your ways, know that a hard judgment
will be upon you.

It differs also from the other verses in that it is not symmetrically positioned. The couplet extends from the left edge of the lintel approximately two-thirds of the way across to the right. The portion of the lintel above the right door is blank, although traces of light blue paint which seem to form letters can just be made out. Possibly another verse was once painted here.[28] It is difficult to believe that this asymmetry is accidental. The final word *futurum* is stretched out so that the inscription reaches to, but not beyond, the gate of Hell above it. Since it addresses the pilgrims entering the church, the obvious conclusion is that they entered on the left. The visual image of Hell above the right portal may have suggested too powerfully an association with hell-mouth to have permitted it to be used for the pilgrims' entrance.

There can be no reasonable doubt that the poet worked closely with the master of the tympanum.[29] If we knew when the poet wrote, it would give us an approximate date for the tympanum.

In addition to the verses of the tympanum, a number of other leonine inscriptions survive at Conques. When Prosper Mérimée visited the abbey in June 1837 in his capacity as Inspector General of the Historic Monuments of France, he saw two doors with leonine inscriptions on their lintels. One of the lintels is now displayed with the treasure of Conques. It reads:

(8) HAS BENEDIC VALVAS QVI MVNDVM REX BONE SALVAS
ET NOS DE PORTIS SIMVL OMNES ERIPE MORTIS
Bless these doors, good King, you who save the world, and at the
same time snatch us all from the gates of death.

In a report to the Minister of the Interior, Mérimée remarked of it, ''I have transcribed [these] verses which can be read above a ruined door which opened into the cloister, but I do not know to what part of the monument it led.''[30]

Mérimée did not give details about the condition or situation of the other portal, except to say that he was puzzled as to the function of the room to which it led.[31] The lintel is now exhibited in the west walk of the cloister (see fig. 4). It is gable-shaped, like the double lintel of the tympanum. The horizontal and vertical guidelines for the inscription are visible. The inscription is carefully laid out so that the two verses stop precisely at the right vertical guideline. The inscription implies that the chamber behind this portal was a kind of storage room connected with the monastic school:

> (9) ISTE MAGISTRORVM LOCVS EST SIMVL ET PVERORVM
> MITTVNT QVANDO VOLVNT HIC RES QVAS PERDERE NOLVNT
> This is the place both of the masters and the boys. When they wish,
> they send here the things which they do not want to lose.

Both portals can be plausibly associated with the construction of the cloister.

The tomb of Abbot Bego gives us a fixed point of reference. Bego III was the last of the great eleventh-century abbots of Conques. Under his rule and that of his predecessors Odolric (before 1031–1065) and Stephen II (ca. 1065–1087), the abbey reached the summit of its prosperity and influence. Bego was appointed ca. 1087 and with one brief hiatus remained in his post until his death sometime between October 1106 and July 1107.[32] His tomb is now placed in a niche in the exterior south wall of the nave. A bricked-up door behind the tomb shows that this was not its original emplacement. Doubtless, like some other great abbots of the end of the eleventh century (e.g., Abbot Durand at Moissac), Bego was buried in the cloister. The nineteenth-century architect who finished dismantling the cloister probably moved the tomb to its present location.[33] In all likelihood, the tomb dates from ca. 1107, the year of Bego's death. The sarcophagus itself has disappeared, but the base, the end columns, and a sculpted group of Christ in Majesty seated between Ste.-Foy and Abbot Bego remain.[34] Two green marble plaques are

Figure 4. Storage-room lintel. (Photograph by Calvin B. Kendall)

set into the wall on either side of the sculpted group. These carry the carved epitaph in leonine hexameters:

(10) HIC EST ABBA SITVS DIVINA LEGE PERITVS
      VIR DOMINO GRATVS DE NOMINE BEGO VOCATVS
      HOC PERAGENS CLAVSTRVM QVOD VERSVS TENDIT AD
         AVSTRVM
      SOLLERTI CVRA [BONA *suprascript*] GESSIT ET ALTERA PLVRA
      HIC EST LAVDANDVS PER SECVLA VIR VENERANDVS   (5)
      VIVAT IN ETERNVM REGEM LAVDANDO SVPERNVM
      Here is buried an abbot, skilled in divine law, a man pleasing to God,
      who was named Bego. He completed this cloister which extends to the
      south and accomplished many other useful works, all with expert
      care. This man should be venerated and praised through the ages.
      May he live forever, praising the King on high.

The phrase *abba situs* in the first line has always been misread as *abbas situs*. *Abbas* is the regular form of the nominative, but it spoils the meter. The poet deliberately substituted the rare form *abba* in order to secure a necessary short syllable.[35]

Conques possesses one of the greatest surviving medieval French treasures. Among the items from the Romanesque period are four reliquaries which are ornamented with leonine verses: a reliquary (perhaps of the true cross) called *the A of Charlemagne,* a reliquary monstrance called *the Lantern of Bego,* another reliquary of the true cross called *the Reliquary of Pope Pascal,* and the coffer of the relics of Ste.-Foy.

The A of Charlemagne is a triangular frame covered in silver gilt. Inscriptions run along the outer surface of either arm. The inscription on the right arm is fragmentary[36]; the word *crux* suggests that the reliquary contained a piece of the true cross. The inscription on the left arm reads:

(11) ABBAS FORMAVIT BEGO[37] RELIQVIASQVE LO[CAVIT][38]
      Abbot Bego fashioned (this reliquary) and put relics (in it).

The Lantern of Bego is shaped like an antique funerary monument. It may have been designed to hold a skull. The reliquary is covered in silver gilt. There are inscriptions on the circular band around the cupola, and on three of the four faces of the square base. Regrettably, none of the inscriptions is completely intact. From what can now be seen, and has been reported, I believe that the inscription on the circular band around the cupola probably consisted of two leonine hexameters.[39] On the base of the reliquary beneath a medallion of Samson wrestling the lion (Judges 14:5) appears the inscription:

(12) SIC NOSTER DAVID[40] S[ANCTVS (?) SA]TANAN SVPERA[V]IT[41]
      Thus our holy (?) David conquered Satan.

The spelling *Satanan* suggests that the poet took *Satan* to be a Greek form and therefore gave it a Greek accusative ending.[42] The inscriptions remaining on two other faces of the base are fragmentary. One is the beginning, the other is the end of a hexameter verse.[43] We may be sure that these too were leonines. Gaillard assigns the reliquary to the "end of the eleventh century."[44]

The Reliquary of Pope Pascal acquired its present form in the fifteenth century. The plaque on its face depicting the Crucifixion, with Mary and John, was perhaps originally made to be the cover of a book.[45] On its socle is a long prose inscription which says, "In the year of the Lord's incarnation 1100 the lord pope Pascal II sent from Rome these relics of the Cross of Christ and of his tomb and of many saints."[46] An inscription at the base of the plaque on its face reads:

(13) ME FIERI IVSSIT BEGO CLEMENS CVI DOMINVS SIT
      Bego ordered me to be made; may the Lord be merciful to him.

It is unusual to find a leonine rhyme spreading over two words: *iussit/dominus sit*. The poet may have been in a playful mood. Because of the composite nature of the reliquary, the inscription on the socle cannot be used to date this verse. But the reference to Bego puts it between ca. 1087 and 1107.

The coffer of the relics of Ste.-Foy is a rectangular box ornamented with thirty-one medallions, two of which have circular inscriptions around their bases. The first reads:

(14) SCRINIA CONCHARVM MONSTRANT OPVS VNDIQVE CLARVM[47]
      The coffers of Conques display brilliant work everywhere.

And the second:

(15) HOC ORNAMENTVM BONE SIT FACII MONIMENTVM
      May this ornament be a memorial of Boniface.

Bone . . . facii is tmesis for *Bonefacii*. It can be compared with the splitting of the leonine rhyme in (13). Boniface, who succeeded Bego as abbot of Conques, ruled from ca. 1107 to 1125. The coffer must fall within these limits.

This body of inscriptions from the tympanum and from buildings and artifacts known to have been constructed or fashioned at Conques in the late eleventh and twelfth centuries adds up to twenty-eight hexameter[48] and two pentameter verses.

The question is, were these verses the work of one man or of several? It is worth asking, because if one poet wrote them all, then we have evidence for the date of the tympanum.

In my judgment, the case for single authorship is overwhelming. The verses are of a piece, they have the same tone, the same quirks of style. The poet (to speak of him in the singular) was an accomplished Latinist and a thoroughly competent versifier who could express himself clearly in meter and rhyme. He must have known a little Greek.[49] Certain personal qualities shine through. For all the sternness of the verses on the tympanum, one senses good humor, a playful spirit, certainly a love of clever verbal combinations.

Let me back up these impressions with some examples. To put my observations in a context, I will compare the verses of Conques with the leonine hexameters inscribed on thirteen other tympana in France—thirty verses in all.[50] The Conques poet has two favorite ways of bridging the fourth and fifth feet of the hexameter. Both involve a connective. He twice adds the enclitic -*que* to an anapestic or choriambic form (*cupidique*, tympanum [6], *reliquiasque*, A of Charlemagne [11][51]) and twice uses the anapestic phrase *simul et* (*simul et scelerati*, tympanum [6], *simul et puerorum*, lintel to storage room [9]). There is only one instance of an anapestic form plus -*que*[52] and none of *simul et* among the non-Conques verses.

There are two Grecisms on the tympanum (*Tartara* [2], *Demonas* [4, pentameter]) and one on the Lantern of Bego (*Satanan* [12]). No Grecisms appear among the non-Conques verses.

The Conques poet employs unusual forms for the sake of the meter (*Homnes* [2], *Tartara* [2], *Demonas* [4] on the tympanum; *abba* [10] on the tomb of Bego; *Bone . . . facii* [15] on the coffer of Ste.-Foy). There are no comparable forms in any of the non-Conques verses.

Such stylistic features may not rule out the possibility of imitation. But there is a different feature which, when taken with the above, is decisive for single authorship. A masculine caesura in the fifth foot is the metrical signature of the Conques poet. On the tympanum we find two final tetrasyllables:

nil ‖ *metuentes* (5)
et ‖ *scelerati* (6),

and one pair of final disyllables:

transmutetis ‖ *nisi mores* (7).

On the cloister lintel there is a pair of final disyllables:

Rex ‖ *bone salvas* (8),

and on the storage-room lintel, a final tetrasyllable:

et ‖ *puerorum* (9).

There is a final tetrasyllable on the tomb of Bego:

> *vir* ‖ *venerandus* (10.5).

Among the various pieces in the treasure, there are two tetrasyllables. On the Lantern of Bego:

> *Satanan* ‖ *superavit* (12),

and on the coffer of Ste.-Foy:

> *facii* ‖ *monimentum* (15).

And finally there is a combination of a trisyllable and a monosyllable on the Reliquary of Pope Pascal:

> *cui* ‖ *Dominus sit* (13).

This caesura is purely a word break; it has no expressive or rhetorical function. It is not a caesura which is commented on in medieval manuals of verse composition.[53] There is no reason to suppose that a master would have directed the attention of his pupils to it, or that they should have singled out this feature to imitate. The masculine caesura in the fifth foot occurs *nine* times in twenty-six hexameter lines of Conques (thirty-five percent). In contrast, there are *three* such caesuras in the thirty non-Conques verses (ten percent).[54] What makes this caesura truly revealing is not its frequency, but its even distribution throughout all the hexameters of Conques—on the tympanum, on both lintels, on the tomb of Bego, and on three of the four pieces in the treasure. The caesura must be the unconscious mannerism of one individual.

A less striking metrical characteristic of the Conques poet is his marked preference for a spondee in the second foot. There are only three second-foot dactyls among twenty-seven hexameters: one on the tympanum (5), one on the storage-room lintel (9), and one on the tomb of Bego (10.1). In contrast, there are seven second-foot dactyls in the non-Conques verses, and seventeen in the first thirty lines of Vergil's First Eclogue. (The search for leonine rhymes explains why the number of spondees in all the medieval inscriptions is greater than in Vergil. A closed penultimate syllable in the rhyme at line-end precludes a second-foot dactyl; a spondee can always be used.)

The conclusion that one man composed all the leonine inscriptions at Conques permits an inference about the date of the tympanum based on what we know of the dates of the other verses. The two lintels have not been precisely dated, but they seem to be connected with the completion of the cloister under Bego.[55] The tomb of Bego can be dated very nearly to 1107.

Three of the four items from the treasure belong to the time of Bego (ca. 1087–1107). The prose inscription on the Reliquary of Pope Pascal proves that fragments of the true cross and other relics arrived at Conques in 1100. Could this event have been the inspiration for the selection of the theme of Last Judgment for the tympanum, which permitted the tympanum master to feature so prominently the cross? It was in any case the probable occasion for the creation of the A of Charlemagne, and it may have been the stimulus for a new workshop which created several reliquaries and other objects.[56] This workshop continued its activities into the time of Boniface with the fabrication of the coffer of Ste.-Foy. However, the coffer is the only twelfth-century piece in the treasure which is positively dated after Bego's death.[57] The concentration of the other surviving pieces in the period before 1107 makes a date early in the abbacy of Boniface seem likely for this one. We can assign the peak years of the workshop with some assurance to the decade 1100–1110.

In summary, there is indisputable evidence that the Conques poet was active from about 1100 to about 1110. The twenty-year span 1095–1115 may be regarded as the probable limits within which all of the verses except those of the tympanum were written. Monasteries, like universities, are by nature conservative. The responsibility for composing these verses would no doubt have devolved upon an older master in the monastic school. If the poet were at least thirty years old in 1100, it is certainly possible that he might have been writing verses twenty-five or thirty years later in 1125 or 1130, but the odds are against it.[58] In light of the evidence, I think that the close collaboration of the poet with the tympanum master is most likely to have taken place sometime between 1105 and 1115. If it did, then the design and at least a substantial portion of the carving of the tympanum probably belong to this same ten-year period.

Appendix
Disyllabic leonine hexameters on tympana in France

(1) Cuncta Deus feci homo factus cuncta refeci.   (Autry-Issards)

(2) Omnia dispono solus meritosque corono
Quos scelus exercet me iudice pena coercet.   (Autun)

(3) Quisque resurget ita quem non trahit impia vita
Et lucebit ei sine fine lucerna diei.   (Autun)

(4) Terreat hic terror quos terreus alligat error
Nam fore sic verum notat hic horror specierum.   (Autun)

(5) In gremio Matris residet sapientia Patris.   (Beaucaire)

(6) Inponunt pulcrum corpus sine fraude sepulcrum
Filius ad Patrem facit almam scandere Matrem.   (Bourges)

(7) Heredes vite Dominam laudare venite
     Per quam vita datur mundus per eam reparatur.   (Corneilla-de-
                                                       Conflent)
(8) Mactant non dignum tam seva morte
     Benignum.   (Dijon)
(9) Cum rudis ante forem dedit hunc michi Petrus
     honorem
     Mutans horrorem forma meliore priorem.   (Dijon)
(10) Est humilis multum lascivum neglige cultum.   (Luz-St.-Sauveur)
(11) Ad portum vite sitientes quique venite
     Has intrando fores vestros componite mores
     Hinc intrans ora tua semper crimina plora
     Quicquid peccatur lacrimarum fonte lavatur.   (Maguelone)
(12) Tres sunt atque decem qui cernunt scandere
     Regem
     Celum cunctorum Cristum Dominum
     dominorum.   (Mauriac)
(13) Scandit sublimis celestia Iesus ab imis
     Quod bene testantur qui iugi luce beantur.   (Mauriac)
(14) Rex sum caelorum merces condigna meorum
     Me quicumque colit pro vita perdere nolit.   (Morlaas)
(15) Vos qui transitis qui crimina flere venitis
     Per me transite quoniam sum ianua vite
     Ianua sum vite volo parcere. . . venite.   (St.-Marcel-lès-
                                                       Sauzet)
(16) Abbas querebat Paulum faunusque docebat.   (St.-Paul-de-Varax)

Notes

    1. Research for this paper was made possible by grants from the Bush Foundation and the Graduate School of the University of Minnesota, and by a fellowship from the Camargo Foundation.
    Fundamental studies include: Marcel Aubert, *L'église de Conques* (Paris: H. Laurens, 1939); Christoph Bernoulli, *Die Skulpturen der Abtei Conques-en-Rouergue* (Basel: Birkhäuser Verlag, 1956); Jean-Claude Bonne, *L'art roman de face et de profil: le tympan de Conques* (Paris: Le Sycomore, 1984); A. Bouillet and L. Servières, *Sainte Foy: vierge et martyre* (Rodez: E. Carrère, 1900); Jacques Bousquet, *La sculpture à Conques aux XIᵉ et XIIᵉ siècles: essai de chronologie comparée* (thesis, Toulouse, 1971; photographically reproduced in 3 vols., Lille, 1973); Georges Gaillard et al., *Rouergue roman*, 2d ed. (La Pierre-qui-Vire: Zodiaque, 1974).

    2. According to Émile Mâle in *Religious Art in France, the Twelfth Century: A Study of the Origins of Medieval Iconography*, trans. Marthiel Mathews (orig. French ed., Paris: A. Colin, 1922; translation based on 6th ed., 1953; Princeton: Princeton

University Press, 1978), 415–16, "[it] can scarcely be earlier than the second quarter of the twelfth century, but neither can it be, as has been said, of the late twelfth century." Paul Deschamps, in *French Sculpture of the Romanesque Period: Eleventh and Twelfth Centuries* (1930; rpt. New York: Hacker Art Books, 1972), 58, assigns it to "about the end of the first quarter of the twelfth century." Later, in "Étude sur les sculptures de Sainte-Foy de Conques et de Saint-Sernin de Toulouse et leurs relations avec celles de Saint-Isidore de Léon et de Saint-Jacques de Compostelle," *Bulletin monumental* 100 (1941): 241, Deschamps dates it around 1120–30. Aubert, 93, on the authority of Deschamps, suggests ca. 1140. He is followed by Marcel Rascol in *Le portail de Sainte-Foy de Conques: sa disposition primitive* (Toulouse, 1947), 12 [cited by Bernoulli, 67–68]. Bernoulli, 68, argues for ca. 1125. Frans Carlsson, in *The Iconology of Tectonics in Romanesque Art* (Hässleholm, 1976), fig. 10, gives ca. 1140. M. F. Hearn, in *Romanesque Sculpture: The Revival of Monumental Sculpture in the Eleventh and Twelfth Centuries* (Oxford: Phaidon Press, 1981), 182, fig. 136, proposes ca. 1130–40.

3. Don Denny, "The Date of the Conques Last Judgment and Its Compositional Analogues," *The Art Bulletin* 66 (1984): 7. Denny's argument is based on comparisons of the composition and iconography of the tympanum with other twelfth-century items, especially the tympanum of Cahors and manuscript paintings in the Winchester Psalter.

4. Gaillard et al., 49, "beginning of the twelfth century" (see also p. 93). Roberto Salvini (*Medieval Sculpture* [Greenwich, Ct.: New York Graphic Society, 1969], fig. 123, and p. 327), "about 1110." However, it is Bousquet, in his monumental thesis, who offers the most convincing case for an earlier dating. His conclusion, 942, "vers 1110–20? . . . Vers 1130 au plus tard," seems to me more cautious than his own arguments have led the reader to expect. In an earlier summation, he states, 461: "Le tympan ne peut venir longtemps après [the Annunciation and certain other sculptures] et c'est donc autour de 1107 que le plus grand sculpteur de Conques a pu commencer de travailler, en liaison avec le 'grand abbé' Bégon. Il a pu continuer et achever son oeuvre au cours de l'abbatiat de Boniface, mais guère au-delà." See also Raymond Oursel, *Floraison de la sculpture romane*, vol. 2 (La Pierre-qui-Vire: Zodiaque, 1976), 388–89.

5. The hand of the tympanum master has been seen in the Flagellation relief in the right tympanum of the south portal of Santiago de Compostella. Unfortunately, this too has not been securely dated. See Deschamps, *Bulletin monumental* 100: 249–51, and Hearn, 145 n. 53.

6. Bousquet, 458–61, summarizes his view of the stages of construction, which I have followed, except that the estimate "about 1110" is mine. He emphasizes the role of Abbot Bego (ca. 1087–ca. 1107) in pushing the project to completion, and limits Boniface (1107–ca. 1125) to giving the finishing touches. Kenneth John Conant, in *Carolingian and Romanesque Architecture 800 to 1200* (Harmondsworth: Penguin Books, 2d integrated ed., 1978), 163, puts the date of completion at about 1130, apparently to accommodate the tympanum, which, with A. K. Porter, he dates ca. 1124. The argument of Marcel Deyres in "La construction de l'abbatiale Sainte-Foy de Conques," *Bulletin monumental* 123 (1965): 7–23, that the present basilica, or

what he calls Conques III, was a product of the early twelfth century has not been generally accepted. See Whitney S. Stoddard, *Art and Architecture in Medieval France: Medieval Architecture, Sculpture, Stained Glass, Manuscripts, the Art of the Church Treasures* (New York: Harper and Row, 1972), 35–37; originally published as *Monastery and Cathedral in France* (Middletown, Ct.: Wesleyan University Press, 1966). Stoddard, 35, assigns the completion of the galleries of the nave and the vaults of the transept and nave to Bego and Boniface.

7. The tympanum is protected from a fairly harsh climate only by a shallow gable. Louis Balsan and Dom Angelico Surchamp (Gaillard et al., 29–37) have advanced a theory of displacement to explain why, after so many centuries, it shows so few signs of weathering. According to this theory, the tympanum was originally erected one bay east of its present location (like Vézelay). Then, in a major remodeling of the church at the end of the Gothic period, it was moved to the outer facade. However, the way the tympanum is integrated into the facade makes the theory untenable. See Bousquet, 127, and 163 n. 12.

8. Bousquet, 163 n. 12.

9. Ibid., 420–22, 492 n. 45.

10. For example, on capitals: Agen, Aulnay (?), Cluny, Elne, Lugo, Poitiers (St.-Porchaire), St.-Sever, Santo Domingo de Silos; on socles: Luz-St.-Sauveur, Vézelay; on keystones: Cluny, Vézelay; on banderoles and books: Arles; on arches and backgrounds: St.-Aventin, Silos, Toulouse (St.-Sernin).

11. See Oursel, 2: 346.

12. As at Autry-Issards, Autun, Beaucaire, Bourges (St.-Pierre-le-Puellier), Cassan, Clermont-Ferrand, Condeissiat, Conques, Corneilla-de-Conflent, Déols, Dijon (St.-Bénigne), Ferrara, Jaca, La Lande-de-Fronsac, Luz-St.-Sauveur, Maguelone, Mauriac, Morlaas, Nevers, St.-Denis, St.-Georges-de-Camboulas, St.-Marcel-lès-Sauzet, St.-Paul-de-Varax, Santa Cruz de la Seros, Vandeins, Verona (Cathedral, San Zeno).

13. Unrhymed verses are found at Clermont-Ferrand, Condeissiat, Dijon (St.-Bénigne), La Lande-de-Fronsac, Nevers, St.-Sever, Toulouse (St.-Sernin).

14. Disyllabic rhyme appears at Arles, Déols, Dijon (St.-Bénigne), St.-Denis, St.-Paul-de-Varax, Vandeins.

15. Cited by Bousquet, 225 n. 150.

16. See Paul Deschamps, "Étude sur la paléographie des inscriptions lapidaires de la fin de l'époque mérovingienne aux dernières années du XIIᵉ siècle," *Bulletin monumental* 88 (1929): 35. Deschamps observes that in the epigraphy of the second half of the eleventh and the beginning of the twelfth century it is rare to find two forms of a letter in the same inscription except for the following: capital and square *C*, capital and uncial *D*, capital and uncial *E*, capital and square *G*, and sometimes *H* with a looped bar or uncial *H* beside the capital, and uncial *M* beside the capital. On the tympanum of Conques we find capital *C* (26X) beside square *C* (9X), capital *D* (14X) beside uncial *D* (3X), capital *E* (22X) beside uncial *E* (36X), capital *G* (6X) beside

square *G* (2X). The only *H* has a bowed bar. There is one uncial *M* with inward-turned, pointed legs, and one closed uncial *M* beside 16 capitals. There are two other letters on the tympanum which have two forms: capital *A* with either a horizontal or a V bar, and capital *Q* beside uncial *Q*. All forms are current in the eleventh and twelfth centuries; both forms of *A* appear at Conques in the epitaph of Bego, ca. 1107. None of the characteristics which Deschamps gives to describe developments from about 1125 on appear on the tympanum. Deschamps himself, in "Les sculptures de l'église Sainte-Foy de Conques et leur décoration peinte," *Monuments Piot* 38 (1941): 183–85, points out the epigraphical resemblances between the script of the epitaph of Bego and the tympanum, but still thinks it necessary to date the tympanum ca. 1125–30.

17. All transcriptions and translations of inscribed verses are mine, unless otherwise noted.

18. Mâle, 413; Gaillard et al., 49.

19. Prosper Mérimée, "Extrait d'un rapport adressé au Ministre de l'Intérieur, sur l'abbaye de Conques," *Bulletin monumental* 4 (1838): 235, was the first to point out the lively contrast between the king and the abbot.

20. The vernacular form goes back to Vulgar Latin. Cf. C. H. Grandgent, *An Introduction to Vulgar Latin* (1934; rpt. New York: Hafner Publishing Co., 1962), secs. 232, 235.

21. See, for example, Vergil, *Aen.* 4.243; 6.135. See Bousquet, 146, and 210–11 n. 119, for these and other details on the use of *Tartarus/Tartara*.

22. Minimal hexameters are not uncommon among Romanesque verse inscriptions, e.g., Cluny, Dijon (St.-Bénigne), Morlaas, and St.-Paul-de-Varax. Obviously, poets were aware that shorter verses could more easily fit small spaces. Abbot Suger composed a minimal elegiac couplet (13 + 12 syllables) for the anagogical window at St.-Denis.

23. *Bulletin monumental* 4 (1838): 236.

24. See Jean-Claude Fau, *Conques* (La Pierre-qui-Vire: Zodiaque, 1973), 125.

25. The word appears to read *cruciatur* with the *t* joined to the *a*. But this ligature was apparently intended as a triple joined letter, the *n* being formed by the sloping verticals of the *a* and the vertical of the *t*. There is a triple joined letter = *a me* on the right banderole on the mandorla.

26. The first two letters of *casti* are damaged, but their outlines can still be made out under certain light conditions.

27. *Falsi* was erroneously carved *falsd*.

28. Mérimée, 238, could make out "une vingtaine de lettres que le temps a rendues illisibles." Elsewhere on the tympanum, the names of the virtues were alternately painted and inscribed. Cf. Bousquet, 194 n. 86.

29. Bousquet, 151, reaches a similar conclusion.

30. *Bulletin monumental* 4 (1838): 240.

31. Ibid.

32. Bousquet, 262.

33. Ibid., 300–301 n. 20.

34. The sculpture is not the work of the tympanum master (cf. ibid., 259–60).

35. Albert Blaise, *Dictionnaire latin-français des auteurs chrétiens* (Turnhout: Brepols, 1954), s. v. *abba,* cites several examples of the use of *abba* for *abbas.* Cf., also, the pentameter inscription on the donor bust of the limestone relief of Christ in Majesty in the portal of St. Emmeran, Regensburg, ca. 1050, which begins *Abba Regenwardus* (text in Hearn, 57). Here, too, the choice of the learned form is *metri causa.*

36. All that can now be read is: . . . VM DOMINV QVE CRVX C. . . . Alfred Darcel (*Trésor de l'église de Conques* [Paris: Librairie archéologique de Victor Didron, 1861], engraved plate facing p. 33) saw: . . . SSVM DOMINV QVEm CRVX C. . . . The engraving shows a looped mark of suspension over the E of QVEM, but nothing over the V of DOMINV[M]. Probably this was another full leonine hexameter.

37. In the epitaph of Bego, the first syllable of his name is long; here and in the Reliquary of Pope Pascal (13) it must be short. Cp. the similar variation in length in Suger's name in the inscriptions at St.-Denis.

38. Mérimée, 241, reported *locavit.* Only the first two letters remain.

39. According to Gaillard, 142, the inscription reads: . . . ORVM DANIELIS TRI / HIC / HA . . . / ABBAS SANCTORVM BEGO PARTE / ET H . . .; "elle laisse deviner que 'Bégon' commande 'ce' réceptacle, pour les reliques 'de Daniel' 'des trois' (Jeunes Hébreux) et (du prophète) 'Ha(bacuc)', comme le texte de l'inventaire du XVIIᵉ siècle, publié par C. de Linas en 1887 permet de le restituer." The editors of *Les trésors des églises de France,* Musée des arts decoratifs (Paris: Caisse national des monuments historiques, 1965), 302, read: ABBAS SANCTORVM BEGO PARTES HIC HAB . . . "(manquent de 7 à 9 lettres)" ET HORVM DANIELIS TRI . . . "(manquent de 16 à 18 lettres)." The nineteenth-century engraving of Darcel, facing p. 15, shows three fragments: [1] ABBAS SANCTORVM BEGO PARTES; [2] ORVM DANIELIS TR [*sic*] HIC HAB; [3] ETH. Fragment 3 appears to fit into the beginning of fragment 2. The reliquary is now in a display case against the wall, which means that the visitor is unable to see the whole of it. What I can make out is: ABBAS SANCTORVM BEGO PARTE [break] HIC HA [break]. The fragments apparently have been rearranged. The portion beginning *abbas sanctorum* was plainly meant to be a hexameter verse. Given the uniform practice at Conques, we can assume that the verse was leonine. What follows was very likely leonine as well, although no definitive conclusions can be reached.

40. As Gaillard et al., 142, point out, *noster David* = Christ. Therefore, the verse is typologically relevant to the medallion of Samson which was added later. But we have no way of knowing what was originally represented on this face. The poet may have intended to spell the name *Davit* in order to make the Leonine rhyme visually exact. Cf. Chaucer's couplet in the *Summoner's Tale* (III, 1933–34):

Whan they for soules seye the psalm of Davit:
Lo, 'buf!' they seye, *'cor meum eructavit!'*

41. A break occurs between the *a* and the *i* in *supera(v)it*. Gaillard et al., 142, read: SIC NOSTER DAVID S[A]TANAN SVPERAVIT. The editors of *Les trésors,* 302, read: SIC NOSTER DAVID S . . . "(manquent de 8 à 9 lettres)" . . . TANAM (*sic*) SUPERAVIT. Cf. Darcel, plate facing p. 15. I propose *sanctus* only to demonstrate that the assumption that this is a leonine hexameter is plausible.

42. Cf. Alexander Souter, *A Glossary of Later Latin to 600 A. D.* (Oxford: Clarendon Press, 1957), s. v. *Satanas*.

43. 1) *Auctorem mortis* . . . ("The author of death . . ."); 2) . . . *stet Pastor et Agnus* (". . . stands the Shepherd and the Lamb").

44. *Rouergue roman,* 141.

45. Ibid., 142.

46. For the inscription, see *Rouergue roman,* 142, and (in a slightly different version) *Les trésors,* 305. The inscription also may not originally have been intended for this reliquary (*Les trésors,* 305–06).

47. The texts of (14) and (15) are cited from Bouillet, 190.

48. Including three fragments and one partially restored line.

49. Bousquet, 426ff., remarks on the learned Latinity and knowledge of some Greek words of the second redactor of the Book of Miracles of Ste.-Foy in the second half of the eleventh century at Conques.

50. See the appendix to this chapter. These are from my collection.

51. Similarly in the pentameter: *perpetuusque, perpetuoque,* tympanum (3, 4).

52. Appendix: Autun, *meritosque* (2).

53. For example, Bede, following Maximus Victorinus, describes only four caesuras: the penthemimeral, the hepthemimeral, the *cata triton trocheon* (the feminine caesura), and the bucolic (diaeresis). *De Arte Metrica* xii. 23–41 (ed. Calvin B. Kendall, in *Corpus Christianorum series latina* 123A [Turnhout: Brepols, 1975], 117–18). Classical Latin poets avoided it (see Rosenmeyer, Ostwald, and Halporn, *The Meters of Greek and Latin Poetry* [Indianapolis and New York: Bobbs-Merrill, 1963], 70). The practice of eleventh- and twelfth-century poets varied. It is fairly common in the leonine verse of Marbod of Rennes (died 1125).

54. Appendix: Autun, *horror specierum* (4); Corneilla, *eam reparatur* (7); Mauriac, *Dominum dominorum* (12). There are no masculine fifth-foot caesuras in the first 30 lines of Vergil's First Eclogue.

55. Bouillet, 154, asserts categorically that the "deux inscriptions [on the lintels] ont été gravés au XIᵉ siècle."

56. See ibid., 183–86; Gaillard et al., 143.

57. The portable Altar of Ste.-Foy has been hesitantly associated with the workshop of Bego. See Bouillet, 205; Gaillard et al., 144.

58. I don't have any special insight into life expectancy at Conques in the eleventh and twelfth centuries. For what it is worth, the average tenure of the five eleventh-century abbots for whom dates are relatively well established is 17.2 years.

14. *Andreas* and the Formula in Transition

ANITA RIEDINGER

There are many things that this chapter will not do. It will not redefine the formula, argue the oral origins of any Old English poem, or test the relationship between *Andreas* and *Beowulf*. Instead, it will try to illuminate the meaning of *Andreas* by considering the poet's use of the formula in relation to its use throughout the Old English poetic corpus. In the process, I shall demonstrate that in his manipulation of traditional formulas, the *Andreas* poet helps break up oral-formulaic tradition and, as he does so, reveals some characteristics of a literate mind acting upon the product of the oral mind that lies behind the whole tradition.

As Helen Damico and Patrick J. Gallacher suggest in their introduction, "To understand a text is to discover the meaning that emerges from the reciprocal relationship between the whole and its parts." In the case of Old English poetry, the "whole" must be regarded as twofold: the tradition and the poem. The formulaic "parts" that this essay will consider belong to both. The *Andreas* poet knew the Old English formulaic tradition intimately. At times he embraced it fully, but at others, he deliberately modified it in order to fuse a Germanic tradition of which he did not always approve with a saint's life recorded in a Latin text that was derived from a Greek source.[1] His poetic techniques were many, and an essay this brief can merely point out a few of his more salient devices: he changed traditional formulas,[2] created new ones, and used old formulas in new contexts. The results were not always successful, and *Andreas* is not a great poem. But to watch the poet's formulaic manipulations is to understand better his intent, the poem's meaning, and the changing nature of the formula in the hands of an indisputably literate poet.

That *Andreas* is densely formulaic has long been known. But its author did not just parrot old verses, as it sometimes seems. He fully understood traditional formulaic usage, a fact that is evident, for example, in his handling of a verse such as *"in* [or *to*] *þære beorhtan byrig"* (in [or 'to'] the bright fortress).[3] This formula occurs once in each of seven very disparate poems. An examination of each context shows that in five of these poems, the verse is used as a traditional thematic formula, by which I mean one that signifies a recurrent image, idea, or event.[4] In all five contexts, *in þære beorhtan byrig* signifies a place where treasure belongs. For example, in *Beowulf*, it is the destination of Hama, the otherwise unidentified place to which he bears the fabulous Brosings' necklace (1199a). In *Judith*, *þære beorhtan byrig* is Bethulia, when the victorious Hebrews take their Assyrian booty homeward— their *dyre madmas . . . golde gefrætewod* (326a, 318a, 328b). In *Ruin*, the formula designates the Ruin itself, when long ago it had been filled with treasures—"gold-bright" men among their silver, gems, and jewels (37a). In *Christ II*, the "bright fortress" is no earthly place; it is heaven, Christ's destination at the Ascension. But the angels who accompany Him to "the bright fortress" of heaven are specifically described as *frætwum blican* (glittering with treasures; 519a, 507b, 522b). In these four poems, then, the formula retains a traditional thematic meaning. Twice elsewhere, however— in *Guthlac B* (1191a) and *Elene* (821a)—the poets use the formula atraditionally: it alludes to heaven, but not as a repository for treasures, for none are mentioned. The traditional thematic context, for them, has vanished.

The *Andreas* poet observes the thematic tradition signified by *in þære beorhtan byrig*, but he does so in a carefully circumscribed context—reserving treasures for Christians only. He might have chosen not to use this formula at all, of course, for no treasure is mentioned in his source. Yet he deliberately introduces this Germanic treasure-motif into his poem, and then, throughout most of the poem, expressly negates its appropriateness to the Mermedonians; he defines them, in part, by what they do not possess: *næs him to maðme wynn, / hyht to hord-gestreonum* (for them there was no joy in treasure, hope in hoard-wealth, 1113b–14a); *welan ne benohton* (they possessed no wealth, 1159b). These, too, are traditional treasure-formulas, found elsewhere in the corpus, but for the unconverted Mermedonians, the formulas are cast in the negative. The *Andreas* poet delays the introduction of the thematic formula "to the bright fortress"—that repository for treasures— until nearly the end of the poem. Earlier, his characters have frequently approached the "fortress" of Mermedonia via the same system, but by different formulas: they go three times *to þære mæran byrig* (to the famous fortress) and twice *in þære hæðenan byrig* (into the heathen fortress, 40b, 287b, 973b; 111b, 1491b). But they do not go to the *beorhtan byrig*. Then at last the Mermedonians are baptized (1630) and a church is built (1633). After this conversion to Christianity, the nature of the fortress changes entirely: first it becomes a *win-burg* (wine-fortress; 1637a), and, finally, all reside *in þære beorhtan byrig* (1649a). Now it is a treasure fortress, full of rings and gold and treasure-adorned halls: furthermore, it is a *gold-burg, beorht beag-selu* (golden fortress, bright ring hall), full of *sinc-gestreon* (treasure-wealth) and *secga sele-dream* (the hall-joy of men), who rejoice in their conversion in *salu sinc-hroden* (treasure adorned halls).[5] Thus the poet knows the Old English formulaic tradition, but he uses it very selectively.

In his analysis of *Andreas*, T. A. Shippey speaks of the "tug-of-war between native and alien traditions'' that permeates this critically controversial poem:[6]

> The main point is that its local successes and failures often come from the same root, a reluctance or inability to abandon the syntax and vocabulary appropriate for a secular epic. This poem's ''garment of style'' is a ready-made one, and it fits where it touches.

One of the causes of this recurrent tension was the fact that imbedded in Old English prosody—inextricably inter-twined with it, where formulas were concerned—were ideas that were antithetical to the Christian doctrine in the poet's subject and source. It is well known, for example, that if an Old English poet needed to express the idea of a ''good leader'' using dual *b* alliterators, he might traditionally say *beaga brytta,* or, if an *s* alliterator were required, *sinces brytta*—but these formulas literally mean ''giver of rings,'' or ''of treasure,'' and are hardly appropriate to Mermedonians who are denied wealth. And they are especially inappropriate to a disciple to whom God has said, *''Ne ðurfan ge on þa fore frætwe lædan, / gold ne seolfor''* (''You need not carry treasure on that journey, gold nor silver''; 337–38a). The spirit of this directive (without mention of gold and silver treasure) is derived from the *Andreas* poet's source, so he cannot escape it. Yet he seems aware of the conflict between his source and the Old English tradition, for Andrew twice apologizes to the Navigator: *''þeh ic þe beaga lyt''* (''though I have few rings for you''; 271b, 476b). This apology is not in the source. Nor is it found elsewhere in the corpus. It is what I call an ''occasional'' formula, by which I mean a formula that is used in one poem only. One way in which the *Andreas* poet solves the problem of the indivisibility of substance and form in Old English poetry, then, is by creating a completely new formula, ad hoc—in this case, one that explicitly acknowledges the tradition and its values, even as it departs from them. When he creates new formulas, as he does here, or selectively limits the context of old formulas, as he does with the *beorhtan byrig,* the adaptation is smoothly done, and the garment of style fits.

Other forms of adaptation seem less successful. This is especially true when the poet uses traditional formulas in such a way that they explicitly contradict their traditional contexts. But if we examine even one such passage closely, it becomes apparent that the poet does not always want the traditional Old English style to fit. Instead, he deliberately reshapes the secular ethos inherent in the formulaic tradition. This fact is evident in the passage below:

F	*Gewat* him þa *Andreas*	inn *on ceastre*	F
F	glæd-mod gangan,	to þæs ðe he gramra gemot,	F
F	fara folc-mægen,	gefrægen hæfde,	F
NF	*oððæt he gemette*	be mearc-paðe	F
NF	*standan* stræte neah	*stapul ærenne.*	NF

NF	*Gesæt him þa be healfe,* hæfde hluttre lufan,	F
NF	ece up-gemynd engla blisse;	F
NF	þanon *basnode* under burh-locan	F
NF	*hwæt him* guð-weorca gifeðe *wurde.*	F

(1058-66)

(F = Formula; NF = Non-Formula; Italics = Greek and Latin sources)[7]

(Then *Andreas went* inside *into the city,* the glad-minded one going to where he had heard of a meeting of the angry ones, a mighty-tribe of foes, *until he came to a brass column standing* next to the street, beside the border-path. *Then he sat down beside it,* had pure love, the eternal celestial thought of the bliss of angels; from *there he awaited what* battle-deeds *would be* granted *to him* beneath the fortress walls.)

These lines afford us a glimpse of the poet at work on his poem. It is important to note, in passing, that when the poet translates from his source, most of the verses are not formulas. But let us examine closely only the verse-pairs that are not italicized; that is, not dictated by the source.

This passage takes place shortly before Andrew's so-called "battle" with the Mermedonians. It should be noted that the poet himself introduces the battle-context to the poem with the words *"guð-weorca"* (1066a). The three verse-pairs with no italics at all—the second, third, and seventh lines—are neither prosodically nor syntactically necessary, so one might presume they were added to enhance the disciple's heroic stature prior to the coming battle. Two of the verses seem to do that by calling attention to the ferocity of the enemy: *to þæs ðe he gramra gemot / fara folc-mægen.* But two other additions—*glæd-mod gangan* and *ece up-gemynd engla blisse*—do not enhance a warrior's stature. This hero is "glad-minded" before battle. His joy is even emphasized by its alliterative juxtaposition with the antithetical *gramra.*[8] Yet that state of mind, when associated with conflict at all, usually occurs after a battle is over: Judith slays Holofernes before she returns to Bethulia, *glæd-mode* (140a); and the youths are saved from the fiery furnace before they honor God *glæd-mode (Dan* 259a). Hrothgar praises Beowulf for having slain both Grendel and his dam, and only then *Geat wæs glæd-mod, geong sona to / setles neosan* . . . (The Gautar was glad-minded, went at once to seek his seat; *Bwf* 1785–86a). Before battle, however, traditional warriors are furious: Byrhtnoth and Beowulf approach their enemies *yrre ond an-ræd* (angry and resolute; *Mld* 44a, *Bwf* 1575a). And Beowulf "waited enraged" for Grendel—*bad bolgen-mod* (709a)—while Grendel entered Heorot to the same formula: *eode yrre-mod* (moved enraged; 726a). In *Beowulf,* villain and hero alike are wrathful. But in *Andreas,* wrath belongs to the devil's party. Andrew is never angry. In fact, anger is the concept that the author directly opposes in this passage. He knows the tradition, for he himself uses it elsewhere: the Mermedonians are *bolgen-mode* (128a, 1221a) before they attack. By introducing *glæd-mod* into this context, the poet does more than merely shun anger: he corrects it. Had he merely wanted to eschew anger and still make his hero conform more to the tradition than he has done, he might have selected some more neutrally appropriate compound, such as *guð-mod* (battle-minded; *Bwf* 306a), which suits the context and also provides the necessary *g* alliterator, without anger. But when Mermedonians, Guthlac's devils, Beowulf, Heremod, and Nebuchadnezzar all initiate a battle or terrible action *bolgen-mod,* to cite just one such adjective,[9] and Andreas approaches his battle *glæd-mod*—and is the only character in Old English poetry ever to do so—then I believe the poet is trying to make a point. He is not incompetently trying to make a hero fit a tradition; he is actively emending the tradition.

His final revision in this passage also occurs in an addition to the source: *ece up-gemynd engla blisse* ([had] the eternal celestial thought of the bliss of angels). It will be remembered that Old English heroes traditionally think about, or are mindful of, something before going into battle. Thus, for example, the heroes before the battle at Finnsburh are to *hicgeaþ on ellen* (think on valor; *Fnb* 11b); and the heroes of Maldon are to remember boasts made on the mead-bench (*Gemunaþ þara mæla þe we oft æt meado spræcon; Mld* 212). I believe that the *Andreas* poet remembered this tradition, too, as he introduced this seemingly superfluous verse-pair into this particular context. But Andrew's thoughts are again contextually atraditional. Once more, the poet changes the tradition as he uses it. In effect, he edits it: formula has become text.

In his introduction to *The Daemon in the Wood,* David Bynum makes a distinction between methods of literary and oral composition that is relevant here. Bynum says that for the oral poet, "the ideas in the tradition are ever present"; only the metrical phrase must be called to mind. But for the literary poet, "it is the phrase that brings an idea to mind." The literary poet, Bynum explains, must at some time consciously inspect "the sense of all his phrases no matter how often he may later routinely repeat them."[10] This is the phenomenon I find in *Andreas:* the poet consciously inspects the sense of his phrases, as though it is the phrase—in this case, the formula—"that brings an idea to mind." It is as though he has thought, as he wrote, "No, my hero won't approach battle full of wrath, *bolgen-mod,* but *glæd-mod;* he'll not think of vows made on mead benches, or even of valor—he'll think of heavenly angels, instead." Thus, the *Andreas* poet uses formulas to "discuss" the ideas contained in other—traditional—formulas. He critiques the formulaic tradition—a very literary act.[11]

And as he does so, he shapes a new hero: God, not man, is the true Hero of the poem, and formulaic evidence suggests that the poet would not have it any other way. His techniques are again varied, and some are quite simple. For example, he uses nearly one hundred different whole-verse nominal epithets for God, most of them several times, suggesting the importance of that particular portrait.[12] Only about twenty-five such epithets denote Andrew. In turn, the skill with variation evident in the many epithets for God makes the poet's twenty-two nearly verbatim repetitions of the colorless phrase *ond þus wordum cwæð* [or *becwist*] (and spoke these words) all the more remarkable.[13] The effect of this formula, of course, is to stress the words which are to follow, which in *Andreas* nearly always concern God. Further, when God is the speaker, He is always elaborately and specifically identified. Andrew is rarely so identified. The poet formulaically suppresses his saint.

God's heroic supremacy, as well as the poet's literate mind, are evident in my last example, which is an instance of the hero-on-the-beach theme, hitherto unnoted. David Crowne identifies this theme as one wherein a hero is on the beach with his retainers in the presence of a flashing or shining light as a journey is completed or begun.[14] Andrew is such a hero as he leaves Mermedonia: his followers, *leoda weorode,* go with him *to lides stefnan . . . æt brimes næsse* (to the ship's prow, at the sea's headland; 1706b, 1707b, 1710b). Only the "shining light" is missing. It is supplied a few lines later, however, by God in the closing hymn: *ond his blæd ofer eall in heofon-þrymme halgum scineð* (and over all His glory shines on the holy ones in heavenly might; 1719b–20). The hero-on-the-beach theme, then, as well as the poem, appropriately concludes with the light of the glory of God.

But glory is an abstraction. In every other recorded instance of this theme, the light emanates from a concrete object—such as armor, spears, or the sun.[15] Walter Ong, in *Orality and Literacy,* notes that illiterate minds tend to think concretely, rather than abstractly.[16] When the *Andreas* poet alters this particular thematic formula, he probably does not deliberately alter the tradition: he merely thinks in such a way that the alteration becomes inevitable. That is, he is literate, and the way his mind works must change an oral tradition.

Walter Ong also says:

> Traditional expressions in oral cultures must not be dismantled: it has been hard work getting them together over the generations, and there is nowhere outside the mind to store them. So soldiers are brave and princesses beautiful and oaks are sturdy forever. . . . [But] once a formulary expression has crystallized, it had best be kept intact. Without a writing system, breaking up thought—that is, analysis—is a high-risk procedure.[17]

I believe that in *Andreas,* we often see the Old English poet, with his writing system, in the process of "breaking up thought"—and with it, the Old English oral-formulaic tradition.

Notes

1. The immediate source no longer exists, but was probably in Latin. In *Critical Studies in the Cynewulf Group* (1949; rpt. New York: Haskell House, 1967), Claes

Schaar, however, demonstrates that the extant Greek version is closer to the Old English poem than is either the Latin or the later Old English prose. I have therefore consulted Alexander Walker's translation of the Greek ("Acts of Andrew and Matthias in the City of the Man-eaters," in *The Ante-Nicene Fathers,* Vol. 8 [1870; rpt. New York: Scribners, 1926], 517–25), as well as Franz Blatt's edition of *Casanatensis* in *Die lateinischen Bearbeitungen der Acta Andreae et Matthiae apud anthropophagos* (Giessen: Topelman, 1930). It is to these source-analogues that I refer when I use the term "source" in this essay.

2. I use the word "traditional" to mean a formula that is used by more than one poet, as does Albert Bates Lord in *The Singer of Tales* (1960; rpt. New York: Atheneum, 1965), 130. The definition of the formula that I use throughout this paper is my own and was explained at length in my article, "The Old English Formula in Context," *Speculum* 60 (1985): 294–317. In it, I described a formula as any verse that was part of a "set," which I defined as "a group of verses usually sharing the same function and system in which one word, usually stressed, is constant, and at least one stressed word may be varied, usually synonymously, to suit the alliterative and/or narrative context. . . . all the verses in a set constitute the same formula, whether or not they repeat one another verbatim" (306).

3. All Old English quotations are from *The Anglo-Saxon Poetic Records: A Collective Edition,* 6 vols., ed. George Philip Krapp and Elliott Van Kirk Dobbie (New York: Columbia University Press, 1931–53). I have supplied the hyphens. My abbreviations for the Old English titles are those listed in *A Concordance to the Anglo-Saxon Poetic Records,* ed. Jess B. Bessinger, Jr., and programmed by Philip H. Smith, Jr. (Ithaca: Cornell University Press, 1978), xiii–xv, which I have used to locate both formulas and contexts. I am indebted to Professor Bessinger for reading an early draft of this paper.

4. The thematic significance may or may not be semantically apparent in the formula itself. This idea, too, is developed at length in my "Old English Formula in Context." Much earlier, however, Paul B. Taylor touched on a similar formulaic function in his "Themes of Death in *Beowulf,*" in *Old English Poetry: Fifteen Essays,* ed. Robert P. Creed (Providence: Brown University Press, 1967), 251. Taylor primarily traced themes, however, rather than formulas. In "Caedmon in Context: Transforming the Formula," *Journal of English and Germanic Philology* 84 (1985), Constance B. Hieatt has more recently suggested that there are perhaps "formulas which could lead us to identify themes and type-scenes of which they may be characteristic parts" (497).

5. Lines 1655a, 1657a, 1656b, 1656a, 1673a. Kathryn Hume has argued: "In *Andreas,* we find total rejection of the hall imagery. The author could not accept the compromise of transforming the secular ideal. . . ." ("The Concept of the Hall in Old English Poetry," *Anglo-Saxon England* 3 [1974]: 72). But the poet does not reject the secular ideal of the hall; he merely reserves it for Christians.

6. T. A. Shippey, *Old English Verse* (London: Hutchinson, 1972), 117 and 119. In *Old English Literature* (New York: Schocken, 1983), Michael Alexander, too, among recent critics, comments on "the strange tension between a story whose reason for existence is religious, and a narrative version of it which constantly reminds us of secular values and a different tradition" (162).

7. Supporting evidence for formulas (F): **1058a:** *Gen* 2083b, 2162a, 2885a; *And* 118a, 225a, 977a; *Bwf* 1963a, 2949a. **1058b:** *And* 1174b; *Ele* 845b; *Jln* 21a; *P106.6* 4a. **1059a:** *Ele* 1095a; and reversed words at *Chr* 576a; *Phx* 519a. **1059b:** *Glc* 127b. See also *Mld* 301a. **1060a:** contextual analyses show that it is probably a variant of one of the following: *And* 1593a, 1346a; *Bwf* 554a. See also *Exo* 342a. **1060b:** *Wds* 17b; *Bwf* 1196b; *Exo* 1a; *Dan* 328b; *Ele* 155b; *MB9* 27b; *P50* 5b; *And* 687b. **1061b:** *Ele* 233a; *And* 788a. **1063b:** *ECL* 8b. **1064b:** *DrR* 153b. **1065b:** *Gen* 2539b; *Bwf* 1928a; *And* 940a, 1038a. **1066b:** *Gen* 1726b; *Bwf* 299b, 555b, 2491b, 2682b; a traditional thematic formula (except in *Gen*). See also *Jud* 157b and *Wld* 1 25a for *gifeðe* in the same context. Most of this supporting evidence consists of near-verbatim repetitions, which proves formularity; more evidence might be possible had proofs included full sets of formulas. I have called **1061a** "non-formulaic" because the only other instance of this verse in the whole corpus is *obþæt ic gemete* (*P131.5* 1a); both poets are translating their sources. It is an example of "incidental" repetition, by which I mean repetition that occurs as a natural concomitant to something else, usually to the high frequency of common words. This verse is a colorless phrase in which both stressed words are very, very common in Old English poetry. In this case, a single repetition does not constitute a formula.

8. See Edward B. Irving, Jr., "A Reading of *Andreas*: The Poem as Poem," *Anglo-Saxon England* 12 (1983): 218, for a discussion of other contrastive collocations in *Andreas,* as well as for an interesting reading of the poem. Randolph Quirk, of course, was the first to analyze the poetic effects of alliterative collocations, as well as to identify them as "complementary" and "contrastive," in "Poetic Language and Old English Meter," in *Early English and Norse Studies Presented to Hugh Smith,* ed. Arthur Brown and Peter Foote (London: Methuen, 1963), 150.

9. *Glc* 287a, 447b; *Dan* 209a; *And* 128a, 1221a; *Bwf* 709a, 1713a. Other contexts in which battle is approached with some form of the verbs *belgan/abelgan* are *Bwf* 723b (Grendel); 2220b, 2280b, 2304a (the dragon); 1539b, 2401b, 2550b (Beowulf).

10. *The Daemon in the Wood: A Study of Oral Narrative Patterns* (Cambridge: Harvard University Press, 1978), 12.

11. The literate mind at work is evident in alliterative collocations, too. For example, *min* and *mægen* (my and might) collocate twice in *Andreas* (1214, 1433), both times in battle contexts and both times referring solely to God. No such divine attribution is present in similar contexts elsewhere in the corpus (*R27,* 10; *Bwf* 418, 445, 1706, 2084, 2837). Again the *Andreas* poet uses the vehicle of the formula (in this case a formulaic collocation) to comment on the traditional substance of the vehicle itself: "might" belongs not to mortal creatures, but to God. For an especially interesting discussion of "the habitual mode of thought" (411) of an *oral* poet, see John Niles, "Formula and Formulaic System in *Beowulf,*" in *Oral Traditional Literature,* ed. John Miles Foley (Columbus: Slavica, 1981), 394–415.

12. David Hamilton says that the poet "partially follows traditional form in that he supplies speakers with epithets, but by making his identifications theological rather than genealogical he alters the received tradition" (*"Andreas* and *Beowulf*: Placing the Hero,*"* in *Anglo-Saxon Poetry: Essays in Appreciation for John C. McGalliard,* ed.

Lewis Nicholson and Dolores W. Frese [Notre Dame: University of Notre Dame Press, 1975], 96).

13. *And* 62b, 173b, 354b, 539b, 716b, 727a, 743b, 850b, 913a, 1206a, 1280b, 1450a, 896a, 1172b, 1299b, 1361b, 1400b, 1663a, 210a, 193b, 304b, 418b.

14. "The Hero on the Beach: An Example of Composition by Theme in Anglo-Saxon Poetry," *Neuphilologische Mitteilungen* 61 (1960): 368.

15. For a convenient table of the sources of light in the various recurrences of this theme in Old English poetry, see Donald K. Fry, "The Heroine on the Beach in *Judith*," *Neuphilologische Mitteilungen* 68 (1967): 168–84.

16. *Orality and Literacy: The Technologizing of the Word* (London: Methuen, 1982), 51.

17. Ibid., 39.

15. "The Rewards of Piety": Two Old English Poems in Their Manuscript Context

FRED C. ROBINSON

In the course of preparing a forthcoming volume in the series *Early English Manuscripts in Facsimile,*[1] I had occasion to examine a large number of Old English poems in their manuscript state, and the experience yielded some startling surprises. Scholars and students are accustomed to reading Old English poetry in the standard editions, where each poem is clearly titled and lineated, precisely punctuated, and set off in a frame of clean space on the page—all of which gives the texts that impression of authority and finality which commands respect and discourages subversive questions about the readings presented in the edition. In the manuscripts in which these poems are preserved, the individual texts make a very different impression: they almost never have titles; they are written as prose from margin to margin and are never lineated;[2] they are often part of a continuous flow of texts, poetry sometimes being mingled with prose, and Latin with the vernacular. One text is separated from the other very often by nothing more than a capital letter and indentation. The divisions between text and text and the divisions between sections within texts are often somewhat similar, and one begins to pay close attention to what goes before and after any single text and to wonder about possible connections. In their manuscript context, the poems seem integrated with the surrounding flow of texts, and that integration is lost when the poem is abstracted by the scholarly editor from its place on the manuscript page and presented as an isolated artifact in the modern printed edition. In an earlier study I have called attention to this loss of significant context.[3] My purpose here is to give a specific example of how this loss can seriously impair our understanding of an Old English poem, in the hope that when the volume of facsimiles of Old English poems is published in *Early English Manuscripts in Facsimile* scholars will be encouraged to ask subversive questions about more Old English verse texts. We have studied these texts too long in the modern editions, and too little in the actual state in which they come down to us from the Anglo-Saxon period.

The poem which modern scholars have called "An Exhortation to Christian Living" is a fairly standard piece of religious instruction in which the reader is told how to conduct his life if he wishes to earn a place in heaven. Humility, almsgiving, prayer, fasting, and attendance at church "in cold weathers" are repeatedly urged, and avoidance of gluttony, excessive sleep, drunkenness, fornication, and the devil are advised, as is fear of the secret thoughts that come in the night causing sinful lusts. The message is underlined through repetition and through reminders that the world's end is near. The style is striking, as Dobbie points out,[4] in its "direct address to the reader or hearer" who is constantly referred to with second-person singular pronouns.

"A Summons to Prayer" also addresses a specific reader or hearer[5] and urges prayer and piety so that heaven may be attained. This poem begins with the word *þænne* (then), which is unusual, since the adverb would seem to imply some foregoing context. The spelling of the word with *æ* is also rather unusual, and the same relatively rare spelling is used for the word in "An Exhortation to Christian Living." These two poems have, in fact, a number of other features in common. As Leslie Whitbread pointed out thirty years ago, there are striking similarities between the two texts, both in subject matter and in style.[6] Some of the Latin tags in "A Summons to Prayer," he suggests, actually seem to be translations of verses in "An Exhortation" (129). He argues persuasively that the two poems are by the same author (128). In both poems, a confessor addresses a penitent: in the first poem, the confessor explains how to repent and live properly; and, in the second, he promises a happy afterlife to the friend who follows this advice (127).

Whitbread never doubts that "An Exhortation to Christian Living" and "A Summons to Prayer" are two separate poems, and one is a little surprised at his confidence in the separate integrity of each text in view of the many points of continuity which he discerns between them. If he had examined the poems in their manuscript state, very likely the question would have occurred to him; for in the single manuscript which preserves them (Corpus Christi College, Cambridge MS. 201, pp. 165–67), they appear together, "A Summons" following immediately the text of "An Exhortation." Preceding "An Exhortation" is a rubricated *explicit* ending unambiguously the preceding poetic text.[7] Following "A Summons" there is an equally emphatic visual break marking the end of that text: the closing words of "A Summons" are broadly spaced, and a generous blank space separates it from the ensuing poem, which is an elaborate versified rendition of "The Lord's Prayer." But between "An Exhortation" and "A Summons" there is only an orange capital letter marking the two texts off from one another, and this orange capital looks exactly like the five colored letters marking off sections within "An Exhortation." The visual evidence of the manuscript considered by itself indicates clearly that these two poems (so-called) are in fact one continuous text subdivided into sections, as most longer Old English poems usually are divided.

If we assume that "An Exhortation" and "A Summons to Prayer" are in fact one continuous text rather than a pair of separate poems, how would they fit together logically and stylistically? "An Exhortation" begins by saying, "Now I shall instruct you as a person must do to a dear friend. If you wish to ascend to that flourishing realm [i.e. heaven], then be liberal with alms and humble. . . ."[8] The speaker's instructions continue for seventy-seven lines, until we reach the last sentence of what is now called "An Exhortation to Christian Living" followed by the opening of "A Summons to Prayer": "If you wish to seek out that celestial dwelling, then you must think on it while still here on earth and restrain yourself severely and abandon all vices which you previously practiced and loved in this life; then will the King of nations who rules the world sitting on his throne show mercy to your soul, to you forever."[9] The semicolon following "life" marks the point at which present editions end one text and begin another. To my mind this bisection of the text results in one poem, "An Exhortation," which simply breaks off in the middle of its list of instructions and another, "A Summons," which begins in mid-thought with an adverb which seems to connect it to the foregoing text. Joined together, the two make one poem with beginning, middle, and end.

Once we notice how clearly the supposed pair of poems merge into a single unified text with "A Summons" providing an apt conclusion to "An Exhortation," the question arises as to how scholars for nearly three centuries could have consistently read them as two separate works. The two-poem interpretation has apparently remained unquestioned ever since Humphrey Wanley first presented this text as two separate poems in his catalogue and J. Rawson Lumby, following Wanley's lead in his *editio princeps,* first printed it as two poems (entitled, respectively, "Exhortation" and "Oratio Poetica," the latter title being appropriated from Wanley, 147).[10] Do Wanley and Lumby really enjoy such extraordinary prepotency that no scholar has dared dissent from their interpretation of the text? First impressions are of course powerful, and it seems a fact that once a text is edited in a certain form it is difficult for scholars to reconceive it in alternative shapes. But in this case there is something else at work which has discouraged scholars from seeing these two verse texts as one. "An Exhortation to Christian Living" is written entirely in Old English, while "A Summons to Prayer" is a Latin-Old English macaronic poem. Even though the style of the Old English verses in the two poems is so similar as to have suggested common authorship, evidently scholars have found it inconceivable that a poet writing a poem exclusively in Old English would suddenly shift into macaronics as his poem drew toward its close. This shift must have persuaded Wanley to divide the text, despite the evidence of the manuscript page, and subsequent scholars have concurred.

But is it so improbable that an Old English poem would have a macaronic conclusion? The most famous example of macaronic verse in Old English is in the poem "The Phoenix," where the poet recounts the story of the mythical bird for 667 lines of Old English verse and then, as he draws near the end of his poem, switches to macaronic Latin-Old English verses to provide a suitably flamboyant ending. Given the example of "The Phoenix," it would seem more probable that the so-called "Summons to Prayer" is in fact the conclusion to "An Exhortation" than that it is not. It is true that the Old English poem "Aldhelm" is always printed as an independent text, so here at least we seem to have one example of a free-standing macaronic poem in Old English, Latin, and Greek. This evidence would not, of course, be probative of the two-poem interpretation of the text, but some might find it suggestive.

Even here, however, it is important to consider manuscript context in weighing the evidence. In the manuscript where the poem "Aldhelm" is uniquely preserved (Corpus Christi College, Cambridge, MS. 326, pp. 5–6), it is not an independent text but rather is presented as the beginning of Aldhelm's prose treatise *De virginitate*, which is preserved completely in this manuscript. Preceding the poem is the table of contents to Aldhelm's Latin treatise. The poem ensues, after which comes the salutation and preface to *De virginitate*. Both the poem and the salutation begin with capital letters, but there is no punctuation mark separating them. The preceding table of contents does not make separate reference to the poem; it describes the opening part of *De virginitate* simply as *Salutatio et prologi præfatio*, as if the macaronic poem were part of the salutation and preface. And indeed, the speaker of the poem is Aldhelm's treatise, and the opening word *Þus* refers to the ensuing Latin treatise. (If the treatise did not immediately follow the macaronic verses, then the *Þus* would have no meaning.) It will help to have Dobbie's text of the poem before us:

> þus me gesette   sanctus et iustus
> beorn boca gleaw,   bonus auctor,
> Ealdelm, æþele sceop,   etiam fuit
> ipselos on æðele   Angolsexna,
> 5 byscop on Bretene.   Biblos ic nu sceal,
> ponus et pondus   pleno cum sensu,
> geonges geanoðe   geomres iamiamque,
> secgan soð, nalles leas,   þæt him symle wæs
> euthenia   oftor on fylste,
> 10 æne on eðle   ec ðon ðe se is
> yfel on gesæd.   Etiam nusquam
> ne sceal ladigan   labor quem tenet
> encratea,   ac he ealneg sceal
> boethia   biddan georne

15 þurh his modes gemind   micro in cosmo,
   þæt him drihten gyfe   dinams on eorðan,
   fortis factor,   þæt he forð simle

Thus the good, saintly, and righteous author Aldhelm, a man learned in books and a noble poet, composed me: also, he was eminent in the land of the Anglo-Saxons, a bishop in Britain. I, a book, an opus and an authority, must now say with full sense the truth, not falsehood at all, with the complaint of a troubled youth [must say] that there was for his help always fame in abundance in his homeland [?] more often than on whom evil is spoken [?]. Also, he who has self-control must on no occasion excuse himself from toil but must always in this little world eagerly pray for help through the thoughts of his mind so that the Lord, the Creator of strength, may give him power on earth so that he henceforth always. . . .

This is a tentative attempt at a translation, for the sense of "Aldhelm" is notoriously difficult, apparently because the poet's ambition to compose a poem in three languages at once exceeded his talents. Especially difficult are lines 10 and 11, where two of the half-lines are hopelessly unmetrical as well as unclear, and where faulty transmission probably compounds the problem. Elsewhere too the poet's clumsy flourishes and often uninflected Latin and Greek words make it difficult to follow his sense.

The end of the poem is of particular concern. Scholars have always assumed that the sentence fragment at the end signals a loss of text, which is very likely. Because of the very obscurity of the macaronic poem, however, it is barely possible to imagine a syntactical connection between the poem and the following text of Aldhelm's salutation. According to the age-old epistolary formula, the verb is unexpressed in the Latin salutation: "To the most reverend virgins of Christ . . . Aldhelm, dilatory worshipper of Christ and humble servant of the Church, [sends his] best wishes for perpetual prosperity."[11] If we assume that the "him" and the "he" of the last clause of the poem refer to Aldhelm (and it is difficult to see how they could refer to anyone else), then the unexpressed verb "sends" or "may send" of the epistolary formula beginning the Latin treatise could be wrenched into service as the verb which completes the last clause of the poem and unites it to the treatise: ". . . so that the Lord, the creator of strength, may give him power on earth so that he henceforth always [may send] to the most reverend virgins of Christ . . . his best wishes for perpetual prosperity." That is, through his support and divine assistance to the book and its author, God may enable him to continue through the ages to greet the nuns of Barking and bring to them and to all readers Aldhelm's inspirational treatise on virginity.

There is precedent for a single sentence in Old English linking prose and verse discourse,[12] and so it is not impossible that the magniloquent Anglo-Saxon who wrote these verses would interweave them with Aldhelm's own words. But the connection is strained and, because of the obscurity of the poem, nebulous. The possibility seems worth mentioning only because the whole performance *is* so grandiloquently strained and blurred that almost anything seems possible. But the safer course, perhaps, would be to assume, as scholars have usually assumed, that some text has been lost at the end of the poem we call "Aldhelm." This missing text would probably have established a transition or connection between the poem and the Latin treatise since, as we have seen, the speaker of the poem *is* the Latin treatise, and the table of contents implies that poem and Latin preface are one. If this is so, then "Aldhelm," like the macaronic verses in "The Phoenix," would be part of another text, not an independent poem. It would also resemble the use of macaronics in other medieval poetry, such as the *Carmina Burana,* where vernacular poems sometimes end with a stanza of macaronic verses.[13] The use of a macaronic close to a vernacular poem seems to have been a traditional way of making a brilliant ending to a poem. The "Aldhelm" poet reversed the procedure and made a macaronic introduction in order to provide a suitable opening for a work by Aldhelm who, with his Greek and Hebrew ornamentation of his Latin prose, was himself a sort of macaronic writer.

This excursus on "Aldhelm" (which might more appropriately be named "The Book's Prologue to *De virginitate*") must not distract us further from our central concern with "An Exhortation to Christian Living" and "A Summons to Prayer." As the above discussion illustrates, the assumption of a macaronic conclusion to "An Exhortation to Christian Living" would be in keeping with the use of macaronic verses elsewhere in Old English. That these texts are in fact one poem seems to me certain, and an appropriate name for that poem would be "The Rewards of Piety," for both parts of the previously separated text describe how a Christian should conduct himself in order to earn the meed of salvation. When seen as a single integrated text dealing with "The Rewards of Piety," these 113 lines take on a shape and direction which they lacked when they were divided. To be sure, it is not a great poem, but it is a better poem than the previously assumed pair of poems were.

But my primary purpose in reuniting a text which had been split by editors is not to improve the quality of this particular work but rather to illustrate how important it can be to reconsider long-studied Old English texts in the light of their manuscript settings. My hope is that when Volume 23 of *Early English Manuscripts in Facsimile* (containing photographs of the manuscripts of all Old English poems not in the four major poetic codices and *The Paris Psalter*) is published, other scholars will take the opportunity to study these works in the form in which they came to us from the Anglo-Saxons. If they do, I am confident that more questions about the textual integrity of familiar Old English poems will be raised, and the result should be a more accurate understanding of the literary corpus we are concerned to study.

Notes

1. Volume 23 of *Early English Manuscripts in Facsimile,* which I am preparing in collaboration with Professor E. G. Stanley of Pembroke College, Oxford, will be entitled "Old English Verse Texts from a Variety of Sources" and will include photographs of the manuscripts and (in the case of poems preserved in inscriptions) artifacts containing all Old English poems except for those in the *Beowulf* Manuscript, the Exeter Book, the Junius Manuscript, the Paris Psalter, and the Vercelli Book, all of which have already been published in facsimile. The volume will be published by Rosenkilde and Bagger in Copenhagen next year.

2. The only exception which I have noticed is "Gloria II" in B. L. MS. Cotton Titus D.xxvii, fol. 56^{rv}. But this poem consists of only three lines of verse, and it is likely that the congruence of manuscript lines with metrical lines is a coincidence.

3. "Old English Literature in Its Most Immediate Context," in *Old English Literature in Context: Ten Essays,* ed. J. D. Niles (Totowa, N.J.: Rowman & Littlefield, 1980), 11–29, 157–61.

4. *The Anglo-Saxon Minor Poems,* ed. Elliott Van Kirk Dobbie, *Anglo-Saxon Poetic Records,* 6 (New York: Columbia University Press, 1942), lxxii. Dobbie notes several familiar features of the speaker's tone and mentions the phrase *har hilderinc* in l. 57, which he takes to be a mere "archaizing conceit" rather than an indication that the friend whom the poet addresses is literally an old warrior. I suspect *har hilderinc* had only the most general meaning such as Modern English "old man," which in familiar address could be said to a twelve-year-old boy as well as to a mature adult.

5. In this poem too (Dobbie, 69–70) second person pronouns are used, and in one place the interlocutor is actually addressed by name; see n. 9.

6. "Notes on Two Minor Old English Poems," *Studia Neophilologica* 29 (1957): 123–29.

7. The preceding poem is "Judgment Day II," and the rubricated *explicit* reads, *"Her endað þeos boc þe hatte inter florigeras. ðæt is on englisc betwyx blowende þe to godes rice farað. ᚷ hu ða þrowiað. þe to helle farað."* The words *blowende . . . rice* are echoed in the second line of "An Exhortation." This could be the result of the medieval "compiler's adapting the phrasing of his texts to forge a verbal link between them" ("Old English Literature in Its Most Immediate Context," 28). Such links are lost by those who read Old English exclusively in edited versions of individual texts rather than in their manuscript setting.

8. Dobbie, 67, lines 1–3.

9. Dobbie, 69, lines 78ff. of "An Exhortation" combined with lines 1–4 of "A Summons." Following *þē* (you) in line 1 of "A Summons" is the Latin abbreviation for *nomen,* indicating, apparently, that the speaker of the poem, like a confessor, should speak the name of the individual he is addressing. This would seem to continue the intimate tone of "An Exhortation," with its frequent use of second-person singular pronouns and the inclusion of words like *leofne* (1) and *har hilderinc* (57).

10. Humphrey Wanley, *Librorum Veterum Septentrionalium . . . Catalogus* (Oxford, 1705), 147, and J. Rawson Lumby, *Be Domes Dæge. De Die Judicii, An Old English Version of the Latin Poem Ascribed to Bede.* Early English Text Society, o.s. 65 (London: N. Trübner & Co., 1876), 28–37.

11. *Aldhelm: The Prose Works,* trans. Michael Lapidge and Michael Herren (Totowa, N.J.: Rowman & Littlefield, 1979), 59.

12. Fred C. Robinson, " 'Bede's' Envoi to the Old English *History:* An Experiment in Editing," in *Eight Anglo-Saxon Studies, Studies in Philology, Texts and Studies,* volume 78, no. 5 (1981): 6–7.

13. See, for example, *Carmina Burana* ed. Alfons Hilka and Otto Schumann vol. I: Text, 2. *Die Liebeslieder* (Heidelberg: C. Winter, 1941), 194 and 295.

16. Old and Middle English Prosody: Transformations of the Model

THOMAS CABLE

I. Misreadings of Old English Meter

Metrists studying English alliterative poetry have always tended to emphasize the continuity of the tradition. This continuity is said to be characterized, from Cædmon to Langland, by "strong-stress meter." W. K. Wimsatt, Jr., and Monroe C. Beardsley present a model that is often cited because of its succinctness and clarity: ". . . the clutter of weaker syllables in a strong-stress meter is against an accurate syllable-stress reading, most often prevents it entirely. A few lines of *Piers Plowman* or of *Everyman* ought to suffice to show what is what."[1] The authors quote from those two texts and continue to say that

> this other kind of meter is older in English poetry and may be more natural to the English tongue, though again it may not be. Here only the major stresses of the major words count in the scanning. The gabble of weaker syllables, now more, now fewer, between the major stresses obscures all the minor stresses and relieves them of any structural duty. . . . Thus we have *Beowulf, Piers Plowman, Everyman,* Spenser's *February Eclogue,* Coleridge's *Christabel,* the poetry of G. M. Hopkins (who talks about 'sprung rhythm' and 'outrides'), the poetry of T. S. Eliot, and many another in our day (p. 592).

One of the main arguments in my *Meter and Melody of Beowulf* was that *Beowulf* and the rest of Old English poetry did not belong in this group.[2] A main argument of the present essay is that *Piers Plowman* and other poems of the fourteenth-century Alliterative Revival do not belong either—or rather that to use the rubric "strong-stress meter" to group *Piers Plowman* and *Christabel* is to misrepresent the fourteenth-century meter in an essential way. The *Piers* meter is obviously strong stress, but, I shall argue, not essentially so (as the phrase is usually understood), just as it is alliterative, but not essentially so.

Contemplating the essence of a meter may seem overly Platonic in a field of inquiry that has mainly been positivist. However, the philosophical assumptions that run through my prosodic analyses, which in various contexts have affinities with Platonism and rationalism, may as well be acknowledged at the outset. I shall suggest that there has been both more and less continuity between Old and Middle English alliterative meter than has usually been seen. Scholars have developed these misapprehensions of continuity and discontinuity by focusing on facts that are true enough, but less relevant than the essential facts that provide the significant generalizations. In the following oppositions, the left-hand term (with representative metrists) is the one that I see deflecting the focus from the more essential right-hand term: alliteration (Oakden, Sapora) vs. rhythm; assumed metrical stress (Borroff, J. Turville-Petre) vs. linguistic stress; the manuscript archetype (Duggan) vs. historical grammar; concrete contours (my own misreading) vs. the abstract paradigm; strong stress (Wimsatt and Beardsley) vs. the patterning of unstressed syllables.[3] There is space in this essay to deal only with the last two oppositions.

In its most abstract form, the model of Old English meter is simply four positions:

1   2   3   4

The internal dynamics of clashing stress, intermediate stress, resolution, strings of unstressed syllables, etc. produce the realization of those four positions as five different series of three binary relationships:

A	$1\diagdown2\diagup3\diagdown4$	´ x ´ x wuldres Wealdend
B	$1\diagup2\diagdown3\diagup4$	x ´ x ´ on sidne sæ
C	$1\diagup2\diagdown3\diagdown4$	x ´ ´ x of brydbure
D	$1\diagdown2\diagdown3\diagdown4$	´ ´ ` x heardhicgende
E	$1\diagdown2\diagdown3\diagup4$	´ ` x ´ wonsæli wer

These series of relationships can be manifested as five contours:

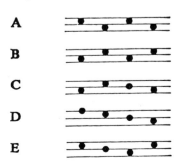

My reasons for originally hypothesizing the five contours as tunes had to do with what I saw as problems in the perception of secondary stress, or more accurately, intermediate metrical ictus. The idea of intermediate ictus is an odd one from the view of familiar Western binary meters. Typically, elements of metrical value are oppositions such as long vs. short, stress vs. unstress, or in syllabic verse, the presence of a syllable vs. the absence of one. In the Old English type E, however, we have ictus, less ictus, and less ictus again. In type D we have four such levels.

My own conclusion is that this system of intermediate ictus operated only in Old English. It did not operate in Old Norse, Old High German, or Old Saxon, and not in Middle English. It makes Old English unique among Western verse forms. The closest parallel that I have been able to find is in certain structures of Gregorian chant.

The perceptual model that especially influenced my thinking at the time of *The Meter and Melody of Beowulf* was that of Philip Lieberman.[4] A great deal of subsequent work in intonation, acoustics, and perception has challenged some of the main features of that model, including features that were significant in my application of it to Old English meter. Lieberman's model has been criticized for being both overly concrete and reductionist, and I now see my own use of the model as going wrong in the same ways.[5]

The implication for Old English poetry that I drew from intonational studies during the early 1970's was that normal intonation would not distinguish the various levels of stress needed to differentiate the Five Types. Therefore, I posited a stylized method of recitation or chant that took the form of discrete tunes. This manifestation of the abstract pattern solved the perceptual problem, but it also removed the advantages that I had gained from an abstract explanation of the concrete patterns. My own paradigm had become concrete again, and Sievers' Five Types had become five contours.

Developments since 1974 in acoustics and in the analysis of the perception of suprasegmentals have included work influenced by studies of "downstep," or "declination," falling levels of pitch. Shinji Maeda has applied these insights to English and has found, contrary to Lieberman, that pitch can differentiate ambiguous structures such as "small-school boy" and "small school-boy."[6] Janet Pierrehumbert and others have shown that the declination is steeper, and the differentiations sharper, as the phrase is shorter.[7] The short average length of half-lines in Old English would produce steep, maximally differentiated contours.

Such findings indicate a more direct relationship between the contours of the spoken voice and the contours of the singing voice than earlier models suggested. This is especially true when patterns are limited in length, as by a metrical form. There is clearly a spectrum of increasingly stylized methods of performance shading from heightened recitation into chant. The complex issues require further experimentation and further developments of theory.[8]

The most relevant theoretical issues for Old English meter concern the perceptual and acoustic problems just sketched, but they also reach back to

Dwight Bolinger's work on pitch accent in English in the 1950's. The constant concern has been with the relationship between the whole and the parts, between the overall intonational contour and the individual elements of stress, pitch, and time. Bolinger expressed the tension between the two basic theoretical orientations as "Levels vs. Configurations," the individual pitch levels versus the line of melody that the levels define.[9]

More recently the two orientations have been characterized as a "Tone Sequence" theory and a "Contour Interaction" theory. The Contour Interaction theory (corresponding to Bolinger's Configurations) begins with the overall shape of the line of speech-melody and sees various local disturbances in that shape as resulting from individual accents along the line, or from the interaction of another contour superimposed on the first.

The Tone Sequence theory, on the other hand, assumes that there *is* no line of melody separate from the individual phonological units that combine to make what is then perceived, after the fact, as a tonal contour. But it is not a matter of making those units fit an idealized or Platonic contour. The contour results from the internal dynamics of the units themselves.

Robert Ladd has distinguished the two approaches succinctly:

> The Contour Interaction model assumes that the individual accent-related pitch movements are specified by a separate component, and then *interact with* an over-all tune; the Tone Sequence view assumes that those pitch movements are simply concatenated to *make up* the tune, so that 'sentence intonation' is merely the sum of its accent-related parts.[10]

The bulk of my analysis in *The Meter and Melody of Beowulf* was parallel to the Tone Sequence approach, and this method, I believe, was correct. I was mainly interested in the relationships of consecutive syllables and metrical units: clashing stress, strings of unstressed syllables, anacrusis, resolution, etc. It was only after finding and stating individual constraints for the various parts that the simpler, more abstract pattern for the whole emerged.[11] The Five Types, manifested as unitary contours without feet, could be seen as the logical result of a paradigm of four positions.

The conclusion to draw from all of this is that there is more of a continuum between speech and song than the modern reader is likely to imagine, and a single metrical abstraction is compatible with a wide variety of styles of recitation. I remain convinced that Old English poetry contained five melodic contours, but it is a mistake to reify those contours as the paradigm itself (just as it was a mistake to reify Sievers' Five Types). They are the result of a more abstract paradigm, but because of that very abstractness we are far from knowing many phonetic details that would be relevant to a performance, such as the intervals between the levels of pitch.

II. Misreadings of Middle English Meter

The quotation from Wimsatt and Beardsley at the beginning of this essay typifies descriptions of strong-stress meter in the handbooks. If no pattern can be found among the unstressed syllables, it is natural to conclude that the patterning occurs in the count of stresses. However, I have found that by supplying the full historical form of each word as it appeared in Old English, Old French, and Old Norse, the unstressed syllables of alliterative meter can suddenly be seen to be regulated from the first syllable in the line to the last. For example, in these two lines from *Cleanness,* most modern readers would scan 797a as x/xx/x and 817a as /xx/x, making each first half-line more or less like the second half-line (depending on whether the reader pronounced the *-e*'s at the ends of the lines). I would read the lines, however, as follows:[12]

797	x / x x / xx He ros vp ful radly	x / x x / x and ran hem to mete
817	/ x x x / xx Loth þenne ful ly3tly	/ x x x / x loke3 hym aboute

Radly comes from Old English *hrædlice,* and *ly3tly* from Old English *lehtlice.* There is compelling evidence that *-ly* adverbs generally retained a trisyllabic form in Middle English. One piece of evidence is that they are strictly avoided at the end of the line. What, then, was required at the end of the line to account for their absence? The two lines above are not very helpful, because both end with the uncertain *-e.* However, it is important to note that both *-e*'s represent a syllable that occurred historically: *mete* < OE *metan, aboute* < *abutan.* Indeed I have found that more than ninety-eight percent of the 1,812 lines in *Cleanness,* and a comparable percentage in other poems, end either with an unambiguous unstressed syllable or with an unstressed syllable that can be justified historically in Old English, Old French, or Old Norse. It appears that the end of the line required exactly one unstressed syllable.

To illustrate, these second half-lines all have masculine endings as written in the manuscript, but all of them had a final unstressed syllable historically:

so sore forþo3t (<OE forþohte) (*Cleanness* 557b)
bot drepe3 in hast (<OF haste) (*Cleanness* 599b)
with bantelles quoynt (<OF cointe) (*Cleanness* 1459b)
in we3tes to heng (<ON hengja) (*Cleanness* 1734b)
þay sued hym faste (<OE fæst) (*Gawain* 1705b)
som worde at this tym (<OE tima) (*Morte* 9b)
and holdys 3ow styll (<OE stille) (*Morte* 15b)
with bignes of will (<OE willa) (*Wars* 105b)
their life for too spill (<OE spillan) (*Alexander A* 126b)

too fonden his myght (<OE miht, f.) (*Alexander A* 108b)
& blame my hert (<OE heorte) (*William* 486b)

Final words that do not have an obvious unstressed syllable generally turn out
to be plural or weak adjectives, or weak nouns, or infinitives, or adverbs that
had an -e in Old English, or loanwords that had an -e. The same methods that
establish final -e in these and other categories, show that a few categories
have changed since Old English. For example, dative -e appears to be no
longer productive, occurring only in "petrified datives"; the preterites of
second class weak verbs end in only one unstressed syllable instead of two;
and feminine nouns acquired analogical -e's. For the most part, however, a
strict following of the historical forms makes the metrical principles clear.

   The lines below suggest that the historical -e is also necessary elsewhere,
and is not simply a characteristic of the end of the line. In these verses the -e
that is not written but should be pronounced occurs between the two stresses:

> and gryspyng harde (*Cleanness* 159b)
> þat fest to haue (*Cleanness* 164b)
> and pertly halden (*Cleanness* 244b)
> ful fiften dayes (*Gawain* 44b)
> ne wowyng nauþer (*Gawain* 2367b)
> wyth sexten kynges (*Morte* 105b)
> her fleshlych sinnes (*Alexander A* 38b)
> with rufull deedes (*Alexander A* 81b)
> for leeflich Knightes (*Alexander A* 139b)
> of grounden tooles (*Alexander A* 210b)
> to karp þe soþe (*William* 503b)

The manuscript indicates an even alternation of unstressed and stressed syllables: di dum di dum di. But in each instance the second dip can be shown to
have another unstressed syllable historically: di dum di di dum di. In fact,
nearly every b-verse in these poems can be shown to have the possibility of at
least two syllables between the stresses or at least two syllables before the first
stress (but not both). However, the patterns for the a-verse are quite different.

   By focusing on the known historical forms of the words (which turn out
to be the essential facts) rather than on the orthographic forms of the manuscripts (which turn out to be irrelevant facts), we come to the conclusion that
final -e is not erratic at all. The distribution of patterns into first and second
half-lines makes the point. Here are the fifteen most common patterns in
Cleanness. The names of the patterns refer in obvious ways to Sievers' Five
Types and the count of syllables (e.g., 2B2A means a combination of Sievers'
B and A, with two syllables in the first dip and two in the second). The sample
is the first half (900 lines) of the poem:

		First half-line	Second half-line	Percentage
B2A	x/xx/x	3	244	98.9%
B3A	x/xxx/x	6	174	96.7%
2BA	xx/x/x	3	98	97.0%
2A	/xx/x	0	94	100.0%
3A	/xxx/x	4	65	94.2%
2B2A	xx/xx/x	62	4	93.9%
2B3A	xx/xxx/x	57	2	96.6%
3B2A	xxx/xx/x	58	1	98.3%
3BA	xxx/x/x	3	53	94.6%
3B3A	xxx/xxx/x	39	0	100.0%
2B2	xx/xx/	33	0	100.0%
2B3	xx/xxx/	31	0	100.0%
3B3	xxx/xxx/	30	0	100.0%
2C	xx//x	0	30	100.0%
3C	xxx//x	0	27	100.0%

The column of percentages indicates the frequency of the pattern in whichever half of the line it occurs in most. Because the percentages of these patterns range between 93.9 and 100, it appears that a given pattern, for whatever reason, tends decisively toward one half of the line or the other.

As it happens, the tendency for the patterns of the two halves of the line to be mutually exclusive holds up for the other 152 types. In the first 900 lines of the poem, 93.2 percent of the half-lines have a characteristic rhythmic pattern for that half of the line. Of the first half-lines, ninety-four percent have a characteristic a-verse pattern; of the second half-lines 92.4 percent have a characteristic b-verse pattern. Similar distributions hold for *Sir Gawain and the Green Knight, Morte Arthure, The Parlement of the Thre Ages, The Wars of Alexander, William of Palerne,* and other poems of the Alliterative Revival. What remains to be determined is exactly what makes a pattern appropriate for one half of the line or the other.

It is well known that the first half-line is generally longer than the second. Overall length, however, is not the whole story: 3BA (xxx/x/x) and 2B2A (xx/xx/x) have exactly the same number of syllables, and they both end with an unstressed syllable (as required in the b-verse), but they have strikingly different distributions in the two halves of the line: 93.9 percent of 2B2A (xx/xx/x) patterns are in the first half-line; 94.6 percent of 3BA (xxx/x/x) patterns are in the second half-line. If we consider the arrangement of stressed and unstressed syllables within each type, it is clear that the more balanced pattern (xx/xx/x) occurs primarily in the a-verse; the unbalanced pattern (xxx/x/x), for whatever reason, occurs primarily in the b-verse. It appears that something in the internal rhythm of the pattern compels a type toward one half of the line or the other.

We can hone the concept of balanced rhythm by following the traditional idea that the texts before us are in strong-stress rhythm, a rhythm that contrasts with the regularly rising rhythm of the iambic pentameter. For a pattern to follow regularly rising rhythm strictly, there should be only one unstressed syllable before each stress. Therefore, let us define strong-stress rhythm as the obverse of this: any pattern that has two or more unstressed syllables before each stress. A metrical type is balanced as long as it stays in strong-stress rhythm. It becomes unbalanced if a regularly rising, or iambic, rhythm intrudes.

Thus, unexpectedly, the key to the solution of the Middle English alliterative line lies in the patterning of the unstressed syllables, which have always been perceived as unregulated. I propose the following principles for the Middle English alliterative line, in descending order of generality:

1. The rhythmic patterns of the two halves of the line are mutually exclusive.
2. The first half-line is generally heavier than the second. It is heavier by virtue of having either two strong dips or three metrical stresses.
3. The second half-line must contain only two metrical stresses and rhythmic dissimilation: One strong dip and one weak dip in either order, and a single, final unstressed syllable.

In one sense the alliterative long line is bewilderingly flexible. The configurations of stressed and unstressed syllables in *Cleanness* form 167 different half-line patterns by my count. Yet a few general principles of rhythm give order and precision to the metric variety. These principles can be made more precise:

a. First half-line
   i. Normal verses
      Two stressed syllables and at least two strong dips.
   ii. Extended verses
      Three stressed syllables with any pattern of dips.
b. Second half-line
   Two stressed syllables, one and only one of which is preceded by a strong dip.[13] Exactly one weakly stressed syllable at the end.
Definitions:
   Strong dip: A run of two or more weakly stressed syllables.
   Stressed/weakly stressed: Following the grammatical hierarchy of Old English poetry: (1) N, Adj, Inf, PP; (2) V, Adv; (3) Pro, Conj, Prep, Art, etc.

The paradigm for the normal (four-stress) line can be further abstracted and schematized as follows:

First half-line   **Second half-line**

~ / ~ / (-) ~ α ~ / $-\alpha$ ~ / x

   or

α ~ / $-\alpha$ ~ / ~

The tilde represents the strong dip, a pattern of two or more weakly stressed syllables. The variable α represents the coefficient of the feature "strong dip," with a value of + or −. The combination of $+\alpha$ and $-\alpha$ in a single pattern functions as in segmental phonology to show a form of dissimilation. A minus value for tilde represents one syllable or no syllable, the normal dip of the iambic pentameter. Therefore, the iambic pattern ideally occurs before one (but not both) of the stressed syllables in the second half-line. However, it cannot occur before either stressed syllable of the first half-line unless, by compensation, the verse ends with a strong dip (xx).

III. *From Old English Meter to Middle English Meter*

It remains to say something in closing about the transformations of the title. In a sense, all that has been said to this point is a prelude to a discussion of the "transformations of the model"—the evolution of the alliterative tradition. The course of the discussion should be clear. If the separate models of Old and Middle English meter resembled anything like those presented above, then getting from the earlier stage to the later is not to be done in the usual terms. J. P. Oakden presents a succinct account of the traditional view:

> Let us, however, endeavour to trace the development throughout the peri-
> od. . . . [W]e discussed the changes which took place in late O.E. verse,
> including the gradual disappearance of the *D.* and *E.* rhythmical types,
> owing to the loss of the poetic compounds. The loss often involved the *C.*
> type in those cases where the latter consisted of a compound with level
> stress . . . but in those cases in which this was not so, the *C.* type would
> naturally remain. . . . There is absolute continuity in rhythm from the O.E.
> period to the close of the M.E. period, despite a few important changes.[14]

The crucial argument against this view is that the alliterative long line did not evolve in lock step with changes in the language. Middle English meter, in following closely the Old English categories of inflectional syllables and grammatical stress, is more conservative than is usually recognized. However, if one assigns a different priority to specific principles of general prosody, it also becomes more innovative. The long line evolved because poets misread the earlier tradition (whether intentionally or not). The far-reaching effects of subtle differences in our own misreadings show clearly that a focus on a particular part of the surface can be used to derive a general principle, which might or might not conform to the original whole. It was possible for poets of the fourteenth-century Alliterative Revival to derive a brilliantly new model without ever understanding fully, or understanding and rejecting, the series of models that preceded and inspired it.

Notes

1. W. K. Wimsatt, Jr., and Monroe C. Beardsley, "The Concept of Meter: An Exercise in Abstraction," *Publications of the Modern Language Association,* 74 (1959): 592.

2. Thomas Cable, *The Meter and Melody of Beowulf* (Urbana: University of Illinois Press, 1974).

3. See J. P. Oakden, *Alliterative Poetry in Middle English,* 2 vols. (Manchester: Manchester University Press, 1930–35); Robert W. Sapora, Jr., *A Theory of Middle English Alliterative Meter with Critical Applications* (Cambridge, MA: Medieval Academy, 1977); Marie Borroff, *Sir Gawain and the Green Knight: A Stylistic and Metrical Study* (New Haven: Yale University Press, 1962); and Joan Turville-Petre, "The Metre of *Sir Gawain and the Green Knight,*" *English Studies* 57 (1976): 310–28. For Duggan, see n. 13, below.

4. See Philip Lieberman, "On the Acoustic Basis of the Perception of Intonation by Linguists," *Word* 21 (1965): 40–54, and *Intonation, Perception, and Language* (Cambridge: MIT Press, 1967).

5. See, for example, D. Robert Ladd and Anne Cutler, "Introduction. Models and Measurements in the Study of Prosody," in *Prosody: Models and Measurements,* ed. A[nne] Cutler and D. Robert Ladd (Berlin: Springer Verlag, 1983), 3.

6. Shinji Maeda, "A Characterization of Fundamental Frequency Contours of Speech," *Quarterly Progress Report, Research Laboratory of Electronics, MIT,* 114 (1974): 199.

7. See Janet Pierrehumbert, "The Perception of Fundamental Frequency Declination," *Journal of the Acoustical Society of America* 66 (1979): 363–69, and "Synthesizing Intonation," ibid., 70 (1981): 985–95.

8. See George List, "The Boundaries of Speech and Song," *Ethnomusicology* 7 (1963): 1–16. I have been experimenting with various forms of recitation and chant in collaboration with the professional medieval musician, Benjamin Bagby.

9. Dwight L. Bolinger, "Intonation: Levels versus Configurations," *Word* 7 (1951): 199–210.

10. D. Robert Ladd, "Phonological Features of Intonational Peaks," *Language* 59 (1983): 723.

11. For a similar view in medieval musicology, see Leo Treitler, "The Early History of Music Writing in the West," *Journal of the American Musicological Society* 35 (1982): 239–40.

12. Lines of Middle English are quoted from the following editions: *Cleanness,* ed. J. J. Anderson (Manchester: Manchester University Press, 1977); *Sir Gawain and the Green Knight,* ed. J. R. R. Tolkien and E. V. Gordon, 2nd ed. rev. Norman Davis (Oxford: Clarendon, 1968); *The Alliterative Morte Arthure,* ed. Valerie Krishna (New York: Franklin, 1976); *The Wars of Alexander,* ed. W. W. Skeat, Early English Text Society, E. S. 47 (London: N. Trübner, 1886); *Alisaunder of Macedoine* (or *Alexander A*), ed. W. W. Skeat, Early English Text Society, E. S. 1 (London: N. Trübner, 1867); *William of Palerne,* ed. W. W. Skeat, Early English Text Society, E. S. 1 (London: N. Trübner, 1867).

13. This constraint was discovered independently by Hoyt N. Duggan. At the 1985 MLA meeting we presented our respective findings at the same session: Duggan, "The Shape of the Alliterative Long Line," and Cable, "The Unperceived Strictness of Strong-Stress Meter." Now see Duggan, "The Shape of the B-Verse in Middle English Alliterative Poetry," *Speculum* 61 (1986): 564–92.

14. Oakden, *Alliterative Poetry,* I, 174.

17. The Authority of Elde in The Parlement of the Thre Ages

DONALD K. FRY

Critics of *The Parlement of the Thre Ages* have focused on three issues: an apparent lack of, proportion, especially of the Nine Worthies section; the problematic presentation of Elde; and the relationship of frame and dream. This essay analyzes the first two issues, not as problems, but as modes of characterization, and applies the results to the frame. I shall argue that Elde, the most prominent speaker in the poem, undercuts his own pronouncements about death by his untenable attitudes and egregious factual errors. Ironically, the audience must discover the theme of the poem by doubting its ostensible authority figure. As a corollary, I argue that the condescension of modern editors toward the medieval author and scribes has caused textual emendations that hide the intended characterization of Elde from the critics.

I

Most scholars view Elde as an authority figure. This supposed authority, coupled with Elde's preoccupation with death, leads them inevitably to see mortality as the poem's theme. Russell Peck typifies this response:

> The unifying topic of the poem is Death, the master-hunter whom none can escape. Although the theme is not explicit stated until Elde holds forth towards the end of the dream, the whole poem is a "parlement" of responses to life's foe.[1]

Dennis Moran argues that, "as the debate develops, [Elde's] voice assumes the didactic and authoritative tone of the poet himself."[2] But if we see *Parlement* as a poem about death with Elde as spokesman, we accuse the poet of sloppy art, for he distracts the audience with fits and starts and hunts, blows the Nine Worthies out of all proportion, and speaks from a sadly flawed persona.[3]

Parlement contains 665 lines, 390 spoken by Elde, or 59 percent. The Nine Worthies, Wise Men, and Lovers occupy 334 lines, 86 percent of Elde's speech and half of the poem. No wonder the first editor, Israel Gollancz, called it *"The Parlement of the Thre Ages/An Alliterative Poem on the Nine Worthies and the Heroes of Romance."*[4] Elde dominates the poem, and the Worthies dominate his speech. Evidently audiences enjoyed the Worthies motif, even imitated them in their own lives. Moran notes:

> The Nine Worthies do not represent a merely conventional grouping of illustrious men from an obscure and literary past, nor are they conventional pieces in a faded ubi-sunt mosaic. They were . . . figures with whom *Parlement*'s audience passionately identified, personages whose presumed exploits they reverenced as history and whose character they emulated.
>
> (Moran, 630)

Elde holds the record for a lengthy Nine Worthies exposition, but he retells the motif badly. John Speirs complains of the motif's length and lack of proportion, and D. J. Williams of its dullness (Speirs, 249; Williams, 119–20). I agree with Speirs and Williams on the long-winded tedium. But they attribute it to the poet, while I assign it to Elde as a speaking character.

And I add another charge: Elde simply does not know what he is talking about; he makes egregious errors of fact. For example, in line 329, he tells us, against all traditions, that Ulysses and Hercules died at Troy:

> For there Sir Priamus the prynce put was to dethe,
> And Pantasilia þe quene paste him by-fore.
> Sir Troylus, a trewe knyghte þat tristyly hade foghten,
> Neptolemus, a noble knyghte at nede þat wolde noghte fayle,
> Palamedes, a prise knyghte, and preued in armes,
> Vlixes and Ercules þat full euerrous were bothe,
> And oþer fele of þat ferde fared of the same,
> As Dittes and Dares demed[e]n to-gedir.
>
> (324–31)

M. Y. Offord explains "Ercules" as "probably a mistake for 'Achilles,' " but does not deal with the Ulysses problem.[5]

In the Alexander section, Elde garbles the argonauts' expedition, calling Jason a Jew. The Thornton manuscript reads: "Ther ientille Iazon þe Iewe wane þe flese of golde" (338). In the Ware manuscript, Elde tells us: "There Ientill Iosue þe Iewe wan þe slevis of gold," turning Joshua into an argonaut. Gollancz comments:

I am inclined to think that "Jewe" of the MSS. is a scribal error for "Grewe" (*i.e.* Greek); the emendation relieves the author of a gross error, and at the same time restores the alliterative effect to the line.

(Gollancz, n. 337–38)

Offord agrees: "Perhaps the poet himself was inaccurate about the Jason story, and 'Iosue' in W[are] was an attempt to make sense of 'Iewe' " (Offord, n. 338).

Then Elde begins his section on the second group of the Nine Worthies, the three Jews, with a falsely labeled source:

> Of thre Iewes full gentill iugge we aftir,
> In the Olde Testament as the storye tellis,
> In a booke of the Bible that breues of kynges,
> And renkes þat rede kane Regum it callen.
> (422–25)

Gollancz comments petulantly:

Our author has not improved on his original in amplyifying the simple reference to "the Old Testament." The writer certainly did not read of Joshua and Judas Maccabeus in "Regum" (Gollancz, n. 423–25).

I suspect that "men who know how to read" (line 425) might snicker at Elde's erroneous pretensions to learning. And the whole audience probably burst out laughing when Elde allows Joshua to part the Red Sea in lines 428 to 438. Offord (n. 426ff) attributes this error to the poet's confusion of Joshua and Moses, although I assume most medieval Christians knew the difference.

In the section on Arthur, where we might expect special interest and expertise in the English audience, Elde makes three notable errors. First, he describes Gawain as "the gude, that neuer gome harmed" (475). Whether we translate "who never harmed a man" or "who [was] never harmed by a man," the statement violates everything we know about Gawain's violent career. Then Elde gives Arthur the wrong opponent on Mount Saint Michael:

> Vppon Sayn Michaells Mounte meruaylles he wroghte,
> There a dragone he dreped, þat drede was full sore.
> (487–88)

As everyone knew and all sources report, Arthur fought a giant there.[6] In lines 495 to 512, Elde has Gawain play the role of Bedevere after the Last Battle. The Ware manuscript changes Gawain to Ewan, equally aberrant. Offord notes: "No other source mentions either Gawain or Ywain in this connection, but the poet may have known some other version" (Offord, n. 497ff). I think the poet knew essentially the same versions we know, and so did his audience.

Toward the end of the Nine Worthies (513–519), Elde anachronistically places Godfrey of Boulogne before Charlemagne, causing Gollancz to sputter at the poet:

> It is difficult to understand why Godfrey precedes Charlemagne, unless it is due to the author's utter ignorance of chronology; his knowledge of the last of the Nine Worthies is certainly vague.
> (Gollancz, n. 515–19)

In lines 520–29, Elde lists the Twelve Peers, a familiar set piece which, as Offord notes, "differs almost from text to text"; but this enumeration matches no known source (Offord, n. 522–29). And finally, Elde has Charlemagne kill "Salamadyne the Sowdane" at "Polborne" or "puerne" (532–33). Even if we follow Gollancz and Offord in taking these muddled place-names as reflecting Paderborn in Saxony, we still have Charles fighting Arabs in Europe anachronistically (Gollancz, n. 531–540; Offord, n. 532, 533).

My list of Elde's errors only touches the most glaring instances, and I invite the reader to scan the notes in Gollancz and Offord for more examples. Neither editor notes any factual errors outside of Elde's speech. Notice that the two editors attribute all these errors to the author or the scribes, never to the speaker, Elde. Both editors labor mightily to correct the author and the scribes, completely overlooking the possibility that the poet meant his audience to see Elde as simply, even outrageously, wrong. We would expect a half-alert audience to notice many of Elde's errors. They would find Elde offensive, a figure without authority.

Previous critics have noticed the less attractive side of Elde. For example, Thorlac Turville-Petre calls him a "senile, long-winded dotard, blinded by his hatred of the world."[7] Indeed, the poet introduces Elde negatively:

The thirde was a laythe lede lenyde one his syde,
A beryne bownn alle in blake, with bedis in his hande;
Croked and courbede, encrampeschett for elde;
Alle disfygured was his face, and fadit his hewe,
His berde and browes were blancheded full whitte,
And the hare one his hede hewede of the same.
He was ballede and blynde, and alle babirlippede,
Totheles and tenefull, I tell ȝowe for sothe;
And euer he momelide and ment and mercy he askede,
And cried kenely one Criste and his crede sayde,
With sawtries ful sere tymes, to sayntes in heuen;
Envyous and angrye, and Elde was his name.
I helde hym be my hopynge a hundrethe ȝeres of age,
And bot his cruche and his couche he carede for no more.
                (152–65)

Both Moran and Turville-Petre ascribe the source of this portrait to Innocent III's *De Miseria Humane Conditionis,* I.x.[8] This familiar text creates a devastating image of the physical and mental decay of the elderly. A daring poet might choose such a character as his spokesman, but he would need to counterbalance the repulsive ugliness, spiteful nature, and inept storytelling with overwhelming wisdom, clarity, and insight. Elde displays none of these positive qualities.

II

Having demolished Elde as an authority (admittedly an easy target), I wish to offer a new interpretation of the poem as a whole. I propose a new theme: the serial consequences of obsessive behavior, of materialistic self-absorption. Anyone who patterns himself on Youthe will inevitably turn into Middle Elde, and any Youthe who acts like Middle Elde will end up as Elde. The dreamer most resembles Youthe, and his dream predicts the consequences of his own behavior.

Elde tells us in lines 270–91 that he recapitulates Youthe and Middle Elde:

> While I was ʒonge in my ʒouthe and ʒape of my dedys,
> I was als euerrous in armes as ouþer of ʒoure-seluen,
> And as styffe in a stourre one my stede bake,
> And as gaye in my gere als any gome ells,
> And as lelly by-luffede with ladyse and maydens.
> My likame was louely es lothe nowe to schewe,
> And as myche wirchip I wane, i-wis, as ʒe bothen.
> And aftir irkede me with this, and ese was me leuere,
> Als man in his medill elde his makande wolde haue.
> Than I mukkede and marlede and made vp my howses,
> And purcheste me ploughe-londes and pastures full noble,
> Gatte gude and golde full gaynly to honde,
> Reches and renttes were ryfe to my-seluen.
> Bot Elde vndire-ʒode me are I laste wiste,
> And alle disfegurede my face and fadide my hewe,
> Both my browes and my berde blawnchede full whitte—
> And when he sotted my syghte, than sowed myn hert—
> Croked me, cowrbed me, encrampeschet my hondes,
> þat I ne may hefe bam to my hede ne noghte helpe my-seluen,
> Ne stale stonden one my fete bot I my staffe haue.
> Makes ʒoure mirrours bi me, men bi ʒoure trouthe—
> This schadowe in my schewere schunte ʒe no while.

This passage echoes the earlier descriptions of Youthe and Middle Elde, and combines Elde as a character and an abstraction: "Bot Elde vndire-ʒode me are I laste wiste" (283). Elde says, in effect, "I began as Youthe, became Middle Elde, and then Elde made me into Elde." This logical sequence leads to the mirror image in 290–291: "Makes ȝoure mirrours bi me, men bi ȝoure trouthe—This schadowe in my schewere schunte ȝe no while." I take this image to mean that Youthe and Middle Elde will become Elde, perhaps even that the poet equates the three characters as one person. At the end of the poem, Elde restates the sequence:

> Thou man in thi medill elde, hafe mynde whate I saye!
> I am thi sire and thou my sone, the sothe for to telle,
> And he the sone of thi-selfe, þat sittis one the stede,
> For Elde es sire of Midill Elde and Midill Elde of ȝouthe.
> (649–52)

These genealogical statements reverse the sequence of Youthe becoming Middle Elde becoming Elde, probably because the speaker Elde sees the pattern from his own selfish point of view. Like father, like son. Young Elde acted like Youthe and became like Middle Elde. The sequence will repeat itself as long as the characters maintain their present attitudes and actions.[9]

The narrator carefully specifies the ages of the three characters as thirty, sixty, and one hundred (lines 133–35, 149–51, 163–64). Each character has reached the end of a phase of his life (Kernan, 264; Turville-Petre, 74). At thirty, Youthe will shortly become middle-aged, and predictably act like Middle Elde. Middle Elde at sixty will awaken momentarily to discover that Elde has undermined him into Elde. And 100-year-old Elde hears death knocking for him in line 654.

The poet also presents these characters as extremes in behavior as well as in age.[10] Youthe and Middle Elde devote themselves exclusively to selfish materialistic concerns.[11] Elde seems as arrogant and egotistical as the two younger characters. As his speech begins in lines 266 to 299, thirty-four lines in all, he uses forty-four first-person pronouns. As it ends in 649–54, six lines contain eight personal references.[12] And Elde's supreme arrogance surfaces in the main thrust of his speech, the implied comparison of himself with the Nine Worthies. Earlier we see Elde in a religious mode:

> And euer he momelide and ment and mercy he askede,
> And cried kenely one criste and his crede sayde,
> With sawtries full sere tymes, to sayntes in heuen.
> (160–62)

But the next line undercuts this positive picture with two adjectives, "envyous and angrye" (163). Elde uncharitably savages the other two characters for their materialistic obsessions, identical with his own earlier activities. But none of Elde's 390 spoken lines contains one word of repentence of *his* actions or attitudes. He chiefly regrets death's approach. At the end of his speech, he says that death sweeps away all the obsessions of the other two characters:

> And ther-to paramours and pride puttes he full lowe;
> Ne there es reches ne rent may rawnsone ȝour lyues,
> Ne noghte es sekire to ȝoure-self in certayne bot dethe,
> And he es so vncertayne that sodaynly he comes,
> Me thynke þe wele of this werlde worthes to noghte.[13]

He advises the other two to reform, but goes to his grave without one syllable of personal remorse. He may provide corrective words, but hardly a corrective example.[14]

III

The most vexing interpretative problems in dream vision scholarship always seem to concern the relation of the frame and the dream, especially the closing of the frame and the ending of the poem. What scholar has not secretly wished that the author would step to the footlights and tell us what the dream meant and how the audience should act? Unfortunately for us but fortunately for poetry, medieval authors and audiences seemed to prefer problematic endings, where the dream simply stops, sometimes in the middle of a sentence promising great authority, or where birds sing, or the dreamer resolves to go on reading. *Parlement* has especially perplexing difficulties because the dreamer does not appear in his own dream, nor does he seem to react to it at the end.[15]

Critics have noticed resemblances between the dreamer and the Three Ages, especially Youthe.[16] I see Youthe as the dreamer writ large, or, put psychologically, Youthe represents the dreamer's aspirations. The dreamer would probably prefer to trade the anxiety of poaching for open hunting; perhaps he would like a gaggle of pretty ladies and a nice horse. He openly admires Youthe, whom he calls "the semely[este] segge that I seghe euer."[17]

The Three Ages do not represent everyman's life, but only this dreamer's life. I think the narrator experiences a prophetic dream of himself, in which he sees Youthe as a projection of all he would like to become. But he also sees that such a Youthe becomes such a Middle Elde, who inevitably ends up as such an Elde. All dreamers grow old, and all die. But the dreamer does not have to turn himself into Elde by obsessive, selfish behavior.

At the end of the poem, the dreamer apparently shows no recognition of mortality, or the consequences of bad attitudes, or indeed of anything else in his dream. He simply wakes up and goes back to town. Kernan suggests an affective reading of the ending:

The narrator's attitude is left a blank, inviting the reader to fill in his own. In itself the awakening and turning back toward town brings the statement made by the vision into the real world and suggests application to everyday life.

(Kernan, 277; cp. Moran, 631)

The poet does not need to hit the audience over the head with a potentially sinful narrator realizing the point of his own dream. The audience would probably identify with this attractive narrator, who speaks so familiarly to them. They would probably see his potential future, for good or ill, as theirs. In fact, the narrator's last words include the audience in the pronouns. He does not ask Mary to save *him* from *his* sins. He says:

And Mary þat is myld quene amend *vs* of *oure* nysse.[18]

Notes

1. R. A. Peck, "The Careful Hunter in *The Parlement of the Thre Ages*," *English Literary History* 39 (1972): 332–41; this quotation, 334.

2. D. V. Moran, "*The Parlement of the Thre Ages:* Meaning and Design," *Neophilologus* 62 (1978): 620–33; this quotation, 628. For similar views, see C. W. Dunn and E. T. Byrnes, eds., *Middle English Literature* (New York: Harcourt Brace Jovanovich, 1973), 238; Anne Kernan, "Theme and Structure in *The Parlement of the Thre Ages*," *Neuphilologische Mitteilungen* 75 (1974): 253–78; H. L. Savage, "Notes on the Prologue of *The Parlement of the Thre Ages*," *Journal of English and Germanic Philology* 29 (1930): 74–82; W. H. Schofield, *English Literature from the Norman Conquest to Chaucer* (London: Macmillan, 1906; reprint 1921), 316; J. Speirs, " 'Wynnere and Wastoure' and 'The Parlement of the Thre Ages,' " *Scrutiny* 27 (1950): 221–52; R. A. Waldron, "The Prologue to 'The Parlement of the Thre Ages,' " *Neuphilologische Mitteilungen* 73 (1972): 786–94; and D. J. Williams, "Alliterative Poetry in the Fourteenth and Fifteenth Centuries," in W. F. Bolton, ed., *The Middle Ages* (London: Barrie and Jenkins, 1970), 107–58.

3. J. P. Oakden, *Alliterative Poetry in Middle English,* 2 vols. (Manchester: Manchester University Press, 1930, 1935; reprint New York: Archon, 1968), II, 54.

4. I. Gollancz, (London: Milford, 1915); Gollancz first edited the poem for the Roxburghe Club in 1897. Line counts and all quotations refer to the standard edition, M. Y. Offord, ed., *The Parlement of the Thre Ages,* Early English Text Society 246 (London: Oxford University Press, 1959). I quote the Thornton manuscript text unless I specify the Ware manuscript.

5. Offord, 54, n. 329. The Ware manuscript gives line 324 as "For þere Sir piramus þer prynce put was to were," saving their lives, if we take *were* as 'war,' as Offord does, 96. But *were* might also mean 'defense' or 'doubt,' as in "þe Inglis men put þam to were," in J. Hall, ed., *The Poems of Laurence Minot,* 2nd ed. (Oxford:

Clarendon Press, 1897), III, line 95. Cf. F. H. Stratman and H. Bradley, eds., *A Middle-English Dictionary* (Oxford: Clarendon Press, 1891), 681.

6. Since Arthur earlier dreamed of a dragon, we might emend *dreped* to *dremed*, but then we join the editors in correcting errors ostensibly scribal, but likely intentional.

7. Thorlac Turville-Petre, "The Ages of Man in *The Parlement of the Thre Ages*," *Medium Ævum* 46 (1977): 66–76; this quotation, 72.

8. Moran, 628; Turville-Petre, 71–72; and *Patrologia Latina* 217: 706, conveniently quoted and translated in Moran, n. 27. See D. R. Howard, ed., Lothario De Segni, *On the Misery of the Human Condition*, trans. M. M. Dietz (Indianapolis: Bobbs-Merill, 1969), 13. Moran also cites Horace's *Ars Poetica,* 169–78.

9. For similar notions, see Turville-Petre, 73; Speirs, 241, 248–249.

10. B. Rowland, "The Three Ages of *The Parlement of the Thre Ages*," *Chaucer Review* 9 (1975): 342–52; this quotation, 348. See also Turville-Petre, 68, 73, and J. Speirs, *Medieval English Poetry/The Non-Chaucerian Tradition* (London: Faber and Faber, 1966), 301.

11. D. Lampe, "The Poetic Strategy of *The Parlement of the Thre Ages*," *Chaucer Review* 7 (1973): 173–83.

12. Elde uses a higher density of first-person pronouns than Arthur does in his egotistical tirade in *Morte Arthure* 4275–4290, fourteen in sixteen lines; L. Benson, ed., *King Arthur's Death* (Indianapolis: Bobbs-Merill, 1974), 236.

13. 633–37, my emphasis. For similar diction concerning Youthe and Middle Elde, see lines 141, 186, and 282.

14. Elde's final Bible quotation, "Et ecce omnia munda sunt vobis" (and behold, all things are clean unto you; Vulgate, Luke 11.41), appears in a context of Christ's warning against hypocrisy. Offord incorrectly attributes this quotation to Luke 17.14; Dunn and Byrnes, 263, ascribe it to Luke 17.21, and mistranslate, "And behold all the world is yours."

15. T. Bestul, *Satire and Allegory in Wynnere and Wastoure* (Lincoln: University of Nebraska Press, 1974), 84; cp. *Book of the Duchess, House of Fame, Parliament of Fowls, Legend of Good Women, Piers Plowman, Divine Comedy, Assembly of Ladies, Pearl, Dream of the Rood, Romance of the Rose,* and *Consolation of Philosophy.*

16. Waldron, 793, 794. Speirs also sees the Three Ages as a "universal human application," 248. See also J. Gardner, *The Alliterative Morte Arthure / The Owl and the Nightingale and Five Other Middle English Poems* (Carbondale: Southern Illinois University Press, 1971), 262–63.

17. In view of the interpretation developing here, we might be tempted to de-emend line 135 back to the manuscript reading, "the semely segge that I seghe euer," as a hint that the dreamer sees the same *segge* all the way through the vision (*euer*).

18. Ware manuscript, 665, my emphasis; Thornton has "amende *vs* of synn. Amen. Amen."

Part IV
Bridging Historical Distance

In any hermeneutic activity, the interpreter brings to a text the preoccupations of his own time and culture. Interpretation is often an act of mediation between the present and the past, in which the two time frames interact. Joseph M. P. Donatelli discusses how Thomas Percy, in the course of compiling the *Reliques*, used medieval metrical romances to reshape ballads for late eighteenth-century tastes. Paul E. Szarmach examines Ælfric's awareness and use of traditional biblical commentary wherein he describes the act of understanding in terms of a response to the beautiful letters of a manuscript. Giles Constable provides a moving portrait of a twentieth-century historian, William Mendel Newman, whose unhappy life gave motive and even focus to his study of medieval institutions. And Madeline H. Caviness demonstrates how the new insights of Post-Impressionist movements were the vehicle by which the modern world came to understand early medieval art.

18. Old Barons in New Robes: Percy's Use of the Metrical Romances in the Reliques of Ancient English Poetry

JOSEPH M. P. DONATELLI

The publication of Thomas Percy's *Reliques of Ancient English Poetry* in 1765 changed the course of English literature. Wordsworth claimed that England's poetry "had been absolutely redeemed by it," and he acknowledged the debt which he and other Romantic poets, most notably Coleridge, owed to the *Reliques*.[1] In later life, Scott recounted how his happy discovery of Percy's anthology "beneath a large platanas tree in the ruins of an . . . old fashioned arbour" caused him to miss his dinner hour, "notwithstanding the sharp appetite of thirteen."[2] The *Reliques* went through four editions during Percy's lifetime, and the more than fifty editions of the work which have been published since Percy's death in 1811 attest to the continuing importance and stature of this collection of ballads, songs, and lyrics.

Even Dr. Johnson, an inveterate ballad-hater, had praised "the grace and splendour" which Percy had given to his studies of antiquity, while wryly observing that the "mere antiquarian is a rugged being."[3] Yet the very qualities that made Percy's work so attractive to a wide audience have been Percy's undoing among literary scholars. Because of his decision to alter his texts radically to cater to an eighteenth-century audience that had little taste for "unadulterated antiquity," Percy has been scorned as an unscrupulous editor and dismissed as a popularizer. One of Percy's contemporaries, Joseph Ritson, set the tone for the attack when he impugned Percy's judgment and morals, and viciously accused him of secretly suppressing original texts and substituting his own fabrications.[4]

I would like to continue the rehabilitation of Percy's reputation undertaken by more recent scholars, including Walter Jackson Bate, Albert Friedman, and Cleanth Brooks,[5] by looking at the famous Folio manuscript (BL Add. 27879) which clearly sparked Percy's interest in early English poetry, and provided him with many of the "select remains of our ancient English bards and minstrels" which were published in the *Reliques*. I would suggest that this manuscript molded Percy's highly influential view of the close relationship between the ballad and the metrical romance, and that this view may explain, though perhaps not justify, the editorial procedures for which Percy has been so roundly condemned.

In what must be one of the most charming bibliographic discoveries, Percy rescued this "unbound and sadly torn" volume from the house of his friend, Sir Humphrey Pitt, where it lay under a bureau, being used by the maids to light the fire.[6] In this remarkable manuscript, Percy found late medieval versions of metrical romances, ballads, two alliterative poems (*Death and Liffe* and *Scottish Feilde*), and Tudor and Stuart lyrics and songs. The texts date from the late medieval period to the reign of Charles I. As we shall see, Percy believed this grand historical sweep to be even greater, and he put what he considered to be a survey of hitherto neglected medieval literary forms to good use, producing influential studies on the ballad and the role of the minstrel, the metrical romances, and alliterative poetry, all of which he included in the *Reliques*. Happily, this manuscript, which now bears his name, preserved unique copies of some of the best English ballads, yet the extraordinary corruption, in both sense and language, which characterizes these and other texts has led many a modern editor to wish that Percy had left the maids to their incendiary work.

The bulk of the Percy Folio manuscript is devoted to seventeen late versions of metrical romances. Although Percy did not include any romances in the *Reliques,* apparently because of their length, an essay on the metrical romances introduced the third volume of ballads on "romantic subjects," and it reveals the extent of Percy's scholarly knowledge.[7] Using the romances in his manuscript as a starting point, Percy published the first bibliography of Middle English romances in this essay. Percy had, in fact, transcribed twenty-six romances himself, and intended to publish a collection of them, although his plan was but one of many literary projects that the bishop never realized.[8] Percy also took up the apology for the genre begun by Bishop Hurd and Thomas Warton by providing a synopsis of the Folio manuscript version of *Libeaus Desconus* (entitled *Libius Disconius*) to demonstrate that a romance, despite its "barbarous unpolished language," could be "as regular in its conduct as any of the finest poems of antiquity."

The sheer volume of metrical romances largely determined Percy's assumptions about the entire contents of the manuscript, for he interpreted the discrete parts of his model, the ballads, against a background formed by a gestalt of romances, even though the romances themselves were strangely absent from the *Reliques*. The juxtaposition of ballads and romances in the Folio MS convinced Percy that the ballads were also medieval "reliques," closely related to the metrical romances. In an era with little firsthand knowledge of Middle English metrical romances, Percy believed that the ballads and romances in the manuscript describing heroes named in Chaucer's *Sir Thopas* (such as Guy of Warwick, Libeaus Desconus, and Sir Gawain) dated from before Chaucer's time. He concluded that Chaucer had borrowed the *Wife of Bath's Tale* from the ballad *The Marriage of Sir Gawaine,* and that Malory had only thrown together into a regular story "the Subject of a hundred Old Ballads."[9] Moreover, the highly corrupt and modernized state of the late romances in the Folio manuscript, which Derek Pearsall has described as half way to becoming ballads,[10] blurred the distinction between ballads and romances in Percy's mind, since there seemed to be little difference between the style and content of these works. His terminology is often tentative and uncertain: he calls *Libius Disconius* and *Sir Lambwell* ballads, while referring to *Sir Cauline* as a "romantic tale."[11]

Despite the wretched state of the Folio MS texts, Percy believed that both the ballads and romances were originally composed and recited by minstrels, to whom Percy accorded an exalted function comparable to that of a Homeric bard or skald. Percy's conception of the medieval minstrel as a companion of kings and nobles, "who got their livelihood by singing verses to the harp at the houses of the great," is a powerful, evocative image with a long history in Romantic poetry and subsequent medieval scholarship.[12] According to Percy, this order eventually became debased, transmitting and producing the inferior entertainment found in the Folio MS, as well as in the journalistic, hack efforts of ballad-mongers.

Percy's extensive reading in the metrical romances afforded him the opportunity to compare the Folio manuscript versions of romances with older witnesses. Upon comparing *Sir Lambwell* to *Sir Launfal* or *The Squier* to *The Squire of Low Degree,* for example, he realized how inferior his "mutilated, incorrect" texts were, and blamed latter-day minstrels for their "wretched readings," which in many places were nothing more than "unintelligible nonsense" (*Reliques,* I, 11). Percy inferred that the ballads had met a similar, if not a worse, fate. Although Percy was also able to compare versions of ballads, he seems to have used romance transmission as a model to explain how these poems, which he believed to have been originally composed for the court, had fallen so low. Percy could therefore envision a more perfect version of ballads, especially those on "romantic subjects," where in fact none existed, and he set about to "supplement," "correct," and "complete" these narratives by using the romances to restore something of their former splendor and glory. These efforts resulted in the introduction of poetry that was written by Percy, and his failure to report these alterations has consigned him to what Albert Friedman has termed "the special hell reserved for bad editors."

The blame for Percy's editorial decision has often been put on the shoulders of William Shenstone, who collaborated with Percy on the first edition of the *Reliques.*[13] As early as 1757, Percy had informed Shenstone of the Folio MS which had come into his possession. In his reply, Shenstone expressed concern that Percy would produce the letter, rather than the spirit of its contents. He advised Percy not to publish the contents of the MS, but rather to use its roughly hewn materials as a *materia informis* for his own poetic invention. In a sense, Shenstone counselled hermeneutic rather than editorial activity, for he recognized that Percy's success depended on his ability to mediate between a past that was something of an embarrassment and the fastidious taste of the present: the Folio MS, he argued, ought to be considered as a "hoard of gold, somewhat defac'd by Time" that could be restored "under more current Impressions."[14] Accordingly, these alterations could be compared to "a Modern Toe or Finger, which is allowably added to the best statues."[15]

Percy's revisions to many of the ballads included such "toes" and "fingers" typical of the "improving" editions and ballad *rifacimenti* fashionable during the period: he regularized the meter, corrected and improved rhymes, reworked the diction, and straightened syntax.[16] But these emendations are minor compared to the extensive interpolations and alterations introduced into ballads on "romantic subjects" in the *Reliques. Sir Cauline* and *The Marriage of Sir Gawaine* were swollen to twice their original length; *The Child of Elle*, a mere fragment of thirty-nine lines in the Folio MS, was amplified to 201 lines, while little of the original was left untouched. The term *reliques* was particularly apt for these ballads, for Percy seems to have conceived of them as mere vestiges of complete narratives, and as partial realizations of the promise inherent in his text. His headnote to *Sir Cauline* is instructive: "the whole appeared so far short of the perfection it seemed to deserve that the Editor was tempted to add several stanzas in the first part, and still more in the second, to connect and compleat the story in the manner which appeared to him most interesting and affecting" (*Reliques*, I, 61). Percy's conception of these ballads as fragmentary productions (or, as mere parts of a whole) seems to have depended upon his viewing them against a background of romance narratives, a perception which was prompted by their juxtaposition in his Folio manuscript.

In these ballads, Percy set about to reverse the process by which these works had become so threadbare, and the romances provided a ready, if not logical, source for his alterations, since he believed that the romances and ballads had been similarly composed, and that both had suffered by an oral transmission directed to a popular audience. Percy had grasped the conventional and episodic nature of romance narratives, and he applied this knowledge in his ballad restorations. As Percy read ballads that described romance commonplaces, he freely supplied plot incidents and details taken from the fuller expositions found in the romances to amplify and expand the terse, often fragmentary narrative of these ballads. In a sense, Percy composed in a manner similar to that of the medieval minstrels whom he so admired, for just as the composers and reciters of such pieces "made no scruple" in altering each other's productions, Percy felt free to change and enrich these ballads by borrowing materials from the romances.

In his restoration of these ballads, Percy appropriated elements that were originally details of other texts, in other words, parts of different wholes. In his introductions to a few ballads, Percy uncovered his method and openly avowed his large debt to romance materials. In *Valentine and Ursine,* the ballad which he fashioned from a couplet version of *Valentine and Orson* in the Folio MS, Percy acknowledged not only that he had drawn details from the romance itself, but that he had gratuitously introduced a marvellous bridge (lined with bells) described in *Beues of Hampton* into the poem (*Reliques,* III, 265). This image had come to Percy's attention when he discovered that Richard Johnson had borrowed this bridge from *Beues* in his sixteenth-century romance, *The Seven Champions of Christendom,*[17] and he was so impressed with both the detail and his scholarly discovery of it in both texts (his headnote dwells on the latter) that he made use of it in this ballad. In a creative reworking of *King Arthur's Death,* Percy had relied upon a more congruous source, having turned to Malory for details concerning Arthur's death and the tossing of Excalibur into the water (*Reliques,* III, 27–8). But it is in his restoration of the ballad *The Legend of King Arthur* that Percy most closely approximates a modern editor, and his success in restoring this ballad testifies to his scholarly acumen. In his headnote to *The Legend* (*Reliques,* III, 39), Percy stated that he had relied upon the chronicles of Geoffrey of Monmouth and Caxton to correct corrupt forms of proper names and to transpose stanzas which were apparently misplaced. Charles Millican's discovery of the source for this ballad, an Elizabethan account of the Nine Worthies composed by Richard Lloyd, has shown that both of Percy's transpositions, as well as many of his emendations, were absolutely correct.[18] Percy knew the Arthurian tradition so well that he succeeded in reconstructing the exact continuity of the original text without ever seeing it.

The fifteenth-century ballad *The Marriage of Sir Gawaine* (*Reliques,* III, 13–24) provides a particularly interesting example of Percy's method. The *Marriage* is a loathly lady tale in which Arthur is charged with answering the question what women want most, and Gawain must marry the hag who provides the answer. Its narrative is most similar to the late romance *The Weddynge of Sir Gawen and Dame Ragnell.*[19] The unique text of the *Marriage* which survives in the Folio MS is indeed fragmentary since half of each folio on which the poem appears has been torn away.[20] The wretched physical state of this manuscript invited Percy to hermeneutic activity (see also Professor Robinson's essay, *supra,* pp. 193–200). Percy faced the task of bridging rather large narrative gaps, which he estimated to be nine stanzas in length, and he drew upon conventional romance episodes to replenish these lacunae.

The first few lines of the ballad describe a Christmas feast at Arthur's court at Carlisle; after the first gap, Arthur declines to fight a "bold baron" at Tarn Wadling, and is told that he must ransom himself by answering the question what it is that women want most. To get Arthur out of his court and to Tarn Wadling, Percy introduces a damsel who interrupts the feast and asks that Arthur avenge her since this bold baron has imprisoned her lover in his "bowre," and then "misused" her. From his reading in the Folio MS, Percy was familiar with the conventional opening of a romance at the king's court, and with the interruption of the feast by one who delivers a message or a challenge: *The Grene Knight* and *The Turke and Gowin* begin in precisely this way, and *The Boy and the Mantle,* yet another Arthurian ballad in the MS, begins with the court in residence at Carlisle.[21] But perhaps the closest episode is that found in the Folio MS version of *Libeaus Desconus,* in which Helen, a fair maiden, interrupts a feast, kneels before the king, and, according to Percy's synopsis, "comes to implore King Arthur's assistance to rescue a young princess . . . who is detained from her rights, and confined in prison."[22] Although the details of *Libeaus* do not correspond exactly, the underlying dramatic situation is similar to the one Percy introduces into the *Marriage,* and Percy may well have thought of *Libeaus* because it also tells a transformation story involving Gawain and his kin.

From his reading Percy had also concluded that Arthur's knights were characterized with certain attributes and manners: "thus *Gawaine* is always drawn courteous and gentle: *Kay* rugged and brutal: *Guenever* light and inconstant."[23] Although this observation seems only too obvious now, at the time Percy had excitedly communicated his discovery to a grateful and attentive Thomas Warton. In the *Marriage,* Arthur is unwilling to fight the "bold baron" and is discourteous to the loathly lady, a characterization which would have been unthinkable to a reader of romances and chronicles, let alone to a reader of Spenser.[24] Percy set about to alter the portrayal of a cowardly and rude Arthur in the ballad. The baron becomes a giant, who now lives in a castle built on "magicke ground" that saps Arthur of his strength when he sets foot upon it. The original detail of the baron carrying "a great club upon his back" may have first suggested Percy's transformation of this character into a giant, but the idea behind this scene may well have come from *The Faerie Queene,* for with the changing of a few details it is reminiscent of Red-Cross's defeat by the giant Orgoglio after the knight has drunk from a spring that has sapped him of his powers. Red-Cross is then imprisoned in Orgoglio's castle, and his release is only obtained when Una encounters Prince Arthur and begs his assistance (Book I.vii–viii).

Further, in Percy's version Arthur's silence upon meeting the hag is no longer interpreted as a sign of discourtesy; instead, Percy emphasizes how thunderstruck he is by her loathsome appearance. Percy also rejects Arthur's unprompted and unceremonious offer of Gawain as a husband. In his version, Arthur agrees to whatever the hag wishes, leaving Gawain an opportunity to exhibit his "old Courtesy" when he offers himself as a bridegroom in a subsequent interpolation: "Then bespake him Sir Gawaine, / That was ever a gentle knighte: / That lothly ladye I will wed; / Therefore be merry and lighte" (*MSG* II.21–4).

Since Percy believed the *Marriage* to have been Chaucer's source for the *Wife of Bath's Tale,* it is hardly surprising that he went to the Wife's tale for a number of scenes. For example, the ballad omits a description of Arthur's fruitless search for an answer before he meets the hag. In Percy's version, Arthur rides everywhere in search of the answer immediately after being set the question, just as the knight does in the Wife's tale (*WBT* III.919–21).[25] Arthur receives answers which seem to be modernizations of the various responses given in Chaucer: Percy's "riches, pompe, or state," correspond to "richesse" and "honour"; "rayment fine and brighte" to "riche array"; "mirthe" and "flatterye" to "jolynesse" and "flaterye," and "a jolly knighte" may well represent a censored version of "lust abedde" (*MSG* I.81–4; *WBT* 925–34). The encounter with the loathly lady also contains hints of the *Wife of Bath's Tale*. Percy has Arthur offer the hag whatever she wishes in return for the answer, and he, just as the knight in Chaucer, must swear to keep his promise before learning what her request will be (*MSG* I.109–20; *WBT* 1008–13). Percy's reference to the answer as a "secrette" (*MSG* I.115) may owe something to Chaucer's image of the hag whispering it in the knight's ear (*WBT* 1021).

Much of the bedroom scene after the marriage of Gawain and the loathly lady is also missing from the ballad, although it is clear that the transformation of the hag into a beautiful woman takes place before the knight yields his sovereignty to the lady, as it does in the *Weddynge* as well as in Gower's *Tale of Florent*. The original states that the lady's enchantment is the work of a wicked stepmother; Percy adds that this "spelle" could not be lifted until "a yong faire courtlye knight" married her, and agreed to be ruled by her. Percy may have inferred this explanation from the events described in the ballad, with the help of the clue provided by the *maistrie* won at the end of the *Wife of Bath's Tale;* however, the interpolation is sufficiently close to Gower's conclusion to make one wonder if Percy did not know the *Tale of Florent* as well. Yet Percy only mentions Gower in passing, and then merely to condemn his "tedious allegories" (*Reliques,* III, 354). On the other hand, Warton seems to have been one of the first scholars to have noticed the similarity between the loathly lady stories of Gower and Chaucer, and Percy may have benefited from this insight.[26]

It is possible to analyze *Sir Cauline* in a similar fashion. This ballad was cited by Henry Wheatley, who published what has become the standard edition of the *Reliques* in 1876, as Percy's "most flagrant violation of manuscript authority"; ironically, *Sir Cauline* was singled out for praise by Wordsworth, who judged it to be "an exquisite ballad," and Coleridge borrowed heavily from it in *Christabel*.[27] The numerous romance commonplaces in this ballad, notably a vassal's love for a king's daughter and the deeds of valor undertaken by Cauline to win the princess, were familiar to Percy from his reading of *King Horn, Guy of Warwick, The Squire of Low Degree,* and two Folio romances, *Sir Degree* and *Eglamore*.

Since Percy had not postulated a source for this ballad, he freely introduced and blended scenes and images from many of these romances in his version of *Sir Cauline*. From *Eglamore*, for example, he borrowed the name *Christabel*, with which he christened the unnamed lady of the ballad, and perhaps he modelled his reworking of Cauline's battle with a giant on Eglamore's defeat of the giant Marrocke and his brother. Imagery from *Eger and Grime*, which was also collected in the Folio manuscript, seems to have been introduced in Percy's handling of the relatively uncommon Eldridge king episode, for he seems to have observed parallels between Sir Gray-Steel and the Eldridge king which have not gone unnoticed by modern editors of these works.[28]

Yet Percy's rejection of the ending of the ballad, in which Cauline marries the princess and she bears him fifteen sons, reveals his willingness to sacrifice an authentic romance episode (confirmed by his reading in the *Earl of Toulouse*) if it did not cater to eighteenth-century sensibility. Having heeded Shenstone's advice, Percy is well aware that he is mediating between the past and an age that had little taste for "unadulterated antiquity." Percy seeks to bridge this historical distance by substituting a pathetic, tragic ending in which Cauline is mortally wounded and Christabel dies from sorrow. His reworking recalls the sentimental conclusions of ballad imitations, and demonstrates just how far Percy would stray from romance materials to create an "interesting and affecting" scene.

The theme of the present volume indicates perhaps that our modern critical sensibility is now prepared to acknowledge, though perhaps not to endorse, Percy's hermeneutic enterprise in the *Reliques*. Percy's extensive revisions and interpolations have received kinder assessments from more recent critics, who have called attention to the audience that this method won for previously neglected poetry, to the notoriously corrupt texts of the Folio MS, and to the superior poetry found in some of Percy's versions, which had impressed Scott, Wordsworth, and Coleridge. Undoubtedly, Percy's methods, if considered from the point of view of a modern scholarly editor, are absolutely indefensible. I would argue, however, that Percy never saw himself as an "editor" of these ballads in the modern sense of the word, but rather envisioned himself as a latter-day minstrel, trying to reshape the romance ballads of the Folio MS so that they might better please his eighteenth-century audience. In doing so, Percy was following in the steps of the antiquarian scribe who had compiled the Percy Folio MS in the preceding century, for he too had revived and remade forgotten poems and songs.

Shenstone had once remarked to Percy that his "improved" copies could still rank as old barons, however modern their robes might be.[29] But Percy had clothed these ballads according to his understanding of medieval minstrel activity, and he had woven his texts from romance materials that were originally medieval. It was this re-creation of minstrel activity in the eighteenth century, rather than the insipid and fussy emendations and modernizations suggested by Shenstone, that won Percy such a high place in English literature and captured the imagination of the Romantic poets.

Notes

1. *The Prose Works of William Wordsworth,* ed. W. J. B. Owen and Jane Worthington Smyser, 3 vols. (Oxford: Clarendon Press, 1974), 3:78.

2. *Scott on Himself,* ed. David Hewitt (Edinburgh: Scottish Academic Press, 1981), 28.

3. *Boswell's Life of Johnson,* ed. G. B. Hill, rev. L. F. Powell, 6 vols. (Oxford: Clarendon Press, 1934–50), 3:278. Despite this praise, Dr. Johnson's attitude towards Percy is not easily understood; Johnson's well-known parodies of Percy's ballad scholarship and compositions suggest a contempt for such projects. On this apparent contradiction, see Albert Friedman, *The Ballad Revival* (Chicago: University of Chicago Press, 1961), 188–94.

4. "To correct the obvious errors of an illiterate transcriber, to supply irremediable defects, and to make sense of nonsense, are certainly essential duties of an editor of ancient poetry, provided he act with integrity and publicity; but secretly to suppress the original text, and insert his own fabrications for the sake of providing more refined entertainment for readers of taste and genius, is no proof or either judgment, candour, or integrity," *Ancient English Metrical Romances,* ed. J. Ritson, rev. E. Goldsmid, 3 vols. (Edinburgh: E. and G. Goldsmid, 1884–86), 1:58. For an account of the Percy-Ritson feud, see Bertrand H. Bronson, *Joseph Ritson: Scholar-at-Arms,* 2 vols. (Berkeley: University of California Press, 1938), vol. 2, chap. 8.

5. Walter Jackson Bate, "Percy's Use of His Folio-Manuscript," *Journal of English and Germanic Philology* 43 (1944): 337–48; Friedman, *The Ballad Revival,* chap. 7; Cleanth Brooks, ed., *The Correspondence of Thomas Percy and William Shenstone,* vol. 7 of *The Percy Letters* (New Haven: Yale University Press, 1977), xv–xxiii.

6. Percy recorded the circumstances relating to this discovery in a note which appears on the inside cover of the Folio MS. The contents of the MS (including Percy's notes) have been edited by John W. Hales and Frederick J. Furnivall in *Bishop Percy's Folio Manuscript,* 3 vols. (London: N. Trübner and Co., 1867–68); a fourth volume, *Loose and Humorous Songs,* was edited and published by Furnivall in 1868. For the note in question, see Hales and Furnivall, 1: lxxiv. On the date of Percy's discovery, see Bertram H. Davis, *Thomas Percy* (Boston: Twayne Publishers, 1981), 75–6.

7. "On the Ancient Metrical Romances," in *Reliques of Ancient English Poetry,* ed. Henry B. Wheatley, 3 vols. (London: Swan Sonnenschein and Co., 1910), 3:339–76. Unless otherwise noted, all subsequent references to the *Reliques* are to Wheatley's edition.

8. "The favourable light in which Mr. Hurd and he [Warton] set the old Romances, I think will be an excellent preparative for such a collection of the old ones in metre as I think sometime or other to publish," *The Correspondence of Thomas Percy and Richard Farmer,* ed. Cleanth Brooks, vol. 2 of *The Percy Letters* (Baton Rouge: Louisiana State University Press, 1946), letter dated Sept. 9, 1762, p. 9; see also *The Correspondence of Thomas Percy and David Dalrymple, Lord Hailes,* ed. A. F.

Falconer, vol. 4 of *The Percy Letters* (Baton Rouge: Louisiana State University Press, 1954), 55–6.

Arthur Johnston has discussed Percy's contribution to early romance scholarship in *Enchanted Ground: The Study of Medieval Romance in the Eighteenth Century* (London: Athlone Press, 1964), 75–99. See also Leah Dennis, "Percy's Essay 'On the Ancient Metrical Romances,' " *Publications of the Modern Language Association* 49 (1934): 81–97, and E. K. A. Mackenzie, "Thomas Percy's Great Schemes," *Modern Language Review* 43 (1948): 34–8.

9. *The Correspondence of Thomas Percy and Thomas Warton*, ed. M. G. Robinson and Leah Dennis, vol. 3 of *The Percy Letters* (Baton Rouge: Louisiana State University Press, 1951), 2.

10. *Old and Middle English Poetry* (London: Routledge and Kegan Paul, 1977), 260–4.

11. The relation between the ballad and medieval romance remains a vexed question; for a recent discussion, see H. O. Nygard, "Popular Ballad and Medieval Romance," in *Ballad Studies*, ed. E. B. Lyle (Cambridge: D. S. Brewer, 1976), 1–19.

12. Percy's famous views on the subject, which gave rise to considerable debate about the status of the medieval English minstrel, can be found in "An Essay on the Ancient Minstrels in England," *Reliques*, 1:345–430; Percy was willing to admit, however, that some of the longer romances may have been originally composed in writing (1:404–5).

13. Irving L. Churchill, "William Shenstone's Share in the Preparation of Percy's *Reliques*," *Publications of the Modern Language Association* 51 (1936): 960–74; Leah Dennis, "Thomas Percy, Antiquarian *vs.* Man of Taste," *Publications of the Modern Language Association* 57 (1942): 140–54; and Cleanth Brooks's introduction to the Percy-Shenstone *Correspondence*.

14. Percy-Shenstone *Correspondence*, letter dated Nov. 24, 1757, 3–4.

15. Ibid., 73.

16. For a detailed account of these emendations, see Bate, 337–48; also Eileen Mackenzie, "Thomas Percy and Ballad 'Correctness,' " *Review of English Studies* 21 (1945): 58–60, and Friedman, 204ff.

17. Percy-Warton *Correspondence*, 38–42; Percy's bridge, in fact, has one hundred bells like Johnson's, not sixty as in *Beues*.

18. Charles Millican, "The Original of the Ballad 'Kinge: Arthurs Death' in the Percy Folio MS.," *Publications of the Modern Language Association* 46 (1931): 1020–24.

19. Laura Sumner, in her edition of *The Weddynge*, has argued that both works derive from the same source: see *Smith College Studies in Modern Languages*, vol. 5, no. 4. (Northampton, Mass., 1924): xx–xxvi.

20. For the Folio MS version of the *Marriage*, see Hales and Furnivall, 1:103–

18; in response to Ritson's attacks, Percy produced a faithful transcription of the MS version in the fourth edition of the *Reliques* (published in 1794, and nominally edited by Percy's nephew) to demonstrate the extreme corruption of his MS texts.

21. Hales and Furnivall, 1:90–2; 2:58–62; 2:304–5; *The Marriage* follows *The Turke and Gowin* in the Folio MS.

22. Hales and Furnivall, 2:419–23, lines 109–77.

23. Percy-Warton *Correspondence,* 3.

24. In March, 1764, Evan Evans, an expert in Welsh poetry, had sent, at Percy's request, notes on the *Marriage,* in which he observed that "we never read of King Arthur's being ever worsted in any of his battles or single combats in any of our romances" (*The Correspondence of Thomas Percy and Evan Evans,* ed. Aneirin Lewis, vol. 5 of *The Percy Letters* [Baton Rouge: Louisiana State University Press, 1957], 70).

25. All references to Chaucer's poetry from *The Works of Geoffrey Chaucer,* ed. F. N. Robinson, 2nd ed. (Cambridge, Mass.: Houghton Mifflin, 1957).

26. Thomas Warton, *The History of English Poetry,* ed. W. Carew Hazlitt, 4 vols. (London: Reeves and Turner, 1871), 3:32.

27. On Coleridge's borrowings, see Donald Reuel Tuttle, "*Christabel* Sources in Percy's *Reliques* and the Gothic Romances," *Publications of the Modern Language Association* 53 (1938): 445–74.

28. See, for example, *Eger and Grime,* ed. James Ralston Caldwell (Cambridge, Mass.: Harvard University Press, 1933), 58–60; *The English and Scottish Popular Ballads,* ed. F.J. Child (1882–98; rpt., New York: The Folklore Press, 1957), 2:56–7.

29. Percy-Shenstone *Correspondence,* 137.

19. Ælfric as Exegete: Approaches and Examples in the Study of the Sermones Catholici

PAUL E. SZARMACH

If we take the long view of the history of medieval exegesis, Ælfric of Eynsham does not appear on the horizon. In her magisterial study of the Bible and medieval exegesis, the late Beryl Smalley gives Ælfric two notices, one of them more or less favorable in a comparison with Andrew of St. Victor and the other, an aside about Ælfric's literalism, rather more critical.[1] Indeed, Norman Cantor suggests that Ælfric may have further missed his chance because by writing in the vernacular he could not hope that his intellectual discourse, however interesting or important it might be, could have the impact of work written in Latin.[2] Ælfric might then have become a "later Carolingian," an Anglo-Saxon Haymo or Heric or Rabanus. If, however, we take a closer view of Ælfric, that is, if we first consider his actual attempts to interpret the Bible in themselves, then Ælfric might be seen to have earned a place in the longer view of medieval exegesis.

There is no dominant, authoritative view of Ælfric's exegesis. While there is always some risk in espousing a "genetic" explanation for this situation, the problems in studying Ælfric's exegetical writings begin at the beginning. It is easy now to dismiss Frederick J. Snell's remark that Ælfric's *Sermones* reflect "a demand for ready-made sermons by lazy, ignorant, or inefficient clerks" as the observation of a crank, or John Lingard's somewhat more thoughtful complaint that Ælfric loves allegory too much: "There is not an action, an event, a name mentioned in the sacred writings, which does not, in his opinion, teem with mystery."[3] Lingard's impatience with allegory certainly dates him, for interpreters of both early and late medieval texts in the last generation have been very ready to celebrate the allegorical. Curiously, this interest in allegory has had no great effect on Ælfric studies. Anglo-Saxonists, when they pursue secular or Christian allegories in *Beowulf*, or when they take a Christian view of the *Wanderer* or *Seafarer*, will go to the *Patrologia Latina*, and not to Ælfric.[4] If the movement to date poems closer

to the date of the manuscripts wins the day, then Anglo-Saxonists may yet
have to consider this premier vernacular interpreter of the Bible, who is
roughly contemporaneous with the poetic codices.[5] As things stand, however,
where there is literary interest in Ælfric, it is in his style.[6] Aside from studies
of style and Milton McC. Gatch's important interpretive study emphasizing
Ælfric's eschatology, the study of Ælfric remains broadly philological, i.e.
showing an interest in manuscripts and sources, not at all in hermeneutics.[7] In
short, the study of Ælfric's exegesis is still at a nascent stage and often
emerges as an adjunct to studies with other objectives in mind. Even this
present, quite circumscribed attempt to give a brief overview of Ælfric's
hermeneutics may prove complex. Still I hope I will keep the object of this
study—the nature of Ælfric's exegetical method—constantly in view, while
doing justice to the assumptions and approaches that other scholars, both
older and contemporary, have brought to Ælfric and his work.

It is possible at this stage in the subject to envision a real beginning that
sees Ælfric as a medieval "father" and an authoritative exegete whose views
on the Bible have their own validity and interest. This beginning can be
welcome, if it is introduced with appropriate caveats and germane contexts, as
I hope to do here. What Ælfric himself says about interpretation, often self-
reflexively, is an appropriate starting point.

At a number of junctures in the *Sermones Catholici*, Ælfric brings into
the foreground the basis for his reading or his interpretation. These reflections
on how to read the *sacra pagina* are only rarely extensive, but they are
numerous enough to point to what is, as will be seen, Ælfric's flexible
approach to biblical hermeneutics. Perhaps the most important of these reflections on method is the simile that Ælfric presents in *Dominica in media
Quadragesima, Sermones Catholici, First Series* where he is seeking to explain the miracle of the five loaves and two fishes:

> þis wundor is swiðe micel, and deop on getacnungum. Oft gehwa
> gesihð fægre stafas awritene, þonne heraþ he þone writere and þa stafas,
> and nat hwæt hi mænað. Se ðe cann ðæra stafa gescead, he heraþ heora
> fægernysse, and ræd þa stafas, and understent hwæt hí gemænað. On oðre
> wisan we sceawiað metinge, and on oðre wisan stafas. Ne gæð na mare to
> metinge buton þæt þu hit geseo and herige: nis na genóh þæt þu stafas
> sceawige, buton ðu hí eac ræde, and þæt andgit understande. Swa is eac on
> ðam wundre þe God worhte mid þam fif hlafum: ne bið na genóh þæt we
> þæs tacnes wundrian, oþþe þurh þæt God herian, buton we eac þæt gastlice
> andgit understandon.

> This miracle is very great, and deep in its significations. Often some
> one sees fair characters written, then praises he the writer and the characters,
> but knows not what they mean. He who understands the art of writing praises
> their fairness, and reads the characters, and comprehends their meaning. In
> one way we look at a picture, and in another at characters. Nothing more is
> necessary for a picture than that you see and praise it; but it is not enough to

look at characters without, at the same time, reading them, and understanding their signification. So also it is with regard to the miracle which God wrought with the five loaves: it is not enough that we wonder at the miracle, or praise God on account of it, without also understanding its spiritual sense.[8]

For an audience which would doubtlessly include many marginally literate members, the comparison Ælfric makes between the nature of painting (*mēting*), the nature of written characters (*stafas*), and the nature of a sacred historical event seems apt and cogent. The unreflective experience he is describing has point and application to audience perception and understanding regarding a written text. Ælfric is saying that there is the merely visible and the finally meaningful. He is not even saying that there is a literal and allegorical meaning, which readers of medieval literature might expect him to say here. Rather, his distinction is considerably more fundamental and basic, namely, between no understanding at all and its antinomy, understanding: ". . . it is not sufficient to look at the characters, unless you read them and understand the sense." For the illiterate audience, or the one learning to read, the path to understanding is therefore long. Ælfric does not discount immediate human response, however unknowing it may be. In fact, he concludes the simile by emphasizing it. The human element, praise—which both learned and unlearned may give to fair writing, to illustration, or to God—appears to be part of the process of understanding, as it is part of worship. But praise is insufficient by itself without true understanding to complete it: ". . . it is not sufficient that we marvel over this miracle, or praise God because of it, unless we also understand the spiritual sense." By implication those who praise and do not understand are not on the wrong path so much as not far enough along the way.[9]

This complicated simile carries in its structure Ælfric's approach to reading the Bible. Like all similes, this one is built on contrastive or distinctive terms or ideas that operate on a dual or binary level. "Binary" is actually the preferable term because Ælfric consistently sees a complementary unity in the Bible rather than a tension that may divide. Thus, words and images, ignorance and understanding, understanding and reaction, are the main structural pairs of terms underlying the simile. Ælfric's habit of mind is to find such pairing. When it comes to the important pair "understanding and reaction," the grounds change from the text to the audience. This shift of focus or emphasis explains how in other expositions the moral sense of scripture is a natural development; there is a habit of mind that enables Ælfric to move from analysis of text to moral application for the audience.[10]

But in emphasizing Ælfric's binary approach to reading the Bible, which underlies his sense for typology, the twentieth-century interpreter runs a risk of inhibiting valid historical understanding. In a paper on Anglo-Saxon literary history, Thomas D. Hill provides an important caveat when he observes that all too often Anglo-Saxonists think that exegesis is allegory, especially in the critical controversies over Old English poetry.[11] Hill aptly notes that much patristic exegesis tries to explain or explain away the difficulties of the biblical text as text, for understanding what the Bible says was as difficult for the early medieval audience as for the twentieth century one.[12] Thus, it is useful to remember that when Augustine explains John's account of the Passion in the *Tractates,* he tries to determine the precise hour of Christ's Crucifixion, to clarify some muddles in the relationships between Annas and Caiphas, and to elucidate such philological points as the phonemic differences of *hoc* with long and short vowels, the meaning of the word *parasceve,* and the nuances of *exinde.*[13] While Ælfric would not need to follow Augustine deeply into the philological wood, he does feel the need to explain from time to time the geography of the Holy Land, aspects of Roman history, especially those relating to the Emperor, and aspects of Jewish history.[14] Occasionally Ælfric fills in information about the Fathers, when he cites them as sources, and his etymologies of names are often presented as pieces of philological information rather than as allegorical interpretations.[15] He also strives to present, when the occasion warrants, a harmony of the biblical texts. It is easy to see some of this information as a response to the "illiterate Anglo-Saxons" in the audience, but the example from Augustine ought to make it clear that the explanation of what is the literal sense is part of a long tradition and thus implies nothing about Ælfric's audience. If it can be granted that the explanation of the literal plays a proper role in Ælfric's exegesis, then the study of his exegesis can move on to more fruitful discussions of such matters as the *where, when,* and *why* Ælfric chooses to include literal or factual information. Such a shift may lead to a new description of his audience and its needs, but it might give new insights about Ælfric's compositional methods, his habits of mind, his purposes, and ultimately the cultural milieu.

An understanding of the role of the Latin homiliary or, more broadly, the sermon collection, as a source book for Ælfric's *Sermones* has been a signal achievement in the last forty years of study of Old English prose. Cyril Smetana's ground-breaking work on the influence of the collections assembled by Paul the Deacon and Haymo of Auxerre, subsequently amplified and developed by J. E. Cross and others, has given a good answer to the earlier question regarding the size and extent of Ælfric's library: with such patristic anthologies at hand, Ælfric had ready resources indeed for the study of the *sacra pagina.*[16] But the Latin homiliaries surely gave Ælfric more than the material for his own *Sermones.* They gave him examples of exegesis as well as examples of preaching/teaching style. I will leave to another occasion a discussion of style *per se,* here focussing rather more on the exegetical contexts the homiliaries provided. Paul the Deacon's collection, which provides the prime example for my treatment, contains some 244 items, most of them considered to be *sermones* or *homiliae.* Bede, Maximus of Turin, Leo the Great, and Gregory the Great are the dominating figures in this collection, while Augustine, Jerome, Ambrose, and Isidore of Seville are among the other Fathers who help complete the full liturgical cycle. Father Smetana's broad characterizations of these authorities can serve as a guide.[17] Bede is "cloistered" and "scholarly," offering tightly knit and plain comments on the biblical text written with a dense weave of patristic sources and biblical allusion. Maximus of Turin and his imitators going under his name are radically popular in their approach, seeking to move their audience by lively and appealing imagery that, for example, draws upon nature and human experience. Leo's sermons are brief and severe, avoiding the transcendental and the metaphysical while exemplifying the direct and the simple. Gregory the Great, one recalls much to Dudden's horror, takes a special delight in the allegorical significance of things and in the major metaphors of the Bible, but does not lose sight of his obligations as *bonus pastor* who needs to lead his flock to moral conversion.[18]

These one-sentence sketches of the major writers in Paul's homiliary mean only to convey some sense of the range and diversity of the collection. Source critics have generally concentrated on Ælfric's particular borrowings from his patristic sources, but have not made much of the context of interpretations from which Ælfric chose. Paul's anthology offered Ælfric not only specific passages *wendan* (to translate) into English, but it gave him as well examples of exegetical modes to learn from and subsequently apply. Thus, just as some sense of *when, where,* and *why* Ælfric chose to follow the letter rather than the spirit may shed more light on his achievement, so too the idea that Ælfric derived a range of exegetical modes from Paul the Deacon may help define more sharply why he sometimes appears to be more like Gregory than Bede or more like Leo than Augustine of Hippo. This variety of choices may lie at the root of why Ælfric has inspired varied scholarly response.

While a considered and full view of early medieval exegesis and a deeper response to the Latin homiliaries standing behind Ælfric can establish a pattern of caveat and context that might improve understanding, there is a third factor, not yet fully recognized, that should play its part in any characterization of Ælfric's exegesis. This factor is what I would call the "narrative impulse" in the *Sermones Catholici.* In the first edition of his *A Critical History of Old English Literature,* Stanley Greenfield detects an aspect of this narrative impulse when he describes a shift from an exegetical emphasis in the *First Series* to a less didactic, more legendary emphasis in the *Second Series.*[19] But Ælfric's narrative impulse includes more than this shift to the legendary. In the broadest meaning, Ælfric's narrative impulse means his presentation of the Bible primarily as story, secondarily as text for analysis. As far as audience effect is concerned, the audience hears primarily narrative as narrative is heard, not, say, a sequence of embedded moral principles. This narrative impulse would appear to have its roots in the broad tradition in Christian Latin literature of teaching the Bible through the Bible's own words.

Augustine gives the warrant for this kind of preaching and teaching in *De Doctrina Christiana* IV.v.8:

> Huic ergo qui sapienter debet dicere, etiam quod non potest eloquenter, uerba scripturarum tenere maxime necessarium est. Quanto enim se pauperiorem cernit in suis, tanto eum oportet in istis esse ditiorem; ut quod dixerit suis uerbis, probet ex illis et, qui propriis uerbis minor erat, magnorum testimonio quodammodo crescat.

> For one who wishes to speak wisely, therefore, even though he cannot speak eloquently, it is above all necessary to remember the words of Scripture. The poorer he sees himself to be in his own speech, the more he should make use of the Scripture so that what he says in his own words he may support with the words of Scripture. In this way he who is inferior in his own words may grow in a certain sense through the testimony of the great.[20]

We need not ascribe to Ælfric any abject humility or moral modesty for this Augustinian statement to apply, nor indeed do we need theoretical authority to support the genre of biblical paraphrase.

Some sense of this narrative impulse and its effect on exegesis is apparent in Ælfric's Palm Sunday homily in the *Second Series*.[21] Since elsewhere Ælfric indicates his minority opinion that there should be no preaching on Holy Thursday, Good Friday, and Holy Saturday, which are *swigdagas* (days of silence),[22] he has no occasion on those days to tell the biblical events of those days. He thus faces an interesting problem when he promises at the beginning of his Palm Sunday homily that he will relate Christ's Passion and its mysteries.

The narrative of Holy Week is long and complicated. Indeed Ælfric seems self-conscious about the dangers of length, and with a mixture of apparent hope and apology regarding his ability to organize the sermon he proceeds. In fact, after these and other preliminaries, he covers the entire sweep of Holy Week from the entry into Jerusalem through the events of Holy Thursday and Good Friday to the Death, Burial, and, briefly, Resurrection. It is further evident from the whole sermon that Ælfric has the Passion accounts in the Synoptic Gospels and John in mind as well as other sources. Ælfric has clear debts to Matthew, whom he cites explicitly, to Luke for the matter of Herod, and to John for the presence of Nicodemus at the Burial. When Ælfric writes "we" will tell you about the Passion, the simple expression contains within it a self-conscious authorial point of view outside of and above the sources. Ælfric clearly has the confidence that he can relate the Passion and explain its mysteries. He becomes in effect another Gospel-writer, conveying more openly the Christian message. The remarkable thing is that these events and their meanings do not lead to an unduly long homily; this Palm Sunday homily is about the size of the Easter homily and shorter than some others. Ælfric demonstrates a rigorous sense of selection; up until now this sense of selection, when isolated, has been seen to be merely a feature of style.[23] It is more properly a feature of Ælfric's habit of mind, of course, and certainly in this example he is choosing the meaningful as well as abbreviating his biblical and patristic sources. This narrative impulse, one might also argue, is properly a function of a literalist response to the *sacra pagina* in that Ælfric is trying to make sense out of somewhat muddled, unclear, and unharmonious biblical texts. But, finally, the effect of the Palm Sunday homily is the effect of a narrative, shaped and formed to stand as a sequence of events in time. Ælfric has made narrative sense of his varied sources.

The most celebrated attempt to explain holy mysteries, however, is Ælfric's first sermon on Easter Sunday in the *Second Series*.[24] Ælfric is trying to ''explain, through the grace of God, the Holy Eucharist . . . and to instruct the understanding [of the audience] regarding the mysteries, according to the Old Testament and according to the New, lest any doubt afflict [the audience] regarding the life-giving supper.''[25] The texts at the basis of this intention are Exodus 12, the synoptic accounts of the Last Supper as in Matthew 26, and John 6:53ff. After relating briefly the story of Moses and the Passover lamb, Ælfric observes that the OT account should not be followed *lichamlice* (bodily, in the flesh), but rather that Christians should know *hwæt heo gastlice getacnige* (what it signifies spiritually). Accordingly Ælfric equates the lamb with Christ and the Tau-sign with the sign of the Cross. Continuing his parallelism with the history of Israel, Ælfric says that for Christians, Eastertide is the period of Redemption and purification comes from taking the Eucharist. Ælfric then proceeds to explain Christ's words concerning his body and blood, continuing the binary mode he has announced at the beginning and has implied by his choice of typology. To the question, ''how can bread, which is made from grain and baked in an oven, be changed into Christ's body or wine, which is pressed from many grapes, be changed by any blessing to Christ's blood?'' Ælfric gives answer through sets of distinctions.[26] Some things are said about Christ through *getacnunge,* some things through *gewissum ðinge;* thus Christ is a lion according to the former, not the latter. The Eucharist is Christ's body and blood because consecrated bread and wine appear to human understanding *wiðutan* as bread and wine, *wiðinnan* as Christ's body and blood through *gastlicre gerynu:* similarly, a baptized heathen child does not change in appearance. There is, again, a *lichamlice* understanding of Baptism and a *gastlice;* there is a *gesewenlican hiwe* and an *ungeswenlican mihte.* As to the Eucharist: nothing is to be understood *lichamlice,* all is to be understood *gastlice.* The Eucharist is Christ's body and blood, *na lichamlice ac gastlice.*

The first observation one can make about Ælfric's analysis is that he actually does not answer the question he asks. The question is about how things can be changed; his answer or answers describe how things appear or how they are to be understood and, perhaps, how they are. There is no explanation of the process of change. The second observation is that our own understanding of Ælfric's terminology is doubtful. The words *lichamlice* and *gastlice* can be quickly rendered as "bodily" and "spiritual(ly)," of course, but there may be some equivocation in *lichamlice*. It would appear that earlier interpreters of Ælfric have taken the word to apply to the idea of "real presence," meaning that Christ's true Body is not there, but it is there only in a figurative (or spiritual) sense. My suggestion is that Ælfric is really talking about typological understanding, not transubstantiation. He does not overtly say anything about real presence, or more fundamentally, about what is the really "real." The implication is that one might draw out of his concept of *gastlice* the Christian-Platonic notion that only the spiritual is really real, but this gloss has yet to be established in Ælfrician vocabulary. Indeed, there is in the passage so much emphasis on the body, on what one sees, and indeed on what one tastes and touches, that it is easy to see how earlier commentators could readily choose to see Ælfric's apparent denial of 'real presence' and affirmation of 'figurative presence.'

In summary then, Ælfric's Easter Sunday sermon on the Eucharist provides an excellent example of the major issues involved in any estimate of Ælfric as exegete. Anglo-Saxonists must unburden themselves from antecedent scholarship that either blatantly or subtly brings with it assumptions that are invalid for the late tenth century. A self-conscious and proper historicism can help establish a context for discussion. With this context, which must take into imaginative account Ælfric's use of sources, the development of early medieval theology, and the valid meaning of early medieval exegesis, it will be possible to assess more accurately Ælfric's role as medieval "father" and to move on to related cultural issues such as Ælfric's audience, the problem of rendering the Christian message to it (a new form of the *translatio* question, it would appear), and even perhaps a new definition of Christian literature. The new view of Ælfric that will thus result will have to account for issues of Christian genres and Christian styles as well. In this brief paper I have tried to suggest some of the contexts and some of the caveats that could lead to a well-grounded re-evaluation of a hitherto undervalued vernacular father.

Notes

Caveat lector: this essay is part of a larger chapter on Ælfric as exegete, which in turn is part of a book-length study. In abbreviating the treatment, I am aware that important or intricate points have not received full discussion.

I note more happily that I have had the use of Luke M. Reinsma's annotated bibliography on Ælfric in its draft form, and accordingly, I owe him a debt of thanks for making my research less burdensome. The bibliography is now published as *Ælfric: An Annotated Bibliography* (New York: Garland Publishing, 1987). I also must thank my colleague Norman T. Burns, who gave me many helpful suggestions.

1. Beryl Smalley, *The Study of the Bible in the Middle Ages* (Notre Dame, IN: University of Notre Dame Press, 1970), 147 and 244 respectively.

2. Norman Cantor, *The English* (London: George Allen and Unwin, 1968), 59–60.

3. Frederick J. Snell, *The Age of Alfred (664–1154)* (London: Bell, 1912), 218; John Lingard, *The Antiquities of the Anglo-Saxon Church* (London: C. Dolman, 1845), II, 313. Lingard also observes: "[Ælfric] shews very little judgment in his selection of legendary matter, and displays throughout an undue partiality for the typical method of scriptural interpretation. . . ."

4. There are some noteworthy exceptions, of course; see, for example, Joseph Wittig, "Figural Narrative in Cynewulf's *Juliana*," *Anglo-Saxon England* 4 (1975): 37–55.

5. Margaret Goldsmith's *The Mode and Meaning of Beowulf* (London: the Athlone Press, 1970), which argues for an allegorical reading, assumes a seventh- or eighth-century milieu (vii). If Kevin Kiernan's *Beowulf and the Beowulf Manuscript* (New Brunswick, NJ: Rutgers University Press, 1981) holds sway in establishing the eleventh-century date of *Beowulf*, then Professor Goldsmith might be forced to recast her book.

6. See the still very useful essay by Peter Clemoes, "Ælfric," in *Continuations and Beginnings*, ed. E. G. Stanley (London: Thomas Nelson and Sons, 1966), 177–209, as a general introduction. John C. Pope, in his edition of *Homilies of Ælfric: A Supplementary Collection*, 2 vols., Early English Text Society, O. S. 259–60 (London: Oxford University Press, 1967–68), discusses rhythmic prose in I, 105–36. For Ælfric's brief style, see these essays by Ann E. Nichols: "Ælfric and the Brief Style," *Journal of English and Germanic Philology* 70 (1971): 1–12; "Methodical Abbreviation: a Study in Aelfric's Friday Homilies for Lent," in *The Old English Homily and Its Backgrounds*, eds. Paul E. Szarmach and Bernard F. Huppé (Albany: State University of New York Press, 1978), 157–80.

7. This statement is an observation, not a criticism. Anglo-Saxonists eagerly await the completion of the *Early English Text Society* edition of the *Sermones Catholici*. A new edition of the *Lives of the Saints*, which could throw light on Ælfric's methods, is not even in the planning stage, and contemporary revision of older editions has not been a growth industry. John C. Pope's *Homilies of Aelfric: A Supplementary Collection*, cited in n. 6, remains the measure of editions supporting further interpretation.

8. The most serviceable edition for the *First Series* is Benjamin Thorpe's edition of the *Homilies of the Anglo-Saxon Church*, 2 vols. (London, 1844–46), here cited throughout as *SC I* (*Sermones Catholici*). This text appears on p. 186 with facing translation on p. 187. The passage follows Augustine: cf. Radbodus Willems, ed. *Sancti Aurelii Augustini in Iohannis Evangelium Tractatus CXXIV*, Corpus Christianorum, Series Latina 36 (Turnhout: Brepols, 1954), *Trac.* XXIV.2, 244–45.

9. Thus one can read the importance of praise as endorsement for liturgical or monastic observances, which are then rendered complete by understanding.

10. In the main I would say that Ælfric does not follow the famous "four-fold method." Typically his exegesis is three-fold, namely, literal, figurative, and moral, when he appears systematic. Thus, he is Gregorian in this regard. Some sermons end biblical analysis surprisingly with a concluding paragraph of moral application. Ælfric, it would appear, has the pair "text and audience" in mind; thus for him the change in focus is easy. Admittedly, this entire matter requires more discussion and more examples. See Hanspeter Schelp, "Die Deutungstradition in Ælfrics Homiliae Catholicae," *Archiv für das Studium der neueren Sprachen und Literaturen* 196 (1960): esp. 274–81.

11. Thomas D. Hill, "Literary History and Old English Poetry: The Case of *Christ I, II, III,*" in *Sources of Anglo-Saxon Culture,* ed. Paul E. Szarmach, Studies in Medieval Culture 20 (Kalamazoo, MI: The Medieval Institute, 1986), 3–22.

12. Hill, 8.

13. Augustine, *Trac.* CXVII.2, 651–52.

14. As, for example, *SC* I, 402, 404 on Vespasian, Titus, and the Jews, or *SC* I, 488 and Josephus.

15. As, for example, *SC* I, 436 on Jerome, and *SC* I, 194 on Gabriel's name. The meaning of names is, as we can expect, a recurrent feature of Ælfric's interpretation of the Bible. See T. M. Pearce, "Name Patterns in Aelfric's *Catholic Homilies,*" *Names* 14 (1966): 150–56; Fred C. Robinson, "The Significance of Names in Old English Literature," *Anglia* 86 (1968): 14–58.

16. See these essays by Father Smetana: "Paul the Deacon's Patristic Anthology," in *The Old English Homily and Its Backgrounds,* eds. Paul E. Szarmach and Bernard F. Huppé (Albany: State University of New York Press, 1978), 75–97; "Aelfric and the Early Medieval Homiliary," *Traditio* 15 (1959): 163–204; "Aelfric and the Homiliary of Haymo of Halberstadt," *Traditio* 17 (1961): 457–61. Cross makes numerous clarifying points in *Ælfric and the Mediaeval Homiliary—Objection and Contribution,* Scripta Minora Regiae Societatis Humaniorum Litterarum Lundensis, 1961–62, no. 4 (Lund: C. W. K. Gleerup, 1963). Subsequent analysis of Ælfric's sources has had to be written with these works as points of reference.

17. I am summarizing here Father Smetana's discussion in "Paul the Deacon's Patristic Anthology," 79–82.

18. F. Homes Dudden, *Gregory the Great* (1905; rpt. New York: Russell and Russell, 1967), I, 253: "Though essentially popular, [Gregory's] sermons overflow with allegory and mystical interpretations, and it must be confessed that the meanings thus elicited are often extremely far-fetched. . . ." Dudden is clearly of Lingard's party!

19. Stanley B. Greenfield, *A Critical History of Old English Literature* (New York: New York University Press, 1965), 50. In the successor volume, *A New Critical History of Old English Literature* (New York: New York University Press, 1986), 76–77, Daniel Calder makes a similar point as he begins an analysis focusing on Ælfric's style.

20. Joseph Martin, ed., *De Doctrina Christiana,* Corpus Christianorum, Series Latina 32 (Turnhout: Brepols, 1962), 121. D. W. Robertson, Jr., provides an accessible English translation in *Saint Augustine: On Christian Doctrine* (Indianapolis and New York: Bobbs Merrill, 1958), 122.

21. *SC* II, 137–49. I am adapting here my discussion found in "The Earlier Homily: *De Parasceve,*" in *Studies in Earlier Old English Prose,* ed. Paul E. Szarmach (Albany: State University of New York Press, 1986), 390–92, where my overall point is to contrast Ælfric and the anonymous author of Vercelli Homily I.

22. For a discussion of *swigdagas* see Joyce Hill, "Ælfric's 'Silent Days'," *Leeds Studies in English,* n.s. 16 (1985): 118–31, and also my *"De Parasceve,"* cited in the previous note, 384–85, which did not have the benefit of Dr. Hill's analysis.

23. See n. 6 to this essay, and particularly the work of Nichols.

24. For the *Second Series,* Malcolm Godden's edition, *Ælfric's Catholic Homilies: The Second Series,* Early English Text Society, Supplementary Series 5 (London: Oxford University Press, 1979), hereafter cited as *SC* II, replaces Thorpe. The Easter Homily is on 150–60. For a discussion of this sermon, see Theodore C. Leinbaugh, "Ælfric's *Sermo de Sacrificio in Die Pascae:* Anglican Polemic in the Sixteenth and Seventeenth Centuries," in *Anglo-Saxon Scholarship,* ed. Carl T. Berkhout and Milton McC. Gatch (Boston: G. K. Hall, 1982), 51–68. The gross misunderstanding of this text in later religious controversies, its place in the early history of sacramental theology, and its general theological temper are important issues, of course, but too complicated for treatment now.

25. *SC* II, 150: "Nu wille we eow geopenian þurh godes gife be ðam halgan husle . . . and gewissian eower andgit ymbe þære gerynu. ægðer ge æfter ðære ealdan gecyðnysse, ge æfter ðære niwan. þy læs ðe ænig twynung eow derian mage. be ðam liflicum gereorde."

26. *SC* II, 152: ". . . hu se hlaf þe bið of corne gegearcod and ðurh fyres hætan abacen. mage beon awend to cristes lichaman. oððe þæt win ðe bið of manegum berium awrungen. weorðe awend þurh ænigre bletsunge to drihtnes blode."

20. William Mendel Newman

GILES CONSTABLE

I

The reputation of William Mendel Newman rests entirely on his publications.[1] He was an active scholar for less than half of his adult life, taught for only three years at three different institutions, and received none of the honors dear to the hearts of academics. As a publishing scholar, however, he ranks among the leading American medieval historians of the twentieth century. His *Domaine royal sous les premiers capétiens* and *Catalogue des actes de Robert II*, which were his major and minor theses at Strasbourg, are both standard works; and his study of *Les seigneurs de Nesle en Picardie* was described by Georges Duby as "de toute première importance" at the time it appeared in 1971. He also prepared for publication four collections of charters, of which that of St. Fursy of Péronne was published in 1977, the year of his death, and another, that of Homblières, will be published shortly.

For more than thirty years, from 1919—when he went to boarding school—until 1950, he kept a diary, which fills nine volumes and runs to about a million and a half words and which gives a vivid, detailed, and intimate picture of his life and attitudes towards himself, his teachers, and his work. While I hesitated to use this diary on account of its intimacy, my reluctance was overcome by three considerations. First was the fact that although Newman destroyed most of his professional and personal papers, he kept the diary and left no instructions concerning it in his will. Second, certain passages suggest that he anticipated, though less than many diarists, that his diary might be read by others. Third, it would have been impossible without using the diary to write more than half a page about Newman's life. He was a private man and during his life concealed his achievements and his sentiments from the world. Yet he considered himself ill-treated and misjudged, and his diary, though it contains much that is not to his credit, is ultimately an apologia, which helps to explain why Newman felt and acted as he did.

Further, very few scholars have left such a detailed record of their lives, especially during their formative years. It may be argued that scholarly works, like works of art, should speak for themselves, without reference to the lives of their creators. But it is also important to understand the relation between a scholar's life and work, and to appreciate the price society pays for the achievements it values. Newman, as seen in his diary, was a deeply unhappy and in many ways unattractive man. Some readers of this and the longer memoir might be put off by the strength of his dislikes, especially towards other people, including his parents and teachers, and by the harshness of his language, which contrast with the somewhat austere character of his publications and with his retiring, even diffident, external behavior. Yet whether his story repels or simply saddens the hearer, it must be remembered that Newman's historical writings were to some extent the products of his personal difficulties. He turned to scholarship largely because he despaired of finding elsewhere the happiness for which he yearned and of which he felt unjustly deprived.

II

The main facts of Newman's life are quickly told. He was born in Pierce City, Missouri, on 31 January 1902, the second son of Milton Newman and his wife Lenna, born Mendel. His only sibling was his older brother, Joseph. In 1922 his parents moved to Enid, Oklahoma, which remained their home until they died in 1943. William went to school in Pierce City and at Phillips Academy, Andover, and entered Harvard in the fall of 1921. After graduating in 1925, he spent one more year at Harvard and took an M.A. in American history. He taught for two years, one at the University of Iowa and the other at Ohio State University, and in 1928 went to Europe, where his studies shifted from American to medieval history. He earned two doctorates, one from Toulouse in 1929, where he worked under Joseph Calmette, and the other from Strasbourg in 1937, where he worked under Marc Bloch and Charles-Edmond Perrin. He was Bloch's only American doctoral student, and perhaps the only student of any nationality who both began and completed his doctoral work under Bloch's direction.

Newman returned to the United States in 1937, after nine years in Europe, and taught for a year as instructor at the University of Michigan. He was in Cambridge from 1938 until 1942, when he went to St. Louis to do warwork in his brother's factory. After the war he lived in Seattle until 1950, when he gave up keeping the diary on the eve of a visit to France. Two years later he went to live in France and remained there for eleven years. He returned to the state of Washington in 1963, living first in a rented house on Lummi Island and then in his own home—the first and last he ever owned—near the town of Bellingham, where he died on 27 April 1977. It is no accident, I think, that he went to live in one of the most distant corners of the United States, where he had no previous connections, or that he spent his happiest and most peaceful years there, though less is known about them, or about his second period of residence in France, than about the years when he kept a diary.

Because the diary is also missing for the years 1926–30, it is impossible to say why Newman gave up what seems to have been the beginning of a conventional career teaching American history and embarked instead on a new life of solitary research into the history of medieval institutions, for which he was suited neither by training nor by temperament. In principle he preferred a life of action to one of scholarship, and after he left Michigan and stopped looking for a teaching position, he abandoned his research for almost a decade. He enjoyed working in his brother's factory, where he was personnel manager, and after he moved to Seattle he hoped to have a career in business and even considered entering public life. He returned to scholarship only when it became clear that he could find no other employment, and because he had to do something, and he wrote his most important book during his second stay in France. When he left France in 1963, according to an isolated entry written in September 1967, "I realized my return to America was the close of a long chapter in my life—I would no longer be able to do research in Medieval History for which I had lived." He burned many of his old notes, and although there was a library for his books in his new house, he did no more serious historical writing.

Five considerations emerge from the diary which help explain why Newman was a medievalist *malgré lui,* who never really enjoyed historical research and was driven to it only because other possible occupations failed. The first of these was his health, which he was convinced from his boyhood kept him from doing his best work and excluded him from certain occupations. He was rejected by the army in 1942 on account of his health, and in his Fiftieth Harvard Class Report he attributed his inability to continue research to his health. The second consideration was his dislike for his family, which kept him from entering the family business and working, as his father did, in one of the several department stores they owned in Missouri, Iowa, and Oklahoma. The progressive deterioration of William's relations with his parents and his brother is a leitmotif in the early volumes of the diary. It not only cut him off personally but influenced his views on families, women, and life in general, since he was convinced that parents invariably sought to control their children. He particularly disliked his parents' efforts to control him through money, and his own care with money may have resulted from his desire in his student days to be as free as possible from his parents. The financial independence which he achieved after he returned to the United States and especially after the death of his parents, from whom he inherited over $100,000, is the third factor explaining why he lived as he did. Though he continued to worry about his finances and live frugally, and though he took some pride in appearing to be poorer than he was, he was in fact a comparatively wealthy man, and at his death he left an estate of about $1,200,000.

Newman's private income allowed him to devote himself to research, without having to earn a living, but it cut him off from colleagues and imposed upon him a degree of isolation, which was heightened by two more personal factors.

One of these was his consciousness of being a Jew, for although he was not a religious man and rarely went to temple, he had a strong sense of Jewish identity. As a young man, and during his first stay in Europe, he seems to have been comparatively at ease with being Jewish, despite some references he made to anti-Semitic prejudice and a nagging concern that most of his friends were Christians. Without advertising his Jewishness, he made no effort to conceal it. He more than once expressed his own low opinion of eastern European and New York Jews. His attitude changed sharply after he returned to the United States, since he was convinced, and made no secret of it, that he lost his position at the University of Michigan because he was a Jew. It is impossible to say what truth, if any, lay in this charge, since Newman's diary shows that he was an unsuccessful teacher and uncooperative colleague, but he firmly believed from this time on that as a Jew he would never obtain a teaching position in America.

The final factor which tended to isolate Newman and exclude him from a normal career was his dislike for women, which amounted almost to misogyny, and his preference for men as friends. Except for one short period of his life, he did not want a physical relationship, aside from what he regarded as innocent marks of affection, and he was repelled by any specifically sexual contact with either a man or a woman. But he longed more than anything else in the world for the companionship of a gentle, sensitive, and intelligent (and preferably young and good-looking) man: "I am so lonely I do not know what to do," he wrote in Seattle in 1947, "but I do *not* drink, do *not* play golf, nor go to the movies, nor play cards, and can't stand the sort of conversation most men indulge in, *so* how could things be other than they are." He in fact had no difficulty in meeting people, and the records of his conversations with casual acquaintances are among the most interesting passages in the diary. But he formed no lasting friendships aside from the few friends who went back to his days at Andover and Harvard, who occupied a special place in his affections but could not satisfy his desperate need for a loving and sympathetic comrade.

Many entries in the diary are concerned with his unhappiness and loneliness and his sense of outrage at the insensitivity of other people towards himself, since he had no doubts about the purity of his own motives. His own chief strength was uprightness (as he wrote in 1937) and he described himself as having "meant so well, lived cleanly, forcefully, honestly, and yet all those troubles." He was only dimly aware of how many difficulties he brought on himself. Though he knew that he was competitive, touchy, and unforthcoming, he tended to regard these not as faults but as the concomitant aspects of a praiseworthy independence, desire to succeed, sensitivity, and modesty. In fact he was suspicious, envious, and always ready to take offense, especially at anyone he regarded as more able or successful than himself. He was generally better disposed towards the unfortunate than the fortunate and at times went out of his way to advise and assist men who were in trouble.

He had a romantic view of himself as disorderly and irrational, and his sufferings were a source of satisfaction as well as of misery. "Without pain life would not be worth living," he said at one point, and elsewhere he described a personal disappointment as "somewhat like a purification."

"Depend upon it," Dr. Johnson said, "that if a man *talks* of his misfortunes, there is something in them that is not disagreeable to him: for where there is nothing but pure misery, there is never any mention of it."[2]

Though Newman rarely went to museums or concerts, he was fond of art and music and would have liked to have been a professional musician had he been more talented. He formed a considerable collection of china, rugs, silver, glass, and furniture, especially in the 1940s, when his means allowed it and he was dreaming of his own home. His real love was his book-collection, however. His zeal in buying books went hand in hand with his enthusiasm for research, and was at its height in France in the early 1930s and again in the 1950s, when I myself met him in Paris while I was working at the Bibliothèque nationale. "My life here is my work and my library," he wrote in 1932, "and I am very happy that I have the extra money with which to buy books. As Ziegler [Aloysius Ziegler, the historian of Visigothic Spain and future professor at the Catholic University] said in Paris 'one's books are *always* faithful, one's friends are uncertain'."

He tended to swing between moods of extravagant optimism and utter despair, with periods of relative resignation and contentment in between. One of the reasons for his rejection by the army in 1942 (in addition to various physical disabilities which he detailed not entirely without relish) was "manic depression psychosis." While there is no reason to believe that this was more than the snap judgment of an army doctor, based on Newman's own description of himself, he certainly suffered from bouts of severe depression and at times, especially as a young man, contemplated suicide. He was convinced that he lacked both the mental and the physical ability to succeed, and the relative happiness of his later life was owing not only to the solution of some of his personal and financial problems but also to the strengthening of the streak of resignation which had always been in his character. In his Fiftieth Harvard Class Report, in 1975, he wrote,

"My life has been a very simple one devoted almost entirely to research in Medieval French history as an independent scholar. I spent about twenty years in France and Belgium for my work. Health forced me in 1963 to cease research. Since then I have lived quietly in the country growing flowers and reading. I still have some manuscripts to be published. I have had a happy life in my work and feel that I have been fortunate in being able to devote full time to it."

It is difficult to recognize in this description of bucolic peace and scholarly complacency the sad and troubled younger man of the diary, though it is satisfying to know that in his old age he drew something of a curtain over the confusions, disappointments, and bitterness of his earlier life. It is also difficult to appreciate that Newman's achievements as a scholar, to which I now turn, were the result not of his years of peace and satisfaction, but of his difficulty and unhappiness.

III

Almost nothing in Newman's family background or early life prepared him to be an historian, and he had no innate bent towards scholarship or pleasure in it. He was a mediocre student at both preparatory school and at college, and the grades he recorded in his diary confirm his own gloomy view of his academic ability. There is no reference to studying history before 1920, and the principal influence which steered him in that direction at Andover was his teacher Archibald Freeman, of whom he wrote, after Freeman's death in 1948, that "He was one of the few, very few, great teachers I have had. . . . I respected him deeply." As might be expected of a man of Newman's character, the basis of Freeman's influence was personal encouragement rather than intellectual stimulation, and Newman deeply appreciated the fact that Freeman described him as able and asked him to tutor some students in history.

At Harvard he particularly enjoyed the lectures (which he graded according to his own system) of Abbott, Bliss Perry, Haskins, Lake, McIlwain, and Turner, and to a lesser degree those of Channing, Copeland, Edgel, Kittredge, and Munro. At one point he referred to Haskins, McIlwain, and Turner as "the three great historians of Harvard." He later considered himself a student of Haskins, whom he thanked in the preface of *Le domaine royal* for "tant de bonnes directives et de sages conseils," but this was primarily to impress his French professors and to minimize his debt to Marc Bloch, whom he bitterly disliked, and in fact he took only one half-course from Haskins and met him only a few times. Most of his work was in American history, and he wrote his senior thesis on James Mason of Virginia and his Master of Arts thesis on the election of 1800. At Iowa he taught in the introductory course in modern European history. There is no record of his teaching at Ohio, but it may have been there, in conversations with the medievalist Edgar McNeal, whom he also thanked in the preface to *Le domaine,* that he decided to do further work in medieval history. It is unknown whether or not he applied to any American graduate schools or why he decided to study in France, except that he probably wanted to be as far away from home as possible.

By the time the diary begins again late in 1930, it is clear that Newman already felt he had made a mistake. "By nature I am not the slightest bit fitted for the work I have set out to do. . . . [I] might well change to modern History, but I feel it necessary to finish this thesis in Mediaeval in order to keep at least some of myself respect—enough for working purposes, otherwise there might be total demoralization." This view was confirmed by Newman's feeling of neglect by his professors. Late in 1933, he wrote, "Up to the present no professor has given me any aide," and in February 1936, "There is not a single professor in Europe with whom I have really gotten along. . . . They all want to make use of me."

The list of his dislikes reads like an academic Almanac de Gotha of the 1930s, headed by Bloch, Perrin (of whom Newman at first thought better than of Bloch, but soon came to dislike as much), Halphen, and Lot and, in Belgium, where Newman lived from 1933 to 1937, by Bonenfant, Ganshof, and Vercauteren. Even Calmette, who Newman thought at least treated him with courtesy, was not above suspicion of hypocrisy. His opinions of scholars whom he knew only through their writings were hardly better, and his diary is filled with deprecating references to Luchaire, Petit-Dutaillis, Levillain, and others. He had better relations with some younger scholars, both Europeans and Americans, who were studying in Strasbourg, Paris, or Brussels at the same time as himself, and after his return to the United States he kept up fitful friendships with Aloysius Ziegler, whom I have mentioned, and Dayton Phillips, who later taught at Stanford. But on the whole he envied and mistrusted his colleagues in the historical profession and had close relations with none of them. Not until many years later, when his interest in medieval history revived in Seattle in the late 1940s, did he have any good words to say of Bloch, whom he continued to dislike personally, or of Halphen.

The fault for this situation was doubtless to some extent divided. In part it was the result of cultural differences which led his professors at Strasbourg to take Newman, who had an M.A. from Harvard and a doctorate from Toulouse and had been an instructor at Ohio, less seriously than he expected. Bloch (who was never the most considerate of men) was at a critical stage in his own career in the mid-1930s, just before he moved to Paris, and may not have devoted much attention to a somewhat unprepossessing American who showed no special sign of historical talent and who, as time went on, increasingly kept his distance. But the problem was greatly exacerbated by Newman's own inability, which was motivated in part by pride and independence, to obtain the help he needed from either his professors or his contemporaries, and it left a lasting legacy of bitterness. He made no reference to his Strasbourg (unlike his Toulouse) degree in his Twenty-Fifth or Fiftieth Harvard Class Reports, and his growing dislike of France and the French, towards whom he was at first very well-disposed, is amply documented in his diary. "Dante should have had a trip to France," he wrote in May 1935, "the contact with the french would have given fresh material for l'Inferno."

It is hard to believe that a scholar who studied under such eminent masters was in reality more or less an autodidact. Already during his freshman year at Harvard he wrote that he would do better studying alone than in college, and he rarely took advantage of the many opportunities for learning from others which were presented to him. When he came to Europe in 1928, his only preparation for the study of medieval history was Haskins's course in the "Intellectual History of Europe," taken in his sophomore year, and a rusty knowledge of Latin and French. He was keenly aware of these deficiencies yet took no systematic steps to remedy them. Perhaps the most profound source of his growing unhappiness during his years in France, even more than his lack of friends, was his growing realization that he had embarked on a course for which he was unsuited by ability and training as well as by nature. Regrets at having taken up medieval history and complaints at his ignorance of paleography and of Latin and other languages run like a litany through his diary.

Newman's task included not only doing the research for the two theses and writing them in French, but also printing and publishing them, which was done at his own expense. The diary includes some interesting details on his difficulties with the printers (and on their difficulties with him), and in finding a distributor. (He eventually settled on the Recueil Sirey in Paris.) He defended the theses in Strasbourg on 13 February 1937 before a committee of six professors, including Bloch and Perrin, each of whom he had, to his dismay, to visit on the previous day. The defense went smoothly, and he was awarded the doctorate with a "mention très honorable," but Newman believed that the reason for this was Bloch's determination to prevent "all unpleasant remarks on either side," which might reveal the scandalous misdirection of the theses. He left the luncheon after the defense "in a most unhappy mood," and later that evening he felt oppressed by his lack both of the "knowledge necessary for latin editing" and, more seriously, of the "courage to get away from Medieval History."

It is hard to say where the real source of the difficulty lay, aside from Newman's character and some real neglect on the part of his professors. It is even harder to assess Bloch's real influence on Newman, especially because he ostensibly denied and concealed it. He not only disliked Bloch personally, but became increasingly convinced that he was incompetent both as a teacher and as a scholar. "Fool" and "dishonest" are among the milder terms he applied to Bloch in the 1930s. Later, after Bloch's death, he recognized that he was "France's outstanding scholar in Economic History and gave the impulsion so badly needed to many studies" and that "his real contribution was to raise questions in the light of much knowledge and understanding." This is probably true of Newman's own work, where Bloch's contribution was more to raise questions (including the subject of the royal domain) rather than to offer solutions or make substantive suggestions, so that Newman felt that he was working entirely on his own. He feared at one point that Bloch would insist on adding "chapters on comparative history that I cannot give."

Later, however, when Newman returned to Cambridge in 1939, he wrote "I must do more comparative study; it awakens one to problems."

The influence of Bloch and the incipient *Annales* school is more apparent in Newman's diary than in his published works. Already in 1935, when the theses were nearing completion and Newman was beginning to look around for new subjects, he composed in his mind an interesting discourse on "Man's Place in Institutions" which shows that the lectures of Haskins and the teaching of Bloch were not lost on him. In it he faced boldly the conflicting claims of custom and modernity in men of the Middle Ages, and also the significance of technological change, including new methods of horse-harnessing and the development of roads, which interested him for many years. "The history of institutions should not merely be descriptive," he wrote, "but should try to place the man's mind (attitude and thought) in the change." Three years earlier, after a discussion with Dayton Phillips, Newman wrote, "He accepts whole heartedly the modern psychology (I should read some to be in line with what and how people are thinking) and also history of thought, both seem superficial to me. If one could write the history of thinking OK. but the history of expressed thought is likely to get merely the shell." This, like his reference to comparative history, was prophetic, because in 1940 he began to read extensively in psychology. In April 1940 he wrote, "Although I work at history during the day, my interest is in psychology—to which I devote each evening." By this time his interests had increasingly moved out of the Middle Ages into other fields, including factory management during his years in St. Louis. He still read works of history, but as an amateur rather than as a professional. For a time he was interested in the Far East, and in May 1946 he wrote, "Now, I really have not lost faith in history, for it should furnish the background for parallel social studies to that I just read for China—but it is so much more difficult for the period in which I work."

The following year there were signs of his reviving interest in the Middle Ages as he sought something to do in Seattle. After hearing in March 1947 of Marc Bloch's death he wrote that "I plan a lot on finishing the three books I began—the cartulary, the bibliography of printed cartularies, and the study of communications Xth century to 1250." In October 1948 the books and notes which he had stored in St. Louis arrived in Seattle and he resumed work on the cartulary of Homblières and began to plan for an extended research visit to France. For almost the first time since 1933 he expressed some real pleasure in his historical research. "It is paradise to live this way and have so much—books and the time to read them and plan to write," he wrote in October 1948. Twelve days later he wrote "This is near heaven, to live this way," though he could not forbear adding "will it last?" This revival of scholarly interest and activity marked the beginning of Newman's second period of productive scholarship, which lasted until he returned from France in 1963, and of which only the first eighteen months, up to February 1950, is covered by his diary. During these years he wrote his masterpiece, *Les seigneurs de Nesle,* and the associated booklet on the personnel of the cathedral of Amiens, and he prepared the editions of the cartularies of St. Fursy of Péronne, Mont-St-Quentin, Homblières, and Arrouaise. Cartularies were always among Newman's favorite type of source (both to study and to collect), and the use he made of them in these works, especially to show the close interrelations between families and institutions in the twelfth and thirteenth centuries, probably owed more to Bloch and Perrin, as in his other works, than he would have cared to acknowledge. Among his notes is a sheet entitled "Some Ideas for a study of 'noblesse de l'église' " in which he raises many questions which are of interest to historians today, such as the relationship between the lay noblesse and the ecclesiastical noblesse, and the differences between the grande noblesse and the petite noblesse. The "basis of such study is [the] *correct* genealogy of many (?) families or only a few," he wrote. "This should also throw light on the extent to which the church and political life was local." I wish I could cite more of this document, which makes one regret, as did at least one reviewer of *Les seigneurs de Nesle,* that Newman did not address himself to broad questions in his published writings, and that he reserved his more speculative questions and generalizations for his private writings. His published works, like his visible life, are marked by a reticence which gives an appearance of calmness and solidity rather than of inquiry and brilliance, but they were the products of an inner turbulence and spiritual suffering which were almost entirely hidden from the world, and which gave no peace to this unhappy and reluctant scholar.

Notes

1. This essay is based on Newman's private papers, especially his diary, which is deposited in the Houghton Library at Harvard University. The quotations cited here are as he wrote them, without using "sic" for errors. For his later life I have used some letters both to myself and to Professor John Baldwin of Johns Hopkins University, who kindly put them at my disposal. The most useful printed sources are Newman's Harvard class reports, of which copies were sent me by Dr. Harley Holden, the curator of the Harvard University Archives. I am also indebted to Professors Charles Brand (Bryn Mawr), C. W. Bynum (University of Washington), Joseph Lynch (Ohio State University), Steven Rowan (University of Missouri, St. Louis), and Donald Sutherland (University of Iowa) for information about various aspects of Newman's career and family, and to Professor Carole Fink of the University of North Carolina at Wilmington for information on Marc Bloch. A longer version of this essay, with a bibliography of Newman's works, will appear in the edition of the charters of Homblières to be published by the Medieval Academy of America in 1988.

2. *Boswell's Life of Johnson,* ed. G. B. Hill (New York: Oxford University Press, 1891–1904), IV, 36.

21. Broadening the Definitions of "Art": The Reception of Medieval Works in the Context of Post-Impressionist Movements

MADELINE H. CAVINESS

This essay will try to prove a double thesis: that in western art history our appreciation (and ultimately, therefore, our interpretation) of medieval art has progressed in a way that is connected to developments in modern art, and that at the same time that modern artists were expanding the accepted definition of art, the corpus of medieval works that came under the scrutiny of historians was enlarged.[1] This is not a new idea. It has occurred previously both to theorists of style and to art historians who were aware of investigating a category of art that had been neglected.[2] As Hans Belting has remarked, Heinrich Wölfflin laid the foundations for the formalist school of art history at the same time that artists were turning away from representational to purely artistic concerns,[3] although in the case of Wölfflin a personal interest in contemporary art apparently was never acknowledged.

Meyer Schapiro has articulated the relationship between contemporary art and art history several times. In his pioneering essay, ''Style,'' he stated: ''Analysis applies aesthetic concepts current in the teaching, practice, and criticism of contemporary art; the development of new viewpoints and problems in the latter directs the attention of students to unnoticed features of older styles. But the study of works of other times also influences modern concepts through discovery of aesthetic variants unknown in our own art.''[4] Schapiro emphasized the positive effect that the former process had on appreciation, and tended to overlook the reading-in of modern cultural and aesthetic values that is implied in this equation.[5] In a 1957 article significantly titled ''The Liberating Quality of Avant-garde Art,'' he again attributed to twentieth-century painters the discovery of ''whole new fields of form-construction and expression,'' which in turn ''made possible the appreciation of many kinds of old art and of the arts of distant peoples . . . which had not been accessible in spirit before.''[6] Among art historians who have accepted this view, James Ackerman acknowledged in 1962 that despite historical biases against the work of certain artists—such as late Michelangelo, El Greco, Vermeer, and Turner—this "was 'successful' in modern times once our own art had trained us to appreciate it."[7] Yet no one has yet presented detailed case studies to demonstrate this model.

I propose to present some historical cases that suggest how the reception of medieval works progressed in relation to developments in modern art. These models are confined to the period 1895 to about 1950, coinciding with an intense phase of the rediscovery of the art of the Middle Ages. Each case study treats some of the specific relationships that have existed between at least two of three agents: First, modern artists and their work; second, the works of the past; and third, art historians, connoisseurs, and museum curators. In other words, we can think of three points with a potential triangular interaction. I do not wish to deal with questions of influence and primacy, though others may feel impelled to argue over them; for this would require a knowledge of the gestation period that lay behind the dates when the works were exhibited or published. Broadly speaking, the triangular relationships demonstrated here are best described as symbiotic.[8]

Publication by Franz Wickhoff and Wilhelm von Härtel of the *Vienna Genesis* in 1895 was a landmark in the rediscovery of medieval art.[9] The introductory text was translated into English for publication in London and New York in 1900.[10] It was also reprinted in German in 1912, and eventually, in 1947, an Italian version appeared.[11] Wickhoff, whose life spanned the latter half of the nineteenth century (1853 to 1909), was a founding member of the Viennese school of art history.[12] The preface to the English edition of the *Vienna Genesis* comments that: "The scholars occupied with early Christian art had concerned themselves solely with the explanation of the subjects represented, without reference to the artistic questions involved."[13] Wickhoff's and von Härtel's errors in dating—claiming the *Vienna Genesis* as a product of the fourth century—and their use of terms such as "continuous method" for narrative involving several actions in the same frame, have little importance beside this redressing of a balance—in which Alois Riegl is acknowledged as the leader.[14]

Significant comparisons can be drawn between works of the 1880s and 1890s by the German Impressionist painter Max Liebermann (b. 1847), and the "impressionistic" paintings of the *Vienna Genesis*.[15] Perhaps such paintings guided Wickhoff's taste in selecting the manuscript for publication, but even more evident is his debt to Impressionist ideas. In assessing what he calls *illusionist* as opposed to *naturalistic* painting in the late antique period, he clearly used the theory of perception expounded by critics in support of the Impressionist painters in prior decades:[16]

> The moment came, however, when painters of genius, trained by the long practice in seeing which they owed to naturalism, recognised that *appearance* had nothing in common with their ingenious and careful studies

and preparations; that a body seen in its own colours and in a chance light does not exhibit that consistent modelling of a relief seen in the artificial light of the drawing-school; its image is the result rather of contiguous and entirely dissimilar values of light and of their physiological effect upon the eye—in other words, that the image which a given object presents to our eye is not that of a softly modelled relief, but, so to speak, it is a *congeries* of patches and spots differing from each other in colour and in degree of illumination; that these do not by any means produce self-contained forms, but that we first evolve the forms from them by the aid of unconscious (subconscious) reminiscences derived from our previous knowledge of the bodies themselves; above all, that all the objects in a picture are not perceived with equal distinctness at the same time, but only those on which the attention is fixed can be clearly observed, while the others, be they nearer or farther away, become more or less hazy in form and outline; and that this process is quite irrespective of the familiar toning-down effect caused by the intervention of air. The painter who has made these observations and worked them out for himself—they can, of course, be made without being formulated—will no longer try to compose his pictures out of material details, modelled throughout, and out of specially contrived and selected determinations of form, but will juxtapose those tones of colour that correspond to the actual phenomenon, *and their combination into objects will be effected not by means of the brush blending them together upon the picture, but precisely as in the act of vision by the supplementary experience of the spectator.*[17]

Works by Max Liebermann were probably known to Wickhoff; they clearly affirm a lack of concern with exact rendering and the impressionistic use of high lights and darks. Yet he continued to use the grays and browns that he had earlier assimilated from Dutch painting, a palette which brings his paintings closer to the *Vienna Genesis* with its brownish-purple ground color than those of the French Impressionists. Liebermann's work was highly appreciated in Germany by 1900, when a monograph was published by Hans Rosenhagen, and it continued to inspire art historians. Max Friedländer, the great connoisseur of northern late Gothic painting, published a book on Liebermann's work in 1924.[18]

In 1898, three years after Wickhoff's publication of the *Vienna Genesis,* Arthur Haseloff published the *Codex Rossanensis,* a manuscript that had already received praise from Wickhoff, who is frequently quoted in Haseloff's text.[19] Haseloff belonged to the next generation (1872–1955), and the choice seems to indicate that a greater degree of abstraction could now be tolerated—one thinks of Gauguin's flat color patches. Indeed, about 1930, Haseloff published on pre-Romanesque sculpture in Italy, bringing works such as the Cividale Altar reliefs into the canon of art.[20]

A younger scholar who fell under the spell of Liebermann was Adolf Goldschmidt (1863–1944). A portrait sketch of Goldschmidt by Liebermann, dated 1913, attests to their friendship, and in 1935 Goldschmidt wrote a

Gedenkrede for the artist.[21] According to Goldschmidt's student, Kurt Weitzmann, his "artistic sense was developed by his original intention to become a painter. His watercolors show the style of early German Impressionism, related to that of his close friend Max Liebermann. . . ."[22] In fact, Goldschmidt was thirty years old when he began to concentrate, at the University of Berlin, on the study of medieval art—in 1892 still a very new field.[23] Like Haseloff, Goldschmidt seems to have absorbed Post-Impressionist canons of form, corresponding to Gauguin's contours and flat color. From 1914 through the 1920s, Goldschmidt produced five great volumes on *Elfenbeinsculpturen*.[24] A powerfully expressive diptych of the *Incredulity of Thomas* was included in the volume published in 1918 (fig. 9). Any corpus, however, precludes selection according to the taste of the author, and it is thus hard to prove that Goldschmidt responded to an affinity between this ivory and works such as Matisse's relief entitled *The Back I*, of nine years earlier.[25]

Rather different is the story of the rediscovery of Spanish Romanesque. The magnificent Beatus manuscripts of the eleventh and twelfth centuries were first studied by a textual scholar who had written his dissertation at the University of Bonn on the exegesis of the book of Ezekiel: Wilhelm Neuss (1880–1965) went on to become Professor of Theology at Bonn, and then to publish a pioneering stylistic study of Catalan bible illustration in 1922, where he mentions Haseloff's work in the Introduction.[26] Through the Institut d'Estudis Catalans in Barcelona, Neuss was drawn into an extremely active circle of art historians which included, at least by 1951, Jurgis Baltrušaitis and Pierre Lavedan, Walter Cook and Chandler Post. After about 1930, the impact of Picasso's works of 1907 may have transformed this generation's way of seeing early Spanish art. Many compelling comparisons can be made, as, for example, between a study of a *Bust of a Woman* completed in the Spring of 1907 and a detail of the head of Christ from the twelfth-century Altar Frontal of St. Martin de Puigbo, Monterouy, now in the Vic Museum (Figs. 1 and 2). Lines no longer had to render form, and a physiognomy could be arbitrarily reformed by the artist. Primitivism was no longer viewed as a lack of skill, but could convey spiritual intensity.

Here, however, it is interesting to note that the triangular model I suggested at the outset is closed on the third side—not only could the art historians using Neuss's volumes absorb new values from Picasso's work in order to appreciate the early illuminations, but Picasso himself must have absorbed the Catalan Romanesque from his childhood, and its images are among his rich multi-layered source material. It is thus equally possible that publication of the Apocalyse manuscripts paved the way for the acceptance of Picasso.[27]

The process of abstraction demonstrated by Bart van der Leck, for instance, in his 1917 *Studies for Donkey Riders,* had also confirmed for Neuss's generation that the Silos Beatus paintings were not necessarily the products of arbitrary failings on the part of the artist.[28] By 1931 when Neuss published his study of the Spanish manuscripts of the Apocalypse of St. John (illustrated

Figure 1. Pablo Picasso, "Bust of a Woman" (Spring, 1907), Prague, National Gallery. (*Photo:* National Gallery)

here is the San Isidoro Apocalypse of 1047 in Madrid), Joan Miró had developed a less academic abstraction than the Der Stil group had; his *Tilled Field* of 1923–24 offers remarkable visual parallels with the fantasy world of the Mozarabic artist (figs. 3 and 4). Meyer Schapiro, not surprisingly, wrote in 1947: ''by the eleventh and twelfth centuries there had emerged in western

Figure 2. Head of Christ (detail), Altar Frontal of Saint Martin de Puigbo (12th century), Vic, Episcopal Museum. (*Photo:* Ampliactiones y Reproducciones ''Mas,'' Barcelona)

Europe within church art a new sphere of artistic creation without religious content and imbued with values of spontaneity, individual fantasy, delight in color and movement, and the expression of feeling that anticipate modern art.''[29]

Cubist sculpture, such as that of Picasso's contemporary and compatriot, Pablo Gargallo, or the Jacques Lipschitz *Bather* of 1917, also played a role in the reevaluation of Romanesque sculpture, such as that of Moissac, brilliantly studied by Schapiro in his 1929 dissertation and published in the 1931 *Art*

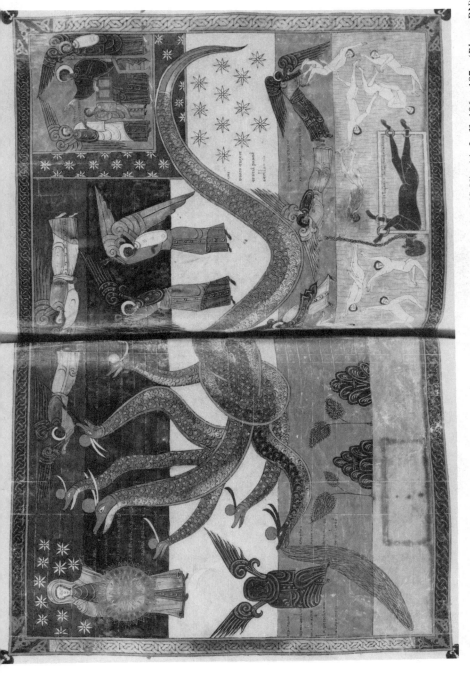

Figure 3. The Woman and the Dragon, San Isidoro Apocalypse, Madrid, Bibliotheca nationale, MS Vit. 14–2, ff. 186v–187r. (*Photo: BN*)

Bulletin.[30] As Hans Belting has pointed out, the theory of art expounded in *Art Concret* in 1930, and perpetuated by Léger, held that art is composed only of purely plastic elements, that is of surface and color.[31] Such a theory broke down historical barriers and invited application to the art of all periods. Celia Betsky Mcgee has said of Schapiro's reprinted essays on Moissac: "Reading this tour de force of observation is a little like watching Picasso paint a woman's face."[32] The implication of this statement is that the art historian not only sees like but also thinks like the artists of his time.

The attribution of aesthetic value to Catalan wall paintings is indicated not only by the inventories made from about 1905 on, but by their removal to the Museum of Catalan Art which opened in 1939, where they are reassembled in full-size spatial settings painstakingly modelled on the churches of origin. This must be one of the most expensive enshrinings of art ever constructed. The buildings themselves were also highly valued. Their detailed study coincided with Antonio Gaudi's experiments with irrational and free form.[33]

Gaudi's younger contemporary, an architect who worked in Barcelona alongside him, was José Puig y Cadafalch (1869–1956). His inventory of Catalan churches was published in 1909–18.[34] It led to broader studies of the international style known to his generation as the "premier art roman."[35] Gaudi had already anticipated this "rustic" aesthetic both in the basement of the Guell Palace of 1886–91, and in the Chapel of 1898–1915. The former is remarkably close to an eleventh-century Burgundian example of the first Romanesque, the lower narthex of Saint-Philibert in Tournus (figs. 5 and 6).[36]

Gaudi also anticipated, in the 1880s–1890s, widespread historical interest in Cistercian architecture: the vista of his white vaults in the Teresian College is remarkably close to those of the side aisles in the nave of Pontigny, although he probably relied on a closer model such as Cuenca.[37] Yet it is to the French art historian Marcel Aubert (1884–1962) that we owe the most extended and systematic study and evaluation of *l'architecture cistercienne*— as he titled his book of 1943, which appeared after several monographic studies—such as his examination of Vaux de Cernay in 1931 and Noirlac in 1932.[38] Aubert's interest, however, is documented earlier; Charles Picaud noted in his obituary that as early as 1908 he went to Germany on a study tour from the Sorbonne, and that on his return he gave a report at the École Pratique des Hautes Études on the Cistercian Churches of the Rhineland.[39] Aubert's father, uncle, cousin, and grandfather were architects, and he seems to have learned to love Gothic architecture from the grandfather, after his own father's early death.[40] Any Parisian architect's family must also have been attuned to the controversies surrounding contemporary architectural design.

It was precisely in 1908 that no less powerful a figure than Franz-Jourdain, President of the Salon d'automne, publically upbraided French designers for continuing to imitate a jumble of decorative styles from the past in the face of a new severe style emerging in Germany, characterized by

Figure 5. Tournus, Saint-Philibert Abbey Church, lower level of narthex (late eleventh century). (*Photo:* Bildarchiv Foto Marburg)

beautiful line and proportion stripped of non-functional decoration, by natural materials and light colors. This style was to be seen in the exhibitions at Munich, Stuttgart and Würtemberg to which the city of Paris had sent an official delegation.[41] In fact the formulation of a "Cistercian aesthetic" that Aubert arrived at is remarkably close to Franz-Jourdain's characterization of the new German style.[42] The Sorbonne study-tour is known to have passed through Bavaria, no doubt including the Munich decorative arts exhibition in its itinerary, and the domestic architecture on exhibit in Stuttgart and Würtemberg may also have been viewed. Certainly the pre-Bauhaus concepts of the Gropius circle, embodied for instance in the Gut Janikov farm buildings of

Figure 6. Barcelona, Guell Palace, basement, Antonio Gaudi, 1886–91. (*Photo:* Archivo Fotográfico, Amigos de Gaudi, Barcelona)

1906, offer certain parallels with those underlying a functional Cistercian building such as the forge at Fontenay.[43] The Fagus Factory designs of 1911 asserted the Bauhaus principle of avoiding ornament in order to achieve an austere and pure beauty; the facade offers a visual similarity to that of the church of Fontenay (figs. 7 and 8).[44]

Figure 7. Fontenay, Cistercian Abbey Church, west entry, 1139–47. (*Photo:* Bildarchiv Foto Marburg)

    Such comparisons, however, risk inviting art historians to transfer onto the Cistercian style a positive aesthetic, despite its predominantly proscriptive intent. The calm of the interior spaces, for instance of the church at Fontenay and the living room and study of a Gropius & Breuer House in Pittsburg, Pennsylvania, is sufficiently similar to seem to negate historical distinctions, and to dissolve the boundaries between secular and sacred, between the essentially functional intent of Bauhaus and the spiritual intent of Cistercian. The visual similarities belie the discrepant ideals. This danger was counteracted in Aubert's case by his insistence on documentary research, and by his exposition of Cistercian ideals as expressed in their own twelfth-century writings. Yet I would claim that a quest for historically-based interpretations was not the impulse that triggered his initial choice of the Cistercian as opposed to other forms of architecture.[45]
    One more extended model of the triangular relationship of artist, art historian, and medieval art is that provided by the two generations of Swarzenskis, who as scholars and collectors had close contact with contemporary art and artists. The father, Georg Swarzenski (1876–1957), shared Adolph Goldschmidt's enthusiasm for early German works and began publishing his important work on the tenth- and eleventh-century Regensberg manuscripts in 1900.[46] He was likewise attracted to the study of crafts and "kleinkunst" which had grown out of Riegl's work.[47] At thirty, Swarzenski became Director of the Städel Kunstinstitut in Frankfurt am Main in 1906. He

Figure 8. Walter Gropius and Adolf Meyer, Fagus Boot-Last Factory, Afeld-an-der-Leine, 1911 (watercolor). (*Photo:* Bildarchiv Foto Marburg)

masterminded the foundation of a Städtische Gallerie, taking over its direction and that of the sculpture collection in the Liebighaus.[48] For the next thirty years, he added to these collections, systematically acquiring the works of Frankfurt artists, both of those established in the nineteenth-century and of young contemporaries like Max Beckmann.[49]

Swarzenski's relationship with Max Beckmann typifies the interaction between museum curator, practicing artist, and medieval art. A portrait sketch of Georg Swarzenski made by Beckmann in New York in 1950 attests to a long association begun in Frankfurt.[50] Bosch's *Ecco Homo,* acquired by the elder Swarzenski along with other late medieval works, has a surface design—irrational space, tonal values, and linear structure—which offers parallels with early works of Beckmann, such as his *Iron Footbridge* (Frankfurt, 1922).

Beckmann's interest in the triptych form, as in his *Acrobats* of 1932, and his brilliant splashes of color and claustrophobic compositions find many parallels in newly rediscovered late Gothic works. Many of those that entered the Städl came from the Historisches Museum, including two grisaille panels by Matthias Grünewald, whose famous Isenheim altar in Colmar has affinities with Beckmann's expressionist works. At the Städl, it seems it was a case of reclassifying these late Gothic works as "art," perhaps taking them out of storage in the historical museum to be hung in the context of contemporary pieces. It is notable that the first monograph on Grünewald was not published by Heinrich Schmid until 1911; he complained that in 1900 he could not find a publisher interested in the subject, but Andrée Hayum has recently established that Schmid was encouraged in his taste for Grünewald by the Basel painter Arnold Böcklin.[51] Beckmann seems also to have admired Grünewald: His *Descent from the Cross* of 1917, for instance, now in the Museum of Modern Art in New York, clearly depends in subject as well as in formal qualities on medieval German works.[52]

With Otto von Falke and Robert Schmidt, Georg Swarzenski catalogued the Guelph Treasure of Brunswick in 1930, and exhibited it at the Städl, in the hope of saving it for the German nation.[53] This too was an almost symbolic rehousing of these works, many of which had such a bizarre reliquary nature that they would have been considered as purely devotional or archaeological objects in an earlier era. They were literally taken from the church treasury and placed in the art museum. Pieces such as the numerous arm reliquaries would surely have been harder to reclassify had it not been for Rodin's 1908 sculpture entitled *The Cathedral* that isolates these limbs as a complete work, or the more modern version by Brancusi, the *Main de Mademoiselle Pogany* of 1920.[54]

The association of Georg's son, Hanns, with Beckmann was no less strong than that of his father. Beckmann's portrait of Hanns with Curt Valentin, dated 1946, was reproduced in Hanns Swarzenski's Festschrift volume.[55] Hanns's preferences in medieval art tended to earlier styles than those favored by his father, especially Ottonian and Romanesque. His personal taste is shown both in his additions to his father's collection of decorative arts and sculpture in the Boston Museum, and in the plates to his *Monuments of Romanesque Art,* first published in 1954. One of the pieces most loved by Hanns was the diptych in the Berlin Museum that had been published long ago by Goldschmidt (fig. 9). The impact of German Expressionism, whether that of Beckmann's paintings, such as *The Dream* of 1921, or of Ernst Barlach's sculptures, such as the *Man in a Pillory,* of 1918 (fig. 10), had endured through the decades in Hanns Swarzenski's sensibility, as it had in American painting. In discussing a manuscript page with the 'portrait' of Gregory, attributed to Trier in the tenth century, that he had acquired for the Boston Museum, he emphasized its emotional suggestion: "As in the art of our own time, this aim is arrived at by means of distortion and abstraction from

Figure 9. Doubting Thomas, wing of an ivory diptych, ?Trier/Echternach (late tenth–early eleventh century), Berlin, Skulpturengalerie der Staatlichen Museen Preussischer Kulturbesitz. (*Photo:* Skulpturengalerie)

Figure 10. Ernst Barlach, Man in a Pillory (wood, 1918), Hamburg, Kunsthalle. (*Photo:* Hamberger Kunsthalle, R. Kleinhempel)

naturalistic forms and colors, which is apparently arbitrary, but in reality obedient to purely aesthetic laws.''[56]

This by no means exhausts the models that could be developed along the same lines, but some conclusions are called for.[57] I have tried to indicate the extent to which early twentieth-century movements in art supported an aesthetic experience of medieval works, especially Romanesque and late Gothic.

One effect seems to have been to free the early works from cultural alterity simply by isolating them from their historical (and iconographic) context. (As a correlary, Goldschmidt even insisted on the isolation of art history from other disciplines.) Often this isolation was accomplished physically, as when the Catalan frescoes were installed in the Barcelona Art Museum, or when late Gothic panel paintings were transferred from the historical museum to the picture Gallery. This wrenching effect sometimes resulted in what we might now—through a closer study of medieval cultural values—regard as irresponsible misinterpretation.[58] The potential problem, though generally avoided by scholars as erudite and as multivalent in their approaches to medieval works as Marcel Aubert and Meyer Schapiro, seems to have caused Schapiro some concern. In a review article published in 1963 he reflected: "The Beatus manuscripts make us realize how limited is our present conception of the artistic process, and how much it depends on the values of art and social life today."[59] The essential gulf between the Middle Ages and the modern period is that there was surely no *art pour art* then; this was the era of André Malraux, of the Ministry of Beaux-Arts, and the Museum without walls.[60] Schapiro was quick to follow with the positive side:

> We are able, however, precisely through our own art and point of view to appreciate these long-ignored medieval works as few observers could do during the last centuries before our time. I have had occasion to look at the older Morgan Beatus with painters and I have observed with satisfaction their strong response to this art. I do not think that I am fanciful in seeing in certain of Léger's works, painted during his stay in New York in the 1940s, the effects of his enthusiasm for this Spanish manuscript.[61]

Because these effects are posited in the words of the art historian, we take him to be an unaffected observer; in fact he was part of the symbiotic relationship, perhaps even "influenced" in his aesthetic judgments by Léger. By a process analogous to intertextuality, it may now be impossible to separate our experience of such a manuscript page from its resonance in Léger, just as some Gothic works (even unrestored) look astonishingly Victorian.[62] Or as Leo Steinberg said: "All art is infested by other art."[63]

As far as medieval art is concerned, the era of discovery—of constantly expanding the corpus to be studied by enlarging the definition of art—may be almost over. The era I have covered, from 1895 to about 1950, followed upon the discovery of Gothic art in conjunction with the revival movements of the nineteenth century. It may have been the most exciting for medieval studies, both because of a delight in discovery and because of a sense of connectedness to modern artistic issues. In discussing the period of discovery in terms of stylistic affinities, I am aware of a certain reflexiveness: The case studies have been presented in terms of predominant art historical theories of the time, which tended to give autonomy to aesthetic choice, and I have relied largely on formal abstraction for visual demonstration.

There is another, far more threatening aspect to closing this chapter of historiography about 1950. In fact taste had changed rather abruptly in the United States by 1940 or so, when William Randolph Hearst dumped his medieval collection on an unenthusiastic market, and interest was perhaps only rejuvenated for a while by an immigrant generation. At the present time medieval art is not taught by a full-time specialist on many American campuses, and many museums are relegating medieval artifacts to storage.[64] The most urgent question for medievalists is how to exit from this circular motion, which, wave-like, seems to cast down grains of sand as it picks up others. We need to deepen our analyses of known and accepted works, and to be more aware of the cultural differences that separate us from them; strenuous efforts can lessen that alterity, especially if we can rediscover the functions these works served within that culture. Perhaps we do not even have to give up the idea of a universal language of visual art so dear to Motherwell's generation and so powerfully stated by Schapiro, despite the fact that the claim arose from the western art of the fifties.[65] There may indeed be a system of visual expression and communication whose exploration would allow us to deepen our understanding of those same works that are already part of the canon.

Notes

1. Versions of this paper were given in the Robert Branner Forum for Medieval Art at Columbia University on December 5, 1985, and at Tufts University the following spring as well as at the Sixty-First Annual Meeting of the Medieval Academy of America in Albuquerque, New Mexico, April 17–19, 1986. In the course of revisions for the present publication, in the spring of 1987, I discussed the material with colleagues at the Institute for Advanced Study in Princeton. On each occasion many colleagues offered comments and constructive criticism, but I am especially grateful to Pamela Allara, Robert L. Benson, Elizabeth Boone, Elizabeth Parker, Charles Nelson, Ronald Salter, and Nancy Troy for their comments and suggestions. A shorter version, in German translation, has appeared as "Erweiterung des 'Kunst'-Begriffs: Die Rezeption mittelalterlicher Werke im Kontext nachimpressionistischer Strömungen," *Oesterreichische Zeitschrift für Kunst and Denkmalpflege* XL (1986): 204–15.

2. The enlargement of the canon in the twentieth century is viewed from a different perspective by Eva Frodl-Kraft, "Kunstwissenschaft—Eine Disziplin in der Krise?," *Anzeiger der phil.-hist. Klasse der Oesterreichischen Akademie der Wissenschaften (Wien)* 122 (1985): 6–31.

3. Hans Belting, *Das Ende der Kunstgeschichte* (Munich: Deutscher Kunstverlag, 1983), 39; he refers to Heinreich Wölfflin, *An Introduction to the Italian Renaissance* (Ithaca: Cornell University Press, 1980), which first appeared in German in 1898. An English translation of Belting's important and controversial paper has just been published by the University of Chicago Press.

4. Meyer Schapiro, "Style," reprinted in *Aesthetics Today*, ed. Morris H. Phil-

ipson (Cleveland and New York: World Publishing Company and New American Library, 1961): 84–85.

5. Some ambivalence is suggested, however, by the use of "nevertheless" in the following passage: "The analysis and characterization of the styles of primitive and early historical cultures have been strongly influenced by the standards of recent western art. Nevertheless, it may be said that the values of modern art have led to a more sympathetic and objective approach to exotic arts than was possible fifty or a hundred years ago. In the past, a great deal of primitive work, especially representation, was regarded as artless even by sensitive people; . . . it was believed that primitive arts were childlike attempts to represent nature—attempts distorted by ignorance and by an irrational content of the monstrous and grostesque. . . . with the change in western art during the last seventy years, naturalistic representation has lost its superior status" (*Aesthetics Today*: 85–86).

6. Meyer Schapiro, "The Liberating Quality of Avant-Garde Art," *Art News* 56 (1957–58): 37.

7. "A Theory of Style," *Journal of Aesthetics and Art Criticism* XX (1962): 237.

8. From biology, symbiosis is: "The living together of two dissimilar organisms, especially when this association is mutually beneficial" (*Random House Dictionary*). A similar relationship between modern art, tribal art, and their western audience was posited by Max Alfert (himself a sculptor and collector), in "Relationships Between African Tribal Art and Modern Western Art," *Art Journal* 31 (1972): 396: "One can conclude that a mutually beneficial interaction between cultures has taken place: The modern artists' range of expression has been extended, and tribal art has profited in turn by a notable gain in Western cultural esteem."

9. Franz Wickhoff and Wilhelm von Härtel, *Die Wiener Genesis, Jahrbuch der Kunsthistorischen Sammlungen des Allerhöchsten Kaiserhauses*, XV & XVI (Vienna: F. Tempsky, 1895); the manuscript, now dated in the sixth century, is in Vienna, Nationalbibliothek, Cod. gr. 31.

10. Franz Wickhoff, *Roman Art: Some of its Principles and their Application to Early Christian Painting*, tr. Mrs. S. Arthur Strong (London and New York: W. Heinemann/MacMillan, 1900).

11. Franz Wickhoff, *Römische Kunst (Die Wiener Genesis)* (Berlin: Meyer & Jessen, 1912).

12. The obituary by Gustav Glück comments on the breadth of his interests, reaching down to the art of his own time, and his assertion of the equal value of all artistic developments.

13. Strong tr., vi.

14. Ibid., 17, where Riegl is quoted on an "ascending line" of development in Roman art.

15. For instance, Liebermann's *Gleaners* of 1888 in Hamburg, and *Joseph sepa-*

rating out the spotted sheep in the *Vienna Genesis,* reproduced in Caviness, "Erweiterung des 'Kunst'-Begriffs," figs. 233, 234.

16. The formulation that follows is very close to that of Jules Laforgue (who refers to the Young-Helmholtz theory of color-vision) in a review of an Impressionist show held in Berlin in 1883, though published only among "Mélanges posthumes," in his *Oeuvres complètes,* 4th. ed., III (Paris: Societé du Mercure de France, 1902–03), III, 133–45. Excerpts in English translation are in: Phoebe Pool, *Impressionism* (New York: Praeger, 1967), 178, and in Barbara E. White, *Impressionism in Perspective* (Englewood Cliffs: Prentice Hall, 1978), 33–34, from *ARTnews* 55 (May 1956): 43–45; according to information in the latter, Laforgue had intended to publish a German translation but it did not appear in print.

17. Strong tr., 120.

18. Hans Rosenhagen, *Liebermann* (Künstler-Monographien, ed. H. Knackfuss, XLV), (Bielefeld and Leipzig: Velhagen and Klasing, 1900); Max J. Friedländer, *Max Liebermann* (Berlin: Propyläen, [1924]).

19. Arthur E. G. Haseloff, *Codex purpureus Rossanensis, Die Minituren der Griechischen Evangelien-Handschrift in Rossano* (Berlin: Giesecke & Devrient, 1898), 48.

20. Arthur E. G. Haseloff, *Die vorromanische Plastik in Italien* (Leipzig: H. Schmidt und C. Gunther, Pantheon Verlag für Kunstwissenschaft [c. 1930]); also published as *La scultura pre-romanica in Italia* (Bologna: Casa Editrici Apollo [1930]), and *Pre-Romanesque Sculpture in Italy* (Firenze and New York: Casa Editrici and Harcourt, Brace, & Co., [1931]).

21. Adolph Goldschmidt, *Gedenkrede auf Max Liebermann* (Hamburg: Kunstverein, 1954); publication was delayed because of Nazi charges against the artist. The sketch of Goldschmidt is reproduced facing p. 5.

22. Kurt Weitzmann, "Obituaries: Adolph Goldschmidt," *College Art Journal,* IV, no. 1 (1944): 49.

23. His earliest publication was concerned with late Gothic German art, but in 1895 his *Albani Psalter* appeared: Adolph Goldschmidt, *Lübecker Malerei und Plastik bis 1530* (Lübeck: Bernh. Nohring, 1889); *Der Albanispsalter in Hildesheim* (Berlin: G. Siemens, 1895).

24. Adolph Goldschmidt, *Die Elfenbeinskulpturen aus der Zeit der karolingischen und sächsischen Kaiser, VIII.-XI. Jarhhundert,* 3 vols. (Berlin: B. Cassirer, 1914–23); *Die Elfenbeinskulpturen aus der romanischen Zeit, XI.-XIII. Jahrhundert,* 2 vols. (Berlin: B. Cassirer, 1926).

25. Now in the Museum of Modern Art, New York: John Elderfield, *Matisse in the Collection of the Museum of Modern Art* (New York: Museum of Modern Art, 1978), 72, illus. 73. The relief was exhibited in London in 1912 and at the Armory Show in New York in 1913. *Back II* (Autumn 1913) is more abstract and in that way closer to medieval works, but it was apparently never shown, and remained in the artist's studio until 1955 (Elderfield, 72, 75–76).

26. Wilhelm Neuss, *Die katalonische bibelillustration um die wende des ersten jahrtausends und die altspanische buchmalerei; eine neue quelle zur geschichte des auslebens der altchristlichen kunst in Spanien und zur frühmittelalterlichen stilgeschichte* (Bonn and Leipzig: K. Schroeder, 1922).

27. Timothy Anglin Burgard, "Picasso's *Night Fishing at Antibes:* Autobiography, Apocalypse, and the Spanish Civil War," *Art Bulletin* 68 (1986): 661–65, figs. 4–7, has traced Picasso's interest in Apocalyptic imagery back to 1901, but relates its reemergence in the late 1930's to art historical publications of the prior decade as well as to the Civil War. An M.A. thesis at Tufts University on Picasso's imagery in a gouache of 28 May, 1936, has demonstrated the occurrence of the eagle-headed Evangelist (John) in local manuscripts, such as one of the late twelfth century in Gerona (Gerona, Museo Diocesano), and in the vault paintings of the Panthéon de los Reyes in León done in the reign of Ferdinand II, 1157–88: see Lasse Antonsen, "The Bird-Headed Demon and the Transfigured Horse: A Study of Iconography, Method and Influence in Picasso's Art of the Years 1933–36, as they conclude in *Composition with Minotaur* of May 28, 1936," unpublished M.A. thesis, Tufts University, May 1986, 61, fig. 68; the image was more easily accessible to Picasso in the Romanesque frescoes from the chancel of Santa Maria, Tahull, now in the Museum of Catalan Art in Barcelona. Similarly, Leo Steinberg has demonstrated an affinity between Picasso's work and late Gothic objects: Picasso, *Head of a Woman*, June 26, 1940, is compared to an ivory bead from a rosary in the Boston Museum of Fine Arts. See Leo Steinberg, "Drawing as if to Possess," in Patricia Kaplan and Susan Manso, eds., *Major European Art Movements, 1900–1945: A Critical Anthology* (New York: Dutton, 1977), 196–97, figs. 62–64.

28. Mildred Friedman, ed., *De Stijl: 1917–1931. Visions of Utopia,* Exhibition Catalogue, Walker Art Center, Minneapolis (New York: Abbeville Press, 1982), 74, fig. 39 (Composition 1917 no. 2), fig. 40 (no. 3), and fig. 41 (no. 5).

29. Meyer Schapiro, "On the Aesthetic Attitude in Romanesque Art," reprinted in his *Romanesque Art: Selected Papers* (New York: G. Braziller, 1977), 1; originally in *Art and Thought,* K. Bharatha Iyer, ed. (London: Luzac, 1947).

30. Caviness, "Erweiterung des 'Kunst'-Begriffs," figs. 239, 240. Compare the animated line and abstraction of the St. Peter of the Moissac portal with Gargallo's "Spanish Ballerina" of 1927 in the Museu de Arte Moderna in Barcelona (illus. Lisbon, Fundaçao Calouste Gulbenkian, *Pablo Gargallo,* Exhibition Catalogue, June–July [Lisbon: A. Fundaçao, 1981], Pl. 74).

31. Hans Belting, "La fin d'une tradition?," (editorial), *Revue de l'art,* 69 (1985): 10.

32. "*The Romanesque Sculpture of Moissac.* By Meyer Schapiro," *The New York Times Book Review* (October 13, 1985), 25.

33. In reference to the Porter's Lodge of the Park Guell of 1900–1914, I am thinking of his use of a cluttered roofline corresponding to the corbel-table friezes of Romanesque, of the extreme contrasts of elements—tall spires next to squat buildings, as in the Romanesque Tahull complex—and the use of natural terrain and rough boulders that blend with the landscape.

34. José Puig y Cadafalch, *L'arquitectura romànica a Catalunya*, 3 vols. (Barcelona: Institut d'Etudis Catalans, 1909–18).

35. José Puig y Cadafalch, *Le premier art roman. L'architecture en Catalogne et dans l'Occident meditérranien aud Xᵉ et XIᵉ siècles* (Paris: H. Laurens, 1928) and *La geografia i els origens del premier art romànic* (Barcelona: Ars Gràfiques, 1930); French translation (Paris: H. Laurens, 1935).

36. For the dates, see Salvador Tarrago, *Gaudi* (Barcelona: Escudo de Oro, 1985), 34; and Kenneth J. Conant, *Carolingian and Romanesque Architecture, 800–1200*, 2nd ed. (Harmondsworth: Penguin Books, 1966), Pl. 45A.

37. Caviness, "Erweiterung des 'Kunst'-Begriffs," figs. 241, 242. He achieved a similar effect in the less grandiose corridor in the attic of Casa Battlo, 1904–1906 (illus. Tarrago, p. 81). It is possible, though doubtful, that earlier historical studies were available to him: H. d'Arbois de Jubainville, *Études sur l'état intérieur des abbayes cisterciennes* (Paris: A. Durand, 1858), and R. Dohme, *Die Kirchen des Cistercienserordens in Deutschland während des Mittelalters* (Leipzig: Seeman, 1869).

38. He of course acknowledges prior studies, including those previously cited, and John Bilson, "The Architecture of the Cistercians," *The Archaeological Journal* 66 (1906): 185–280, and Josef Sauer, *Der Cisterzienser-Orden und die deutsche Kunst des Mittelalters* (Salzburg, 1913).

39. Ch. P[icaud], "Nouvelles archéologiques et correspondence. Marcel Aubert (1884–1962)," *Revue archéologique* I (1963), 95: "dès 1908, avec un groupe d'étudiants de Sorbonne, il participa à une mission en Allemagne; à son retour il présentait à l'École des Hautes Études un rapport sur les églises cisterciennes de la région du Rhin—première apparition sur ses horizons scientifiques de la silhouette de Cîteaux!"

40. I am greatly indebted to our colleague Jean Taralon for contacting Aubert's daughter, Madame François Sermage, who supplied information about the family. His grandfather, André Aubert (1832–1914), had two sons, both architects: Edmond, whose son Pierre died in 1914, and Georges (1858–1891), Marcel's father.

41. Franz-Jourdain, "L'Évolution de l'Art décoratif en Allemagne," *La Revue* 76 (1908): 435–442. The cry was taken up by Jules Huret whose articles from *Le Figaro* of 1908 and 1909 were reprinted as *En Allemagne, la Bavière et la Saxe* (Paris: E. Fasquelle, 1911); he reports the views of other members of the delegation (154–71). I am extremely grateful to Nancy Troy for sharing an extensive bibliography on this question with me, part of her study of Le Corbusier's formative period.

42. Franz-Jourdain (1908, 438): "Les Bavarois ont pris le parti de . . . supprimer, en somme, toute décoration inutile. Plus de faux-fuyants, ni de mensonages. Enserrés dans cette doctrine un peu apre, il sont obligés de chercher la beauté dans les proportions et dans les lignes. . . ." Cf., Aubert, *L'Architecture cistercienne* I (Paris: Les Éditions d'art et d'histoire, 1943), 142: "Car la crainte du luxe, de la richesse, qui est la cause des décisions prises par le Chapitre général, n'étouffe pas chez les abbés le sens de la beauté, de l'art, de la grandeur et de la noblesse dans l'austerité. Elle oblige le constructeur à chercher des solutions simples et logiques, et, bien souvent, nous le verrons, c'est cela même qui l'a conduit à la perfection."

43. Zürich, Kunstgewerbemuseum, *Walter Gropius: Bauten und Projekte 1906–1969*, Ausstellung, 26. Juni bis 22. August (Zürich, 1971), no. 1, illus.). For Fontenay, Aubert (II, 1943), figs. 460, 482, 483.

44. *Walter Gropius*, no. 2.

45. Aubert, *L'Architecture cistercienne*, I, 135–149. A view of Aubert as a pure chartiste, removed from the aesthetic considerations of his time, was vehemently defended by Ernst Kitzinger in his comments on this paper.

46. Georg Swarzenski, *Die Regensburger buchmalerei des X. und XI. jahrhunderts* (Leipzig: E. Hermann, 1900).

47. Georg Swarzenski et al., *Illustrierte geschichte des kunstgewerbes*, ed. Georg H. Lehnert (Berlin: M. Oldenbourg, [1907–09]).

48. Edmund Schilling, "Obituary: Georg Swarzenski," *Burlington Magazine* 664 (1958): 251–52.

49. Staedelsches Kunstinstitut, *Verzeichnis der Gemälde aus dem Besitz des Staedelschen Kunstinstituts und der Stadt Frankfurt* (Frankfurt am Main, 1924), *passim*. By 1923, the Städel paintings catalogue indicates the acquisition of many works by living artists, including the leading Successionists, Lovis Corinth and Max Slevogt, the "Die Brücke" group, Erich Heckel and Ernst Ludwig Kirchener, as well as Peter Becker, Heinrich Campendonk, Philipp Heyl, Ferdinand Hodler, Karl Hofer, Oskar Kokoshka, Franz Marc, Henri Matisse, Oskar Moll, Edvard Munch, Alfred Oppenheim, Max Pechstein, and Wilhelm Trübner; many of these works came directly from the artists, and some were gifts of Georg Swarzenski. There were also representative pre-modern paintings by Henri Edmond Cross, Daubigny, Degas, Franz von Lenbach, Liebermann, Manet, Monet, Adolphe Monticelli (a pupil of Diaz), Renoir and Sisley. Along with those acquisitions are late medieval northern works, such as Bosch's *Ecce Homo*, acquired in 1917. I am grateful to Ron Salter for identifying the less well-known artists.

50. Reproduced as the frontispiece in *Beiträge für Georg Swarzenski*, ed. Oswald Goetz (Berlin & Chicago: Gebr. Mann and H. Regnery, 1951).

51. Andrée Hayum, "Grünewald, The Isenheim Altarpiece, and the Politics of Culture," *Tribute to Lotte Brand Phillip*, ed. William Clark et al. (New York: Albaris Books, 1985), 71.

52. Perry T. Rathbone, in "Introduction" in *Max Beckmann 1948* [retrospective exhibition] (St. Louis: City Art Museum of St. Louis, 1948), 12, comments on Beckmann's early discovery of the triptych when he worked with Hans von Marees in Weimar in 1900; but the full impact of Northern Gothic art seems to have been felt later, in Frankfurt about 1915 (pp. 21–22, 24).

53. Otto von Falke, Robert Schmidt, and Georg Swarzenski, *Der Welfenschatz. Der reliquienschatz des Braunschweiger domes aus dem besitze des herzoglischen hauses Braunschweig-Lüneburg* (Frankfurt am Main: Frankfurter Verlagsanstalt, 1930).

54. Caviness, "Erweiterung des 'Kunst'-Begriffs," figs. 243, 244.

55. Tilmann Buddensieg et al. ed., *Intuition und Kunstwissenschaft: Festschrift für Hanns Swarzenski* (Berlin: Mann, 1973), 7.

56. Hanns Swarzenski, *Early Medieval Illumination* (New York: Batsford, 1951), 11.

57. Lillian Randall tells me that Wilhelm Köhler and Paul Klee were close friends, and that in his courses at Harvard, Köhler used to compare the Ravenna mosaics with works of Klee. Werner Hofmann, "Anstelle eines Nachrufes," *Idea: Jahrbuch der Hamburger Kunsthalle* 3 (1984): 7–17, has offered others from the Vienna school. I am grateful to Tom Kauffmann for this reference.

58. The problem of alterity and misinterpretation is viewed from a different vantage point, that of restoration, by Ernst Bacher, "Kunstwerk und Denkmal— Distanz und Zusammenhang," *Deutsche Kunst und Denkmalpflege* (1986), 124–127.

59. Meyer Schapiro, "The Beatus Apocalypse of Gerona," *ARTnews* 61 (January 1963): 50.

60. André Malraux, *Le Musée imaginaire de la sculpture mondiale* (Paris: Gallimard, 1952), tr. as *Museum without Walls* (Garden City: Doubleday, 1967). The French Ministry's name has again been changed, to Communications. Wayne Dynes, in "The Work of Meyer Schapiro: Distinction and Distance," *Journal of the History of Ideas* 42 (1980): 168, cites an anonymous volume entitled *Towards Modern Art, or King Solomon's Picture Book: Art of the new age and of former ages shown side by side* (London: Phaidon, 1952), as an extreme case of anachronism.

61. Schapiro, "Beatus Apocalypse of Gerona," 50.

62. Malraux is mentioned in conjunction with Kristeva by Germaine Brée, "The Archeology of Discourse in Malraux's Anti-memoirs," in Jeannine Parisier Plottel and Hanna Cherney ed., *Intertextuality—New Perspectives in Criticism*, 2 (New York: New York Literary Forum, 1978), 3–13, where she gives the useful definition: "Intertextuality, in one interpretation (Julia Kristeva's) of the much used term, is the power of a written text to impose a reorganization of the corpus of texts that preceded its appearance, creating a modification in the manner in which they are read."

63. Leo Steinberg, Introduction to Jean Lipman and Richard Marshall, *Art about Art* (New York: Dutton, 1978), 9.

64. These issues have been presented in the *International Center for Medieval Art Newsletter*, 1985–1987.

65. Schapiro, "Style," *Aesthetics Today*, 87: "The same tendencies to coherent and expressive structure are found in the arts of all cultures. . . . As a result of this new approach, all the arts of the world, even the drawings of children and psychotics, have become accessible on a common plane of expressive and form-creating activity. Art is now one of the strongest evidences of the basic unity of mankind." See also Robert Motherwell, "The Universal Language of Children's Art, and Modernism," *The American Scholar* 40 (1970–71): 24–27.

Index